HOMER IN PRINT

ΟΜΗΡΟΣ

HOMER IN PRINT

A CATALOGUE OF THE BIBLIOTHECA HOMERICA LANGIANA AT THE UNIVERSITY OF CHICAGO LIBRARY

Edited by Glenn W. Most and Alice Schreyer

Essays by M. C. Lang, Glenn W. Most, and David Wray

Entries by Alex Lee and Diana Moser

CHICAGO

THE UNIVERSITY OF CHICAGO LIBRARY

2013

The Division of the Humanities at the University of Chicago
helped to underwrite this publication.

Distributed by the University of Chicago Press
www.press.uchicago.edu

COVER: B69

FRONTISPIECE: B9

All illustrations are keyed to catalogue entry numbers.

ISBN: 978-0-943056-41-8

CONTENTS

PREFACE

Homer in Print: A Catalogue of the Bibliotheca Homerica Langiana at the University of Chicago Library is the product of a collaboration between the worlds of private collecting, philanthropy, research libraries, scholarship, and learning. Rarely does a collection formed by a private individual and donated to an academic institution demonstrate within such a short period of time its power to stimulate research, discovery, and knowledge.

This catalogue of the Bibliotheca Homerica Langiana (BHL) traces the transmission and reception of the *Iliad* and the *Odyssey* in printed form from the fifteenth through the twentieth century. Entries for each item provide details of the particular edition's textual, intellectual, printing, and publishing history as well as noteworthy physical features of the BHL copy. As such, it contributes to scholarship in classical studies, the history of printing and print culture, textual editing, and translation studies, and stands as a testament to the enduring influence of the Homeric texts over 500 years.

M. C. Lang describes the formation of the BHL in his introductory essay. His love for the classics began when he was a student at Hamilton College, where he was inspired by his professor, John Mattingly, who received his AB at the University of Chicago in 1926. Mr. Lang's priority in seeking a home for the collection was an institution where students and faculty would actively use the books. We are grateful and proud that he recognized that the vibrant program in classics at the University of Chicago would provide such an environment.

From the beginning of our conversations, we agreed that a catalogue of the BHL would be an important contribution to scholarship. As surprising as it may seem, there is no in-depth study of Homer in print, and the scope of the BHL ensured that this catalogue of an individual collection includes representation of all significant Greek editions and near-complete coverage in English translations. The "gaps" that exist are often present in the University of Chicago Library's circulating and special collections, illustrating how well they complement each other. F. A. Wolf's *Prolegomena ad Homerum* (1795), a cornerstone of modern Homeric scholarship frequently referred to in this catalogue, is a notable example.

The catalogue was shaped in conversations with M. C. Lang; Danielle Allen, former Professor in Classics and Political Science and Dean of the Humanities Division, University of Chicago; Glenn W. Most, Professor, John U. Nef Committee on Social Thought and the College, University of Chicago; and Catherine Mardikes, Senior Humanities Bibliographer, University of Chicago Library. David Wray, Departments of Classics, Comparative Literature, and the College, joined our advisory group early on. We agreed that graduate students would research and write the entries, providing them with the opportunity to work with these magnificent editions and immerse themselves in the fields of bibliography, printing history, and textual criticism to enrich their disciplinary studies. Ally Lamb worked on the project in its initial stages. Diana Moser took on the task of producing entries for the English editions and then extended her work to include the other translations; Alex Lee tackled the Greek editions. Catherine Uecker, Rare Books Librarian, University of Chicago Library, provided extensive and expert bibliographical assistance with the entries. David Vander Meulen contributed to our investigation into the variant first lines of Pope's *Iliad* (see B9).

The individual entries bring to the fore the editor's and/or printer's goals for the edition together with the intellectual, printing, publishing, and reception history. The three essays, contributed by M. C. Lang, Glenn W. Most, and David Wray, place the collection in the context of bibliophily, classical scholarship, and translation studies.

In his essay, M. C. Lang observes that "the purpose of the collection would not be achieved until connections between the books and those who came to use them were established." In achieving this goal, *Homer in Print: A Catalogue of the Bibliotheca Homerica Langiana at the University of Chicago* fulfills a collector's vision, honors his extraordinary gift, and enriches the understanding of the transmission and reception of the Homeric texts.

ALICE SCHREYER
Assistant University Librarian for
Humanities, Social Sciences, and Special Collections
Curator of Rare Books
The University of Chicago Library

THE ARCHITECTURE OF ACCUMULATION: A BOOK COLLECTOR'S APOLOGY

The metaphor is apt. A collection, like any building, whether kennel or cathedral, should be constructed using a good plan and quality materials, so the completed result is both fit for use and pleasing to the senses. In the past, some collections were said to have been "formed," which smacks more of wet clay on a potter's wheel than of books on shelves, and others "created," which seems presumptuously reminiscent of the Deity's role in *Genesis*. This collection of printed editions of the *Iliad* and *Odyssey* and important works of Homeric scholarship was not formed or created, but built, and this essay is an attempt to describe the nature of its plan and give an overview of the materials gathered for its construction.

But first a reasonable question arises, which deserves a reasoned answer: Why build it at all? Why spend years of effort, and considerable capital, in order to accumulate the volumes that make up the Bibliotheca Homerica Langiana (BHL)? Was it an exercise in ego—a desire to attach an ephemeral name to a timeless one in order to gain some bit of renown? In truth, no. Was it to satisfy a primitive longing to feel the thrill of the chase and share in the excitement of the kill—but only in a safe, sedate, civilized, and bloodless way? In part, probably. Was it to enable others to apply, or at least test, the collector's belief regarding what one might call the "substance of format": that study of the physical printed book in which a text first appeared can add to one's understanding not only of the intentions of its author, editor, or publisher, but also of the impact that text had on its first readers? Most definitely, yes. It is neither romantic nor delusory to assert that the thoughtful examination of original editions can reveal information that is absent in a later reprint, online digital surrogate, or facsimile.

Because both readers and printed books are material and, incidentally, biodegradable things, it is understandable that specimens of the former often form attachments to examples of the latter. For centuries, books and readers have left marks on one another: books leave invisible psychological and intellectual marks on readers, whereas readers leave physical marks on books. These visible marks—in the form of inscribed notes, symbols, or other marginalia, or inserted bits of paper, or bookplates, or even particular pages grubbier or more dog-eared than their neighbors—are virtual spoor dropped by earlier readers that, if someone inquisitive enough were to follow them, can lead toward information pertaining not merely to the text itself, but beyond it.

In addition to the marks readers leave, the physical characteristics of even a pristine copy of an original edition—its binding, size, typography, design, margin width, paper quality, and illustrations and ornaments, or lack thereof—may, individually or severally, offer clues to the otherwise undocumented hopes and expectations of the author or editor and publisher who together labored to produce and sell the book. An original edition, whatever else it may be, is an artifact, and from the physical evidence it offers, one can make deductions about, among other things, the nature of some of the invisible marks that book, as the text incarnate, may have left on its original readers.

Availability is another concern: some important editions of Homer, whether of the Greek text, translations, or works of scholarship, are not readily available in a form other than the one in which they first appeared. Some first editions remain the only editions. But even when a text has been reprinted, the preface, other preliminary matter, and the endnotes from the first edition were often heavily edited or sometimes omitted entirely from subsequent editions. This can be a serious loss. In both Pope's *Iliad* (B9) and *Odyssey* (B49), the introductory essays and numerous endnotes, which occupy almost half of each volume, are absent from the majority of later editions, yet they were and remain of much value and interest. Many early editors of the Greek text used the preface to describe their methodology, goals, and justification for offering a new version to the public. And the preface to the first edition of many translations is often the only place in which the translator explains his—or, in the single instance of Madame Dacier (C5, C7), her—philosophy of translation, laying down the principles that guided his attempt to provide an accurate reflection of the Greek text via the mirror of a barbarian tongue.

As the catalogue entries show, the extent and quality of useful "extra-textual" information obtainable from original editions vary. Format was vastly important to Pope (B9, B49) and Ogilby (B7, B47), whereas it was evidently negligible to Hobbes (B1, B48): his books are small, unattractive, and poorly produced. Elegance of format was the *raison d'être* for the original publication of Lawrence's *Odyssey* (B69), whereas Rieu's prose translation of the *Odyssey* (B71), commissioned for a general audience, seems particularly suited to its inexpensive paperback form. To evaluate and consider any of these, or many of the other books in the BHL, without attending to the evidence of the physical book itself, is an experience less rich, less illuminating, less informative, less evocative, and less revealing than it otherwise might be.

Without doubt, information inherent primarily or exclusively in original editions can be of practical use in study and research. It is visible and citable, and its scholarly value has become increasingly recognized. In addition, however, there is another species of "value"—an incalculable, impressionistic one that, at least in library budget requests, dares not speak its name: the one generated by the physical encounter between a student or scholar and original materials. The benefit of such experience does not lend itself to clinical analysis, or even to lucid description. It is neither objective nor logical, and those who have not experienced it often dismiss it as foolish sentimentalism.

Yet, in reality, particular feelings and sensations do occur in otherwise rational humans when, instead of reading a transcript, thumbing through a reprint, or looking at a digital facsimile, they hold in their hands the actual, physical document, first edition, or association copy, that is the subject of their interest. They make a tactile connection with history, and many scholars and students will privately admit that the experience has refined their response to the text to some degree and in ways difficult to describe. It is a close encounter at first hand, not second. Although it is most frequently associated with autograph manuscript materials, the same sort of connection, perhaps with lowered intensity, exists with printed books, when what sits on the table is the very edition, in the exact format, that the author may have planned, possibly demanded, and almost certainly saw and handled. Although it is rarely the author's actual personal copy, it is still the author's book, as the author knew it, which now becomes the author's book as the student knows it—an experience that transcends time, shared by both.

Those engaged in critical analysis or serious scholarship are not immune to sensations of affinity arising from a physical connection with the subject of their study, and it is naïve to discount the subtle effects of such sensations. On the other hand, it is equally naïve to believe that university libraries should operate on romantic principles, plunking down hard cash to acquire original material in the hope that exposure will inspire and promote a greater quality of scholarship than might otherwise be the case. Here is where the private collector, able to act in support of intangible benefits, can play a useful role.

Selectivity in any accumulation of objects invariably reflects the selector. Although relative scarcity or absolute rarity may affect the precise makeup of the final gathering, parameters established at the outset will still determine its primary characteristics. Some book collectors, like magpies, are attracted to the bright and shiny. This attraction has resulted, in its most expensive form, in collections of what are called "high spots": important books, often great books, in fine condition and in important, ideally original, bindings. Each book is an icon, a totem, a fetish of intellectual or artistic achievement, but each book stands alone and bears no relation to its equally iconic shelfmates. The light shed by every "high spot" brightly illuminates itself, but not its neighbors.

Other book collectors, however, including myself, adhere to a principle of connectivity, insisting that relevant connections must exist between and among the books in their collections. For each book, it should be possible to draw lines forward or backward or in both directions reflecting influence, debt, imitation, adoption, or rejection, connecting it to other books in the collection. In addition, I adopted a second connective principle: that the purpose of the collection would not be achieved until connections between the books and those who came to use them were established.

A collector can honor the connective first principle even if the collection is inaccessible and isolated, shown rarely to a select few and then primarily for the purpose of generating envy or applause, rather like the mock Roman temples, monastic ruins, and other architectural follies built in the eighteenth century on the grounds of some English country houses. The second principle, however, demands a different situation. The collection of course must be sited where it can be cared for properly, but the primary role of its custodians is not to promote passive display, but to encourage and supervise active use of the collection by an audience capable of using it. For the BHL, I found the right site, and decided it was time to move the collection there. To delay the latter after achieving the former would frustrate and devalue the second principle of connectivity in return for nothing of comparable value.

It is gratifying that the detailed, extensive, and scholarly notes for each catalogue entry do suggest that the BHL is fit for use in supporting, encouraging, and validating the study of original material. The notes identify some examples of information extractable only from such material, and point out important connections that might elude notice by scholars studying the books in isolation from one another. What catalogue notes cannot reveal, however, is how those who use this collection will value the experience of physically connecting with the books in it. That is a question with only personal answers. For this collector, at least, a room full of books is a great provocation: something tangible that, at a single glance, and without any mediation, makes visible the complexity and continuity of human thought, the vast gulf of one's own ignorance, and proves how robust and efficient the printed book is in enabling voices long dead to speak directly to those now living and to those yet to be born.

PLANNING THE BHL

Inclusiveness must give way to discrimination when attempting to build a collection of significant printed editions of any classical text, especially one as complex and venerable as the Homeric poems. There have been hundreds of editions of the *Iliad* and *Odyssey* in Greek, and hundreds more translations into various modern languages, especially English. The complete published corpus of Homeric scholarship and commentary runs into many thousands of separate titles. Selective acquisition was imperative. And because connectivity was the overarching parameter for inclusion, an accumulation ultimately resulted in which intrinsic relationships, sometimes lying on the surface and sometimes buried, exist between the important and the unimportant, the rare and the common, the valuable and the cheap, the famous and the forgotten, the beautiful and the ugly.

The specific criterion of admission for editions in Greek ("A" entries in the catalogue) was the flexible one of "significance." This allowed for the exercise of rigorous selectivity while permitting the inclusion of a lucky find. But each volume had to evince some worth as an editorial, historical, or typographical exemplar with ascertainable, substantive connections to its predecessors or successors.

After consulting the standard classical bibliographies as well as appropriate collection catalogues I drew up a list of desiderata, a selection of approximately forty key editions of Homer in Greek without deference to the twin gods of collecting, availability and affordability. Had I consulted their oracles at the outset, the potential difficulties then revealed might well have dampened all enthusiasm for the project. It is not stretching the metaphor too far to say that the decision to start building this collection was based on a blissful ignorance of the odds of structural collapse.

In the category of commentary and scholarship ("D" entries in the catalogue), I winnowed the vast field down to a handful of seminal works that, in their time, represented the best and most carefully considered thinking on Homer and the so-called Homeric Questions: Who composed the *Iliad* and *Odyssey*? How? Orally or in writing? When did the composition occur? Of course, no matter which books I selected, all theories about the creation of the two Homeric epics remain speculative. Indeed, over the centuries there have been competing published arguments for virtually any Homeric notion capable of rational embrace, including the existence of one Homer, or two Homers, or a committee of Homers, or of no Homers at all; of illiterate Homers who composed orally; of literate Homers who wrote the poems down; or of yet other Homers who either couldn't or wouldn't write, but who dictated to scribes who did.

When deciding which translations into modern European languages ("C" entries in the catalogue) to include, it seemed sensible to limit acquisitions to the earliest obtainable versions, plus one or two later translations generally acclaimed to be "classic."

Then, while I was pondering what to do about translations into English ("B" entries in the catalogue), something snapped. The concept of selective acquisition faltered, and the notion of completeness took hold.

THE MATERIALS SELECTED

EDITIONS IN GREEK

There are no extant autograph manuscripts of any Greek or Roman classical writers, nor are there any copies that have been collated with the originals. In virtually every instance, the manuscripts on which all printed editions have been based are the surviving offspring of over a millennium of copying—in the case of Homer, probably over two millennia.

On uncounted occasions, the texts of the *Iliad* and *Odyssey* were copied by inattentive scribes; by scribes with bad eyesight; by bored or drunk or sleepy scribes; by students with limited skills; by students with bad handwriting; and by all those who could not resist "improving" a text they were only supposed to reproduce. Then, of course, there were all those unfortunate conjunctions between manuscript and fire, flood, mildew, nasty insects, and peckish rodents.

Consequently, after two thousand years of bad copying, arrogant or ignorant interpolation, accidental destruction, and intentional ingestion, the Renaissance inherited a few precious manuscripts that formed the basis of the earliest printed editions of Homer. In the centuries that followed, editors continually tried—by intuition, by inspiration, or by applying various theories of textual criticism—to strip away corruption and reconstruct the earliest recoverable form of the text. Today, in every serious bookstore, copies of the Greek texts of the *Iliad* and *Odyssey* are available. From these confident modern volumes one can move back along an absolutely solid line of printed editions of Homer. Some are large, beautifully printed folios destined for aristocratic libraries; some are small, inexpensive books intended for student use. Some contain extensive commentary giving variant readings or providing explanatory notes about obscure words or references; some provide a parallel translation in Latin or another language familiar to the reader. Some are very rare, and some are quite common. The succession of printed editions of the Greek text of Homer since 1488 represents, in essence, the successive attempts of individual editors to offer a version closer to the "original" *Iliad* and *Odyssey* than did their predecessors. How well any of them succeeded remains a matter of conjecture.

The *editio princeps,* or first printed edition, of Homer appeared in two elegant folio volumes, printed in Florence at the end of 1488 (A1). Typical of many fifteenth-century printed books, a space for the initial letter of each of the twenty-four books of the *Iliad* and *Odyssey* was left blank to enable the purchaser, according to his own taste and preference, to have a skilled artist add them. In many copies of the 1488 Homer, these spaces remain blank; in others, the rubrication is of a much later date. The original audience for the first printed Homer consisted of the few Europeans capable of reading Greek, and from this physical evidence one can surmise that many of them felt little inclination to spend on decoration. Although the precise history of its printing and publication remains in some doubt, the Florence Homer is arguably the most important first edition in all of Greek literature. It is not an impossible book to find: any collector with a surfeit of assets and a modicum of patience will eventually have the chance to acquire one. In the BHL, the *editio princeps* is represented by a substantial fragment of volume I that, although crippled, possesses sufficient presence to stand in for a complete copy.

The second edition of Homer in Greek was published in 1504 by the great scholar-printer Aldus Manutius (A2). Aldus reprinted his Homer in the same small octavo format in 1517 and 1524 (A6). Each of these editions, being respectively the third and sixth printings of the *Iliad* and *Odyssey* in Greek, corrects misprints existing in its predecessors while adding a new batch of mistakes for later editors to reveal.

For students in the ancient world, the *Iliad* and *Odyssey* were primary resources, with the *Iliad* as the premier guide to noble conduct. Then, after the fall of the Roman Empire in the West, the Greek texts of the poems were unknown in Western Europe for nearly a thousand years, and any familiarity with the Homeric stories was derived from Latin epitomes or from quotations by Latin writers. In Constantinople and other parts of the Eastern empire, however, both the Greek language and the full texts survived. Ultimately, it was from the East that Greek manuscripts of the *Iliad* and *Odyssey* traveled back to Europe in the fourteenth and fifteenth centuries. Thereafter, in the early sixteenth century, as printed editions became more widely available, the Homeric poems once again became important in the classrooms of the West.

The earliest printed Homeric school texts, like most of their modern counterparts, were literally used to pieces, and survivors are scarce. The first schoolbook edition of the *Odyssey* was issued in Basel in 1520 (A4). It is a small, slim volume containing only the first two of the poem's twenty-four books, printed with wide margins and generous leading between the lines to allow space for students' annotations (often, as in this copy, translations of difficult words peculiar to the Homeric vocabulary). The title page of Thierry Martens's 1523 Louvain edition of the complete *Iliad* (A5), the first printing of the *Iliad* in Greek outside Italy, states that it also consists of only the first two books, although the full text follows, printed in three separate parts. It seems probable that although Martens originally intended to publish just the first part for sale to students, he subsequently decided to expand the base of potential buyers by printing the text in full. It is unknown why he failed to supply a new title page to supersede the one issued with the first part. Because of the serial nature of the publication, complete copies of this early edition of the *Iliad* are rare.

The first half of the sixteenth century saw the production of a number of other Greek Homers, each claiming some improvement over its predecessors. In 1535, for example, Johann Herwagen issued the ninth edition of Homer (A8), the first published in Basel, and the first time the Greek text was combined on the page with the explanatory *scholia* of Didymus, previously only available separately. In 1541, Adrianus Turnebus, a scholar who Montaigne praised as a man "who knew more, and knew better what he knew, than any man that lived in his time or for many years before," issued his Paris edition of the *Iliad* (A11) which, along with the great scholar-printer Henri Estienne's magnificent 1556 folio edition of the principal Greek poets (A14), formed the foundation of almost all Greek editions of the *Iliad* until the eighteenth century. In preparing his text of Homer for publication, Estienne collated eighteen earlier printed editions plus additional sources, and thereby created a critical Greek text of Homer unsurpassed for several hundred years. During the eighteenth century, perhaps the two most important critical editions were the work of English scholars, Joshua Barnes (1711, A18) and Samuel Clarke (1729–32–40, A19). The beautiful folio *Iliad* and *Odyssey* of the Foulis brothers in Glasgow (1756–8, A20) is both typographically accurate and aesthetically pleasing. Gibbon commented that "as the eye is the organ of fancy, I read Homer with more pleasure in the Glasgow edition. Through that fine medium, the poet's sense appears more beautiful and transparent."

For sheer size, magnificent simplicity, and presswork approaching perfection, the Bodoni *Iliad* of 1808 (A24) remains unsurpassed. Printed in Parma in an edition of 170 copies on various papers, this massive three-volume set (nearly the size, and approaching the cost, of a small used Fiat) was dedicated to Napoleon, who subsequently awarded Bodoni a pension of 3,000 francs. An earlier, unconsummated Homeric connection between the printer and the emperor is evidenced by a document from 1800 (A24A), conveying a request by Bodoni that Napoleon agree to sponsor a polyglot edition of Homer in Greek, Latin, Italian, and French. Although Napoleon acknowledged the memo by signing it, no offer of support was forthcoming, and Bodoni's idea proceeded no further.

Standing at the farthest extreme from Bodoni's giant is William Pickering's dwarf: the tiny "Diamond Classics" edition of Homer published in London in 1831 (A27). Although the *Iliad* volume cannot fit into a walnut shell like the manuscript copy allegedly known to Cicero (as reported by Pliny), Pickering's is universally acknowledged as the smallest printed Homer, and surely must be the least read. Unlike the Pickering, the lovely 1909 Greek *Odyssey* printed by Oxford University Press in Proctor's "Otter" Greek typeface (A32) can be perused with ease. Typographically, however, the finest twentieth-century Greek Homer, austere and elegant, was that produced by the Bremer Press (A33). It is unlikely that a more beautiful edition of Homer in Greek will ever be printed.

SCHOLARSHIP, CRITICISM, AND COMMENTARY

Critical study of the Homeric poems began no later than the sixth century B.C. and continues unabated. This unbroken chain of criticism, hypothesis, argument, and analysis is unmatched in the history of world literature. Homer has been politicized, allegorized and historicized, deified and debunked, disassembled and rearranged, embraced as an ally and attacked as the enemy in all manner of religious, historical, and academic disputes.

Some early important printed critical works in the collection are Aldus's 1521 edition of Didymus's ancient notes on the *Iliad* (D1); the massive and celebrated four-volume commentary on Homer by Eustathius, Archbishop of Thessalonica, published by Antonio Blado in Rome between 1542 and 1550 (D4); and Wolfgang Seber's concordance of Homer published in Heidelberg in 1604 (D5). Seber's work was not only the first printed concordance of Homer, but also the first separately published concordance of any classical author. It filled such an important void in Homeric scholarship that it remained in print for more than two centuries. In the eighteenth century, the work of incalculable influence was F. A. Wolf's *Prolegomena ad Homerum* (1795), absent from the collection. In this slim volume, Wolf argued that the original short Homeric songs were composed in the mid-tenth century B.C. by various unknown poets, without the aid of writing, and that only in the sixth century B.C. were the poems first written down and edited into what we now call the *Iliad* and *Odyssey*. Wolf's book lies at the beginning of the transition of Homeric scholarship from the hands of amateur generalists into those of professional specialists. Earlier in the century, English amateur scholars made some important contributions to the discussion about the origin of the epics, including Thomas Blackwell's *Inquiry into the Life and Writings of Homer* (1735, D9) and Robert Wood's *Essay on the Original Genius and Writings of Homer* (1775, D10). In the Victorian age, Gladstone's seven volumes on Homer, including his three-volume *Studies on Homer and the Homeric Age* (1858, D11), exceeded, in bulk if not in influence, the work of anyone else writing in English, and Matthew Arnold's *On Translating Homer* (1861, D12) laid down the famous dictum that "Homer is rapid in his movement, Homer is plain in his words and style, Homer is simple in his ideas, Homer is noble in his manner."

Within the mass of twentieth-century criticism, most of it unread by anyone outside the academy, there are few works that have mightily influenced how people now view the origin, composition, and structure of the *Iliad* and *Odyssey*. First among these is Milman Parry's seminal 1928 doctoral dissertation at the University of Paris, *L'Épithète traditionnelle dans Homère* (D14). Parry, using a rigorous scholarly methodology, for the first time demonstrated that the poems consisted to a great extent of traditional formulas and were almost certainly composed orally, without the aid of writing. This quarto pamphlet, serendipitously spotted in a dealer's catalogue listing mostly monographs on modern French artists, was printed in a small edition on fragile, poor quality paper, and is understandably scarce.

TRANSLATIONS INTO ENGLISH

Whether it is ever possible to represent truthfully in one language a poetic work composed in another language is a question that has been long and hotly debated. Despite all the theories, however, the one certainty is that acts of poetic translation, truthful or not, have been issuing forth in unceasing streams for centuries.

The *Iliad* and *Odyssey* are among the most frequently translated literary works, ancient or modern. The challenge and appeal of presenting these poems afresh to new audiences, in the language of those audiences, have proved irresistible to an incredible array of optimists with differing tastes, skills, and abilities. Although multiple versions exist in virtually all Western and many Eastern languages, more have appeared in English than in any other. Hundreds of partial, incomplete translations, as well as "retellings," also exist. At least 105 complete translations into English of the *Iliad* or *Odyssey* have appeared since Chapman's full *Iliad* in the early seventeenth century.

Viewed as a continuum, the printed record of English versions of the Homeric epics presents an evolution not only of the theory and practice of translation, but also of the English language itself, and its use in literary form. In addition, it constitutes an epitome of the history of printing and publishing in English during the past four centuries. The challenge of attempting to obtain a copy of the first edition of each and every complete translation was compelling. In the end, thirteen of the translations identified as complete eluded capture (see the list appended to this essay).

The chronology of the published translations of the *Iliad* and *Odyssey* in English offers at least one insight into the evolution of human thought on a serious subject. Throughout the classical period, the *Iliad*—that great poem of war, extolling the glory and honor of individual combat without suppressing its bloody reality—took precedence, by every measure, over the fantastical and domestic-oriented *Odyssey*. Of the papyri fragments of Homer that have survived (mostly of Egyptian origin, ranging in date from the third century B.C. to the eighth century A.D.), those from the *Iliad* are three to four times more numerous than those from the *Odyssey*. This preference continued to be reflected, in English at least, until the end of World War I. Not surprisingly, by the November armistice, the Western romantic notion of war, first expressed in Homer's portrayal of aristocratic warriors engaged in glorious combat, was utterly shattered. On the battlefields of France and Belgium, the sword and spear were superseded by a chilling, impersonal mix of wire, gas, and artillery. The tactics of modern warfare could no longer accommodate Homeric models. Reflecting this cultural turnabout, the line of translations reveals that during the three centuries between Chapman's version and the November armistice, the *Iliad* was fully translated into English thirty-eight times, compared with just twenty-six versions of the *Odyssey*. In the nine decades after 1918, only sixteen complete *Iliads* appeared, compared to twenty-five *Odysseys*. Thus it seems to have taken almost three thousand years for Homer's tale of Odysseus's long and difficult journey home to finally surpass, in general popularity at least, his pounding tale of war.

From pulpit ministers (B21) to Prime Ministers (B18), from philosophers (B2) to forgers (B10) to poets (B1, B4, B9, B22, B96, and so on), from aristocrats (B101) to adventurers (B69) to astronomers (B20) to academics (B16, B31, B37, B41, B44, and so forth), a diverse fraternity—there is as yet no complete translation by a woman of the *Iliad* or *Odyssey* in English—have succumbed to the temptation to translate Homer. A few, like Alexander Pope, created independently great literary masterpieces (B9, B49). Others, primarily in the nineteenth century, labored to produce volumes that were quickly and rightly forgotten, and as a result are now very hard to find (among them, of course, the missing thirteen). A few were ridiculed for presenting Homer in an English idiom deemed grossly inappropriate to the original, especially the odd and archaic *Iliad* of F. W. Newman (B16), which Matthew Arnold (D12, D13) so famously attacked. Some were simply declared bad, and publicly condemned in unambiguous terms (B10, B15). Others, however, were widely praised and swiftly adopted for classroom use (B24, B31, B37, B55, B64), or found particular favor with the general reading public and sold in relatively large numbers (B44, B55, B71, B74).

No collection of translations of Homer into English can be complete, except for a moment. The fundamental impossibility of a perfect translation ensures that every generation will attempt to convey, in English, the qualities and essential characteristics of the original poems. Each translation will differ from its predecessors, and in each new English version some aspects of the original *Iliad* or *Odyssey* will be preserved, whereas others will inevitably be lost. Some attempts will meet with critical or popular success; others will surely fail. The only certainty is they will never cease.

M.C. LANG.

[NOTE: *An earlier version of several portions of this essay previously appeared in* Matrix 22 *(Whittington Press, Risbury, England, 2002) under the title "On Collecting Homer".*]

APPENDIX OF COMPLETE* TRANSLATIONS INTO ENGLISH NOT IN THE BHL

Of the 105 complete translations identified by M.C. Lang as having been published during the period 1611 through 2004, the BHL lacks the thirteen listed below. Happily, however, some of these were already in the University of Chicago Library, and yet others have been added since the arrival of the BHL.

(*The criterion of "complete" eliminated from consideration all partial translations or "retellings" or paraphrases, some of which have been erroneously cited as complete in various lists of Homeric translations. The exclusion of such versions from the BHL was based on a physical review of the volumes concerned.)

THE *ILIAD*

Brandreth, T. S. London: W. Pickering, 1846. 2 vols.
Norgate, T. S. London: Williams and Norgate, 1864.
Simcox, E. W. London: Jackson, Walford and Hodder, 1865.
Worsley, P. S. (1–12) & Conington, J. (13–24). Edinburgh: Blackwood, 1865–68. 2 vols.
Cochrane, J. A. Edinburgh: [s.n.], 1867.
Calacleugh, W. G. Philadelphia: Lippincott, 1870.
Rose, J. B. London: Clowes [Privately printed], 1874.
Tibbetts, E. A. Boston: R. G. Badger, 1907.

THE *ODYSSEY*

"By A Member of the University of Oxford" [H. F. Carey?]. London: G. & W. B. Whittaker, 1823. 2 vols.
Norgate, T. S. [s.l.: s.n.], 1862.
Bigge-Wither, L. Oxford: Parker, 1869.
Barnard, M. London: Williams and Norgate, 1876.
Mongan, R. London: James Cornish, 1879–80.

NOTE ON THE CATALOGUE ENTRIES

¶ This is a catalogue of the Bibliotheca Homerica Langiana presented to the University of Chicago Library in 2006 and does not include descriptions of other Homeric texts in the Library's collection.

¶ The focus of the entries is on the transmission of the Homeric text and the printing, publishing, and editorial history and critical reception of the editions included rather than on the individual copies. The format statements and notes on physical features are taken from a preliminary checklist prepared by M.C. Lang; early ownership marks and signatures are included selectively.

¶ The forms of authors' names and birth and death dates in the entry headings are in accordance with the Library of Congress Name Authority File. The vernacular forms of names are used in the text.

¶ Unless stated otherwise, the BHL copy described in each entry is the "first edition"—the first manifestation of this version of the text in printed form. Later edition statements are transcribed when they appear on the title page. Where the BHL copy is not a "first edition" as defined above, and the edition statement does not appear on the title page, the difference is identified in the narrative. In such cases, for example, the BHL copy may be (1) a later edition, or (2) the first collected publication of texts previously published separately, or (3) the first publication in one country of a text published simultaneously or previously in another country, or (4) the first trade publication of a text previously issued in a limited edition or printed privately and not offered for sale to the public.

¶ The first two lines of Homer's text have been transcribed in the entries for the English-language editions of the *Iliad* and the *Odyssey* to illustrate the stylistic and interpretive range of the translations.

¶ Alex Lee, currently a Ph.D. candidate in the Department of Classics, researched and wrote the entries in Section A. Diana Moser, currently a Ph.D. candidate in the Department of Classics, researched and wrote the entries for Sections B, C, and D. Glenn W. Most wrote the entry for C13, and Alice Schreyer and Catherine Uecker prepared the entries for Section E.

ΥΠΟΘΕCΙC ΤΗC Χ ΟΜΗΡΟΥ ΡΑΨΩΔΙΑC.

ἀ περὶ τὴν μνηστοφονίαν ἐργασάμενος ὁ ὀδυσσεὺς παρούσης ἀθηνᾶς, ἐν τοῖς ἑξῆς τὰς θεραπαίνας διὰ τηλεμάχου καὶ τῶν οἰκείων κολάζει ἅμα μελανθίῳ.

ΟΔΥCCΕΙΑC Χ ΟΜΗΡΟΥ ΡΑΨΩΔΙΑC.

Χῖ ὀδυσεὺς μνηστῆρας ἐκαίνυτο νηλέϊ χαλκῷ.

ὐτὰρ ὁ γυμνώθη ῥακέων πο
λύμητις ὀδυσσεύς.
ἆλτο δ' ἐπὶ μέγαν οὐδὸν
ἔχων βιὸν ἠδὲ φαρέτρην
ἰῶν ἐμπλείην, ταχέας δ' ἐκ
χεύατ' ὀϊστοὺς
αὐτοῦ πρόσθε ποδῶν, μετὰ
δὲ μνηστῆρσιν ἔειπεν.
οὗτος μὲν δὴ ἄεθλος ἀάατος
ἐκτετέλεσται.
νῦν αὖτε σκοπὸν ἄλλον, ὃν οὔπω τις βάλεν ἀνήρ,
εἴσομαι αἴ κε τύχοιμι. πόρῃ δέ μοι εὖχος ἀπόλλων,
ἦ. καὶ ἐπ' ἀντινόῳ ἰθύνετο πικρὸν ὀϊστόν.
ἤτοι ὁ καλὸν ἄλεισον ἀναιρήσεσθαι ἔμελλε
χρύσεον ἄμφωτον, καὶ δὴ μετὰ χερσὶν ἐνώμα,
ὄφρα πίοι οἴνοιο. φόνος δέ οἱ οὐκ ἐνὶ θυμῷ
μέμβλετο. τίς κ' οἴοιτο μετ' ἀνδράσι δαιτυμόνεσσι
μοῦνον ἐνὶ πλεόνεσσι, καὶ εἰ μάλα καρτερὸς εἴη,
οἷ τεύξειν θάνατόν τε κακὸν καὶ κῆρα μέλαιναν;
τὸν δ' ὀδυσεὺς κατὰ λαιμὸν ἐπισχόμενος βάλεν ἰῷ.
ἀντικρὺ δ' ἁπαλοῖο δι' αὐχένος ἤλυθ' ἀκωκή.
ἐκλίνθη δ' ἑτέρωσε. δέπας δέ οἱ ἔκπεσε χειρὸς
βλημένου. αὐτίκα δ' αὐλὸς ἀνὰ ῥῖνας παχὺς ἦλθεν
αἵματος ἀνδρομέοιο. θοῶς δ' ἀπὸ εἷο τράπεζαν
ὦσε ποδὶ πλήξας, ἀπὸ δ' εἴδατα χεῦεν ἔραζε,
σῖτός τε κρέα τ' ὀπτὰ φορύνετο. τοὶ δ' ὁμάδησαν
μνηστῆρες κατὰ δῶμα, ὅπως ἴδον ἄνδρα πεσόντα.
ἐκ δὲ θρόνων ἀνόρουσαν ὀρινθέντες κατὰ δῶμα
πάντοσε παπταίνοντες ἐϋδμήτους ποτὶ τοίχους,
οὐδέ πῃ ἀσπὶς ἔην, οὐδ' ἄλκιμον ἔγχος ἑλέσθαι.

BIBLIOTHECA HOMERICA LANGIANA

SECTION A

GREEK EDITIONS

A1

Demetrio Calcondila (1423–1511). Ἡ τοῦ Ὁμήρου ποίησις ἅπασα. Florence: Bernardus Nerlius, Nerius Nerlius, and Demetrius Damilas, 1488.

Folio.

Although incomplete, this copy contains a representative amount of the full edition, with 192 leaves out of a possible 440. It begins with the second and third pages of Chalcondylas's preface. This is followed by the texts of Ps.-Herodotus, Ps.-Plutarch, and Dio Chrysostom, most of the *Odyssey* (beginning in book 5), the complete *Batrachomyomachia*, the *Hymn to Apollo*, and part of the *Hymn to Hermes.*

The first printed edition of Homer, this is also one of the earliest printed editions of any ancient Greek author. The inspiration and funding for this edition came from two Florentine brothers, Bernardo and Nerio Nerli, with the help of Giovanni Acciaioli. The text was edited by Demetrius Chalcondylas and produced at the press of Bartolommeo di Libri, who was one of the most prolific printers in the late fifteenth century. According to Proctor, di Libri published approximately 200 books from 1482 to 1500, although few bear his name (pp. 66–69).

The edition contains two prefaces, one in Latin by Bernardo Nerli and the other in Greek by Chalcondylas. This is followed by Ps.-Herodotus's biography of Homer, Ps.-Plutarch's "On the Life and Works of Homer," and Dio Chrysostom's fifty-third oration, "On Homer"; then comes the text of the *Iliad*, *Odyssey*, *Batrachomyomachia*, and *Hymns*.

In his preface, Bernardo dedicates the edition to Piero de' Medici. He explains that the lack of books has proved troublesome for students of Greek literature, himself included, and in response he decided to offer some aid and encouragement by publishing a Greek text. It was on Chalcondylas's suggestion that Bernardo chose to publish the works of Homer. Bernardo notes the sad state of the text as reported by the manuscript sources, although he does not say which specific manuscripts Chalcondylas consulted when preparing it. In assembling and emending the text, Chalcondylas consulted Eustathius's commentary (see

D4 for a copy of the first printed edition). Bernardo justifies the inclusion of the accessory texts (Herodotus, Plutarch, and Dio) not only for the biographical information they provide about Homer, but also for the light that they shed on the meaning of the text and the teaching contained in it.

Chalcondylas was a key figure in the transmission of Greek to Renaissance Italy. Born in Athens, he moved to Italy in the 1440s and was by this time Professor of Greek in Florence. His preface addresses many of the same issues as Bernardo's: the benefit of having more Greek books available, the usefulness of the accessory texts, his consultation of Eustathius. He adds a short discussion of the *Batrachomyomachia* and *Hymns*, which he singles out as especially corrupt textually. He hopes that this edition will lend support to students of Greek literature and inspire a wider interest in Greek culture.

This edition is a fine example of fifteenth-century Greek printing. The type was cast and set by Demetrius Damilas (also known as Demetrius Cretensis), based on a type that he had used earlier for the Ἐπιτομή of Constantine Lascaris, published in 1476 and the earliest dated book printed entirely in Greek. The same type reappears three times in books produced by the Giuntine press (see A3). In contrast to the cursive style that the Aldine press established and that dominated Greek print until the end of the nineteenth century, Damilas's type made only limited attempts to reproduce features of contemporary handwriting; it has, for example, upright letter forms and is relatively free of ligatures.

Deutscher, Thomas B. "Demetrius Chalcondyles." *Contemporaries of Erasmus: A Biographical Register of the Renaissance and Reformation.* Edited by Peter G. Bietenholz. Toronto: University of Toronto Press, 1985–87.

Proctor, Robert. *The Printing of Greek in the Fifteenth Century.* Oxford: Oxford University Press, 1900.

A2

Aldo Manuzio (1449/50–1515). Ὁμήρου Ἰλιάς, Ὀδύσσεια. βατραχομυομαχία. ὕμνοι. λβ = *Homeri Ilias, Vlyssea....* Venice: Aldus, 1504.

Octavo. 2 vols.

Each volume bears a bookplate of early twentieth-century adventurer and book collector Cortlandt F. Bishop. Volume 1 bears an ownership signature dated 1860, apparently that of John S. Blackie, the Scottish classicist who translated B19 (he likely consulted this very volume in the preparation of that text). Volume 2 bears the bookplate of bookseller Leo S. Olschki. Pasted on a blank preliminary leaf of volume one is a small sixteenth-century engraving depicting a triton and a Nereid, signed with a crossed P.

Both volumes contain annotations in various older hands, volume one in

Greek and Latin, volume 2 in French, Greek, and an as yet unidentified script. The front flyleaf of volume one contains a handwritten list of readings.

Aldus Manutius dedicated his life to promoting the study of the classics. He founded the New Academy of Hellenists in 1500 and the following year began printing a series of small editions of classical authors in Greek, Latin, and Italian. This edition of Homer, the second Greek edition to be printed and the first of three from the Aldine press, is one of the fruits of that project. Aldus's pocket-sized editions, which made original texts available to scholars at a reasonable price, greatly contributed to the growth of interest in the classics in Italy.

The text largely reproduces that of the *editio princeps* (A1), although it corrects many errors in the earlier edition. This suggests that Aldus consulted other manuscripts, unlike most other editors, who simply relied on previous print editions. Like other Aldine publications, it was compact and affordable. As such, the virtues of the *editio princeps* notwithstanding, with this edition Homer first became widely accessible to readers in the original Greek. This edition and the second Aldine edition of 1517 (not in the BHL) served as the basis for or had a strong influence on subsequent editions until the print publication of Eustathius (D4).

In the preface to this edition, Aldus Manutius dedicates the work to Jerome Aleander, whom he praises for his great talents and enthusiasm for learning. Aleander was still a young man at the time; Aldus marvels that he is so learned while not yet twenty-four, and he uses Aleander's character and learning as justification for the dedication. The preface to the second edition is also addressed to Aleander; here Aldus remarks that he must say some words about the *Batrachomyomachia* and the *Hymns*, and proceeds to quote Chalcondylas, who Aldus says had already given them sufficient treatment in the preface to his edition (A1).

Aleander had grown up near Venice and studied there. In 1508 he moved to Paris and worked as a teacher of Greek and Latin, eventually becoming the rector of the University of Paris. Most of his efforts following his return to Italy in 1517 were in the service of the church. Most notably, he was the Pope's representative at the Diet of Worms, leading the opposition against Luther.

The type is a typical Aldine cursive. Whereas Demetrius Damilas's type for A1 attempted to recreate a more ancient style, Proctor states that Aldus used contemporary handwriting as his model. Largely because of the success and prominence of the Aldine press, the cursive style became prevalent, finding its ultimate expression in the French Royal Greek (see A14); otherwise, on practical and perhaps also aesthetic grounds, the history of Greek print would have been better served by the alternate tradition represented by Damilas's more legible and elegant type. (Two attempts to return to earlier styles of Greek handwriting, both at the end of the nineteenth century, can be seen in the Macmillan Greek type [see A30] and Robert Proctor's Otter Greek [see A32].) As Scholderer describes it, "By providing books imitating the familiar script of the day, he had given the public what it wanted, with the result that the finer traditions of his predecessors withered at the roots and cursive Greek was in a few decades established as the typographical norm all over Europe" (p. 8). Only with the emergence of Porson Greek at the beginning of the nineteenth century (see A22) would the cursive style find a serious and successful challenger.

A2

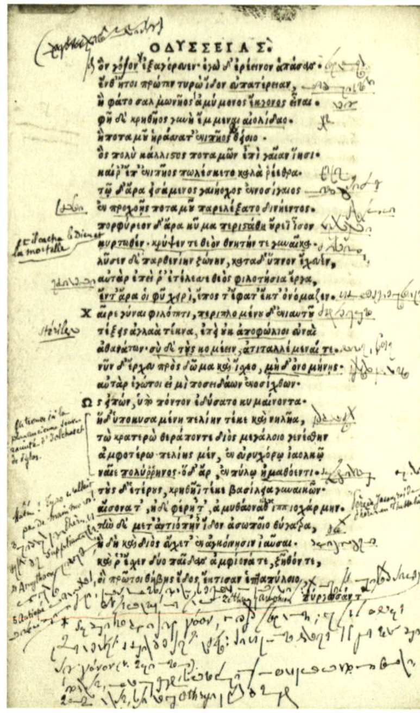

A2

Lowry, M. J. C. "Aldo Manuzio." *Contemporaries of Erasmus.*

Proctor, Robert. *The Printing of Greek in the Fifteenth Century.* Oxford: Oxford University Press, 1900.

Scholderer, Victor. *Greek Printing Types, 1465–1927.* London: British Museum, 1927.

A3

Antonio Francini. Ὀδύσσεια. Βατραχομυομαχία. ὕμνοι. λβ = *Vlyssea.* . . . Florence: In ædibus hæredum Philippi Iuntæ, 1519.

Octavo.

ΟΔΥΣΣΕΙΑ.
Βατραχομυομαχία.
ὕμνοι. λβ.

VLYSSEA.
Batrachomyomachia.
Hymni. xxxij.

A3

A handwritten note on the title page suggests that this was once in the library of a monastery of the Order of the Minims, in the Brie region of France. Pages 3 (signed a5) and 4 (unsigned) are misbound from the *Iliad* and interrupt between page 4 (signed aiiii) and page 5 (unsigned) of the *Odyssey*. The *Iliad* volume of this edition is not part of the BHL.

Bernardo Giunti's family, originally from Florence, was a key player in Italian publishing in the fifteenth and sixteenth centuries. The Florentine branch was founded by Bernardo's father Filippo in 1489 as a stationery shop (following close upon the appearance of A1 in that same city); the first book he published was the Ἐπιτομή of Zenobius, in 1497. The Venetian branch, founded by Filippo's younger brother Lucantonio (see A9) in 1480, was a larger and more successful business, yet the Florentine branch's significance lies in its more scholarly focus. Like the Aldine press, it focused on producing classical and humanist texts.

The editor was Antonio Francini. Originally from Montevarchi, he taught Greek in Florence, and in 1516 began a longstanding collaboration with the Giunti, editing around thirty texts. After the fall of the Florentine Republic in 1532, he moved to Venice to work with Lucantonio Giunti. There he edited, among other works, a revised edition of this Homer (A9).

Francini wrote the prefaces to each volume. He dedicates the *Iliad* volume to Lorenzo Bartolini, at the suggestion of Filippo's son Bernardo, and the *Odyssey* volume to Bartolomeo Cavalcanti. In the latter preface he includes the same text of Chalcondylas that Aldus had quoted in the preface of A2. The main text has been copied from the second Aldine edition, published in 1517 (not in the BHL; this was the intermediate edition between A2 and A6), and Heyne (A23) demonstrates that it even includes some of the errors from that edition.

Following the publication of A1, Filippo Giunti purchased the type and re-used it for the *Proverbs of Zenobios* (1497), *Orpheus* (1500), and an edition of Chrysoloras's *Erotemata* (ca. 1496; although its use for this publication is uncertain). The type used for this edition, however, is an upright cursive, similar to that used in A4 and A5.

Heyne, Christian Gottlob. *Homeri Ilias.* Leipzig: In libraria Weidmannia and London: Apud I. Payne et MacKinlay, 1802.

Pettas, William A. *The Giunti of Florence: Merchant Publishers of the Sixteenth Century.* San Francisco: B. M. Rosenthal, 1980.

A4

Angelo Poliziano (1454–1494). Ὁμήρου Ὀδυσσείας βίβλοι Α. καὶ Β. = *Homeri Vlysseae. . . .* Basel: Ex aedibus Andreae Cratandri, 1520.

Quarto.

Throughout are notes (some canceled) in a contemporary hand, containing translations into Latin, interpretative comments on style, content, and grammatical forms.

This appears to be the first schoolbook edition of the *Odyssey* and the first separate printing of any part of the *Odyssey* in Greek. It was published by Andreas Cratander, a printer and bookseller who was active in Basel from 1518 to 1536. His business only reached a moderate size, and he specialized in shorter texts and texts for university students.

In his preface, Cratander recalls his earlier publications for the teaching of Greek, including a grammar (*Dragmata graecae literaturae*, 1518) and a lexicon (*Dictionarium graecum*, 1519). This edition of Homer was intended to address the scarcity of Greek texts. Although it contains only the first two books of the *Odyssey*, Cratander puts forward the possibility of publishing the remaining books, should the edition be well received by readers (*duos priores* Ὀδυσσεῖας [sic] *libros . . . damus . . . exhibituri et in posterum reliquos, si gratum id tuo studio testeris*). (In A5 one observes the same publication strategy, although that text was eventually completed.)

Cratander names two individuals who strongly encouraged this publication, Caspar Hedio and Jacobus Nepos. Hedio was a scholar and preacher who had recently completed his studies in theology at the University of Basel. Later in life he was actively involved in education in Strasbourg, where he was appointed preacher at the cathedral. He made important contributions to the study and documentation of church history. Nepos was a private secretary to Erasmus and later worked at the Froben press in Basel. He was also a teacher of Greek, and his private teaching, together with a course of lectures on Homer at the University of Basel around this time, would explain his interest in the production of this edition of Homer.

Certain features of the text confirm that it was designed with students in mind. Cratander notes that it is of a manageable size (*in forma portatili*), and that it has been set with generous interlinear spacing, so that the student can easily take notes on prosody (this, he says, aids greatly in students' memory). The text has generous margins suited to additional note-taking.

This edition also includes a preface to Homer by the famed humanist and classical scholar Angelo Poliziano (or Politian), which Cratander believes will give the careful reader more direct access to the poet himself through its treatment of his life, genius, and teaching.

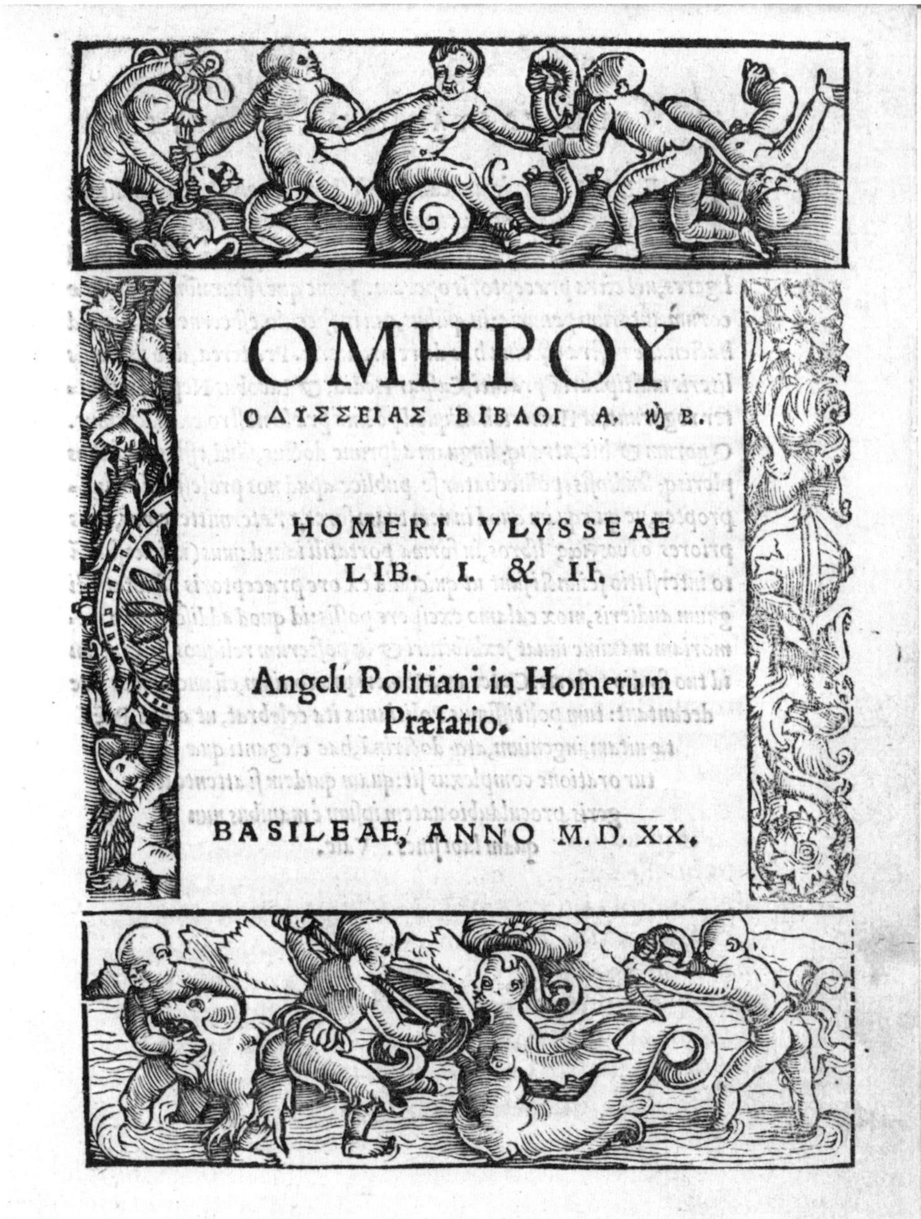

ΟΜΗΡΟΥ

ΟΔΥΣΣΕΙΑΣ ΒΙΒΛΟΙ Α. καὶ Β.

HOMERI VLYSSEAE
LIB. I. & II.

Angeli Politiani in Homerum
Præfatio.

BASILEAE, ANNO M.D.XX.

A4

Νῦν δ' αὖ καὶ πολὺ μεῖζον. ὃ δὴ τάχα οἶκον ἅπαντα
Πάγχυ διαῤῥαίσει. βίοτον δ' ἄπο πάμπαν ὀλέσσει.
Μητέρι μοι μνηστῆρες ἐπέχραον, οὐκ ἐθελούσῃ,
Τῶν ἀνδρῶν φίλοι υἷες οἳ ἐνθάδε γ' εἰσὶν ἄριστοι.
Οἱ πατρὸς μὲν ἐς οἶκον ἀπεῤῥίγασι νέεσθαι,
Ἰκαρίου ὥς κ' αὐτὸς ἐεδνώσαιτο θύγατρα, — unde ἔεδνα dote [illegible]
Δοίη δ' ᾧ κ' ἐθέλοι. καί οἱ κεχαρισμένος ἔλθοι.
Οἱ δ' εἰς ἡμέτερον πωλεύμενοι ἤματα πάντα,
Βοῦς ἱερεύοντες καὶ ὄϊς, καὶ πίονας αἶγας
Εἰλαπινάζουσι, πίνουσί τε αἴθοπα οἶνον — quod adversus facere [illegible]
Μαψιδίως, τὰ δὲ πολλὰ κατάνεται, οὐ γὰρ ἔπ' ἀνὴρ
Οἷος ὀδυσσεὺς ἔσκεν ἀρὴν ἀπὸ οἴκου ἀμῦναι.
Ἡμεῖς δ' οὔ νύ τι τοῖοι ἀμυνέμεν, ἦ καὶ ἔπειτα
Λευγαλέοι τ' ἐσόμεθα, καὶ οὐ δεδαηκότες ἀλκήν. — [illegible]
Ἦ τ' ἂν ἀμυναίμην, εἴ μοι δύναμίς γε παρείη.
Οὐ γὰρ ἔτ' ἀνσχετὰ ἔργα τετεύχαται. οὐδ' ἔτι καλῶς — a τεύχομαι
Οἶκος ἐμὸς διόλωλε. νεμεσσήθητε καὶ αὐτοί.

ἀνέσχετα [illegible]

The type is an early, upright German cursive, modeled on the cursives of Aldus and Callierges. Scholderer describes it as "the first cursive to appear out of Italy, and one which in its turn made its influence felt both in Germany and in France" (p. 9). This same type is used in A5.

Bietenholz, Peter G. "Andreas Cratander." *Contemporaries of Erasmus.*

——— . "Jacobus Nepos." *Contemporaries of Erasmus.*

Chrisman, Miriam U. "Caspar Hedio." *Contemporaries of Erasmus.*

Scholderer, Victor. *Greek Printing Types, 1465–1927.* London: British Museum, 1927.

A5

Ὁμήρου Ἰλιάδος βίβλοι Α. καὶ Β. = *Homeri Iliados....* Louvain: Theodo. Martin. excudebat, 1521–23.

Quarto.

A note written in the inside front cover refers to the second edition of Clarke (A19). The final line explains that many of the handwritten notes in this copy have been taken from Clarke's edition. The text to the first book of the *Iliad* contains marginal and interlinear notes written in two hands, containing Latin translations of Greek words, grammatical forms, and some exegetical notes.

This is the first recorded printing of the *Iliad* outside of Italy, and the first printing of Homer in the Netherlands. It was produced by Dirk Martens, an important figure in early Dutch printing. Trained in Venice, he began printing in Aalst in 1473, later establishing himself in Antwerp and Louvain. He was responsible, among other things, for printing the first book in the Netherlands to contain Greek letters. More generally, he played an important role in the diffusion of classical and humanistic texts. He had a close friendship with Erasmus and printed many of his writings.

This was a serial publication (see A4). The first two books were printed in 1521, the rest in 1523. Book 2 ends on the recto of its final sheet, with the word τέλος ("end"); on the verso is the printer's mark of Dirk Martens. The remainder of the *Iliad* then follows, beginning with a decoration and ΥΠΟΘΕΣΙΣ in large type (the following hypothesis headings are all normal). The type is subtly different between the two printings, perhaps most evident in the shape of the rho. The book ends with another printer's mark, slightly different than the first.

The origins of the text are unclear. Heyne suggests (A23, pp. 3.xv–xvi) that this is a copy of the second Aldine (not in BHL, but see A2 and A6), with occasional readings taken from the first Aldine (A2) and the *editio princeps* (A1). But it is also possible that the printer used a copy of the first Aldine that had

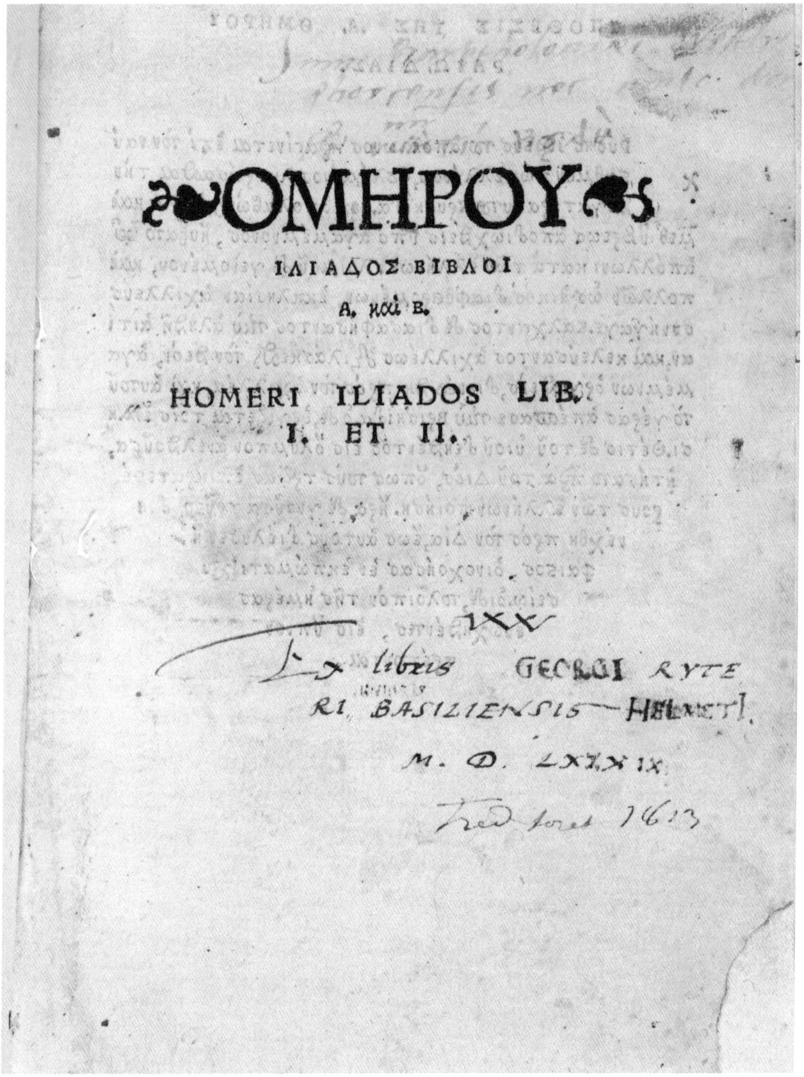

A5

corrections added from the second Aldine. In any event, this edition draws in various ways from these three earlier editions.

The type is the same German cursive that appears in A4.

Heyne, Christian Gottlob. *Homeri Ilias.* Leipzig: In libraria Weidmannia and London: Apud I. Payne et MacKinlay, 1802.

IJsewijn, J. "Dirk Martens." *Contemporaries of Erasmus.*

A6

Aldo Manuzio (1449/50–1515). Ὁμήρου Ἰλιάς, Ὀδύσσεια. βατραχομυομαχία. ὕμνοι. λβ = *Homeri Ilias, Vlyssea....* Venice: In Aedibus Aldi, et Andreae Asulani Soceri, 1524.

Octavo. 2 vols.

Each volume contains a slip of paper with the handwritten note "Complete, / pp. B. Quaritch Ltd. / AB" (on Bernard Quaritch, see A11). A third slip, included with the first volume, reads, "I think this cheap at 3 guineas / it cost 2£."

This is the third and final complete Aldine edition of Homer. It was edited by Franciscus Asulanus, the son of Andreas Asulanus, Aldus's father-in-law. Following Aldus's death in 1515, Andreas managed the business together with his two sons. Franciscus was also responsible for the Aldine editions of the scholia ascribed to Didymus (the D-scholia). The *Iliad* scholia were printed in 1521 (D1; reprinted in A8), the *Odyssey* scholia in 1528.

This edition is largely a reprint of the second Aldine edition of 1517. Comparison with the first Aldine shows that, even with minor variations in spacing and details of the type, the layout is unchanged, following the same pagination and line breaks. Although it contains a handful of textual differences, unfortunately it also introduces many new errors. Heyne (A23) remarks that, even though the *Iliad* scholia ascribed to Didymus had been published, first in 1517, and then in 1521 by Asulanus himself (D1), it appears that they were not used or consulted in the production of this edition (p. 3.ix).

Heyne, Christian Gottlob. *Homeri Ilias.* Leipzig: In libraria Weidmannia and London: Apud I. Payne et MacKinlay, 1802.

A7

Johann Lonitzer (1499–1569). Ὀδύσσεια. βατραχομυομαχία. ὕμνοι. λβ. ἡ τῶν αὐτῶν πολυπλόκος ἀνάγνωσις. Strasbourg: Apud Wolphium Cephalaeum, 1525.

Octavo.

This copy bears a handwritten note along the top of the title page. It is partially cut off—at some point this copy was cut down from its original size—and very faded. At the bottom of the title page another note identifies it as belonging to George Leonbardus Faber, of Graz in Styria.

Handwritten notes appear in the earlier sections of the text, including in the preface, where some passages have been underlined and a printing error has been corrected. The notes consist almost exclusively of Latin glosses of individual words, such as a student would use.

This edition of the *Odyssey*, *Batrachomyomachia*, and *Hymns* was published together with a companion volume containing the *Iliad* (not in the BHL) by Wolfgang Faber Capito (in the colophon he adopts the Hellenized name "Cephalaeus"). The text was edited by Johann Lonitzer. These men were connected not only by their interest in humanistic studies and theology, but also by their allegiance to Martin Luther and his reform movement.

Capito was born near Strasbourg, in Haguenau. He studied theology in Freiburg and was proficient in Hebrew as well as Greek and Latin. From 1515 to 1519 he lived in Basel, where he served as cathedral preacher and professor of theology. He played an active role in the academic community affiliated with the presses of Froben (see A8 on his relation to Herwagen) and Cratander (A4), and during this time he became acquainted with Luther. Back in Strasbourg, where he lived from 1523 until his death, he was an important Reformation leader.

Lonitzer was educated in Wittenberg, taught for a short while in Freiburg, and eventually settled in Strasbourg. Here he worked with Capito not only on this edition of Homer, but also on an edition of the Septuagint (1524–26). From 1527 until his death in 1569 he lived in Marburg, where he taught Greek and Hebrew. He too was involved with publishers in Basel, including Cratander (A4) and Herwagen (A8), producing translations, commentaries, and a Greek grammar. While at Wittenberg, Lonitzer had studied under Philipp Melanchthon, the influential Reformation humanist and theologian. Lonitzer dedicates this edition to his former teacher.

This edition draws heavily from the second and third Aldine editions (A6; see also A2). The pagination is identical throughout the *Odyssey* and *Batrachomyomachia*, and only begins to diverge in the *Hymn to Aphrodite*. The excerpt by Chalcondylas about the *Batrachomyomachia* and *Hymns* (also included in A2 and A3) is placed after the texts.

In preparing this edition, Lonitzer compared the readings of the Aldine editions against those of the *editio princeps* (A1), but rather than silently incorporating this or that reading into the text, he kept track of the variant readings and included them at the back of each volume. These are introduced in this volume under the heading "ἡ τῆς Ὀδυσσείας πολύπλοκος ἀνάγνωσις, ἐκ τῆς Φλωρεντίνης, χ᾽ ἑκατέρας Ἀλδίνης ἐκδόσεων συλλεχθεῖσα" ("The multifarious reading of the *Odyssey*, collected from the Florentine edition and each Aldine edition"); similar headings for the *Batrachomyomachia* and the *Hymns* follow. Although presented in a rather unwieldy layout (the variants are reported in one continuous block of text), the listing itself is an important development in the printed editions of Homer. Later editions that copy or draw from this listing (e.g., A8, A11, A13) adopt more usable tabular layouts for presenting the same information.

This volume ends with a section entitled ΟΜΗΡΟΥ ΒΙΟΣ ("Life of Homer"), containing the same texts of Ps.-Herodotus, Ps.-Plutarch, and Dio Chrysostom that appear in the *editio princeps* (A1); these follow the pagination of the texts as printed in the Aldine editions (A2, A6).

Because of its usefulness as a critical text, this edition influenced many subsequent editions, including that of Herwagen (A8) and the second Giuntine (A9), and it was an important source in the preparation of such influential editions as those of Turnebus (A11) and Estienne (A14).

Guenther, Ilse. "Johannes Lonicerus." *Contemporaries of Erasmus.*

Kittelson, James M. "Wolfgang Faber Capito." *Contemporaries of Erasmus.*

A8

Johann Herwagen (1497–1559?). Ὁμήρου Ἰλιὰς καὶ Ὀδύσσεια μετὰ τῆς ἐξηγήσιος = *Homeri Ilias et Vlyssea....* Basel: Apud Io. Hervagium, 1535.

Folio.

The front inside cover bears the owner's mark of Edward Davies Davenport. Marginal notes in Latin indicate the topics covered in the scholia, with occasional Greek notes dealing with issues of language and style. Latin explanatory notes appear around the main text. The beginning of the *Iliad* has a long marginal note about Achilles's patronymic (Πηληϊάδεω in line 1). A note on the first page of the *Odyssey* appears to be a Latin translation of the opening lines.

Although not the first printed edition of the Homeric scholia, this edition is the first to present the scholia alongside the text of the poems. The Aldine press had already published these scholia (here the D-scholia that have traditionally been attributed to Didymus). The scholia on the *Iliad* appeared in 1521 (D1), followed by those on the *Odyssey* in 1528 (see also A6 on Asulanus, who edited these volumes).

Starting in the second half of the fifteenth century, Basel had become an important humanistic center (see A7). Johann Herwagen operated one of the major presses of the sixteenth century there, the other two being those of Froben and Cratander (A4). Before moving to Basel in 1528, Herwagen had run a productive publishing house in Strasbourg. Once in Basel he joined the Froben press (marrying the widow of the recently deceased Froben), and in 1531 he established his own press, which focused on ancient history and literature.

Following the Strasbourg edition of 1525 (A7), Herwagen provides listings of variant readings. Those for the *Iliad* precede the text, and those for the *Odyssey* follow it. The heading, "*Annotatio locorum quibus Aldino exemplari quod fere secuti sumus, cum Florentino non convenit*" ("Register of passages where the Aldine copy, which I have for the most part followed, does not agree with the Florentine"), sug-

δισυλλάβως. χρὴ γὰρ λέγειν μονοσυλλάβως λᾶν. οἵ δ' οἴτυλον.) καὶ οἴτυλον. ἔστι δὲ καὶ αὕτη πόλις λακεδαιμονίας. ἀπάτερθεν.) ἄπωθεν. χωρίς. κίεν.) παρεγίνετο. ᾗσι προθυμίῃσι.) ταῖς ἑαυτοῦ προθυμίαις. πεποιθώς.) πεπιστευκώς. ὀτρύνων.) παρορμῶν. ἵετο.) προεθυμεῖτο. θυμῷ.) τῇ ψυχῇ. τίσασθαι.) τιμωρήσασθαι. ὁρμήματα.) μεριμνήματα. στοναχάς τε.) καὶ στεναγμούς. Πύλον.) πύλος ὁ ὑπὸ νέστορι τῆς μεσσηνίας, τὸ καὶ κορυφάσιον. ὁ δὲ τῆς ἀρκαδίας οὐ τοῦ Νέστορος πατρίς. ὁ δὲ τῆς ἠλείας παρὰ τὴν ὠλενίαν πέτραν. θρύον.) πόλιν τῆς ἤλιδος ἣν ἑτέρως θρυόεσσαν λέγουσιν.

Ἑξήκοντα νεῶν. ἀπάτερθε δὲ θωρήσσοντο.
Ἐν δ' αὐτὸς κίεν. ᾗσι προθυμίῃσι πεποιθὼς
Ὀτρύνων πόλεμόνδε, μάλιστα δὲ ἵετο θυμῷ
Τίσασθαι ἑλένης ὁρμήματά τε, στοναχάς τε.
Οἳ δὲ πύλον τ' ἐνέμοντο, καὶ ἀρήνην ἐρατεινήν,
Καὶ θρύον ἀλφειοῖο πόρον, καὶ ἐΰκτιτον αἰπύ,
Καὶ κυπαρισσήεντα, καὶ ἀμφιγένειαν ἔναιον,
Καὶ πτελεὸν, καὶ ἕλος, καὶ δώριον, ἔνθα τε μοῦσαι
Ἀντόμεναι, Θάμυριν τὸν θρήϊκα παῦσαν ἀοιδῆς,
Οἰχαλίηθεν ἰόντα παρ' Εὐρύτου οἰχαλιῆος.
Στεῦτο γὰρ εὐχόμενος νικησέμεν, εἴπερ ἂν αὐταὶ
Μοῦσαι ἀείδοιεν κοῦραι Διὸς αἰγιόχοιο,
Αἱ δὲ, χολωσάμεναι, πηρὸν θέσαν, αὐτὰρ ἀοιδὴν
Θεσπεσίην ἀφέλοντο, καὶ ἐκλέλαθον κιθαριστύν.
Τῶν, αὖτ' ἡγεμόνευε γερήνιος ἱππότα Νέστωρ,
Τῷ δ' ἐνενήκοντα γλαφυραὶ νέες ἐστιχόωντο.
Οἳ δ' ἔχον ἀρκαδίην, ὑπὸ κυλλήνης ὄρος αἰπύ,
Αἰπύτιον παρὰ τύμβον, ἵν' ἀνέρες ἀγχιμαχηταί,
Οἳ φενεόν τ' ἐνέμοντο, καὶ ὀρχομενὸν πολύμηλον.
Ῥίπην τε. στρατίην τε, καὶ ἠνεμόεσσαν ἐνίσπην,
Καὶ τεγέην εἶχον, καὶ μαντινέην ἐρατεινήν,
Στύμφηλόν τ' εἶχον, καὶ παρρασίην ἐνέμοντο,
Τῶν, ἦρχ' ἀγκαίοιο πάϊς κρείων ἀγαπήνωρ,
Ἑξήκοντα νεῶν. πολέες δ' ἐν νηῒ ἑκάστῃ
Ἀρκάδες ἄνδρες ἔβαινον ἐπιστάμενοι πολέμοιο.
Αὐτὸς γάρ σφιν δῶκεν ἄναξ ἀνδρῶν Ἀγαμέμνων
Νῆας ἐϋσσέλμους περάαν ἐπὶ οἴνοπα πόντον
Ἀτρεΐδης. ἐπεὶ οὔ σφι θαλάσσια ἔργα μεμήλει,

Οἱ δ'

ἀλφειοῖο πόρον.) καθ' Ὅμηρον ποσὶ διαβατός ἐστιν ὁ ἀλφειὸς ποταμός. πόρον γὰρ τὸ διαβατὸν αὐτοῦ μέρος φησίν. ἔστι δὲ ὁ ἀλφειὸς τῆς ἠλίας χώρας. αἰπύ.) βαρυτόνως λεκτέον. ὄνομα γὰρ ἐστὶ πόλεως. τὸ δὲ ὀξυτονούμενον ἐπίθετόν ἐστι, καὶ σημαίνει τὸ ὑψηλόν. τῶν μέν τοι εἰς .υ. ληγόντων οὐδετέρων γίγνονται τὰ θηλυκὰ εἰς .α. λήγει τῇ .ει. διφθόγγῳ παραληγόμενα. οἷον αἰπὺ καὶ αἰπεῖα κολώνη. ὀξύ, ὀξεῖα. ταχύ, ταχεῖα. ἔνθα.) ὅπου, ἐν τῷ δωρίῳ. ἔστι δὲ ὄνομα πόλεως. ἀντόμεναι.) ἀπαντήσασαι. θάμυριν.) οὗτος παῖς ἦν φιλάμμωνος καὶ ἀρσίης τῆς νύμφης, τὸ γένος θρᾷξ. ὃς ἔσχεν αἰσχρὸν ἔρωτα πρῶτος ἀρξάμενος ἐρᾶν ἀρρένων. οὗτος κάλλει πολλῷ διενεγκὼν, καὶ κιθαρῳδίᾳ περὶ μουσικῆς ἐρίσας ταῖς μούσαις συνέθετο, ἂν μὲν κρείττων εὑρεθῇ πλησιάσαι πάσαις. ἂν δὲ ἡττηθῇ, στερηθῆναι οὗ ἂν ἐκεῖναι θέλωσι. καθυπέρτεραι δὲ αἱ μοῦσαι γενόμεναι, τῶν ὀμμάτων αὐτὸν καὶ τῆς κιθαρῳδίας, καὶ τοῦ νοῦ ἐστέρησαν. θρήϊκα.) θρᾷκα. παῦσαν.) ἔπαυσαν. ἐπέσχον. ἀοιδῆς.) τῆς ᾠδῆς. ἰόντα.) πορευόμενον. οἰχαλίηθεν.) ἀπὸ τῆς οἰχαλίας πόλεως τῆς θεσσαλίας, ἧς ἐβασίλευσεν εὔρυτος. οἰχαλιῆος.) τοῦ ἀπὸ τῆς οἰχαλίας. στεῦτο.) διεβεβαιοῦτο. ἔλεγεν. εὐχόμενος.) μεγαλαυχῶν. νικησέμεν.) νικήσειν. εἴπερ ἂν αὐταὶ μοῦσαι ἀείδοιεν.) εἰ αὐταὶ ᾄδοιεν αἱ μοῦσαι. κοῦραι Διός.) αἱ τοῦ Διὸς θυγατέρες. χολωσάμεναι.) ὀργισθεῖσαι.

πηρὸν θέσαν.) ἤτοι τῆς τέχνης ἔπαυσαν καὶ ἔκφρονα αὐτὸν ἐποίησαν, ἢ περὶ τὴν φωνὴν ἔβλαψαν. πηρὸς γὰρ καλεῖται ὁ κατά τι μέρος τοῦ σώματος βεβλαμμένος. θεσπεσίην.) θείαν. θαυμαστήν. ἀφέλοντο.) ἀφείλοντο. καὶ ἐκλέλαθον κιθαριστύν.) καὶ ἐπιλαθέσθαι ἐποίησαν τὴν κιθαρῳδίαν. ὁ δὲ σχηματισμὸς τῆς λέξεως αἰολικός. ὁμοίως δὲ τῷ κιθαριστὺν καὶ ὀρχηστύν. ἱππότα.) ἱππικός. ἐστιχόωντο.) κατὰ τάξιν ἐπορεύοντο. κυλλήνης.) κυλλήνη ὄρος ὑψηλὸν τῆς ἀρκαδίας. καὶ πόλις οὖσα παρ' αὐτῷ ὁμώνυμος ἐν ᾧ ὄρει δοκεῖ ἑρμῆς γεγενῆσθαι ἐκ μαίας τῆς ἄτλαντος θυγατρὸς καὶ Διός. ὅθεν καὶ κυλλήνιον τὸν θεόν φασιν. αἰπύ.) ὑψηλόν. μέγα. αἰπύτιον, παρὰ τύμβον.) παρὰ τὸν τοῦ αἰπύτου τάφον. ὁ δὲ αἴπυτος ἀρχαιότατος ἥρως, ἀρκὰς τὸ γένος. ἵνα.) ὅπου. ἀνέρες ἀγχιμαχηταί.) οἱ ἐγγὺς καὶ συστάδην μαχόμενοι ἄνδρες. προσληπτέον δὲ τὸ εἰσί. πολύμηλον.) πολλὰ θρέμματα ἔχοντα. ῥίπην τε στρατίην τε.) πόλεις ἀρκαδίας. ἠνεμόεσσαν.) ὑπὸ ἀνέμου καταπνεομένην. ὑψηλήν. καὶ τεγέην.) τέγεα πόλιν ἀρκαδίας. καὶ μαντινέην.) καὶ μαντίνειαν. στύμφηλον.) ἣν οἱ κατοικοῦντες στυμφήλιοι λέγονται. καὶ παρρασίην.) πόλιν ἀρκαδίας. ἀγκαίοιο πάϊς.) ἀγκαίου παῖς ἀγαπήνωρ. κρείων.) καρτερός. ἰσχυρός. ἐπιστάμενοι.) ἐπιστήμονες. εἰδότες. αὐτὸς γάρ σφιν δῶκεν ἄναξ ἀνδρῶν Ἀγαμέμνων.) τοῖς ἀρκάσι φησὶν αὐτὸς ὁ βασιλεὺς Ἀγαμέμνων παρέσχε ναῦς, διὰ τὸ ἐν μεσογείῳ τῆς πελοποννήσου αὐτοὺς οἰκοῦντας ἀπείρους εἶναι τῶν κατὰ θάλασσαν ἔργων. ἐϋσσέλμους.) εὐκαθέδρους. περάαν.) διαπερᾶν. διϊέναι. ἐπὶ οἴνοπα.) μέλανα. ἐπεὶ οὔ σφι θαλάσσια ἔργα μεμήλει.) ἐπεὶ ἄπειροι ἦσαν τῶν κατὰ θάλασσαν ἔργων, καὶ

οὐδαμ…

θαμυρις

Νεστορ

ἀρκαδες

gests that Herwagen used the Aldine edition as the main source for his text. Yet the Strasbourg edition used these same sources, and it seems likely that Herwagen simply took the list of variant readings from that edition. Thus it is quite possible that Heyne was right in asserting (A23, p. 3.xix) that the text of this edition was copied from the Strasbourg edition, either its initial printing of 1525 or the following edition of 1534. In support of this, he notes too that this edition reproduces the errors of the Strasbourg edition while introducing some new errors (*Est ex editione Argentoratensi 1525 aut 1534 ducta, etiam cum vitiis, interdum aliis novis sphalmatibus, quae accessere. Ex eadem petita est varia lectio utrique carmini adiecta, reddita tamen latine: numeris passim turbatis. Scholia ex Ald. Scholiorum editione 1521. expressa esse dubitare haud licet*). Although the text of the scholia is likewise copied, having been taken from the earlier Aldine publications, this edition offers a real innovation in its presentation of poem and commentary together.

The Greek type in this edition first appeared in 1530 and quickly became dominant among the printers in Basel. Erasmus praised it for both its graceful design and its compactness. This latter characteristic is particularly important in an edition such as this, where the inclusion of the scholia frequently demands that a large amount of text be placed on the page.

Heyne, Christian Gottlob. *Homeri Ilias*. Leipzig: In libraria Weidmannia and London: Apud I. Payne et MacKinlay, 1802.

Scholderer, Victor. *Greek Printing Types, 1465–1927*. London: British Museum, 1927.

Vervliet, Hendrik D. L. "Greek Printing Types of the French Renaissance: The 'Grecs Du Roy' and Their Successors." *The Palaeotypography of the French Renaissance: Selected Papers on Sixteenth-century Typefaces*. Leiden: Brill, 2008.

A9

Antonio Francini. 'Ομήρου Ὀδύσσεια. βατραχομυομαχία, / ὕμνοι. λβ. / ἡ τῶν αὐτῶν πολυπλόκος ἀνάγνωσις = *Homeri Odyssea*.... Venice: In Officina Lucaeantonii Iuntae, 1537.

Octavo.

The inner front cover of this copy bears the coat of arms and motto of John William Montagu, seventh Earl of Sandwich.

This edition is based on the earlier Giuntine edition, produced by the Florentine branch of the family business that was established by Filippo Giunti. This revised edition was published by the press run by Filippo's younger brother Lucantonio in Venice. The editor, as in the earlier edition, was Antonio Francini. (For more on the relationship between the two, see A3.)

This edition corrects many of the errors in the earlier edition. It also includes fresh readings: In the preface to the *Iliad* volume, Francini claims that he used additional sources available in Venice to further correct the text. Nevertheless, Heyne (A23, p. 3.xiii) argues that he simply took the new readings from the Strasbourg edition of 1525 (A7).

As with A7, this edition follows the pagination of the Aldine editions, with similar signatures. The alignment stops in the *Batrachomyomachia.* (There is a potentially interesting misalignment in the final pages of the *Odyssey.* The second-to-last page of the Aldine has only 29 lines, not the usual 30, but both A7 and this edition have 30 lines.) The *Hymns* are followed by the oft-reproduced passage by Chalcondylas (also A2, A3, A6, A7, all following A1). The title page announces that there is a listing of variant readings, yet none appears in this copy. Following the title page is a poem by Andrea Dazzi, titled "Epigram of Andrea Dazzi to those who are going to read Homer."

Heyne, Christian Gottlob. *Homeri Ilias.* Leipzig: In libraria Weidmannia and London: Apud I. Payne et MacKinlay, 1802.

A10

Edmée Tousan (d. 1541?). Ὁμήρου Ὀδύσσεια. Paris: Edmée Tousan, 1541.

Octavo.

The hypothesis and opening six pages of book 10 are heavily marked with notes in Greek and Latin, consisting mostly of simple grammatical notes and glosses of word meanings.

This early edition of the *Odyssey* is most likely the first separate printing of the complete poem (A4 is an earlier, but partial, printing). The title page bears the printer's mark of Conrad Néobar, who in 1538 had been appointed the first Royal Printer in Greek by François I. (See C3 for François's commission of the first French Homeric translation by Hugues Salel.) Néobar died soon after his appointment, but was likely responsible for initiating work on the French Royal Greek types before his death (see A14). Robert Estienne, the father of Henri Estienne (see A14), then took up the post; he in turn was succeeded by Adrianus Turnebus (see A11).

This edition was mostly likely issued by Néobar's widow, Edmée Toussain. She was a relative of Jacques Toussain, professor of Greek at the Collège Royal (now the Collège de France) from 1530 until his death in 1547. Edmée Toussain continued to publish under Néobar's mark alongside printer Jacques Bogard, whom she seems to have married after Néobar's death, although there remains some uncertainty about the precise relationship.

Beaud, Marie-Josèphe. "À propos des éditions grecques de trois officines parisiennes (1539–1549)." *Le livre dans l'Europe de la Renaissance. Actes du 28e Colloque d'études humanistes de Tours.* Edited by P. Aquilon and H.-J. Martin. Paris: Promodis, 1988.

Bietenholz, Peter G. "Jacques Toussain." *Contemporaries of Erasmus.*

Proctor, Robert. "The French Royal Greek Types and the Eton Chrysostom." *Bibliographical Essays.* London: Chiswick Press, 1905.

——. *The Printing of Greek in the Fifteenth Century.* Oxford: Oxford University Press, 1900.

Vervliet, Hendrik D. L. "Greek Printing Types of the French Renaissance: The 'Grecs Du Roy' and Their Successors." *The Palaeotypography of the French Renaissance: Selected Papers on Sixteenth-century Typefaces.* Leiden: Brill, 2008.

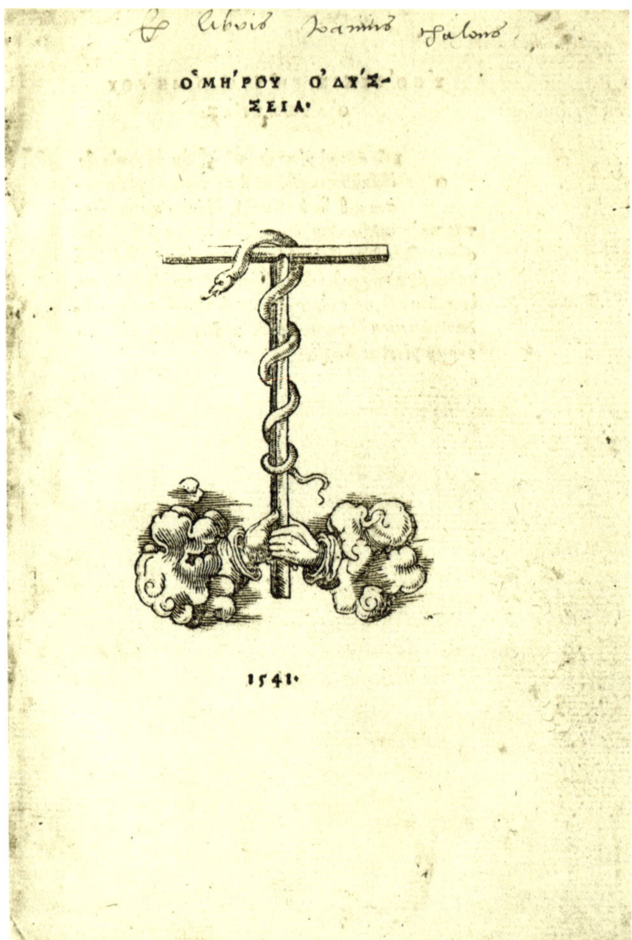

A10

A11

Adrien Turnèbe (1512–1565). Ὁμήρου Ἰλιάς = *Homeri Ilias*.... Paris: Apud Adr. Turnebum typographum Regiu[m], 1554.

Octavo.

This copy was at one point in the collection of Michael Wodhull, the poet, translator, and noted bibliophile. The front flyleaf contains one of his characteristic acquisition notes, recording the source (Davies sale, Feb. 21, 1770), the price paid (10/6), and the cost of binding (4/). Although Wodhull sold a significant portion of his collection during his lifetime, the remainder of his collection was not sold until 1886. This copy would have been in the latter group: The front inside cover contains the owner's mark of Cecily Mary Severne, of the Severne family that inherited Wodhull's estate, and the front flyleaf contains a handwritten note affirming this copy's completeness by the influential London bookseller and publisher, Bernard Quaritch, who is known to have purchased a sizable amount of Wodhull's collection. Although he was the dominant bookseller of his day, Quaritch also supported the production and distribution of scholarly works, especially those he deemed valuable but that lacked popular appeal. The BHL contains another edition once owned by Wodhull (A20), as well as another sold by Quaritch (A6).

A single marginal note is written next to a line in book 3, on p. 55. The line is "αἴθ' ὄφελές τ' ἄγονός τ' ἔμεναι, ἄγαμός τ' ἀπολέσθαι·", and the note marks it as the line frequently spoken by Augustus in his deep despair over his family troubles ("*Citatur ab Augusto apud Sueto. vita Augu. Cap. 65.*"; the precise text in Suetonius differs in that the words ἄγονος and ἄγαμος are reversed). Occasionally lines in the text have been flagged with a faint vertical bar.

Edited and published by the scholar-printer Adrianus Turnebus, this edition is distinctive in its careful preparation and correctness. Although Turnebus included no new sources—according to Heyne (A23, p. 3.xx), he relied on the Aldine editions (see A2 and A6), the recently printed commentary of Eustathius (D4), and the Strasbourg edition (A7)—he inspected and collated them with exceptional care. The result is a text that removes, rather than transmits, errors from previous editions. As with the Strasbourg edition, this edition includes a list of variant readings, and it too follows the Aldine pagination. Together with Stephanus's edition of 1566 (A14), it had a strong influence on later editions until the early eighteenth century, when the editions of Barnes (A18) and Clarke (A19) gained prominence.

From 1547 Turnebus was professor of Greek at the Collège Royal, and in 1551–56 he served as the printer in Greek at the Royal Press. Other publications of his from this period include editions of Aeschylus (1552), Sophocles

πυκνοῖσιν λάεσσι κατεστόρεσαν μεγάλοισι.
ῥίμφα δὲ σῆμ' ἔχεαν, περὶ δὲ σκοποὶ εἵατο πάντῃ,
μὴ πρὶν ἐφορμηθεῖεν ἐϋκνήμιδες ἀχαιοί·
χεύαντες δὲ τὸ σῆμα πάλιν κίον· αὐτὰρ ἔπειτα
εὖ συναγειρόμενοι δαίνυντ' ἐρικυδέα δαῖτα,
δώμασιν ἐν Πριάμοιο διοτρεφέος βασιλῆος.
ὣς οἵ γ' ἀμφίεπον τάφον Ἕκτορος ἱπποδάμοιο.

ΔΙΑ'ΦΟΡΟΙ ΓΡΑΦΑΙ' Ε'Ν τῇ Ἰλιάδι.

Σελ. στίχ. ἀρχή
1 οἰων. οἰωνοῖσι τε· πᾶσι Δι
ὸς δ' ἐτελείετο βουλή.
3 αὐτὰρ, ἐφιεὶς
8 οἷῳ, ὄρητο
ἧς, ὀλέσσῃ
ἦλθον, τὸ σὸν μῦθος
12 Ὣς, κρατερόν τ'
17 ὕψου, ψαμάθου
25 βουλ. βουλίῳ γὰρ ὑπ.
33 ἀγαλ. σὺν νηΐ
χαμ. χαμέελοι
36 ἀγλαά, ἄγχι' ἔθηκεν
45 Αἰτωλ. δ' ἦρχεν Θο.
62 ἐς πεδ. πισσὰ ταμφομένου
65 νῶν δ', χείρεσσιν ἄγῃ
72 ἀμφοτέρ. οὕνεκά σοι
74 ἀγκλ. στάκη
79 τίαι, αἰ αἴπεσσι διοτρε-
φέων
87 τὸν δὲ, ἔπεσσ' ὕμνον
91 Βῶρυ, Μῶρυ, καὶ, Θῶρυ
93 θύνοντ', παρέσθεν
98 Αἰνεί. υἱὸς μὲν ἀμύμονος
99 τῶν, γενέθλη
100 αἰχμὴ, ἐξελύθη
107 κρίν. κρίνῃ
124 Ὣς πε. κήδεαι οὕτως
125 Ἕκτορ, μετοίχεο
εἶ), ἐνὶ μεγάρῳ
ὀβριμώων, μαχέεσθαι
147 σιγῇ, πεπύθωνται
152 ἄκριτον, ἐκ πεδίου
ὄφρα, ἱππηλασίῃ
ἦχ, ἦχ' ἵπποις
153 νῶν, κατὰ πόλιν
159 αὐτὸς, ἀγόρευεν· οἱ δ'
ὑπὸ πάντες
165 ἀρχ. ὑπὸ καπνοῦ

A II

ΟΜΗΡΟΥ ΙΛΙΑΣ.

HOMERI ILIAS, ID EST, DE REBVS ad Troiam gestis.

Βασιλεῖ τ' ἀγαθῷ κρατερῷ τ' αἰχμητῇ.

TYPIS REGIIS.

PARISIIS, M.D.LIIII.
Apud Adr. Turnebum typographum Regiũ.

EX PRIVILEGIO REGIS.

(1553), Cicero's *De legibus* (1552), Theophrastus, and Philo. Although widely learned, Turnebus had particular interest in Greek textual criticism, as seen in his *Adversaria* (1564–65), a collection of explanations and emendations to a range of ancient texts. Turnebus's status as the Royal printer in Greek is indicated at the bottom of the title page; also mentioned here is the text's use of the popular and highly influential French Royal Greek type (see A14).

Only the *Iliad* is given here, and the text is presented without any front matter, aside from a few excerpts from Aelian's *Varia Historia*. Attached to the end of the poem is a page and a half of variant readings.

Freeman, Arthur. "Quaritch, Bernard Alexander Christian (1819–1899)." *Oxford Dictionary of National Biography* [Online edition]. Oxford: Oxford University Press, 2004.

Heyne, Christian Gottlob. *Homeri Ilias*. Leipzig: In libraria Weidmannia and London: Apud I. Payne et MacKinlay, 1802.

Sandys, John Edwin. *A History of Classical Scholarship*. Oxford: Oxford University Press, 1906–10.

Vaulbert de Chantilly, Marc. "Wodhull, Michael (1740–1816)." *Oxford Dictionary of National Biography*.

Vervliet, Hendrik D. L. "Greek Printing Types of the French Renaissance: The 'Grecs Du Roy' and Their Successors." *The Palaeotypography of the French Renaissance: Selected Papers on Sixteenth-century Typefaces*. Leiden: Brill, 2008.

A12

Jean Crespin (d. 1572). Ὁμήρου Ἰλιάς = *Homeri Ilias*.... [Geneva]: E typographia Ioannis Crispini Atrebatii, 1560–67.

Sextodecimo. 2 vols.

William Hayley, poet and biographer, gave this copy to William Cowper Johnson, son of writer John Johnson, who edited Hayley's memoirs following his death. He adapts *Iliad* 23.618 with the quote, "κειμήλιον ἔσται" ("it will be a treasure," although it is written somewhat incorrectly as κειμηλὲον εσται).

This one of the earliest bilingual editions of Homer (the first was printed in 1551 by Nicholas Brylinger, see A13). Originally from Arras, Jean Crespin studied and practiced law in Paris. Because of his religious beliefs (he was a Huguenot) he moved to Geneva in 1548, and there he founded a successful press. The books he produced were mainly religious in content, such as his *Le livre des martyrs* (1554) and *Le Marchand converti, tragédie nouvelle* (1558). Yet he also exercised his proficiency in Greek and Latin when publishing his *Lexicon sive Dictionarium graecolatinum* (1562) and his edition of Theocritus and other ancient pastoral poetry (1569).

In the preface to the *Iliad* volume, Crespin mentions the Greek edition of the *Iliad* that he had published in the preceding year. The present edition is meant to further promote the study of Homer, by aiding the inexperienced reader with a parallel, word-for-word (*ad verbum*) Latin translation of the Greek text, while retaining the convenience of its portable size. Crespin notes that he compared nearly all existing *ad verbum* Latin translations, but above all he used an old manuscript from the library of Guillaume Budé, containing a translation by an unnamed Italian. The translation is that of Andreas Divus (for the first printed publication of this text, see C2; for its use by Chapman see B1), and the version printed here was subsequently copied by Castellio for the Latin translation of the *Iliad* in A13. For the Greek text, Crespin follows the text of Turnebus (A11), including his listing of textual variants (although Heyne suspects that Crespin copied another edition that had been corrected against Turnebus's edition; A23, p. 3.xxi).

In 1567 Crespin published the *Odyssey*, as before in a Greek-only as well as a bilingual edition. In the preface, he attributes the long delay to the care taken in revising the Latin translation. Here he expresses an interest in proper Latin style, and further improvements along these lines would appear in the second edition (1570, which would form the basis of the Latin translation in the edition of Spondanus [A15] and the Elzevier edition [A17]). The 1580 edition published by Crespin's son-in-law, Eustace Vignon, would show even more substantial and consistent improvement because of the extensive revisions by Franciscus Portus (see A16).

The preface to each volume is followed by a list of variant readings. After the text of the *Odyssey* in the second volume are the *Batrachomyomachia* and the *Hymns* (although no variant readings are provided for these), as well as Ps.-Plutarch's *Life of Homer*. Indexes are included at the back of each volume. The text has been set in a version of the French Royal Greek cut by Pierre Haultin. The same type appears to have been used in A16.

Cooper, Thompson. "Johnson, John (1769–1833)." Rev. Rebecca Mills. *Oxford Dictionary of National Biography.*

Heyne, Christian Gottlob. *Homeri Ilias.* Leipzig: In libraria Weidmannia and London: Apud I. Payne et MacKinlay, 1802.

Painting, Vivian. "Hayley, William (1745–1820)." *Oxford Dictionary of National Biography.*

Sowerby, Robin. "The Homeric *Versio Latina.*" *Illinois Classical Studies* 21 (1996): 161–202.

Vervliet, Hendrik D. L. "Greek Printing Types of the French Renaissance: The 'Grecs Du Roy' and Their Successors." *The Palaeotypography of the French Renaissance: Selected Papers on Sixteenth-century Typefaces.* Leiden: Brill, 2008.

A13

Nikolas Brylinger (fl. 1537–1565) and Sébastien Castellion (1515–1563). *Homeri opera graeco-latina, quae quidem nunc extant, omnia. Hoc est: Ilias, Odyssea, Batrachomyomachia, et Hymni....* Basel: Per Nicolaum Brylingerum, 1561.

Folio.

This copy has several handwritten notes in Latin and Greek on the preliminary pages and title page. They include quotes from Lactantius, Plato, and Augustine about Homer. One note on the front inside cover quotes a sentence from Lactantius, *Divine Institutes* 1.5, "Homer could give nothing to us that pertains to the truth, since he wrote of human rather than divine things" (*Homerus nihil nobis dare potuit, quod pertineat ad veritatem, qui humana potius quam divina conscripsit*). The first of two notes on the verso of the front flyleaf quotes from Plato, *Alcibiades 2* 147c, where Homer is called the "wisest and most divine poet"; the second points to "something about Homer" in Plato's *Hippias Minor*. A note on the verso of the title page quotes from Augustine, *Confessions* 1.14, where Homer is called "most sweetly empty" (*Homerus dulcissime Vanus est*). The front inside cover bears the bookplate of the eighteenth-century Freemason writer and actor Joseph Uriot. The indexes have been supplemented in a few places with handwritten notes in the margins.

In 1551, Nicholas Brylinger and Bartholomaeus Calybaeus published the first bilingual Homer. Intended for educational purposes, it was equipped with an *ad verbum* Latin translation parallel to the Greek text, which was taken from Lonitzer's edition (A7). Yet Sowerby argues that the Latin was prepared without sufficient care and expertise, and the resulting text proved lacking in both style and correctness (p. 171). This edition, published ten years later, sought to address those deficiencies. Brylinger was once again the publisher, and he enlisted as his editor Sebastian Castellio, an important scholar and Protestant theologian, who from 1553 until his death was chair of Greek at the University of Basel.

In the preface, Castellio explains that he was induced to undertake this project by Johannes Oporinus, who had overseen the production of Brylinger's earlier 1551 edition. And although he yielded to Oporinus's request, he did so with hesitation, as he "would have preferred to put [his] effort into better things." Castellio spends the bulk of the preface justifying his work, for he expects that people might find it strange that he, ever the proponent of studying sacred writings, would invest effort in producing an edition of Homer. Accordingly, he recalls with regret how in his youth he was strongly drawn to Homer, to the detriment of his other studies, and he implies that his present work could be considered a sort of punishment for his earlier sin. He concludes by warning his reader not to wrongfully elevate Homer and other human writings above the far more important sacred writings.

ILIADIS HOMERI AVT B. COMPOSITIO.

Somnium & Catalogus.

B. autem somnium habet, concionem & naues enumerat.

ALII quidem dijque & uiri equites galeati
dormiebant per totã noctem: Iouem autẽ nõ ceperat dulcis somnus:
sed is cogitabat per mentem, quomodo Achillem
honestaret, perderet autẽ multos in nauibus Achiuorũ.
hoc autem ei in animo optimum uisum est consilium,
mittere ad Atridẽ Agamemnonẽ perniciosum somniũ:
et ipsum compellans uerba cita dixit illi:
Vade, abi perniciosum somniũ citas ad naues Achiuorum
ingressum tentorium Agamemnonis Atridæ
omnia ualde constanter nuncia, sicut iubeo:
armare ipsum iube crinitos Achiuos
omnibus copijs: nunc enim capiat ciuitatem latiuiam
Troianorum: non enim amplius diuersæ cœlestes domos
immortales sentiunt. inflexit enim omnes (habẽtes
Iuno supplicans: Troianis autem mala impendent.
Sic dixit: iuit aũt somniũ, postquã sermonem audiuit.
statim autem peruenit citas ad naues Achiuorum:
iuit autẽ ad Atridẽ Agamemnonẽ: hunc autẽ inuenit
dormientẽ in tentorio: circũ aũt diuinus fusus erat somnus:
stetit autem super capite Neleio filio similis
Nestori: quem maximè senum honorabat Agamẽnon.
huic se aßimilans allocutus est diuinum somnium:
dormis Atrei fili ualde prudentis equũm domitoris?
non oportet per totã noctem dormire consiliariũ uirum.
cui populi sunt commißi, & tot curæ sunt.
nũc uerò mihi mentẽ adhibe cito: Iouis aũt tibi nũcius sum:
qui te longè habitãs ualde curat & miseratur:
armare te iußit crinitos Achiuos
omnibus copijs: nunc aũt capias ciuitatem latiuiam
Troianorũ. non enim amplius diuersa cœlestes domos
immortales sentiunt. inflexit enim omnes (tenentes
Iuno supplicans. Troianis autem mala impendent
ex Ioue. sed tu tuis habe mentibus, neque te obliuio
capiat. quando te dulcis somnus dimiserit,
Sic fatus abijt: illum autem reliquit ibi
hæc cogitantem per animum, quæ non perfici poterant.
putauit enim is capturum Priami urbem die illo
stultus: neque ea sciebat, quæ Iupiter cogitabat opera.
ponere enim parabat insuper doloresq́, singultusq́,
Troianisq́, & Danais per fortes pugnas. (uox:
surrexit aũt ex somno: diuina autem ipsum circumspersit
sedit autem arrectus. mollem autem induit tunicam,
pulchram, nouam: circa autem magnum iecit pallium:
pedibus autem sub teneris ligauit pulchra calciamenta.
circum autem humeros posuit ensem argenteis clauis.
accepit autem sceptrum paternum incorruptum semper.
cum hoc iuit ad naues Achiuorum loricatorum.
Aurora quidem dea conscendit magnum olympum,
Ioui lumen allatura & alijs immortalibus.

Iupiter somniũ mittit Agamẽnoni qui eũ preliari iubeat, falsò ei Troiæ excidium promittens.

sed

ἸΛΙΆΔΟΣ ὉΜΉΡΟΥ Ἦ Β. ῬΑΨΩΔΙΆ.

Ὄνειρος καὶ κατάλογος.

Βῆτα δ' ὄνειρον ἔχει ἀγορὴν, καὶ νῆας ἀριθμεῖ.

ἌΛΛΟΙ μέν ῥα θεοί τε, καὶ ἀνέρες ἱπποκορυσταὶ
εὗδον παννύχιοι. Δία δ' οὐκ ἔχε νήδυμος ὕπνος,
ἀλλ' ὅγε μερμήριζε κατὰ φρένα, ὡς Ἀχιλῆα
τιμήσῃ, ὀλέσῃ δὲ πολέας ἐπὶ νηυσὶν ἀχαιῶν·
ἥδε δέ οἱ κατὰ θυμὸν ἀρίστη φαίνετο βουλὴ,
πέμψαι ἐπ' ἀτρείδῃ Ἀγαμέμνονι οὖλον ὄνειρον·
καί μιν φωνήσας, ἔπεα πτερόεντα προσηύδα,
Βάσκ' ἴθι οὖλε ὄνειρε θοὰς ἐπὶ νῆας ἀχαιῶν,
ἐλθὼν ἐς κλισίην Ἀγαμέμνονος ἀτρείδαο,
πάντα μάλ' ἀτρεκέως ἀγορευέμεν ὡς ἐπιτέλλω·
θωρῆξαί ἑ κέλευε καρηκομόωντας ἀχαιοὺς
πανσυδίῃ· νῦν γάρ κεν ἕλοι πόλιν εὐρυάγυιαν
τρώων, οὐ γὰρ ἔτ' ἀμφὶς ὀλύμπια δώματ' ἔχοντες
ἀθάνατοι φράζονται, ἐπέγναμψεν γὰρ ἅπαντας
Ἥρη λισσομένη· τρώεσσι δὲ κήδε' ἐφῆπται·
Ὣς φάτο· βῆ δ' ἄρ ὄνειρος, ἐπεὶ τὸν μῦθον ἄκουσε·
καρπαλίμως δ' ἵκανε θοὰς ἐπὶ νῆας ἀχαιῶν·
βῆ δ' ἄρ ἐπ' ἀτρείδην Ἀγαμέμνονα. τὸν δ' ἐκίχανεν
εὕδοντ' ἐν κλισίῃ, περὶ δ' ἀμβρόσιος κέχυθ' ὕπνος·
στῆ δ' ἄρ ὑπὲρ κεφαλῆς νηληΐῳ υἷι ἐοικὼς
Νέστορι, τόν ῥα μάλιστα γερόντων τῖ' Ἀγαμέμνων·
τῷ μιν ἐεισάμενος προσεφώνεε θεῖος ὄνειρος,
εὕδεις Ἀτρέος υἱὲ δαΐφρονος ἱπποδάμοιο;
οὐ χρὴ παννύχιον εὕδειν βουληφόρον ἄνδρα,
ᾧ λαοί τ' ἐπιτετράφαται, καὶ τόσσα μέμηλε·
νῦν δ' ἐμέθεν ξύνες ὦκα· Διὸς δέ τοι ἄγγελός εἰμι,
ὅς σευ ἄνευθεν ἐὼν, μέγα κήδεται ἠδ' ἐλεαίρει·
θωρῆξαί σε κέλευσε καρηκομόωντας ἀχαιοὺς
πανσυδίῃ· νῦν γάρ κεν ἕλοις πόλιν εὐρυάγυιαν
τρώων, οὐ γὰρ ἔτ' ἀμφὶς ὀλύμπια δώματ' ἔχοντες
ἀθάνατοι φράζονται. ἐπέγναμψεν γὰρ ἅπαντας
Ἥρη λισσομένη. τρώεσσι δὲ κήδε' ἐφῆπται
ἐκ Διός. ἀλλὰ σὺ σῇσιν ἔχε φρεσὶ, μηδέ σε λήθη
αἱρείτω, εὖτ' ἄν σε μελίφρων ὕπνος ἀνήῃ.
Ὣς ἄρα φωνήσας ἀπεβήσατο· τὸν δ' ἔλιπ' αὐτοῦ
τὰ φρονέοντ' ἀνὰ θυμὸν, ἅ ῥ' οὐ τελέεσθαι ἔμελλε.
φῆ γὰρ ὅγ' αἱρήσειν Πριάμου πόλιν ἤματι κείνῳ
νήπιος. οὐδὲ τὰ ᾔδη, ἅ ῥα Ζεὺς μήδετο ἔργα.
θήσειν γὰρ ἔτ' ἔμελλεν ἐπ' ἄλγεά τε στοναχάς τε,
τρωσί τε καὶ δαναοῖσι διὰ κρατερὰς ὑσμίνας.
ἔγρετο δ' ἐξ ὕπνου· θείη δέ μιν ἀμφέχυτ' ὀμφή·
ἕζετο δ' ὀρθωθείς· μαλακὸν δ' ἔνδυνε χιτῶνα,
καλὸν, νηγάτεον. περὶ δ' αὖ μέγα βάλλετο φᾶρος·
ποσσὶ δ' ὑπαὶ λιπαροῖσιν ἐδήσατο καλὰ πέδιλα·
ἀμφὶ δ' ἄρ ὤμοισιν βάλετο ξίφος ἀργυρόηλον.
εἵλετο δὲ σκῆπτρον πατρώϊον ἄφθιτον αἰεὶ,
σὺν τῷ ἔβη κατὰ νῆας ἀχαιῶν χαλκοχιτώνων.
Ἠὼς μέν ῥα θεὰ προσεβήσατο μακρὸν ὄλυμπον,
Ζηνὶ φόως ἐρέουσα, καὶ ἄλλοις ἀθανάτοισιν.

Ἔχε pro εἶχε. πέμψαι ἐπὶ anastrophe. ἀγορευέμεν Io. et infiniti. est pro imperat. καρηκομόωντας Epẽthesis. o. ἐφῆπται ab ἐφάπτομαι. ἄκουσε pro ἤκουσε systole est. ἐοικὼς, ι abundet prothesi. ἐπιτετράφαται Io. uide Cep. fo. 64. lin. 13. μέμηλεν Ectasis ι in η. ξύνες à συνίημι, Att. σ. in ξ. ἐμέθεν Att. σεῦ dorice. ἀνήῃ ectasis pro ἀνῇ, quãuis & hoc poëticum sit pro ἀνῇ, Cep. 72. li. 9. κείνῳ. αἱρήσειν pro αἱρήσειν. imperatius est, aphæresis ε. ᾔδη Att. pro ᾔδει. ἔγρετο pro ἤγρετο, ὑπαὶ & ὑπὸ pro eodem. φόως ionice. epent.

b αὐτὰρ

Castellio's preface also offers some details about his work in revising the edition of 1551. For the *Iliad* he completely replaced the earlier Greek text and Latin translation with those of Crespin's edition (A12, the *Iliad* volume of which had been published in the preceding year). For the *Odyssey* both the text and translation required extensive corrections, and for the Latin Castellio calls himself not so much a corrector as another translator. He also mentions that, in addition to his marking of *loci communes* in the text, he originally intended to write observations on some of them. He got as far as the nineteenth book of the *Odyssey*, but for some reason he then abandoned the project.

Between the preface and the main text are an index to the *Iliad*, corrigenda, and an index to the *Odyssey*. In the main text, the outer columns contain the Greek, and the inner columns contain the Latin translations. Short printed notes in the inner margins describe the content of each section, whereas outer marginal notes explain the meanings of certain words and make miscellaneous observations. These become less frequent after the first books of the *Odyssey*; no such notes appear beyond the eleventh book. The *Odyssey* is followed by the *Batrachomyomachia*, *Hymns*, and Ps.-Plutarch's "Life of Homer."

Oporinus, at whose instigation Castellio had undertaken this edition, was a prolific editor and printer of classical and contemporary works. He had worked as a corrector for Froben in Basel and briefly pursued medicine as an assistant to the famed physician Paracelsus. Then, from 1538 to 1542 he was Professor of Latin and Greek at the University of Basel. He gave up teaching for financial reasons and devoted himself fully to his printing business until his retirement in 1566. He published around 700 works.

Heckethorn, C. W. "Johannes Oporinus." *The Printers of Basle in the XV & XVI Centuries.* London: Gresham Press, 1897.

Killy, W., and R. Vierhaus, eds. *Deutsche Biographische Enzyklopädie.* Munich: Saur, 1995–99.

Sowerby, Robin. "The Homeric *Versio Latina.*" *Illinois Classical Studies* 21 (1996): 161–202.

A14

Henri Estienne (1531–1598). Οἱ τῆς ἡρωικῆς ποιήσεως πρωτεύοντες ποιηταὶ, καὶ ἄλλοι τινές = *Poetae Graeci Principes heroici carminis, et alii nonnulli.* [Geneva]: Excudebat Henricus Stephanus, illustris viri Huldrichi Fuggeri typographus, 1566.

Folio. 2 vols. in 1.

The inside front cover bears the bookplate of Henry Paul, with the motto "*pro rege et republica.*" The reverse of the title page contains the bookplate of the *Collegium Beatae Mariae de Etona* (Eton College), beside which is a handwritten note identifying it as a duplicate sold in the 1730s.

Homer is but one of the many Greek poets represented in this edition, which also includes Hesiod, Orpheus, Callimachus, Aratus, Nicander, Theocritus, Moschus, Bion, Dionysius, Coluthus, Tryphiodorus, Musaeus, Theognis, Phocylides, and the *aurea carmina* of Pythagoras. This collection ranks among the finest books produced by Henri Estienne the younger, of the famed Estienne family of printers.

Estienne was as much a scholar as a printer, serving as both editor and corrector for his publications. He had taken up the study of Greek at an early age (attending for a while the lectures of Turnebus, see A11), and after a few years of travel settled down in Geneva, where he worked at the press of his father, Robert Estienne. After his father's death, Henri took over the family business, and under his direction the press produced, among other works, a large number of editions of ancient texts, at least fifty-eight in Latin and seventy-four in Greek. Henri was in turn succeeded by his son Paul, who would later publish a bilingual edition of Homer in 1604 (A16).

Perhaps the most notable of Estienne's many publications is the five-volume *Thesaurus Graecae Linguae* (1572). Although it became an important and influential work, the cost of its production placed enormous financial strain on Estienne's business. Further difficulty can be attributed to a competing, single-volume lexicon published by Johannes Scapula in 1579. Scapula had worked as an assistant to Estienne in the production of the *Thesaurus* and allegedly used the larger work as the basis for his smaller, more profitable text. Indeed, Scapula's lexicon was one of the two main sources Chapman used for his translation of Homer (see B1), the other being the edition of Spondanus (A15).

This edition begins with two prefaces by Stephanus and the following accessory texts to Homer: Ps.-Herodotus's "On the Life of Homer," Ps.-Plutarch's "On the Life and Poetry of Homer," and Porphyry's "Homeric Questions" and "On the Cave of the Nymphs." To these is added a series of epigrams to Homer, Hesiod, Callimachus, Theocritus, and Nicander. Then come the text of the *Iliad*, *Odyssey*, *Batrachomyomachia*, and *Hymns*. Estienne also includes a fifty-seven-page appendix of critical notes to the text of both volumes of this edition.

In the second of two prefaces, Estienne discusses editorial issues surrounding the text of Homer. He was led to believe that his work would be made easier by the multitude of editions available to him, yet he was shocked to discover that they did little to illuminate the problematic passages of the text. The two best editions proved to be the Florentine (A1) and the Roman (D4), but even these were corrupt in many places. Few details are given about the other eighteen editions used by Estienne, except that they included, in addition to the two aforementioned editions, the Aldine (see A2 and A6) and the Louvain edition (A5, whose prominence he contests), and "many German and French editions."

In the end Estienne determined it best to rely on a certain old manuscript—he does not name it or describe it further—and the commentaries of Eustathius (see

D4). Support for this decision comes from the fact that the text quoted by Eustathius in his commentaries, which often disagrees with the text of the various editions and even with the very text printed alongside it in the Roman edition, in those same instances tends to agree with the manuscript. This manuscript has been identified as Genevensis 44 and is one of the main sources used for critical work on the text of Homer.

By departing from the established printed versions and relying on new sources, Estienne made a significant contribution to Homeric scholarship. This feature of the edition is in large part responsible for its great influence in succeeding years. The shift toward greater consideration of the manuscript sources would come to fruition with the publication of Barnes's edition in 1711 (A18). In addition to its contributions to the constitution of the Homeric texts, this edition also marks a major advance in the systematic treatment of prepositions and particles.

Printed notes in the inner margins of the main text show variant readings. Various signs (explained at the end of volume 2) above the text mark proper names; pointers in the margin indicate γνῶμαι (maxims and moral generalizations).

This edition, considered to be one of Estienne's typographic masterpieces, is a fine example of the French Royal Greek types in use. This set of types (three sizes were produced) represent the premier example of the cursive style popularized by Aldus (see A2). Their production was commissioned and funded by Francis I of France. They were based on the handwriting of the Cretan scribe Angelus Vergetius and were skillfully executed by the premier type designer and type-cutter of the day, Claude Garamond. First used by Henri's father Robert for his *Alphabetum Graecum* of 1543 and then the *editio princeps* of Eusebius in 1544, the French Royal Greek proved to be an enormous success, dominating Greek typography for the next 200 years and further establishing the preeminence of the cursive style. It is only with the Glasgow Homer of 1756 that a new approach can be observed (see A20).

It is fitting, then, that Estienne composed a four-line poem in Latin, included on the title page of this edition, commenting on the relationship between the elegance of an edition as a book and the elegance of the text that it presents: "What attracts by its appearance attracts more eyes / When it shines with body bright, adorned with handsome refinement. / Earlier these <poets> enticed us through their own elegance, / Your new polish provides attractions anew."

In the imprint at the bottom of the page, Estienne is referred to as "typographer of the distinguished Ulrich Fugger" (*illustris viri Huldrichi Fuggeri typographus*). This was the title Estienne adopted during the ten-year period when he served as printer to Ulrich Fugger, of the prominent banking family, based in Augsburg.

Grafton, Anthony, Glenn W. Most, and Salvatore Settis, eds. *The Classical Tradition*. Cambridge: Harvard University Press, 2010.

Sandys, John Edwin. *A History of Classical Scholarship*. Oxford: Oxford University Press, 1906–10.

Scholderer, Victor. *Greek Printing Types, 1465–1927.* London: British Museum, 1927.

Vervliet, Hendrik D. L. "Greek Printing Types of the French Renaissance: The 'Grecs Du Roy' and Their Successors." *The Palaeotypography of the French Renaissance: Selected Papers on Sixteenth-century Typefaces.* Leiden: Brill, 2008.

West, M. L., ed. *Homeri Ilias.* Stuttgart: B. G. Teubner, 1998.

———. "Geschichte des Textes." *Homers Ilias: Gesamtkommentar, Prolegomena.* Edited by Joachim Latacz. München: K. G. Saur, 2000.

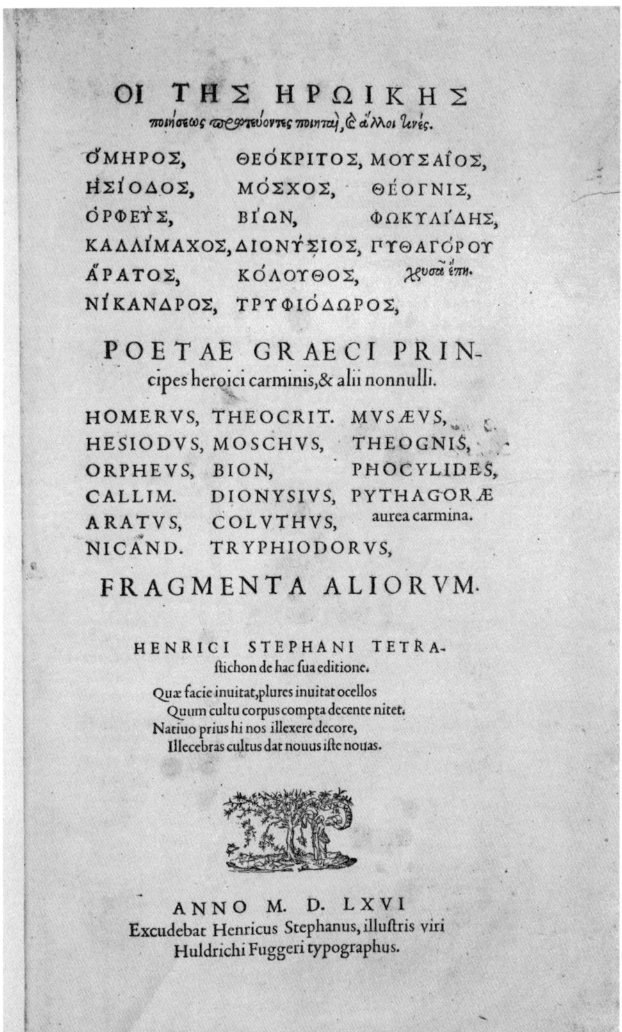

ΟΙ ΤΗΣ ΗΡΩΙΚΗΣ
ποιήσεως πρωτεύοντες ποιηταί, καὶ ἄλλοι τινές.

ὍΜΗΡΟΣ, ΘΕΌΚΡΙΤΟΣ, ΜΟΥΣΑΙ͂ΟΣ,
ἩΣΊΟΔΟΣ, ΜΌΣΧΟΣ, ΘΈΟΓΝΙΣ,
ὈΡΦΕΎΣ, ΒΊΩΝ, ΦΩΚΥΛΊΔΗΣ,
ΚΑΛΛΊΜΑΧΟΣ, ΔΙΟΝΎΣΙΟΣ, ΠΥΘΑΓΌΡΟΥ
ἌΡΑΤΟΣ, ΚΌΛΟΥΘΟΣ, χρυσᾶ ἔπη.
ΝΊΚΑΝΔΡΟΣ, ΤΡΥΦΙΌΔΩΡΟΣ,

POETAE GRAECI PRINcipes heroici carminis, & alii nonnulli.

HOMERVS, THEOCRIT. MVSÆVS,
HESIODVS, MOSCHVS, THEOGNIS,
ORPHEVS, BION, PHOCYLIDES,
CALLIM. DIONYSIVS, PYTHAGORÆ
ARATVS, COLVTHVS, aurea carmina.
NICAND. TRYPHIODORVS,

FRAGMENTA ALIORVM.

HENRICI STEPHANI TETRAstichon de hac sua editione.

Quæ facie inuitat, plures inuitat ocellos
Quum cultu corpus compta decente nitet.
Natiuo prius hi nos illexere decore,
Illecebras cultus dat nouus iste nouas.

ANNO M. D. LXVI
Excudebat Henricus Stephanus, illustris viri
Huldrichi Fuggeri typographus.

A14

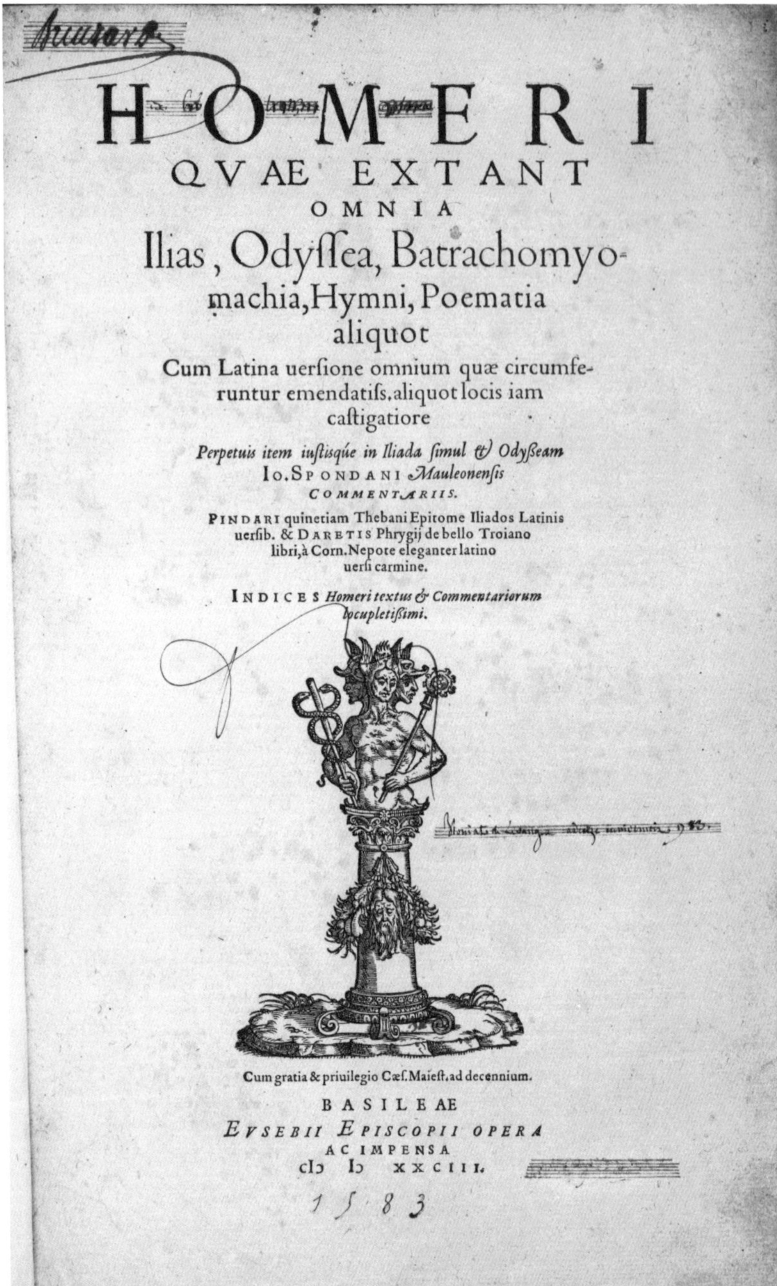

HOMERI
QVAE EXTANT
OMNIA
Ilias, Odyssea, Batrachomyomachia, Hymni, Poematia aliquot
Cum Latina uersione omnium quæ circumferuntur emendatiss. aliquot locis iam castigatiore
Perpetuis item iustisque in Iliada simul & Odysseam IO. SPONDANI *Mauleonensis* COMMENTARIIS.
PINDARI quinetiam Thebani Epitome Iliados Latinis uersib. & DARETIS Phrygij de bello Troiano libri, à Corn. Nepote eleganter latino uersi carmine.
INDICES *Homeri textus & Commentariorum locupletissimi.*

Cum gratia & priuilegio Cæs. Maiest. ad decennium.

BASILEAE
EVSEBII EPISCOPII OPERA
AC IMPENSA
CIƆ IƆ XXCIII.
1583

A15

A15

Jean de Sponde (1557–1595). *Homeri quae extant omnia, Ilias, Odyssea, Batrachomyomachia, Hymni, Poematia aliquot....* Basel: Eusebii Episcopii opera ac impensa, 1583.

Folio.

This edition presents a revised Latin translation of Homer's works as well as extensive commentary by the poet and scholar Jean de Sponde. Although de Sponde was only in his twenties when this edition was produced, his commentary had a lasting influence on subsequent readers and scholars. It was of particular importance to Chapman, who made extensive use of both the translation and commentary when composing his English translation of Homer (B1).

De Sponde's education had been enabled in large part by the patronage of Queen Jeanne d'Albret of Navarre and, following her death, that of her son Henry III, King of Navarre. In a prefatory letter dated June 12, 1583, de Sponde dedicates this edition to Henry, acknowledging his and his mother's support and calling him "my Maecenas." The letter is followed by two poems in praise of Henry, one in Greek and the other in Latin. The latter is based on an anagram of Henry's name which transforms *Henricus Bourbonius* ("Henry of Bourbon") into *hic bonus orbi nervus* ("this good force for the world").

The dedicatory letter is followed by a short letter from de Sponde to Eusebius Episcopius, the printer of the edition. Dated several months earlier, this letter appears to have accompanied the materials sent to Episcopius prior to the edition's typesetting. Here de Sponde praises Episcopius's craftsmanship and acknowledges that what he has produced is the result of *iuvenilis opera* ("youthful effort"). Yet he also believes that this sort of edition is unprecedented and that the two of them will not regret having undertaken such a costly and difficult project.

Eusebius Episcopius was the grandson of the printer Johannes Froben, who had helped establish Basel as an important center for the printing of humanistic and classical texts. After Froben's death the press was managed by Eusebius's father, who had married Froben's daughter, and then his brother Nicolaus. Eusebius partnered for a short while with Nicolaus, but at some point after 1566 he purchased Herwagen's press (see A8). The imprint on this edition reads *ex officina Hervagiana, per Eusebium Episcopium* ("from the workshop of Herwagen, by Eusebius Episcopius").

The main text is preceded by an introduction by de Sponde and a series of epigrams to Homer. Attached to the epigrams are excerpts from Silius Italicus's *Punica* (14.778–97) and Politian's *Nutricia* (the first of his *Sylvae*, giving a review of the history of poetry), along with passages from Pliny's *Natural History* where he praises Homer (7.29, 17.5, and 25.3). More contemporary poems follow, the first of which is titled "On the poetry of Homer, recently edited by J. Spondanus, and explicated with most learned notes by the same" and written by Theodore Beza, the influential Reformation theologian and successor to Calvin at Geneva; he had been one of de Sponde's teachers in Basel.

The source of de Sponde's Greek text is unclear, but it seems likely that he used the editions of Brylinger (A13 or a later printing) and Estienne (A14). The *ad verbum* Latin translation is based on Crespin's edition of 1570 (see A12). In addition to applying his own changes to the translation, de Sponde also incorporated readings from the revised translation of Franciscus Portus, which Crespin's son-in-law had published in 1580 (see A12 and A16). The translation benefits from de Sponde's systematic approach. Above all, he tries to communicate the sense of the Greek through the most literal rendition possible.

Text and commentary are presented in alternating blocks. The text appears in parallel columns, with the Latin in the inner column and the Greek in the outer column. To the Homeric poems and commentary de Sponde attaches two further texts. The first is the *Epitome*, also known as the *Ilias Latina*; here it is ascribed to Pindarus Thebanus, although current scholarship rejects this attribution. The second text is a supposed Latin translation of Dares of Phrygia's "On the Trojan War," traditionally considered to be the work of Cornelius Nepos, although it is most likely a later forgery. The type appears to be a version of the French Royal Greek (see A14) cut by Robert Granjon (as in A17 and A22).

Heckethorn, C. W. *The Printers of Basle in the XV & XVI Centuries.* London: Gresham Press, 1897.

Heyne, Christian Gottlob. *Homeri Ilias.* Leipzig: In libraria Weidmannia and London: Apud I. Payne et MacKinlay, 1802.

Schoell, Frank-Louis. *L'humanisme continental et Angleterre à la fin de la renaissance.* Paris: Champion, 1926.

Sowerby, Robin. "The Homeric *Versio Latina.*" *Illinois Classical Studies* 21 (1996): 161–202.

A16

Paul Estienne (1566/7–ca. 1627). *Homeri poemata duo, Ilias et Odyssea, sive Vlyssea. Eiusdem Batrachomyomachia, hymni, & Epigrammata....* [Geneva]: Excudebat Paulus Stephanus, 1604.

Sextodecimo. 4 vols.

Henri Estienne had originally published Homer's poems in 1566 as part of his larger collection of Greek poets, the *Poetae Graeci Principes* (A14), but in 1589 he produced a stand-alone edition of Homer. In addition to the standard texts—the *Iliad*, *Odyssey*, *Batrachomyomachia*, and *Hymns*—the edition included the *Epigrams* and *Centones*. To this Estienne attached a Latin translation based in large part on the work of Franciscus Portus (see A12; Portus had been responsible for the substantial revisions that appeared in the 1580 edition produced by Crespin's son-in-law).

The edition of 1589 formed the basis of this edition, which Henri's son Paul produced. Here the *Centones* are replaced by Coluthus's *Rape of Helen* and Tryphiodorus's *Taking of Troy*, together with short introductions about the authors.

After briefly discussing in his preface the rich variety of characters and topics that one finds in Homer's poems, Estienne explains that he will refrain from praising Homer, but that he has included a few epigrams taken from *Anthologia Graeca* to that end. These appear before the start of the main text and include: two epigrams in praise of Homer, one in four lines, by Leonidas of Tarentum (book 9, poem 24), the other in six lines, by Philip (book 9, poem 575); a one-line poem in Apollo's voice ("While I was singing, divine Homer was writing") (book 9, poem 455); a couplet by Antipater about the seven cities that lay claim to Homer (book 16, poem 298); and a six-line dialogue by Antipater, in which Homer avoids naming his place of birth (book 16, poem 299).

The type is a version of the French Royal Greek (see A14) that was cut by Pierre Haultin; the same type appears in A12. This copy has been bound in four parts, with two for the *Iliad* and two for the *Odyssey* and the other works. An index appears at the end of the fourth volume.

Sowerby, Robin. "The Homeric *Versio Latina*." *Illinois Classical Studies* 21 (1996): 161–202.

Vervliet, Hendrik D. L. "Greek Printing Types of the French Renaissance: The 'Grecs Du Roy' and Their Successors." *The Palaeotypography of the French Renaissance: Selected Papers on Sixteenth-century Typefaces*. Leiden: Brill, 2008.

A17

Cornelis Schrevel (1608–1664). Ὁμήρου Ἰλιὰς καὶ Ὀδυσσεία, καὶ εἰς αὐτὰς σχόλια, ἢ ἐξήγησις Διδύμου = *Homeri Ilias & Odyssea.* Amsterdam: Ex officina Elzeviriana, 1655–56.

Quarto. 2 vols.

Several notes in the same hand appear on the verso of the front flyleaf, including a discussion of the chronology of Homer (including a play on Horace, *Ars Poetica*, line 78); a reference to book 6 of Clement of Alexandria's *Stromata*, mentioning how Homer took much from Orpheus; a claim reported from French philologist Tanaquil Faber that the scholia commonly attributed to Didymus are spurious; and a blunt evaluation of the scholia printed in this edition as being "not worth much."

This edition is notable for its fine layout and presentation of text, translation, and scholia. The Latin translation is subordinated to the Greek original, placed to the right of it and in a smaller type, and the scholia are placed below in two columns, in sections clearly distinguished by line number (contrast the layout adopted by Herwagen [A8], which is far more unwieldy, although perhaps more faithful to the manuscripts). The Greek types are close copies of the French Royal Greek (see A14). The layout's success is confirmed by the imitations in subsequent editions, such as those of Barnes (A18) and Clarke (A19) (as well as the Cambridge edition of 1689, discussed below).

The editor was the physician and classical scholar Cornelius Schrevelius. He is perhaps best known for his dictionary, the *Lexicon manuale Graeco-Latinum et Latino-Graecum*, which was produced in 1654 at the press of Franciscus Hack in Leiden. Although the same firm printed some copies of this edition, the copy in the BHL was printed simultaneously in Amsterdam by the Elzevier family.

In the opening letter Schrevelius dedicates this edition to Willem Frederick of Nassau-Dietz. A preface addressed to the reader follows, in which Schrevelius discusses Homer's background and genius and then explains the sources for the edition. For the Greek text, he claims that he has used the "most correct" editions and names those of Estienne (A14; see also A16) and Turnebus (A11). The Latin translation is based on the text of Giphanius (1572; this is a reprint of Crespin's second edition of 1570 [see A12]), with corrections from Estienne. Schrevelius mentions that he has added the scholia attributed to Didymus, although he does not specify the sources he used, along with an index and list of variant readings.

Contrary to Schrevelius's expectation that "learned men will by no means disapprove of this edition of ours" (*Confidimus itaque doctos hanc nostram editionem neutiquam improbaturos esse. . .*), it was in fact heavily criticized, in particular by Meric Casaubon (son of the prominent scholar Isaac Casaubon, and the grand-

ὉΜΗΡΟΥ
ἸΛΙΑΣ καὶ ὈΔΥΣΣΕΙΑ,
Καὶ εἰς αὐτὰς σχόλια, ἢ ἐξήγησις
ΔΙΔΥΜΟΥ.
HOMERI
ILIAS & ODYSSEA,
Et in eaſdem ſcholia, ſive interpretatio
DIDYMI.
Cum Latina verſione accuratiſſima,
Indiceque Græco locupletiſſimo
Rerum ac variantium lection.
Accurante
CORN. SCHREVELIO.
AMSTELODAMI,
Ex Officinâ Elzevirianâ.
ANNO CIↃ IↃCLVI.

A17

son of Henri Estienne [see A14]) in his 1659 *Dissertatio,* "On the recent Leiden edition of Homer by Hackius" (*De nupera Homeri editione Lugduno-Batavica, Hackiana*). Casaubon focuses on the numerous errors that Schrevelius committed in the Latin translation—he suggests also that the Portus translation would have made a better starting point than Giphanius (see A12 and A16)—but Schrevelius is also open to criticism for the many typographical errors in the text and the even graver offense of misrepresenting the scholia. Moss provides Gottlieb Christoph Harless's judgment: "this brilliantly deceptive edition presents scholia which, in contrast to the report of earlier editions, have been distorted, mutilated, and disfigured by numerous additions" (*haec enim splendide mendax editio scholia habet contra priorum editionum fidem, detorta, mutilata, et permultis additamentis depravata . . .*).

The note connecting this edition with the 1689 Cambridge edition is only partially correct. The later edition took its Greek text from earlier editions: primarily Estienne's 1566 edition (A14), but also the *editio princeps* (A1), the text of the Roman edition together with the readings in Eustathius's commentary (D4), and the edition of Turnebus (A11). Although the editor attempted to use Schrevelius's Latin translation as a starting point, he quickly abandoned that plan. The scholia, too, are taken from other sources, and the editor explicitly states that the interpolations of Schrevelius have been removed. Nevertheless, the Cambridge edition follows the layout of the Elzevier/Hack edition as closely as possible, thus acknowledging its aesthetic merits.

Lane, John A. "From the Grecs du Roi to the Homer Greek: Two Centuries of Greek Printing Types in the Wake of Garamond." *Greek Letters: From Tablets to Pixels.* Edited by Michael S. Macrakis. New Castle, DE: Oak Knoll Press, 1996.

Moss, Joseph William. *A Manual of Classical Bibliography.* London: Simpkin & Marshall, 1825.

Sowerby, Robin. "The Homeric *Versio Latina.*" *Illinois Classical Studies* 21 (1996): 161–202.

Vervliet, Hendrik D. L. "Greek Printing Types of the French Renaissance: The 'Grecs Du Roy' and Their Successors." *The Palaeotypography of the French Renaissance: Selected Papers on Sixteenth-century Typefaces.* Leiden: Brill, 2008.

A18

Joshua Barnes (1654–1712). Ὁμήρου Ἰλιὰς καὶ Ὀδύσσεια, καὶ εἰς αὐτὰς σχόλια, ἢ ἐξήγησις τῶν παλαιῶν = *Homeri Ilias & Odyssea....* Cambridge: Apud Cornelium Crownfield, 1711.

Quarto. 2 vols.

This edition marks the beginning of a new phase in Homeric scholarship. Other editions since the *editio princeps* (A1) had relied predominantly on earlier printed versions of the Homeric text (the main exception being that of Estienne [A14]). According to West (pp. 37–38), from Barnes's edition onward, editors began to pay greater attention to the manuscripts.

From 1695 until his death, Joshua Barnes held the chair of Regius Professor of Greek at the University of Cambridge. He encountered difficulty in funding his edition, and the apocryphal story is that he secured the financial support of his wife, a highly religious person of independent wealth, by convincing her that Homer was actually King Solomon; however, both the extent of her wealth and her ability to support her husband's publications are unclear. Whether or not the story is true, Barnes did at some point compose a poem in Greek arguing for a causal link between Solomon's principles and those expressed in the works of Homer.

The printer of this edition was Cornelius Crownfield. Originally from the Netherlands, he began working at the University Press in 1698. Around this time the eminent classical scholar Richard Bentley was involved in organizing a revival of the press, with the intention of bringing it more under the control of the university and focusing its efforts on scholarly publications. Crownfield played a key role in this project: He imported new printing types and equipment from the Netherlands and served from 1705 to 1740 as University Printer. Among the many important works published under his management are Bentley's editions of Horace (1711) and Terence (1726) and the second edition of Newton's *Principia Mathematica* (1713).

The first volume begins with a dedicatory letter of September 14, 1710, to Thomas Herbert, eighth earl of Pembroke and fifth earl of Montgomery, whom Barnes praises as being well qualified to judge and appreciate the results of what he characterizes as an extremely difficult and costly undertaking. A preface follows, in which Barnes gives details about various aspects of the edition, including the text, translation, and sources used. In a substantial digression, Barnes condemns those who would be too quick to criticize and judge his work and appeals to those who are mindful of human frailty and have the sense to recognize Barnes's effort and good faith. Attached to the preface is a couplet from the *Anthologia Graeca* (16.302) about Homer:

A18

ΟΜΗΡΟΥ

ΙΛΙΑΣ ΚΑΙ ΟΔΥΣΣΕΙΑ

Καὶ εἰς αὐτὰς ΣΧΟΛΙΑ, ἢ ἘΞΗΓΗΣΙΣ, τῶν Παλαιῶν.

HOMERI

ILIAS & ODYSSEA,

Et in eaſdem SCHOLIA, ſive INTERPRETATIO, Veterum.

Item NOTÆ perpetuæ, in TEXTUM & SCHOLIA, VARIÆ LECTIONES, &c. cum VERSIONE LATINA emendatiſſimâ.

ACCEDUNT

BATRACHOMYOMACHIA, HYMNI & EPIGRAMMATA, *unà cum* FRAGMENTIS, *& Gemini* INDICES.

Totum Opus cum Plurimis MSS. Vetuſtiſſimis, & Optimis EDITIONIBUS Collatum, Auctum, Emendatum, & Priſcæ Integritati Reſtitutum.

———————ὁ δὲ θεῖος Ὅμηρος
Ἀπὸ τοῦ τιμὴν, καὶ κλέος ἔσχε, πλὴν τοῦδ', ὅτι χρήστ' ἐδίδαξε,
Τάξεις, ἀρετὰς, ὁπλίσεις ἀνδρῶν; *Ariſtoph.* Βατραχ. *Act.* IV. *Scen.* II.

Operâ, Studio, & Impenſis,

JOSUÆ BARNES, S. T. B.

In Academiâ CANTABRIGIA Regii GRÆCÆ Linguæ Profeſſoris.

CANTABRIGIÆ,

Apud CORNELIUM CROWNFIELD, Celeberrimæ Academiæ Typographum, apud quem etiam, EDITORIS Nomine, proſtant Venales, MDCCXI.

A18

Εὗρε Φύσις, μόλις εὗρε, τεκοῦσα δὲ παύσατο μόχθων,
Εἰς ἕνα μοῦνον Ὅμηρον ὅλην τρέψασα μενοινήν.

Nature produced him; she produced him by a mighty effort, and after bearing him she ceased from her labor, having spent all her care on Homer alone.

Then come two poems in praise of Barnes, both composed in Latin. The first is the work of Adriaan Reland, professor of Oriental languages at the University of Utrecht; the second is by the lawyer and antiquarian Anthony Allen, then a fellow of King's College, Cambridge. At this point the *Iliad* begins, followed by an index of Greek words at the end of the volume.

The second volume contains a separate dedicatory letter, this time addressed to Laurence Hyde, first earl of Rochester. Next comes a short preface to the *Odyssey* by Barnes. Here, according to the table of contents at the beginning of the volume, the text of the *Odyssey* should begin, but in the BHL copy a lengthy collection of introductory texts, which should have been included in the first volume, is misbound between the *argumentum* of the *Odyssey* and the main text. The minor works (the *Batrachomyomachia*, *Hymns*, *Epigrams*, and *Fragments*) are preceded by their own title page. Barnes prefaces the *Batrachomyomachia* and *Fragments* with short introductory essays. An index to the *Odyssey* follows, similar to the index in the first volume.

At the very end of the volume Barnes has attached a verse "Epilogue" written in Greek. In the first and longest section he offers details about his family, education, and character; he then complains about his environment and the greedy and envious men who surround him, and he expresses a longing to spend his life among men who are wise and have more concern for scholarship; he also recounts (again) the great effort and cost involved in undertaking this edition. To this longer piece are added three short poems, the first two of which affirm the insignificance of other concerns and the ultimate importance of reverence for God, and a final poem that speaks in the voice of Barnes's effort or labor (Βαρνεσίου πόνος εἰμὶ . . .), expressing the great accomplishment as well as the future significance of his work.

The layout of the text in this edition closely follows that of the Elzevier edition (A17). At the top of each page the Greek text appears on the left, with the Latin translation to the right and in smaller type. Below are notes and commentary. For the *Iliad* and *Odyssey*, Barnes includes the scholia, his own notes on the text, his notes on the scholia, and variant readings. To the minor works Barnes attaches his own notes and variant readings.

In his preface Barnes compliments himself on the correctness and completeness of the text, translation, and scholia of his edition, which he considers superior to all earlier ones. Whatever the truth of his claim, Barnes takes pains to note where he diverges from previous editions, reassuring readers that he has made no changes without noting them. He has also taken into consideration a wider range of sources than any of his predecessors, collecting and comparing numerous manuscripts as well as printed editions, and drawing on not only readings transmitted in Eustathius, but also those in Plato, Aristotle, Strabo, Dionysius of Halicarnassus, Plutarch, Longinus, Athenaeus, and others. Barnes mentions at least nine manuscripts that he has examined firsthand, as well as many others whose readings he takes from the report of others. Of the many printed editions that he has consulted, he names the following: the *editio princeps* (A1) and the Aldine (A2 and A6); the editions of Herwagen (A8), Capito (A7), Turnebus (A11), Estienne (A14 and A16), Castellio (A13), Franciscus and Aemilius Portus (see A12), Crespin (A12), Spondanus (A15), and Schrevelius (A17); the Cambridge edition (1689, see A17), the Oxford edition (1675 and 1695), and the Amsterdam edition (1707).

Despite the many merits of this edition, it was quickly overshadowed by the edition of Samuel Clarke (A19; the first volume appeared in 1729). The various criticisms Barnes received, in particular for errors transmitted from the Elzevier edition or otherwise overlooked, were considered excessive. Heyne (A23), for instance, writes that it "experienced unfair judgments from many people" (p. 3.xxxi). Barnes's problems were in part the result of his difficult relationship with Richard Bentley, and according to many accounts the complaints Barnes expressed in the preface and epilogue were targeted at Bentley. Bentley would later become a strong advocate for Clarke's edition of Homer (see A19).

The title page to the first volume is accompanied by an engraved frontispiece, which, according to a letter by Barnes, was procured from Holland by Crownfield. The engraving depicts a monument to the *Iliad* and *Odyssey*, with an inscription identifying the monument with Barnes's edition. The title page contains a quotation from Aristophanes's *Frogs* (lines 1034–36): "And where did the godlike Homer get respect and renown if not by giving good instruction in the tactics, virtues, and weaponry of men?" The title page to volume 2 contains a quotation from Theocritus's sixteenth *Idyll*, line 20: "Homer is enough for all. Him rank I best of poets."

Black, Michael H. *A Short History of Cambridge University Press*, 2nd ed. Cambridge: Cambridge University Press, 2000.

"Cornelius Crownfield." *World Biographical Information System* [Online edition]. Farmington Hills, MI: Gale, 2004.

Haugen, Kristine L. "Barnes, Joshua (1654–1712)." *Oxford Dictionary of National Biography.*

Heyne, Christian Gottlob. *Homeri Ilias.* Leipzig: In libraria Weidmannia and London: Apud I. Payne et MacKinlay, 1802.

Monk, James Henry. *Life of Richard Bentley, D.D.* 2nd ed. London: J.G. & F. Rivington, 1833.

West, M. L. "Geschichte des Textes." *Homers Ilias: Gesamtkommentar, Prolegomena.* Edited by Joachim Latacz. München: K. G. Saur, 2000.

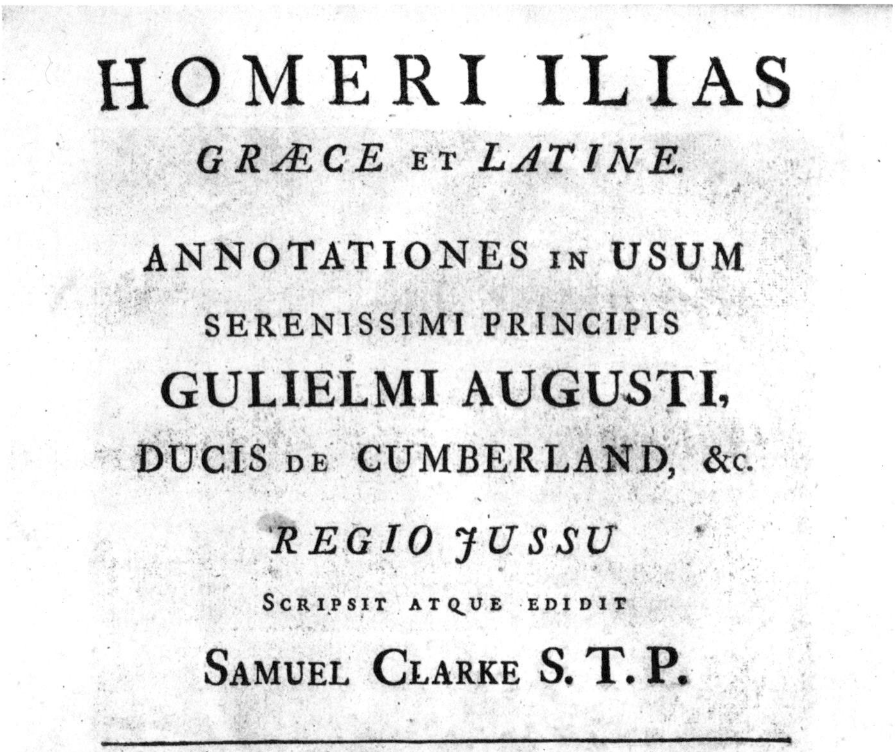

HOMERI ILIAS

GRÆCE ET *LATINE.*

ANNOTATIONES IN USUM
SERENISSIMI PRINCIPIS
GULIELMI AUGUSTI,
DUCIS DE CUMBERLAND, &c.

REGIO JUSSU

SCRIPSIT ATQUE EDIDIT

SAMUEL CLARKE S. T. P.

VOL. I.

Ὅμηρος ——λέξει καὶ διανοίᾳ πάντας ὑπερβέβληκε.
Ariſtot. de Poetic. Cap. 24.

Hic Omnes ſine dubio, & in omni genere eloquentiæ, procul a ſe reliquit. Quintilian. Lib. 10. Cap. 1.

LONDINI.
Typis GULIEL. BOTHAM.

Impenſis JACOBI et JOHANNIS KNAPTON in Cœmeterio D. Pauli. MDCCXXIX.

A19

A19

Samuel Clarke (1675–1729). *Homeri Ilias Graece et Latine. Annotationes in usum Serenissimi Principis Gulielmi Augusti....* London: Typis Guliel. Botham, impensis Jacobi et Johannis Knapton in coemeterio D. Pauli, 1729–32.

Quarto. 2 vols. in 1.

Homeri Odyssea Graece et Latine, item Batrachomyomachia, Hymni, et Epigrammata.... London: impensis Johannis et Pauli Knapton, 1740.

Quarto. 2 vols. in 1.

The front inside cover of each volume contains the bookplate of Edward Lockwood Percival, probably Edward Lockwood Percival the younger, who was lord of Lambourne Manor, Essex, and who spent some time as a book collector in Munich, where he died in 1842.

This edition is notable not only for its value as a scholarly text, but also for its reputation and wide influence. Heyne (A23, p. 3.xxxii) notes that its fame quickly eclipsed that of Barnes's edition. In 1837, Moss proclaimed that the edition was "the most correct and critical which has yet been published" (p. 496). Dibdin wrote that "such was its authority, that no edition of Homer, whether on the continent or in England, was published without being formed on the basis of Dr. Samuel Clarke's" (p. 56)—a statement that, in the context of the BHL, at least holds true for the Glasgow edition (A20) and the Grenville Homer (A22).

Samuel Clarke was one of the most significant British philosophers of his day. He attained mastery over a wide range of subjects, including theology, natural philosophy, and mathematics, as well as classical philology. A close friend and advocate for Newton, he was strongly influenced by Newtonian science and mathematical method. Clarke lived only a short while past the printing of the first volume, and his son Samuel Clarke prepared the remaining three volumes with the aid of his father's notes.

The edition was printed by William Botham and funded by the Knapton family of booksellers, who were active in London in the first half of the eighteenth century. The Knaptons were involved in many important publications of their day, including the Warburton edition of Alexander Pope's *Works* (1751) and the first edition of Samuel Johnson's *Dictionary of the English Language* (1755).

Clarke dedicates the edition to Prince William Augustus, Duke of Cumberland, whose name appears on both the title page and the dedication page. His portrait also appears on the frontispiece, which was engraved by George Vertue, based on the work of Charles Jarvis. Jarvis, a successful portrait painter and translator, was a close friend of Alexander Pope (B9).

In the preface that follows the dedication page, Clarke briefly discusses the text, translation, and notes. He explains that any departures in the Greek text from the vulgate texts have been explained in the notes, but that these instances are few. The Latin translation is for the most part a revision of an existing version, with some parts rewritten. The chief goal of the translation was a word-for-word expression of the Greek text through correct, if not the most elegant, Latin. Clarke does not mention the basis for his version, but he likely used the 1689 Cambridge edition (see A17).

In his discussion of the notes, Clarke explains that they fall into roughly three types: demonstrations of the poet's skill, identifications of rhetorical ornaments, and explanations of the text's meaning. He remarks that the last type of note is seldom required "because the consistent and special virtue of Homeric eloquence is clarity within the most splendidly adorned poems—such clarity that no one has yet attained, not even in prose" (*cum Homericae eloquentiae et perpetua et singularis virtus sit* perspicuitas *in carminibus ornatissimis tanta, quantam ne in soluto quidem scribendi genere unquam assequutus est quisquam*). A selective index of notes by topic further illustrates the sorts of issues that Clarke's notes address, including meter, verb tenses, accentuation, poetic language, the dual, figures of speech, passages in need of emendation, and notable instances of narration and characterization. Clarke felt it necessary to defend the inclusion of such notes (and perhaps he anticipated criticism for not including the scholia), concluding his preface with a general remark:

> Certainly these matters are slight and perhaps of little importance, should they be considered individually. But all things are constituted from elements, all things originate from their principles: And upon a habit of judgment that has been brought to bear in *minute* matters, there very frequently depends, even in the *greatest* matters, true and exact knowledge. (*Levia quidem haec, & parvi forte, si per se spectentur, momenti. Sed ex elementis constant, ex principiis oriuntur, omnia: Et ex judicii consuetudine in rebus* minutis *adhibita, pendet saepissime etiam in* maximis *vera atque accurata Scientia*)

It is not difficult to see how such notes proved useful for students and other readers, and given the popularity and enthusiastic reception of the edition, it would seem that Clarke's defense was unnecessary. (Among the notes that Clarke does not mention here are numerous cross-references and identifications of passages that are of significance to Virgil.)

Clarke died the year he published the first volume and his son, Samuel Clarke, Jr. (d.1778), completed the edition. The second volume of the *Iliad* appeared in 1732; the *Odyssey* and minor works were published together in 1740. Although Clarke gives little detail about his sources in the preface to the first volume, the method his son adopted, which he explains in the preface to the second volume, is more transparent. When Clarke died, he had written notes through *Iliad* book 16, line 359, and had prepared the text and translation through line 510 of the same book. These his son presents as accurately as possible. For the remaining text, he draws from Barnes's edition (A18) or one of the other editions, guided in his choices by his father's notes. For the Latin translation, he mostly follows the Amsterdam 1707 edition, from which he also takes the indexes. According to the preface to the 1740 volume, he followed the same approach in the final two volumes.

While Clarke was preparing the second volume, Richard Bentley (see A18 on his connection to Barnes) discussed with him his ideas regarding the "Aeolic digamma." Bentley had discovered that by altering the spelling of certain words to include the digamma, he could make better sense of and improve the versification of Homer's works. The result of his communication with Clarke is evident in one of the last notes Clarke composed before his death, at *Iliad* 16.172, where he uses the digamma to explain the line's meter. Although Bentley worked in his later years on producing a new edition of Homer that would fully reinstate the digamma, his work was never published, and his plan was ultimately executed by Richard Payne Knight (A25) and further taken up by Thomas Shaw Brandreth (A28).

The first volume of the *Iliad* covers books 1–12, and the second completes the *Iliad* and provides two indexes. The 1740 volumes contain the *Odyssey* (the break occurs between books 13 and 14), the minor works, and two additional indexes. The minor works—the *Batrachomyomachia*, *Hymns*, *Epigrams*, and *Fragments*—are introduced with their own title page. The edition's layout is modeled on that of either the Elzevier edition (A17) or Barnes (A18), although the minor works use a smaller type for the Greek text.

Two epigraphs appear on the title page to volume 1. The first quotes, with slight modification, Aristotle's *Poetics* 1459b16: "Homer excels all [poets] in diction and thought," and the second quotes Quintilian's *Institutio Oratoria* 10, ch. 1: "[Homer], indeed, has undoubtedly left all others, in every branch of eloquence, far behind" (*Hic Omnes sine dubio, & in omni genere eloquentiae, procul a se reliquit*). A further epigraph appears on the title page to volume 3, reporting Aristotle's quotation of Alcidamas in his *Rhetoric* 3, ch. 3: "the Odyssey, a beautiful mirror of human life" (Τὴν Ὀδύσσειαν, καλὸν ἀνθρωπίνου βίου κάτοπτρον).

Bottoms, Edward. "Jervas [Jarvis], Charles (1675–1739)." *Oxford Dictionary of National Biography*.

Dibdin, Thomas Frognall. *An Introduction to the Knowledge of Rare and Valuable Editions of the Greek and Latin Classics*. 4th ed. London: Harding and Lepard, 1827.

Heyne, Christian Gottlob. *Homeri Ilias*. Leipzig: In libraria Weidmannia and London: Apud I. Payne et MacKinlay, 1802.

Monk, James Henry. *Life of Richard Bentley, D.D.* 2nd ed. London: J.G. & F. Rivington, 1833.

Moss, Joseph William. *A Manual of Classical Bibliography.* London: Simpkin & Marshall, 1825.

Nichol, Donald W. "Knapton, John (*bap.* 1696, *d.* 1767x70)." *Oxford Dictionary of National Biography.*

Sowerby, Robin. "The Homeric *Versio Latina.*" *Illinois Classical Studies* 21 (1996): 161–202.

A20

James Moor (1712–1779) and George Muirhead (1715–1773). Τῆς τοῦ Ὁμήρου Ἰλιάδος ὁ τόμος πρότερος / δεύτερος. Τῆς τοῦ Ὁμήρου Ὀδυσσείας ὁ τόμος πρότερος / δεύτερος. Glasgow: In aedibus academicis, excudebant Robertus et Andreas Foulis, 1756–58.

Folio. 4 vols. in 2.

This copy was once in the collection of Michael Wodhull, and like A11 the front flyleaf bears one of his characteristic notes, with details about the copy's purchase.

Although this edition of Homer was, like many of those at the time, based on Samuel Clarke's work (A19), the Glasgow Homer is distinctive in the correctness and quality of its printing and the beauty of its layout and type.

The edition was published by the Foulis Press, under the direction of the brothers Robert and Andrew. Robert had originally trained to become a barber and maltman, like his father, but his studies at the University of Glasgow and in particular the influence of Francis Hutcheson, professor of moral philosophy at the University, led him to different pursuits. In 1741 he founded a bookshop; he began printing his own books in the following year; and in 1743 he was appointed the printer to the University. He and his brother Andrew, who had studied Humanity at the University and was a teacher of Greek, Latin, and French, soon formed a partnership. Focusing on publishing works by professors at the university and producing editions of classical texts, they quickly came to dominate Glasgow printing.

As they often did with their publications, the Foulis brothers collaborated on this project with professors from the University of Glasgow. The editors were James Moor, Professor of Greek, and George Muirhead, Professor of Latin. All four were members of the Glasgow Literary Society, and both Moor and Muirhead, like Robert Foulis, had been students of Hutcheson. The Glasgow Homer is just one of many collaborations between these men. In addition to other editions of classical authors prepared by Moor or Muirhead, the press also published several of Moor's own works.

The sterling reputation of the Foulis Press is due in large part to the care and attention that they gave to proofreading, typography, and materials and binding. Indeed, the preface claims that the proofs for each page were checked six times: twice by the *corrector* of the press, once by Andrew Foulis, and three further times by the editors. The first four rounds involved comparing the text against Clarke's edition. Then the editors compared the text against Estienne's edition (A14), and to a lesser extent against the Cambridge edition of 1689 (see A17), Barnes's edition (A18), and several others. According to the preface, the sixth and final round of proofreading was done as the pages came off the press.

In the preface, the editors acknowledge a conscious intent to follow the aesthetics of Estienne's edition, although they have made improvements in both layout and choice of type. The type itself marks an important shift in the history of Greek printing types. Although it is loosely based on the popular French Royal Greek (see A14), it departs from the established cursive/handwritten style and contains fewer ligatures and abbreviations; according to Scholderer, a more definite break would come with "Porson Greek" (see A22). Astronomer and typefounder Alexander Wilson specially designed it for this edition; it was one of several types that he supplied to the Foulis brothers.

The first two volumes contain the *Iliad*. The third and fourth volumes contain the *Odyssey*, *Batrachomyomachia*, *Hymns*, *Epigrams*, a listing of spurious verses, and the *Fragments*. An index of books and their titles is appended to each of the major works, and an index of sources for the spurious verses and fragments appears at the end of the fourth volume.

The title page to the first volume contains a quotation from Horace's *Epistle* 1.2, lines 5–6: "[Homer], who tells us what is fair, what is foul, what is helpful, what not, more plainly and better than Chrysippus or Crantor" (*Qui, quid sit pulchrum, quid turpe, quid utile, quid non, / Planius ac melius Chrysippo et Crantore dicit*). The quotation appearing on the title page of the third volume comes from the same text: "Again, of the power of worth and wisdom he has set before us an instructive pattern in Ulysses" (*rursus, quid virtus, et quid sapientia possit, utile proposuit nobis exemplar Ulyssem*). The edition is dedicated to George William Frederick, Prince of Wales (then only seventeen or eighteen years of age; four years later he would be crowned King George III of Great Britain).

Ovenden, Richard. "Foulis, Robert (1707–1776)." *Oxford Dictionary of National Biography.*

Scholderer, Victor. *Greek Printing Types, 1465–1927.* London: British Museum, 1927.

Sher, Richard B. "Moor, James (*bap.* 1712, *d.* 1779)." *Oxford Dictionary of National Biography.*

———. "Muirhead, George (*bap.* 1715, *d.* 1773)." *Oxford Dictionary of National Biography.*

Νύξ', ἐκ δ' ἔσπασεν ἔγχος· ὁ δ' ἑσπόμενος πέσε δουρὶ
Πρηνής, ἀμφὶ δέ οἱ βράχε τεύχεα ποικίλα χαλκῷ.
Σαρπηδὼν δ' ἄρ' ἔπαλξιν ἑλὼν χερσὶ στιβαρῇσιν,
Ἕλχ', ἡ δ' ἕσπετο πᾶσα διαμπερές· αὐτὰρ ὕπερθεν
Τεῖχος ἐγυμνώθη, πολέεσσι δὲ θῆκε κέλευθον.
Τὸν δ' Αἴας καὶ Τεῦκρος ὁμαρτήσανθ', ὁ μὲν ἰῷ
Βεβλήκει τελαμῶνα περὶ στήθεσφι φαεινὸν
Ἀσπίδος ἀμφιβρότης· ἀλλὰ Ζεὺς κῆρας ἄμυνε
Παιδὸς ἑοῦ, μὴ νηυσὶν ἔπι πρύμνῃσι δαμείη·
Αἴας δ' ἀσπίδα νύξεν ἐπάλμενος· ἡ δὲ διαπρὸ
Ἤλυθεν ἐγχείη, στυφέλιξε δέ μιν μεμαῶτα·
Χώρησεν δ' ἄρα τυτθὸν ἐπάλξιος, οὐδ' ὅγε πάμπαν
Χάζετ', ἐπεί οἱ θυμὸς ἐέλπετο κῦδος ἀρέσθαι.
Κέκλετο δ' ἀντιθέοισιν ἑλιξάμενος Λυκίοισιν·
Ὦ Λύκιοι, τί δ' ἄρ' ὧδε μεθίετε θούριδος ἀλκῆς;
Ἀργαλέον δέ μοι ἐστὶ, καὶ ἰφθίμῳ περ ἐόντι,
Μούνῳ ῥηξαμένῳ, θέσθαι παρὰ νηυσὶ κέλευθον·
Ἀλλ' ἐφομαρτεῖτε· πλεόνων δέ τοι ἔργον ἄμεινον.
Ὣς ἔφαθ'· οἱ δὲ ἄνακτος ὑποδδείσαντες ὁμοκλὴν,
Μᾶλλον ἐπέβρισαν βουληφόρον ἀμφὶ ἄνακτα.
Ἀργεῖοι δ' ἑτέρωθεν ἐκαρτύναντο φάλαγγας
Τείχεος ἔντοσθεν, μέγα δέ σφισι φαίνετο ἔργον.
Οὔτε γὰρ ἴφθιμοι Λύκιοι Δαναῶν ἐδύναντο
Τεῖχος ῥηξάμενοι θέσθαι παρὰ νηυσὶ κέλευθον·
Οὔτε ποτ' αἰχμηταὶ Δαναοὶ Λυκίους ἐδύναντο

41

A20

ΤΗΣ ΤΟΥ

Ο Μ Η Ρ Ο Υ

Ο Δ Υ Σ Σ Ε Ι Α Σ

Ο ΤΟΜΟΣ ΠΡΟΤΕΡΟΣ.

RURSUS, QUID VIRTUS, ET QUID SAPIENTIA POSSIT,
UTILE PROPOSUIT NOBIS EXEMPLAR ULYSSEM.

G L A S G U A E;
IN AEDIBUS ACADEMICIS,
EXCUDEBANT ROBERTUS ET ANDREAS FOULIS
ACADEMIAE TYPOGRAPHI,
MDCCLVIII.

A20

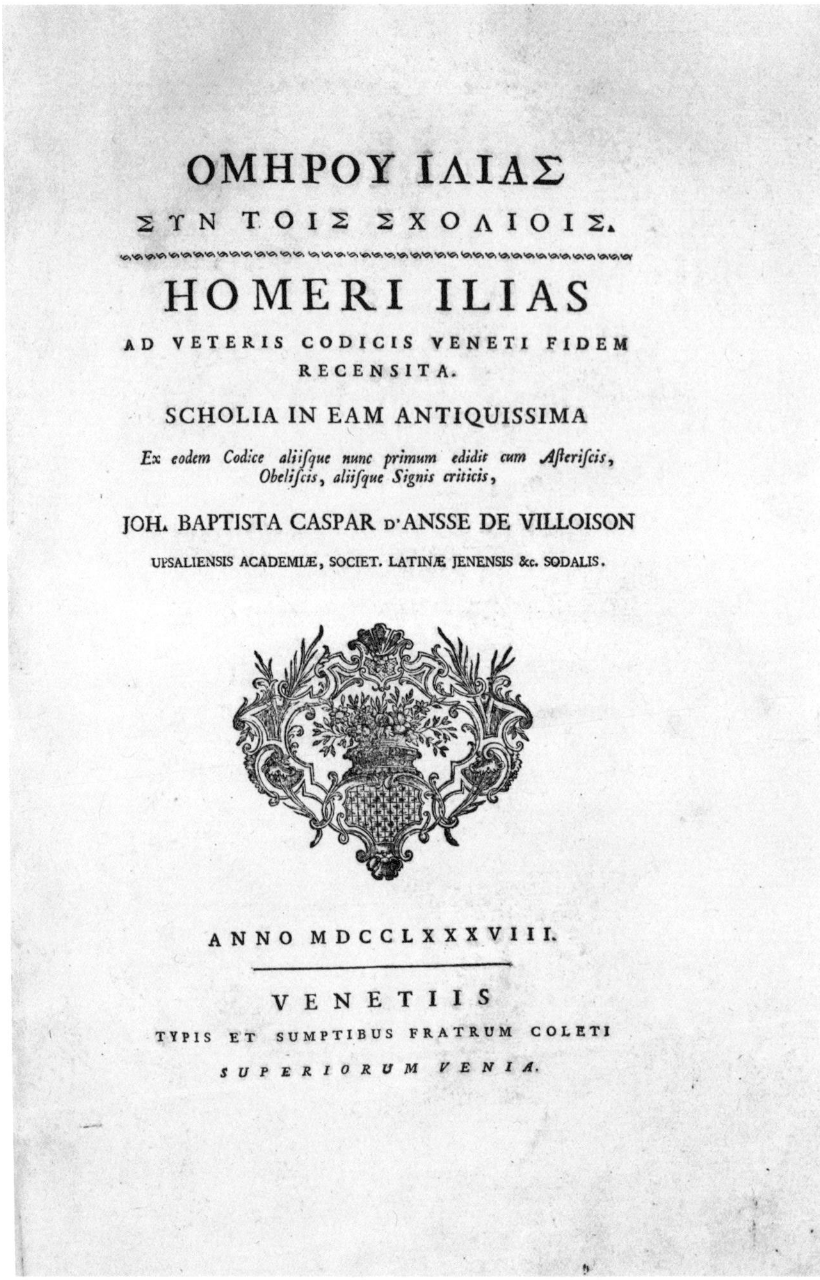

ΟΜΗΡΟΥ ΙΛΙΑΣ

ΣΥΝ ΤΟΙΣ ΣΧΟΛΙΟΙΣ.

HOMERI ILIAS

AD VETERIS CODICIS VENETI FIDEM RECENSITA.

SCHOLIA IN EAM ANTIQUISSIMA

Ex eodem Codice aliisque nunc primum edidit cum Asteriscis, Obeliscis, aliisque Signis criticis,

JOH. BAPTISTA CASPAR D'ANSSE DE VILLOISON

UPSALIENSIS ACADEMIÆ, SOCIET. LATINÆ JENENSIS &c. SODALIS.

ANNO MDCCLXXXVIII.

VENETIIS

TYPIS ET SUMPTIBUS FRATRUM COLETI

SUPERIORUM VENIA.

A21

A21

Jean Baptiste Gaspard d'Ansse de Villoison (1750–1805). Ὁμήρου Ἰλιὰς σὺν τοῖς σχολίοις = *Homeri Ilias....* Venice: Typis et sumptibus Fratrum Coleti, 1788.

Folio.

This edition brought to light the long-neglected Venetian scholia on Homer, most notably the scholia contained in the tenth-century "Venetus A" manuscript (Marcianus Graecus Z. 454). The publication of these scholia provided crucial evidence about the activity of ancient scholars and their influence on the transmission of the Homeric text. It helped spur important developments in modern Homeric scholarship, making it possible for the first time to study the development of the Homeric text and the history of ancient Homeric scholarship.

The manuscripts containing these scholia had been available for many years in the Library of St. Mark's in Venice, yet their scholarly significance was unrecognized until 1781, when the French classical scholar Villoison traveled to Venice and began a three-year examination of the sources available there. He published the results of his studies in this edition, which presents new scholia and a new text of the *Iliad*, accompanied by a lengthy introduction. From the Venetus A he takes the main text, together with critical signs (*paragraphos*, *koronis*, *diple*, and *asterisk*) and scholia. Also included are the scholia from the Venetus B and another manuscript.

This edition represents the culmination of decades of interest in ancient scholarship on Homer throughout the middle of the eighteenth century. Homer increasingly came to be seen not as the cultured poet established by tradition but rather as a primitive, illiterate bard (see for example the work of Robert Wood, D10). Coupled with this was a growing recognition of the many changes that ancient scholars made to the Homeric text. To Villoison and many of his contemporaries, the Venetian scholia seemed like the crucial evidence needed in order to return Homer's text to its original, unaltered form. Yet these scholia ultimately found their greatest significance as a considerable part of Friedrich August Wolf's evidence in his highly influential *Prolegomena ad Homerum* (Halle, 1795). Rather than occupying himself with restoring the poems to their state prior to the ancient critics' intervention, Wolf presented a history of the Homeric text, the first "history of a text in antiquity."

Allen, Thomas W. *Homeri Ilias.* Oxford: Clarendon Press, 1931.

Grafton, Anthony, Glenn W. Most, and James E. G. Zetzel, eds. *Prolegomena to Homer, 1795.* Princeton: Princeton University Press, 1985.

Scholderer, Victor. *Greek Printing Types, 1465–1927.* London: British Museum, 1927.

Wolf, Friedrich August. *Prolegomena ad Homerum.* Halle: 1795.

A22

Ὁμήρου Ἰλιὰς καὶ Ὀδύσσεια. Oxford: Ex ergastēriou typographikou Akadēmias tēs en Oxonia, 1800.

Quarto. 4 vols.

In the preface to this edition—also known as the "Grenville Homer"—the editors express one overriding goal: to set forth an accurate text of the *Iliad* and *Odyssey* in large, easy to read type. To this end, they adopt a larger typeface and set the text in a simple, yet elegant and attractive layout. The text itself is based on Clarke's edition (A19), but the editors also took readings from the more recent editions by Johann August Ernesti (Leipzig, 1759–64) and Villoison (A20). (Although Ernesti's edition was likewise based on Clarke, it incorporated further manuscript sources.)

For the *Iliad* the editors also consulted a manuscript from the library of New College, Oxford, probably *Oxon. Novi Collegii* 298, which remains today one of the chief manuscripts that editors of the *Iliad* use. Similarly, for the *Odyssey* they took into account the readings of what is now considered one of the best manuscripts for that text, *Harleianus* 5674. This was achieved through a collation against Ernesti's edition by the prominent classical scholar Richard Porson. The editors consider the collation to be of such quality and scholarly value that they include it in full. When they wrote the preface, the editors intended to integrate the collation into the text of the *Odyssey*. At some point they abandoned this idea (perhaps because of the cost), and the collation appears as a standalone section immediately following the preface.

The edition was funded by three brothers of the prominent Grenville family: George Nugent-Temple-Grenville, first marquess of Buckingham; Thomas Grenville; and William Wyndham Grenville, Baron Grenville. All three were active in politics, holding seats in parliament for Buckinghamshire, and Baron Grenville, following his father, served for a time as prime minister. Politics aside, Thomas was an enthusiastic book collector (at his death his collection of over 20,000 volumes was donated to the British Museum), and he likely played a more involved role in the preparation of this edition. The names of the editors are not indicated anywhere in the text, and different sources give different names. Jebb and Brunet list the editors as Randolph, Cleaver, and Rogers. Of these Cleaver would be the clergyman William Cleaver, bishop of St. Asaph. Elsewhere, Thomas Grenville and Porson are credited as the editors. Yet if anything is clear, Porson was not one of the editors; he merely supplied the collation with Harleianus 5674.

In addition to being an accomplished scholar, Porson had remarkable ability as a calligrapher. He developed this skill in his youth and pursued it throughout his life: his notes were meticulously written, and he did not shy away from the laborious task of transcribing his own copies of manuscripts and books. From 1806 to 1808 Porson worked closely with typecutter Richard

Austin to produce a new Greek type for the Cambridge University Press. The resulting Porson Greek departs sharply from the cursive styles that had dominated since the popularization of the Aldine types at the end of the fifteenth century (see A2). The letterforms introduce a fresh simplicity and uniformity, and ligatures and contractions are avoided entirely. In Scholderer's estimation "the Porsonian Greek as a whole marks a very great step forward. The ghost of the French Royal letter is now effectually laid, and Greek printing in England, especially the standard types adopted by the University Presses of Oxford and Cambridge, had but to follow Porson's lead to rank as the best in contemporary Europe" (p. 14). This type appears in A29 and A31, both published in Oxford by the Clarendon Press. Even today it is widely used and immediately recognizable, appearing in the venerable series of Oxford Classical Texts as well as many student texts.

The publication of this edition brought about a noteworthy correspondence between Porson and Villoison (see A21). Villoison had returned to Paris, yet the Revolution had ruined him financially and he found himself without the means to purchase a copy on his own. Still, he wanted this edition enough to contact Porson directly. In an 1802 letter, he praises Porson's scholarship and introduces himself (offering his credentials by mentioning his work on Apollonius's *Lexicon* and his edition of the Venetian scholia); he then asks, from one scholar to another, whether Porson might prevail upon the Grenville brothers to add him to the list of recipients of gift copies. Evidently Porson was successful in this mission, and a letter from Villoison three months later acknowledges his receipt of the edition, which he praises highly for both its text and typography, as well as for the quality of Porson's collation.

The edition is divided into four volumes, two for the *Iliad* and two for the *Odyssey*. The title page follows the sparser style popularized by the Foulis Press (see A20). On it is a quotation from Eustathius's commentary on the *Iliad*, 1.25–26: ΕΣΤΙΝ ΑΛΗΘΩΣ ΒΑΣΙΛΙΚΟΝ ΠΡΑΓΜΑ Η ΟΜΗΡΟΥ ΠΟΙΗΣΙΣ ("Truly, the poetry of Homer is a kingly thing"). In accordance with the editors' vision of an attractive and accurate reading text, they provide only the Greek text of the poems, without any accompanying notes, translation, or variant readings. The type is a copy of the popular French Royal Greek (see A14). This particular version appears to come from the set of types cut by Robert Granjon, which even as a reproduction had a wide influence on the history of Greek type—it appears that Granjon's versions are also used in A15 and A17.

The date of publication is 1800, according to the title page, but the prefatory letter is dated March 27, 1801. In addition to the standard copies (such as the BHL copy), the press produced twenty-five large paper copies. These include engravings of the Grenville brothers according to Brunet; according to Dibdin, extra pages of variant readings have been added to some of them.

Bowman, John H. "Greek Type Design: The British Contribution." *Greek Letters: From Tablets to Pixels*. Edited by Michael S. Macrakis. New Castle, Delaware: Oak Knoll Press, 1996.

Brunet, Jacques-Charles. *Manuel du libraire et de l'amateur de livres*. Paris: G.-P. Maisonneuve & Larose, 1965–66 [1860–80].

Davis, R. W. "Grenville, George Nugent-Temple-, first marquess of Buckingham (1753–1813)." *Oxford Dictionary of National Biography*.

Jebb, R. C. *Homer: An Introduction to the Iliad and the Odyssey*. Boston and Glasgow: 1887.

Jupp, P. J. "Grenville, William Wyndham, Baron Grenville (1759–1834)." *Oxford Dictionary of National Biography*.

Lane, John A. "From the Grecs du Roi to the Homer Greek: Two Centuries of Greek Printing Types in the Wake of Garamond." *Greek Letters: From Tablets to Pixels*. Edited by Michael S. Macrakis. New Castle, Delaware: Oak Knoll Press, 1996.

Luard, H. R., ed. *The Correspondence of Richard Porson, M.A.* Cambridge: Cambridge Antiquarian Society, 1867, letters 38, 40, 42.

Morson, Geoffrey V. "Porson, Richard (1759–1808)." *Oxford Dictionary of National Biography*.

Scholderer, Victor. *Greek Printing Types, 1465–1927*. London: British Museum, 1927.

Smith, G. B. "Grenville, Thomas (1755–1846)." Rev. R. W. Davis. *Oxford Dictionary of National Biography*.

Vervliet, Hendrik D. L. "Greek Printing Types of the French Renaissance: The 'Grecs Du Roy' and Their Successors." *The Palaeotypography of the French Renaissance: Selected Papers on Sixteenth-century Typefaces*. Leiden: Brill, 2008.

A23

Christian Gottlob Heyne (1729–1812). *Homeri Ilias. . . .* Leipzig: In libraria Weidmannia and London: Apud I. Payne et MacKinlay, 1802.

Octavo. 8 vols.

This massive edition of the *Iliad*, consisting of eight large volumes, collected and synthesized nearly all the scholarship that preceded it, and it provided the most comprehensive reporting of manuscript evidence to date. In his *editio maior* of the *Iliad* (1931), T. W. Allen calls Heyne's edition a "second princeps" and observes that it "for many years dominated Homeric study, and still holds the key to statements in the most modern editions" (p. 1.267). Indeed, the appearance of this edition marked a break in scholarship on the text of Homer that would last for the next sixty years. During this time, scholars stopped focusing on the text of Homer and instead investigated other aspects of the poems. This was partly due to the new questions raised by Villoison's publication of the Venetian scholia (A18) and Wolf's *Prolegomena ad Homerum*, but also because of the sheer magnitude and thoroughness of Heyne's work.

Christian Gottlob Heyne was one of the most prominent classical scholars of his day. At the University of Göttingen, he served as Professor of Poetry and Eloquence from 1763 until his death; he also directed the University Library and held various other posts. His philology seminar produced many influential teachers and scholars, including F. A. Wolf (see A21). Included among his publications are a popular edition of Virgil (1767–75) and an edition of Pindar's *Odes* (1798).

Heyne played an important role in expanding the scope of classical studies beyond language and literature. In particular, he introduced the study of art and archeology, taking up Winckelmann's historical approach and developing it further and more thoroughly. Together with Wolf, he is considered one of the founders of the comprehensive study of antiquity known as *Altertumswissenschaft*, and he played a central role in giving classical philology its modern form: he broadened its scope, organized its subdisciplines within a coherent system, and established the practice of bringing it into dialogue with the present.

The inspiration for this project came in large part from Robert Wood's *Essay on the Original Genius of Homer* (D10, published in 1769), which Heyne had reviewed positively. Heyne may have intended to give similar treatment to the *Odyssey* and perhaps also to the minor works. This is in part suggested by the second of the two title pages: the first, which is transcribed at the top of this entry, accurately describes the work as "Homer's *Iliad*," but the second title page reads "Homer's poems" (*Homeri Carmina*).

Heyne dedicates the edition to the genius of King George II of Great Britain, who founded the University of Göttingen. The first volume contains a preface, an explanation of the sigla that are used, a list of handwriting specimens (the specimens themselves are included at the end of this volume), and a description of the engravings. The Greek text of *Iliad* books 1–12 follows, with the remaining books presented in the second volume. The third volume begins with a detailed treatise on the sources and materials used for the study of Homer. Here Heyne discusses previous editions and translations, the available manuscripts, and the scholia and other sources of ancient scholarship. The bulk of the volume consists of a prose Latin translation of the *Iliad*, which is a revision of the translation from Ernesti's edition (this in turn was based on Clarke, A19).

The remaining five volumes contain variant readings, together with notes and discussions of the text. (A ninth volume, not in the BHL, consisting of an index to this edition was published in 1822.) The material in these volumes gives a detailed treatment of variant readings, sources, ancient scholarship, and other issues, but a more limited set of notes is attached to the Greek text in the first two volumes. These are meant to facilitate quick reading and deal mainly with the action of the poem. The text is also accompanied by a limited apparatus, which

HOMERI
ILIAS
CVM
BREVI ANNOTATIONE
CVRANTE
C. G. HEYNE
VOLVMEN PRIMVM
LIB. I–XII
LIPSIAE
IN LIBRARIA WEIDMANNIA
LONDINI
APVD I. PAYNE ET MACKINLAY
MDCCCII
HOMERI CARMINA HEYNE
TOM V VARIÆ LECT LIB V IX
TOM IV VARIÆ LECT LIB I IV
TOM III VERSIO LATINA
TOM II TEXTUS LIB XIII XXIV
TOM VIII VARIÆ LECT LIB XX XXIV
TOM VII VARIÆ LECT LIB XV XIX
TOM VI VARIÆ LECT LIB X XIV

primarily reports divergences from the text as it was commonly printed. A second apparatus provides readings of lines that incorporate the digamma. Heyne relied on Richard Bentley's (see A25) extensive notes in the annotated copy of the Estienne edition (A14) that Bentley loaned him. His general treatment of the digamma appears in the excursuses attached to *Iliad* book 19, which appear in the seventh volume of this edition. The process begun by Bentley and taken up in part by Heyne would be pursued more completely by Richard Payne Knight (A25) and Thomas Shaw Brandreth (A28).

Although the breadth and detail of Heyne's work are impressive, it has been open to criticism. For example, Sandys (pp. 3.36–44) argues that it fails to give enough weight to the Venetian scholia (A21) and is too dependent on the work of Clarke (A19) and Ernesti.

Allen, Thomas W. *Homeri Ilias.* Oxford: Clarendon Press, 1931.

Homeri Carmina. Edinburgh Review 2, no. 4 (July 1803): 308–29.

Jebb, R. C. *Homer: An Introduction to the Iliad and the Odyssey.* Boston and Glasgow: 1887.

Platt, Arthur. "T. S. Brandreth." *Classical Review* 7, no. 3 (March 1893).

Sandys, John Edwin. *A History of Classical Scholarship.* Oxford: Oxford University Press, 1906–10.

Schindel, Ulrich. "Christian Gottlob Heyne." *Classical Scholarship: A Biographical Encyclopedia.* Edited by Ward W. Briggs and William M. Calder III. New York: Garland, 1990.

Wilamowitz-Moellendorff, Ulrich von. *History of Classical Scholarship.* Edited by Hugh Lloyd-Jones and translated by Alan Harris. Baltimore, MD: Johns Hopkins University Press, 1982.

A24

Luigi Lamberti (1759–1813). Ἡ τοῦ Ὁμήρου Ἰλιάς. Parma: Typis Bodonianis, 1808.

Imperial folio. 3 vols.

Included with the BHL copy is a trial proof of the first two pages of the main text. Aside from variations in capitalization and punctuation, the chief difference between this and the final version is in the diacritics: ultimately Bodoni chose to use simpler forms of the breathing marks. He also simplified the design of the running heads.

Bookplates on the front inside cover show that this copy comes from the collection of John Hayford Thorold. In like manner with his father, Thorold was an avid book collector and bibliophile, and he amassed an impressive library at his Syston Park estate. Thorold's collection was auctioned off in December of 1884, and a listing for this very copy appears in the auction catalog. The entry includes a mention of the trial proof: "This edition is undoubtedly the 'CHEF D'ŒUVRE' of Bodoni's typographical skill, and is now extremely rare. Inserted is a leaf showing Bodoni's first attempt."

This magnificent edition of Homer's *Iliad*, of which only 170 copies were printed, is among the greatest productions of Giambattista Bodoni, the foremost printer and typographer of his day. Bodoni began his career as a compositor at the press of the Propaganda Fide in Rome, and in 1768 he was appointed director of the Royal Press of the Duke of Parma. Bodoni brought renewed attention to the quality of materials and presswork at a time when care in such matters was on the decline. But his most lasting influence lies in his work as a typographer. Inspired by the work of Baskerville and Didot, Bodoni further developed and popularized the "modern face" style, in which the thick and thin strokes of the letterforms exhibit a high degree of contrast.

The results Bodoni achieved in his roman and italic designs, widely praised at the time, did not, however, carry over with equal success to his Greek designs. Scholderer argues that, despite the other merits of his Greek editions, he "had no understanding of the principles on which a Greek fount should be designed" (p. 13), and Zapf finds fault with what he considers uneven character weight, improper spacing, and excessive ornamentation. At a moment when Greek type seemed ready for a clear departure from the dominant cursive tradition (see A2 and A14), Bodoni's designs "not merely failed to improve upon their predecessors but did positive harm when carried to general favour by the typographic excellence of the editions in which they were used." Scholderer specifically condemns the type used in this edition of Homer as "an aggressively ugly fount which endeavours to disguise its poverty of design by exaggerated contrasts of thick and thin strokes" (p. 13).

The edition is dedicated to Napoleon in three languages (Italian, French, and Latin) and set in three different types (italic, roman, and small capitals, respectively). This is followed by a preface by the editor of the text, the Hellenist and poet Luigi Lamberti. In the preface the edition is offered as the newest contribution in a distinguished tradition of Homeric texts printed in Italy, which have been represented thus far by the *editio princeps* (A1, Florence), the first printing of Eustathius's commentary (D4, Rome), and Villoison's edition of the Venetian scholia (A21, Venice). Lamberti distinguishes the present edition for its magnificence and carefulness; Bodoni's presswork and typography supply the former, and Lamberti's own effort the latter. In his editorial approach, Lamberti relies first on the manuscript evidence, but in passages that pose difficulties he refers to his predecessors, the foremost among which are Heyne (A23) and Wolf.

In 1810, Napoleon awarded Bodoni a pension of 3,000 francs. There had already been some contact between the two men a decade previously, when Bodoni had solicited Napoleon's patronage for a polyglot edition of Homer (see A24A).

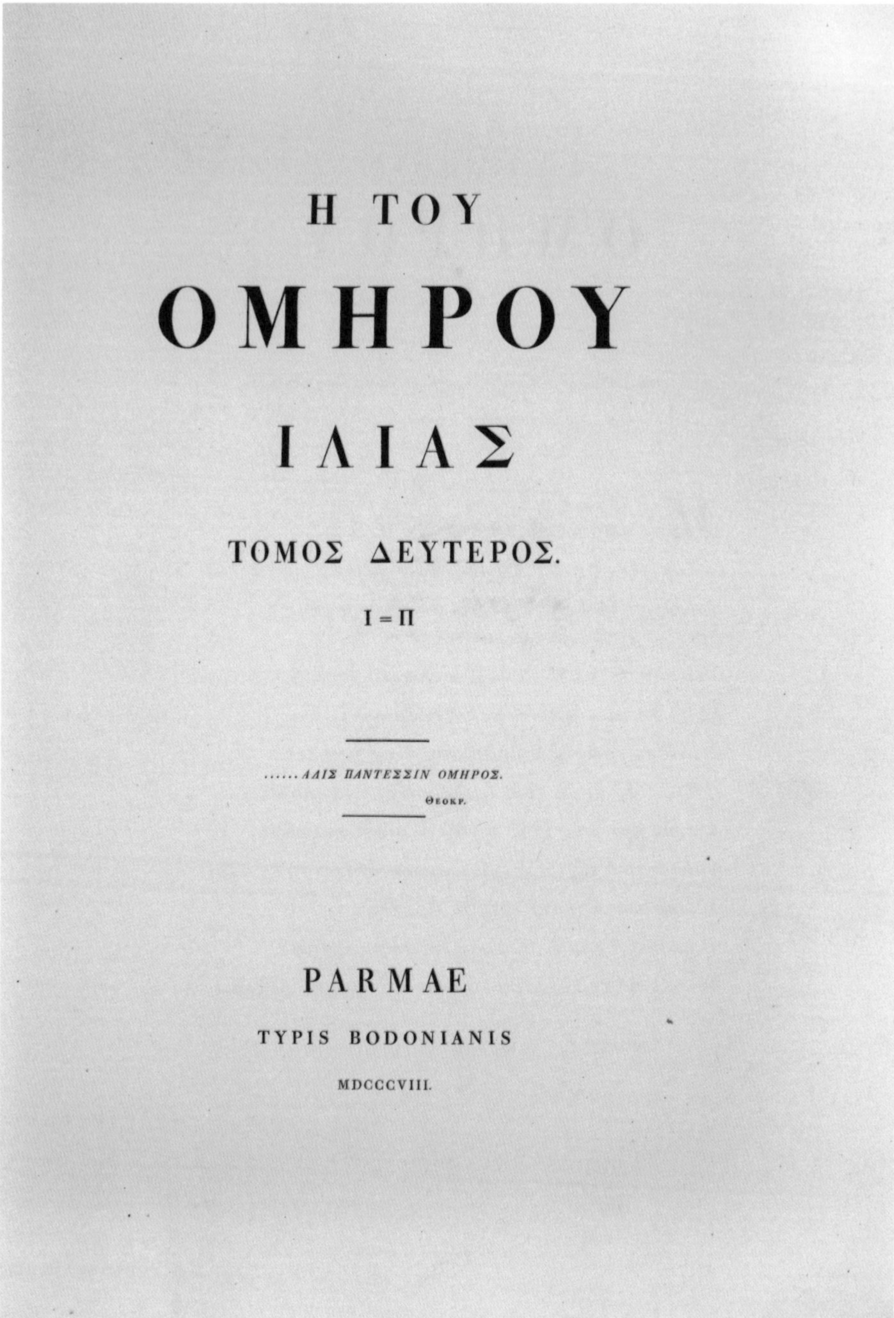

Η ΤΟΥ

ΟΜΗΡΟΥ

ΙΛΙΑΣ

ΤΟΜΟΣ ΔΕΥΤΕΡΟΣ.

Ι = Π

......ΑΔΙΣ ΠΑΝΤΕΣΣΙΝ ΟΜΗΡΟΣ.

ΘΕΟΚΡ.

PARMAE

TYPIS BODONIANIS

MDCCCVIII.

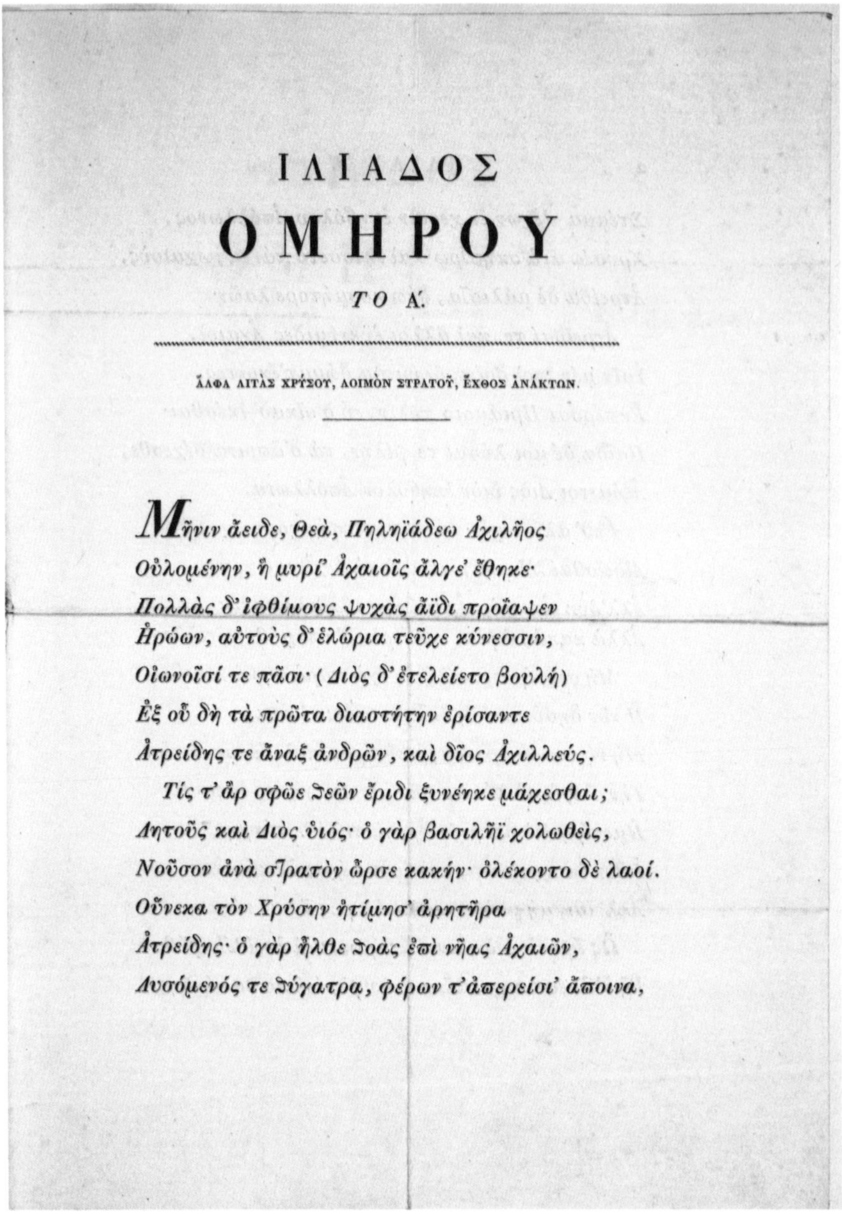

ΙΛΙΑΔΟΣ
ΟΜΗΡΟΥ

ΤΟ Α΄.

ἌΛΦΑ ΛΙΤᾺΣ ΧΡΎΣΟΥ, ΛΟΙΜῸΝ ΣΤΡΑΤΟΥ͂, ἜΧΘΟΣ ἈΝΆΚΤΩΝ.

Μῆνιν ἄειδε, Θεὰ, Πηληϊάδεω Ἀχιλῆος
Οὐλομένην, ἣ μυρί' Ἀχαιοῖς ἄλγε' ἔθηκε·
Πολλὰς δ' ἰφθίμους ψυχὰς ἄϊδι προΐαψεν
Ἡρώων, αὐτοὺς δ' ἑλώρια τεῦχε κύνεσσιν,
Οἰωνοῖσί τε πᾶσι· (Διὸς δ' ἐτελείετο βουλή)
Ἐξ οὗ δὴ τὰ πρῶτα διαστήτην ἐρίσαντε
Ἀτρείδης τε ἄναξ ἀνδρῶν, καὶ δῖος Ἀχιλλεύς.
Τίς τ' ἄρ σφῶε ϑεῶν ἔριδι ξυνέηκε μάχεσθαι;
Λητοῦς καὶ Διὸς υἱός· ὁ γὰρ βασιλῆϊ χολωθεὶς,
Νοῦσον ἀνὰ στρατὸν ὦρσε κακήν· ὀλέκοντο δὲ λαοί.
Οὕνεκα τὸν Χρύσην ἠτίμησ' ἀρητῆρα
Ἀτρείδης· ὁ γὰρ ἦλθε ϑοὰς ἐϖὶ νῆας Ἀχαιῶν,
Λυσόμενός τε ϑύγατρα, φέρων τ' ἀϖερείσι' ἄϖοινα,

A24

PROOF SHEET

ΙΛΙΑΔΟΣ

ΟΜΗΡΟΥ

Α.

Μῆνιν ἄειδε, θεὰ, Πηληϊάδεω Ἀχιλῆος,
Οὐλομένην, ἣ μυρί' Ἀχαιοῖς ἄλγε' ἔθηκε,
Πολλὰς δ' ἰφθίμους ψυχὰς Ἄϊδι προΐαψεν
Ἡρώων, αὐτοὺς δὲ ἑλώρια τεῦχε κύνεσσιν
Οἰωνοῖσί τε πᾶσι· Διὸς δ' ἐτελείετο βουλή·
Ἐξ οὗ δὴ τὰ πρῶτα διαστήτην ἐρίσαντε
Ἀτρείδης τε, ἄναξ ἀνδρῶν, καὶ δῖος Ἀχιλλεύς.
Τίς τ' ἄρ σφωε θεῶν ἔριδι ξυνέηκε μάχεσθαι;
Λητοῦς καὶ Διὸς υἱός. ὁ γὰρ βασιλῆϊ χολωθεὶς,
Νοῦσον ἀνὰ στρατὸν ὦρσε κακὴν, ὀλέκοντο δὲ λαοὶ,
Οὕνεκα τὸν Χρύσην ἠτίμησ' ἀρητῆρα
Ἀτρείδης. ὁ γὰρ ἦλθε θοὰς ἐπὶ νῆας Ἀχαιῶν,
Λυσόμενός τε θύγατρα, φέρων τ' ἀπερείσι' ἄποινα,

A24

Caputo, V., ed. *Italia poetica antica e moderna.* Rome: Istituto editorale del Mediterraneo, 1967.

Cleland, T. M. *Giambattista Bodoni of Parma.* Boston: Society of Printers, 1916.

Purcell, Mark. "Thorold, Sir John, ninth baronet (1734–1815)." *Oxford Dictionary of National Biography.*

Scholderer, Victor. *Greek Printing Types, 1465–1927.* London: British Museum, 1927.

The Syston Park Library. Catalogue of an Important Portion of the Extensive and Valuable Library of Sir John Hayford Thorold, Bart. London: 1884.

Zapf, Hermann. "The Development of Greek Typefaces." *Greek Letters: From Tablets to Pixels.* Edited by Michael S. Macrakis. New Castle, DE: Oak Knoll Press, 1996.

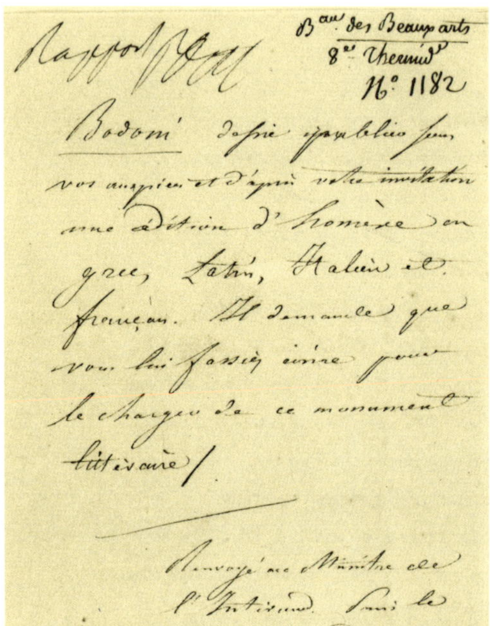

Rapport

Bau. des Beaux arts
8e Thermidor
No. 1182

Bodoni désire publier sous vos auspices et d'après votre invitation une édition d'homère en grec, latin, italien et français. Il demande que vous lui fassiez écrire pour le charger de ce monument littéraire.

Renvoyé au Ministre de l'Intérieur Paris le sept thermidor an 8
Le 1er Consul
Bonaparte

A24A

A24A

Rapport. Bureau des Beaux arts. Paris, 8th thermidor [i.e. July 25, 1800], No 1182. Manuscript, signed by Napoleon.

This proposal for a polyglot edition of Homer in Greek, Latin, Italian, and French was submitted to Napoleon eight years before the publication of Bodoni's magnificent *Iliad* (see A24). Napoleon's signature indicates that he read the memorandum, which was returned to the Ministry of the Interior, but apparently he did not provide the patronage for the publication that Bodoni sought.

A25

Richard Payne Knight (1751–1824). *Carmina Homerica, Ilias et Odyssea . . . cum Notis ac Prolegomenis. . . .* London: In ædibus Valpianis and Paris and Strasbourg: Apud Treuttel et Wurtz, bibliopolas, 1820.

Quarto.

In the eighteenth century, Richard Bentley had put forward the theory that the digamma, a letter that fell out of use in ancient Greek speech and writing at an early stage, was still in use when Homer's poems were composed. Bentley believed that its restoration would correct various metrical problems found in the Homeric poems. Bentley himself started work on an edition of Homer that would fully restore the digamma, but he soon found that its consistent application raised many problems; although he left copious notes, he never finished the project. Both Clarke (A19) and Heyne (A23) accepted Bentley's ideas, although neither incorporated the digamma into the text of his edition: Clarke discusses it in one of his notes, and Heyne (who had direct access Bentley's notes in his copy of Estienne's edition, A14) selectively restores it in his textual apparatus, having decided that fully restoring it would be too disruptive of the text. With this edition, however, after nearly a century's delay, Bentley's plan was at last brought to completion.

The editor was the antiquarian and dilettante Richard Payne Knight, a man of wide-ranging interests who was deeply involved in contemporary debates concerning aesthetics and taste. One of his more influential works was *Analytical Inquiry into the Principles of Taste* (1805). He was prone to stirring up controversy, as with his *Account of the Remains of the Worship of Priapus* (1786), which attracted widespread criticism for its claims about the pervasiveness of sexual symbolism in all religions. Later in life he would severely damage his reputation by insisting that the Elgin marbles were Roman copies of little artistic value.

Just the prolegomena to this edition were published in 1808 in London, at the press of William Bulmer. The same material later appeared with additional notes in the *Classical Journal* (vols. 7–8, 1813, printed by the same printer as this edition) and as a separate publication in Leipzig in 1816. The full text of the *Iliad* and *Odyssey* were added in the present edition of 1820. Many years earlier Payne Knight had put forth his views on the digamma in his *Analytical Essay on the*

Greek Alphabet (London, 1791), in which he used the language of Homer almost exclusively in developing his argument. Porson (see A22) reviewed this work critically, although not entirely unfavorably.

The edition was printed in London at the press of Abraham John Valpy, who had aspirations of becoming an influential printer-editor of classical texts, on a par with Aldus or Estienne. One of his major undertakings was a new edition of Estienne's *Thesaurus Graecae Linguae* (1816–28; see A14). His trademark and monogram—fittingly, in this case—was the digamma, which is visible on the title page of this edition, above the imprint.

Payne Knight's prolegomena deal in large part with Homeric language and grammar. He discusses the historical development of the Greek language, including the use of the digamma. Payne Knight argues for the traditional view of Homer, placing himself in opposition to the recent German scholarship represented by Wolf and Heyne. In contrast to Wolf, who did not have the goal of determining how the text looked prior to the work of the ancient critics (see A21), Payne Knight attempts to construct a text that reaches closer to the poems as Homer would have composed them.

Following the title page and prolegomena are a page of corrigenda and two maps of the Troad, one Homeric and one contemporary, and then the text of the poems, with the digamma fully restored according to Payne Knight's system. At the end of the edition are notes on the text, which are mostly variant readings and discussions of lines that Payne Knight considers spurious. They also include points of language, grammar, and meter.

Many critics regarded Payne Knight's work as impressive, learned, and even entertaining; yet he has often been criticized for his lack of discipline and restraint in pursuing his theories. Reviewing Payne Knight's *Analytical Essay on the Greek Alphabet,* Porson said, "The author is a man of reading, learning, and inquiry . . . but when he traces the history of the language, and the etymology of words, he gives too much scope to conjecture and imagination."

In the case of the text he reconstructs for this edition, the result is inconsistent and jarring, for, as Bentley had discovered, the many changes imposed on the Homeric poems over time seriously complicate any attempts to restore fully the digamma and the old orthography. The following comparison of *Iliad* 1.1–3 in Payne Knight's version and in a recent scholarly edition illustrates the extent to which Payne Knight alters the text:

West (1998):

ΙΛΙΑΣ

Μῆνιν ἄειδε, θεά, Πηληϊάδεω Ἀχιλῆος
οὐλομένην, ἣ μυρί' Ἀχαιοῖς ἄλγε' ἔθηκεν,
πολλὰς δ' Ἰφθίμους ψυχὰς Ἄϊδι προΐαψεν

Payne Knight (1820):

ΓΙΛϜΙΑΣ

Μηνιν αϜειδε, θεα, πηλεϜιαδαϜ' αχιλεϜος
ολομενην, ƕη μυϜρι' αχαιϜοισ' αλγε' εθῆκε,
πολλας δ' ἰφθῖμοϜς πσυϜχας αϜιδι προϊαπτσεν

Clarke, M. L. *Greek Studies in England, 1700–1830.* Cambridge: Cambridge University Press, 1945.

Courtney, W. P. "Valpy, Abraham John (1787–1854)." Rev. Richard Jenkyns. *Oxford Dictionary of National Biography.*

Jebb, R. C. *Bentley.* London: 1882.

Monk, James Henry. *Life of Richard Bentley, D.D.* 2nd ed. London: J.G. & F. Rivington, 1833.

Porson, Richard. "Mr. Knight's *Analytical Essay on the Greek Alphabet.*" *Monthly Review* 13 (January 1794): 7–16, 379–85.

Watson, J. S. *The Life of Richard Porson, M.A.* London: 1861.

A26

Edward Robinson (1794–1863). *Homeri Iliadis libri novem priores librique xviii, et xxii. . . .* Catskill: Veneunt apud N. Elliott, 1822.

Octavo.

The BHL copy includes a pamphlet from a bicentennial exhibition on Edward Robinson, held at his *alma mater* Hamilton College in 1994.

This selection of eleven books of the *Iliad* is almost certainly the first Greek edition of Homer produced by an American scholar. It was the first book written by its editor, Edward Robinson, who after this publication devoted the rest of his career to biblical studies. Yet this edition played some role in setting the direction of Robinson's work. He had gone to Andover in 1822 to finish work on the edition and see to its publication, but once there he took up the study of Hebrew. Thereafter, Robinson engaged in biblical scholarship and teaching, and he would spend several years studying in Europe and traveling in the Holy Land. Robinson played an important role in establishing America's presence in biblical scholarship and in building connections with the German academic community. He founded and for several years edited the *Biblical Repository* (1831–35), and his *Biblical Researches in Palestine* (1841 and 1856) is considered a major contribution to biblical geography.

The title of the work indicates that it was intended for educational use (*in usum iuventutis academicae*). In the prefatory letter, Robinson states that the edition is not meant for more advanced students of the Greek language; rather, his goal is to excite and encourage young American students toward further study. He further explains that he has collected the notes from various sources, chiefly from Heyne (A23), and he has selected and adapted them for use by students.

Included in this edition is the text to *Iliad* books 1–9, 18, and 22. Following the text are the notes, two appendices, and an index of the Greek terms discussed in the notes. As with the notes, the material in the appendices has been collected from various sources. The first appendix, "On the reckoning of days in the *Iliad*, and the distribution of battles across them" (*De computatione dierum in Iliade, et pugnarum per eos distributione*), is taken from Heyne's first excursus on *Iliad* 18. The second appendix, "On the *Iliad* and its author" (*De Iliade, et de eius auctore*), includes excerpts from Heyne's second excursus on *Iliad* 24, Wolf's *Prolegomena ad Homerum* (see A21), Bentley (see A19, A23, A25), and others.

The typeface in this edition bears a close resemblance to the original Greek type that appeared in editions of the Bibliotheca Teubneriana, and thus will be instantly recognizable to most scholars. According to Scholderer (pp. 13–14), these typefaces were heavily influenced by the work of Giambattista Bodoni (see A24).

Duyckinck, Evert A., and George L. Duyckinck. "Edward Robinson." *Cyclopaedia of American Literature.* New York: Charles Scribner, 1866.

Scholderer, Victor. *Greek Printing Types, 1465–1927.* London: British Museum, 1927.

Williams, Jay G. *The Times and Life of Edward Robinson: Connecticut Yankee in King Solomon's Court.* Atlanta: Scholars Press, 1999.

A27

William Pickering (1796–1854). Ὁμήρου Ἰλιάς. Ὁμήρου Ὀδύσσεια.... London: Gulielmus Pickering, 1831. *Diamond Classics.*

Sextodecimo. 2 vols.

Printed in 4½ point type, this miniature edition of the *Iliad* and *Odyssey* is remarkable for its high production quality and the clarity of its print. Scholderer calls it "one of the best printed of Greek tiny books" (p. 15). William Pickering's work can be credited with several important developments in book production, most of all through his attention to quality typography and his pioneering use of cloth binding. According to Keynes, Pickering "had done more than any other single man to raise the standard of book production in all its details, whether of subject matter, typography, or binding" (p. 41).

As with many of Pickering's publications, this edition was printed by Charles Whittingham the younger. In 1828 the two men established a close friendship and longstanding business partnership. They complemented one another effectively, with Whittingham supplying the necessary technical and typographical expertise that Pickering's ambition and originality demanded.

In that same year, Pickering adopted the printer's device that would become closely associated with his name. He took up the anchor and dolphin from the Aldine device and attached to it the motto *Aldi Discipulus Anglus* ("English student of Aldus"). The association with Aldus (see A2 and A6) was motivated by Pickering's interest in producing convenient and affordable editions. It also reflected his understanding and appreciation of the history of printing. Before the expansion of his publishing business, he was primarily an antiquarian bookseller. His experience with secondhand books appears to have influenced not only his literary tastes but also his aesthetic sense.

One of Pickering's earliest ventures was the Diamond Classics, a series of miniature volumes printed from 1821 to 1831. Initially focused on Latin and Italian classics, the series soon expanded to include works in English and Greek as well. This edition of Homer is the last publication in this series.

Keynes, Geoffrey. *William Pickering Publisher: A Memoir and Checklist of His Publications*, rev. ed. London: Galahad, 1969.

Scholderer, Victor. *Greek Printing Types, 1465–1927*. London: British Museum, 1927.

Spielmann, Percy E. *Catalogue of the Library of Miniature Books*. London: Edward Arnold, 1961.

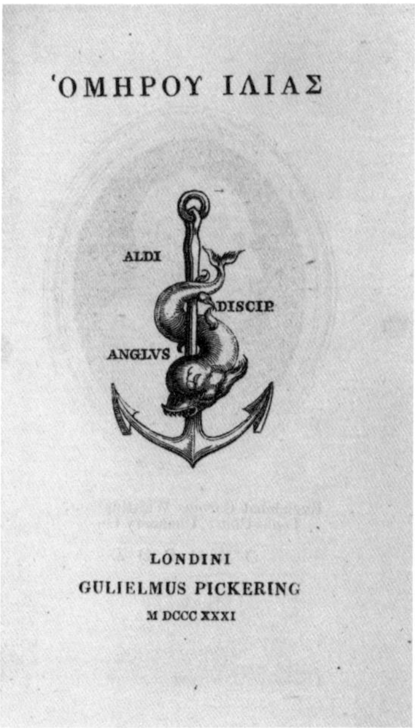

A27

A28

Thomas Shaw Brandreth (1788–1873). ʽΟμήρου Fιλιάς. *littera digamma restituta ad metri leges redegit et notatione brevi illustravit Thomas Shaw Brandreth.* London: Gulielmus Pickering, 1841.

Octavo.

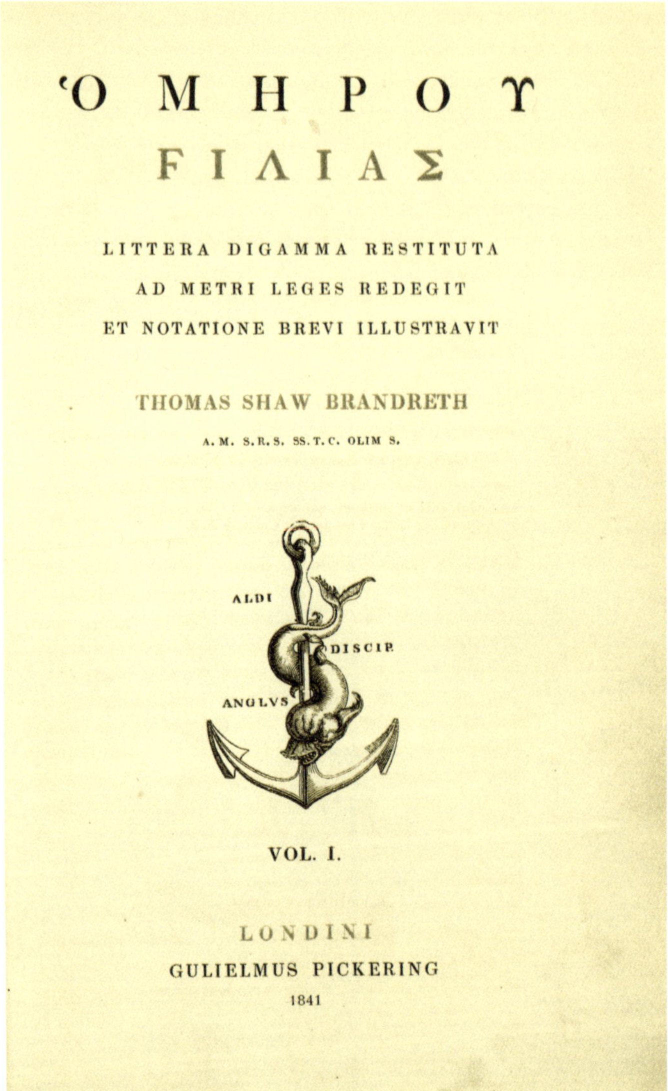

A28

Through his studies of the digamma (see A19) and his efforts at restoring it to the text of the Homeric poems, Richard Payne Knight (A25) had done much to advance the understanding of Homeric language and the development of ancient Greek. Yet his excessive insertion of the digamma into the text and his willingness to condemn lines as interpolations exposed him to criticism and hindered the acceptance of his ideas. Two decades later this edition of the *Iliad* took up the question again, but with a more measured approach.

Although Brandreth was a lawyer by profession, his interests lay in inventing, and such pursuits led him to work for a time as a director of the Liverpool and Manchester Railway. He returned to classical studies after his retirement. Following the publication of this edition of Homer in 1841, Brandreth produced two related works: *A Dissertation on the Metre of Homer* (1844) and a blank verse translation of the *Iliad* (1846).

The *Dissertation* reviews past scholarship related to the restoration of the digamma, starting with Bentley. Brandreth criticizes what he sees as the deficiencies and errors in the approaches of his predecessors. For example, he finds fault with Payne Knight's edition (A25) for its extreme and inconsistently applied orthography and liberal condemnation of verses. For example, Brandreth indicates that he has given the familiar spelling "ουλομενην" in the text but mentions that Payne Knight "printed ολομενην, which was the ancient word-form" (*Knightius ολομενην edidit, quae forma antiqua erat*) (p. 23). Brandreth then presents his own discussion of the digamma and how it is to be restored to the text.

A more abbreviated treatment of these issues appears in the short, two-page preface to this edition. Brandreth begins by describing his editorial approach. His stated policy is to refrain from using the digamma when there is reasonable doubt as to its use in a word. Above all he strives to remove instances of hiatus from the text: By his reckoning, the digamma is used to resolve around 1,750 instances of hiatus, and a further 100 are handled by other means. He does not hesitate to incorporate the more certain modifications into the main text, although he does note such changes. Next, Brandreth briefly recounts the history of the publication of the Homeric text (many of which are in the BHL, such as the *editio princeps* [A1], the Aldine [A2, A6], and others), as well as the work done thus far on the digamma, beginning with Bentley and on to Richard Dawes, Heyne (A23), and Payne Knight (A25). Of his predecessors he acknowledges the greatest debt to Clarke (A19) and Heyne. With specific regard to the digamma, he claims that he has conducted a thorough examination both of words that take a digamma and of all troublesome passages.

The greater conservatism of Brandreth's approach is evident in a comparison of the first three lines of the *Iliad* (for Payne Knight's text, see end of A25). Where Payne Knight inserts nine digammas, Brandreth has only one. The difference between the two is further evident in Brandreth's note to the second line. He asserts that, to the extent that it is possible, he follows the established practices of writing (*mihi tamen propositum est scripturam usitatam, quoad possim, retinere*). Payne Knight, by contrast, seeks to recreate an older, more authentic orthography.

The edition was published by William Pickering and printed by Charles Whittingham the younger (see A27 for both), and the title page displays Pickering's customary Aldine device. On the facing page is a map of the Troad, and on the verso of the title page appear two epigraphs. The first quotes Aristotle, *Poetics* 1459b16, "Homer excels all [poets] in diction and thought" (Ὅμηρος λέξει καὶ διανοίᾳ πάντας ὑπερβέβληκε; the text differs from the current reading, but it is the same as the text quoted in Clarke's edition [A19]). The second comes from Horace, *Epistles* 1.2, lines 3–4, "[Homer], who tells us what is fair, what is foul, what is helpful, what not, more fully and better than Chrysippus or Crantor" (*Qui, quid sit pulchrum, qui turpe, quid utile, quid non, / Plenius ac melius Chrysippo et Crantore dicit*).

After the preface the text begins, with notes arranged at the bottom of the page. The first volume contains *Iliad* 1–12. The second volume continues with books 13–24, followed by extensive back-matter: (a) an index of Greek words; (b) a table of words spelled with a digamma; (c) transcription, translation, and remarks on a bronze tablet inscription found at Olympia, which provides important evidence about the use of the digamma; (d) brief remarks by Brandreth justifying his decision, contrary to the usual practice, to omit accents from the text; (e) a grammatical index; (f) a summary of the metrical rules followed in the edition; and (g) an index of names.

As a result of Brandreth's more moderate approach, the text of this edition appears far less eccentric than Payne Knight's. It helps greatly that the shape of the digamma blends more harmoniously with the other letters. Diacritical marks are mostly absent; only rough breathings and diaereses are indicated. The typeface is a version of the French Royal Greek (see A14), but contrary to the spirit of the type's original design (and in accordance with nineteenth-century trends in Greek typography), it refrains entirely from using ligatures and variant letterforms.

Brandreth did not meet much greater success than Payne Knight. *The North American Review* sharply criticized his edition. In a short review article over fifty years later, Arthur Platt found it necessary to call attention to Brandreth's neglected work—"rescuing [him] from undeserved oblivion" (p. 107–8), as he puts it—and demonstrate what he recognized as the work's many useful insights and observations.

Lane-Poole, Stanley. "Brandreth, Thomas Shaw (1788–1873)." Rev. R. C. Cox. *Oxford Dictionary of National Biography.*

Platt, Arthur. "T. S. Brandreth." *Classical Review* 7, no. 3 (March 1893): 107–8.

"Review of *ΟΜΗΡΟΥ FΙΛΙΑΣ. Litera Digamma restituta, ad Metri Leges redegit et Notatione brevi illustravit Thomas Shaw Brandreth.*" *North American Review* 57, no. 121 (October 1843): 501–5.

A29

W. Walter Merry (1835–1918) and James Riddell (1823–1866). *Homer's Odyssey. . . .* Rev. 2nd ed. Oxford: Clarendon Press, 1886. *Clarendon Press Series.*

Vol. 1, Books I–XII.

D. B. Monro (1836–1905). *Homer's Odyssey. . . .* Oxford: Clarendon Press, 1901.

Vol. 2, Books XIII–XXIV.

Octavo. 2 vols.

The BHL copy of the first volume contains interlinear and marginal pencil notes on morphology and word meanings.

James Riddell, fellow and tutor of Balliol College, Oxford, began the initial work on this edition. Following his untimely death, his friend and former student William Walter Merry completed the work. The first edition, with text and notes to the first twelve books of the *Odyssey*, was published by the Clarendon Press in 1876. The BHL contains a copy of the second edition of 1886.

In 1859 Merry was elected a fellow of Lincoln College; he would later serve as its rector. He also held the curacy of All Saints Church beginning in 1862. During his lifetime, he became well known in Oxford for his preaching and his English and Latin oratory. From 1904 to 1906, he was Vice-Chancellor of Oxford University, succeeding David Binning Monro, the scholar who prepared the second volume of this edition.

In 1870, Merry had produced the first volume of a smaller edition of the *Odyssey*, which was intended for use in schools (the second volume appeared in 1878). In the preface to this volume he acknowledges his debt to Riddell's notes and mentions the forthcoming larger edition. Merry also undertook a series of school editions of Aristophanes's plays; commentaries to seven plays were published between 1879 and 1900.

D. B. Monro spent most of his career at Oriel College, Oxford. He was elected a fellow in 1859 and took up the position of Provost in 1882. He had expertise in a variety of subjects, but the focus of his scholarly work was Homer. His *Grammar of the Homeric Dialect* (1882, second edition 1891), which he dedicated to Riddell, remains an important resource for Homeric studies even today. In 1902 he coedited, with T. W. Allen, what would become the standard text of the *Iliad* in the twentieth century (A31, first edition, vols. 1–2).

The first volume contains both the original preface from 1876 and the preface to the revised edition. Books 1–12 of the *Odyssey* follow, with notes arranged below the text. The text has been taken nearly unaltered from the edition by J. La Roche

(Teubner, 1867); Merry offers only a limited critical apparatus and refers the reader to La Roche for fuller information about the text. The volume ends with three appendices: "The Homeric Ship," "On some various forms of the legend of the blinded cyclops," and "Ithaca." In the second preface, Merry notes that, in addition to many other revisions, the most substantial change to the second edition is that references have been made throughout to Monro's *Grammar of the Homeric Dialect* (the first edition of which had appeared a few years earlier). The volume concludes with an index of the principal Greek words and names that appear in the notes.

The second volume is arranged much like the first, with the addition of a table of contents. Monro's notes are not as extensive as Riddell and Merry's, but this difference is offset somewhat by the large amount of material contained in the appendices. Monro explains his motivation for this in the preface, noting, "In the present state of scholarship an editor of Homer is almost obliged to form some opinion on the multifarious issues which make up the 'Homeric Question.'" The volume contains two indexes, one of Greek words appearing in the notes and another of English terms and names. It is dedicated to Monro's *alma mater*, the University of Glasgow, which was then celebrating its 450th anniversary.

The main text in both volumes is set in Porson Greek (the lemmata in the notes are set in Greek Thick Face). The choice of capital letters in each volume deserves mention. Porson's original design called for capitals with serifs, and although the lowercase letters were slanted, the capitals were upright. Neither volume of this edition conforms to this design, however. In the first volume a set of slanted, sans serif capitals has been paired with the lowercase letters. The visual harmony between the letters is strained somewhat by the fact that the capitals are of uniform thickness, whereas the lowercase letters exhibit a moderate degree of contrast. The second volume uses a different set of capitals, closer to Porson's design but nevertheless slanted. (By contrast, the text in A31, for example, has been set according to the original design.)

Bowman, John H. "Greek Type Design: The British Contribution." *Greek Letters: From Tablets to Pixels.* Edited by Michael S. Macrakis. New Castle, DE: Oak Knoll Press, 1996.

Carlyle, E. I. "Merry, William Walter (1835–1918)." Rev. Richard Smail. *Oxford Dictionary of National Biography.*

Monro, D. B. *A Grammar of the Homeric Dialect.* 2nd ed. Oxford: Clarendon Press, 1891.

Phelps, L. R. "Monro, David Binning (1836–1905)." *Oxford Dictionary of National Biography.*

West, M. L. "Monro, David Binning (1836–1905)." *Dictionary of British Classicists.* Edited by Robert B. Todd. Bristol, England: Thoemmes Continuum, 2004.

A30

Walter Leaf (1852–1927). *Homeri Ilias.* London: Macmillan and Co., 1895. *Parnassus Library of Greek and Latin Texts.*

Octavo.

This edition is representative of an important moment in the development of Greek type. It was part of Macmillan's "Parnassus Library of Greek and Latin Texts," a series intended to provide high-quality and attractive reading texts, accompanied by introductions (but not notes or commentaries). One of its key features was that the Greek editions used a new typeface known as Macmillan Greek. Squarish, heavy, and uniform in the appearance of its letterforms and lacking any ligatures, it expresses a sharp departure from the dominant tradition in Greek type design, which was based on the fifteenth-century cursive handwriting that Aldus had popularized (see A2). In designing Macmillan Greek, Selwyn Image, an artist best known for his stained glass pieces, took the Greek type used in the New Testament of the Complutensian Polyglot Bible of 1514 as a starting point. That design had in turn been based on the handwriting in tenth-century manuscripts. Thus, Image's type shares certain features with the type designed by Demetrius Damilas for the *editio princeps* (A1). Robert Proctor's Otter Greek, which appeared in 1903, was developed in a similar spirit (see A32). An earlier effort to depart from the cursive tradition can be seen in the type that was designed for the Glasgow Homer (A20); similarly with Porson Greek, a half century later (see discussion in A22).

Walter Leaf had produced a two-volume text and commentary of the *Iliad* in 1886–88. This edition takes up the earlier text, although Leaf revises it to reflect additional manuscript evidence (he points specifically to the "Paris group" of manuscripts, which represent an ancient textual tradition distinct from the mainline "vulgate"). As he explains in the preface, "the present text is in fact an endeavour to get the best that can be got from the MSS., including MS. variants attested by ancient authorities"; and in his overall assessment, "on the whole I have followed the MSS. even more closely than in my edition with commentary." The modifications to the earlier text are given after the preface in a "List of the principal variations from the text of the *Iliad, with English Notes and Introduction.*" In 1900–02 Leaf issued a revised edition of the text and commentary.

Leaf had studied at Trinity College, Cambridge, on a classical scholarship and graduated as Senior Classic in 1874. He was elected a fellow of Trinity in the following year but was soon forced to return to the family textile business. From 1892 he pursued a successful second career in banking.

Because Leaf was not a professional academic, he took a broader view of classical studies. In particular, he recognized the importance of making classical texts accessible to those who could not read Latin or Greek. Along these lines, he contributed to a popular and well-received English translation of the *Iliad* (1882, with Andrew Lang and Ernest James Myers; B24) and wrote *A Companion to the Iliad for English Readers* (London: Macmillan, 1892). At the same time, Leaf conducted important research within the traditional line of Homeric studies. For example, T. W. Allen (see A31) praises Leaf's contributions to manuscript collation and methodology in his *editio maior* of the *Iliad* (1.270–71).

In his preface, Leaf sets forth the problem that faces any editor of Homer: What text does he want to present? He finds fault with the efforts that reach back to some more archaic and original form (an extreme example being Payne Knight, A25), finding that such editions are unable to apply their methods consistently. Moreover, he determines that "All such editions are in effect essays in the reconstruction of early Greek rather than texts of Homer; they are meant for scholars who can criticize them and correct them, rather than for readers whose aim it is to read Homer as literature" (p. viii–ix). Leaf's alternative is to present the text as it stands in a particular historical moment, "to fix within the history of the text a period which we consider to be within the domain of external evidence" (p. vii).

After a discussion of the textual tradition and his own editorial approach, Leaf concludes by mentioning two matters of presentation: the use of the new Macmillan Greek type and his decision to abolish the iota subscript. He anticipates some surprise on the reader's part, but is optimistic: "As they get accustomed to the new fount—and from its beauty they cannot but do so—they will have the opportunity of growing accustomed also to seeing iota in its place as much after a long as after a short vowel" (p. xiv).

W. G. Rutherford, while acknowledging that it took some time to become accustomed to the type, was similarly optimistic: "I am convinced that they need only to be well known for a universal verdict to be given in their favour." He found that the letters "do not worry and weary the eye so much as the ordinary types" and that the type "has evenness without monotony, and seen in the mass has a singularly rich and decorative effect" (p. 82).

Despite the positive reception from some quarters, the type never attained any significant popularity. In a review of R. Y. Tyrrell's edition of Sophocles, also a part of Macmillan's Parnassus series, T. W. Allen remarked that the "publishers have penalised [the text] with ... their own particular black type, unaesthetic and unhistorical" (p. 408). Ultimately the type was used for the main text in just a handful of publications. The second edition of Leaf's text and commentary (1900–02) restricts the use of Macmillan Greek to the headings, critical apparatus, and lemmata.

Allen, Thomas W. *Homeri Ilias.* Oxford: Clarendon Press, 1931.

———. "Two Editions of Sophocles." *Classical Review* 12, no. 8 (1898): 408–409.

Calder, William Musgrave. "Allen, Thomas William (1862–1950)." *Dictionary of British Classicists.* Edited by Robert B. Todd. Bristol, England: Thoemmes Continuum, 2004.

——. "Leaf, Walter (1852–1927)." *Dictionary of British Classicists.* Edited by Robert B. Todd. Bristol, England: Thoemmes Continuum, 2004.

Dyer, Louis. *Century Guild Hobby Horse,* no. 3 (1893).

Jones, Helen Caroline. "Image, Selwyn (1849–1930)." *Oxford Dictionary of National Biography.*

Leaf, Walter. *Iliad, with English Notes and Introduction.* London: 1886–88.

——. *Iliad, with Apparatus Criticus, Prolegomena, Notes, and Appendices.* London: 1900–02.

"Notes and Announcements." *Book Reviews* 3, no. 1 (May, 1895): 102.

Rutherford, W. G. "A New Fount of Greek Type." *Classical Review* 8, no. 3 (1894): 81–85.

A31

D. B. Monro (1836–1905) and Thomas W. Allen (1862–1950). *Homeri Opera....* Oxford: E typographeo Clarendoniano, 1908–12.

Octavo. 5 vols. in 1.

The BHL copy, printed on India paper, contains the second edition of the *Iliad* and the first editions of the *Odyssey* and the minor works. A label on the front inside cover shows that this copy was originally a prize for Greek verse composition, awarded by Trinity College, Cambridge in 1914 to C. A. Stott. Below is the signature of Henry Montagu Butler, who served as the Master of Trinity from 1866 until his death. It is fitting for him to have presented this award, as he was himself known for his skill at composing Latin and Greek verse.

This volume contains an earlier version of what would become the definitive edition of Homer's works in the twentieth century. In 1902 David Binning Monro (see A29) and Thomas William Allen collaborated on a new edition of the *Iliad* (vols. 1–2) for the well-known series, the Oxford Classical Texts. After Monro's death in 1905, Allen continued the project, supplementing the two volumes of the *Iliad* with two further volumes of the *Odyssey* (1907) and a final, fifth volume containing the minor works (1912). This final volume also presents the lives of Homer, reediting the accessory texts that Chalcondylas had included in the *editio princeps* (A1) as well as the "Contest of Homer and Hesiod," first published in 1573 by Henri Estienne (see A14). Allen also revised the texts as further evidence from recent papyrus finds and additional manuscript collations came to light: a second edition of the *Iliad* appeared in 1908, followed by a third edition in 1920; and a second edition of the *Odyssey* in 1917–19.

Allen completed his undergraduate studies at Queen's College, Oxford in 1885. After obtaining a Craven Travelling Fellowship, he spent the years 1887–90 examining Greek manuscripts, primarily in Italy. It was during this time that he acquired much of his expertise in paleography. In 1890 he was elected a fellow of Queen's, where he remained for the remainder of his career. Among his most significant works are this edition of Homer and a three-volume edition of the *Iliad*, published in 1931. One of his earlier works, *Notes on Abbreviations in Greek Manuscripts* (1889), remains a useful resource for specialists.

The 1912–20 edition of Monro and Allen became the dominant text of Homer's works in the twentieth century. However, the value and accuracy of Allen's work on the manuscripts and textual transmission of Homer has at times been questioned. In Haslam's view, however, such criticism needs to be qualified: "[Allen's] methods were rudimentary but not, as is often charged, fundamentally flawed" (p. 90). There are limits to Allen's grouping of manuscripts into families—limits that Allen himself recognized—but the application of such groupings is nevertheless a useful scholarly tool.

Calder, William Musgrave. "Allen, Thomas William (1862–1950)." *Dictionary of British Classicists.* Edited by Robert B. Todd. Bristol, England: Thoemmes Continuum, 2004.

Haslam, M. "Homeric Papyri and Transmission of the Text." *A New Companion to Homer.* Edited by I. Morris and B. Powell. Leiden: Brill, 1997.

Shepherd, Janet. "Butler, Henry Montagu (1833–1918)." *Oxford Dictionary of National Biography.*

Wilson, N. "Thomas William Allen, 1862–1950." *Proceedings of the British Academy* 76 (1990): 311–19.

———. "Allen, Thomas William (1862–1950)." *Oxford Dictionary of National Biography.*

A32

D. B. Monro (1836–1905). Ὁμήρου Ὀδύσσεια. Oxford: Printed at the University Press with Greek types designed by Robert Proctor, 1909.

Folio.

The front flyleaf contains a handwritten note about the edition, citing Scholderer's praise of the typeface, but the unopened gatherings indicate that this copy has never been read.

This finely produced, limited edition of the *Odyssey* was clearly inspired and influenced by the modern fine press movement. The layout is elegant in its simplicity, with the main text accompanied by the argument to each book and marginal headings in red, and no ornamentation. The most notable feature of the edition is its use of Proctor's Otter Greek type. Like Selwyn Image's Macmillan Greek (see A30), Proctor's design is based on the Greek type used in the New Testament of the Complutensian Polyglot Bible of 1514. But whereas Image merely took the Complutensian Greek as a starting point for his own design, Proctor followed it very closely. However, he had to design additional diacritical marks and a new set of capitals, as these were mostly absent in the original. Pollard characterizes the difference between the two as follows: "Unfortunately in the type he designed for Messrs. Macmillan, Mr. Selwyn Image had introduced modifications and compromises which completely altered its character. Proctor, on the other hand, accepted it in its entirety, but as in its original form it had only one upper-case letter, he was obliged to design the rest himself" (p. xxxvi).

Proctor spent the bulk of his short career as a bibliographer at the British Museum, where he specialized in early printed books and typography. His *The Printing of Greek in the Fifteenth Century* (Oxford, 1900) and a paper on "The French Royal Greek Types and the Eton *Chrysostom*" are important contributions to the history of Greek type. Proctor had an interest in the private press movement, fueled in part by his friendship with William Morris (see A33). Morris's work helped inspire Proctor to produce the new Greek type.

The punchcutter was Edward Philip Prince, who cut the types for numerous private presses, most notably for the Doves Press. The type was produced in 1903 and used the following year in a limited edition of Aeschylus's *Oresteia* (London: Chiswick Press). After this edition of Homer, it was used once more in a 1932 edition of the Gospels (Oxford: Clarendon Press).

Although the type has been widely praised, it is generally acknowledged that its design restricts its usefulness. In Scholderer's view, "Few would deny that Proctor's fount, completing the Complutensian type as it does, stands out as the finest Greek face ever cut, and it is much to be regretted that it will not bear reduction to a commercial size" (p. 15). Bowman agrees, but points to the influence of Otter Greek on the subsequent development of Greek type: "The type's large size made it unsuitable for ordinary editions and any reduction would have destroyed its character. But although it had no *direct* effect on Greek type, it led the way back to a revival of fifteenth and sixteenth-century letter-forms and showed that a type based on them was a practical possibility" (p. 143). Indeed, one of the most successful Greek typefaces of the twentieth century, Scholderer's New Hellenic, followed Proctor's approach, to greater success. In his review of Scholderer's monograph, T. D. Barlow considered New Hellenic superior to its predecessor: "Mr. Scholderer reiterates the praise which Proctor's type has received. I cannot agree with him. I have never understood why it has attained to such universal approbation. It seems to me if not actually clumsy, much too broad and ponderous in face and its general effect is oppressive. . . . The most beautiful type in this book is not Proctor's but the 'New Hellenic'" (p. 363).

The colophon to this edition contains an excerpt from the 1904 edition of the *Oresteia*, in which Proctor explains the origins and design of the Otter Greek type. Below this is a note giving details about the source edition, a single-volume collection of Homer's works edited by David Binning Monro, in which Monro reproduces the text of earlier editions, with revisions. The text of the *Odyssey* derives from W. W. Merry's edition of 1870–78 (see A29 and A31).

Barlow, T. D. "Review of V. Scholderer, *Greek Printing Types, 1465–1927*." *Library* 4, no. 8 (1927): 361–4.

Bowman, John H. "Greek Type Design: The British Contribution." *Greek Letters: From Tablets to Pixels*. Edited by Michael S. Macrakis. New Castle, DE: Oak Knoll Press, 1996.

Cave, Roderick. *The Private Press*. 2nd ed. New York: R.R. Bowker, 1983.

Pollard, A. W. *Bibliographical Essays*. London, 1905.

Proctor, Robert. *The Printing of Greek in the Fifteenth Century*. Oxford: Oxford University Press, 1900.

———. "The French Royal Greek Types and the Eton *Chrysostom*." *Transactions of the Bibliographical Society* 7 (1902): 49–74.

Scholderer, Victor. *Greek Printing Types, 1465–1927*. London: British Museum, 1927.

A33

Eduard Schwartz (1858–1940). Ὁμήρου ποίησις. Ἰλιάς. Ὀδύσσεια. Munich: Impensis officinae Bremensis, 1923–24.

Folio. 2 vols.

The modern fine press movement began with the founding of the Kelmscott Press in 1891 by the designer, author, and social reformer William Morris (see his translation of the *Odyssey*, B59). Although the aesthetic principles and historic models varied widely, private presses shared a devotion to using materials of the highest quality and achieving excellence in printing, design, and typography. The Bremer Presse was one of the most prominent and successful of the German private presses established in the early years of the twentieth century. Founded in Bremen in 1911 by a group of artists under the direction of Willy Wiegand, it took as its model the Doves Press, one of the greatest of the English private presses. The press produced large-format editions of the classics with specially designed typefaces and ornamental initials. The press moved to Munich in 1922 and closed at the start of World War II in 1939.

As with the other types used by the press, the Greek type was designed by Wiegand. Its most notable feature is its calligraphic appearance: Hutner and Kelly state that "The type has a degree of movement, letter strokes tilting left and right so that one almost senses a scribal hand" (p. xxxiv). Hermann Zapf observes: "The forms show exactly the movement of the pen strokes with an intended emphasis on the horizontal. This creates the harmony in the lines for which the books of the Bremer Presse are so famous" (p. 21). And Ransom praises the type for producing a "happy blending of classic form and free rendering" (p. 177). Nevertheless, Scholderer criticizes it for appearing "rather too deliberately calligraphic" (p. 15). Barlow agrees with this assessment, adding: "It has the appearance of a script designed by a cultivated and skilful scribe who knew no Greek and had learnt it

ΟΔΥΣΣΕΙΑΣ Α

ἌΝΔΡΑ μοι ἔννεπε, Μοῦϲα, πολύτροπον, ὃς μάλα πολλὰ
πλάγχθη, ἐπεὶ Τροίης ἱερὸν πτολίεθρον ἔπερϲε,
πολλῶν δ' ἀνθρώπων ἴδε ἄϲτεα καὶ νόμον ἔγνω·
πολλὰ δ' ὅ γ' ἐν πόντωι πάθεν ἄλγεα ὃν κατὰ θυμόν,
ἀρνύμενος ἥν τε ψυχὴν καὶ νόϲτον ἑταίρων,
ἀλλ' οὐδ' ὣς ἑτάρους ἐρρύϲατο ἱέμενός περ·
αὐτῶν γὰρ ϲφετέρηιϲιν ἀταϲθαλίηιϲιν ὄλοντο,
νήπιοι οἳ κατὰ βοῦς Ὑπερίονος Ἠελίοιο
ἤϲθιον, αὐτὰρ ὃ τοῖϲιν ἀφείλετο νόϲτιμον ἦμαρ.
τῶν ἁμόθεν γε, θεὰ θύγατερ Διός, εἰπὲ καὶ ἡμῖν.
Ἔνθ' ἄλλοι μὲν πάντες, ὅϲοι φύγον αἰπὺν ὄλεθρον,
οἴκοι ἔϲαν πόλεμόν τε πεφευγότες ἠδὲ θάλαϲϲαν·
τὸν δ' οἶον νόϲτου κεχρημένον ἠδὲ γυναικὸς
νύμφη πότνι' ἔρυκε Καλυψὼ δῖα θεάων
ἐν ϲπέεϲι γλαφυροῖϲι, λιλαιομένη πόϲιν εἶναι.
ἀλλ' ὅτε δὴ ἔτος ἦλθε περιπλομένων ἐνιαυτῶν,
τῶι οἱ ἐπεκλώϲαντο θεοὶ οἶκόνδε νέεϲθαι
εἰς Ἰθάκην, οὐδ' ἔνθα πεφυγμένος ἦεν ἀέθλων
καὶ μετὰ οἷϲι φίλοιϲι, θεοὶ δ' ἐλέαιρον ἅπαντες
νόϲφι Ποϲειδάωνος, ὃ δ' ἀϲπερχὲς μενέαινεν
(ἀντιθέωι Ὀδυϲῆι πάρος ἣν γαῖαν ἱκέϲθαι).
ἀλλ' ὃ μὲν Αἰθίοπας μετεκίαθε τηλόθ' ἐόντας,
Αἰθίοπας τοὶ διχθὰ δεδαίαται, ἔϲχατοι ἀνδρῶν,
οἳ μὲν δυϲομένου Ὑπερίονος, οἳ δ' ἀνιόντος,
ἀντιόων ταύρων τε καὶ ἀρνειῶν ἑκατόμβης.
ἔνθ' ὅ γ' ἐτέρπετο δαιτὶ παρήμενος, οἳ δὲ δὴ ἄλλοι
Ζηνὸς ἐνὶ μεγάροιϲιν Ὀλυμπίου ἁθρόοι ἦϲαν.
τοῖϲι δὲ μύθων ἦρχε πατὴρ ἀνδρῶν τε θεῶν τε·
μνήϲατο γὰρ κατὰ θυμὸν ἀμύμονος Αἰγίϲθοιο,
τόν ῥ' Ἀγαμεμνονίδης τηλεκλυτὸς ἔκταν' Ὀρέϲτης·
τοῦ ὅ γ' ἐπιμνηϲθεὶς ἔπε' ἀθανάτοιϲι μετηύδα·
Ὢ πόποι, οἷον δή νυ θεοὺς βροτοὶ αἰτιόωνται.

α 1–32

for the purpose of designing this fount. It is pretty and refined, but has, so to speak, no 'background'" (p. 363).

The *Iliad* appeared in 1923 and was followed in 1924 by the *Odyssey*. The colophon identifies Eduard Schwartz's rescension of the text as the source for this edition, of which 615 copies were printed. Schwartz was one of the great classical philologists of his day. He made important contributions to church history and the study of Thucydides, and did significant work in the many other areas over which his interests ranged. Around the same time that these editions of Homer were produced, he published a monograph entitled *Die Odyssee* (Munich: Max Hueber, 1924), in which he argued that the poem we now have had evolved from the reworkings and revisions of a succession of four competing poets.

Following the text of the poem is a letter to the reader, in which Schwartz explains that in such an edition the editor's work should remain somewhat hidden. Accordingly, he provides only a limited critical apparatus, whose primary function is to explain emendations to the text and indicate the lines that he regards as interpolations.

Because the apparatus is placed separately, between the letter and the colophon, the reader is given unobstructed access to the main text, which takes on a certain crispness and elegance. On each page, the only accompaniment to the lines of the poem are the book and line count, placed unobtrusively below the last line, toward the outer margin.

Barlow, T. D. "Review of V. Scholderer, *Greek Printing Types, 1465–1927*." *Library* 4, no. 8 (1927): 361–64.

Clark, H. W. *Homer's Readers*. Newark: University of Delaware Press, 1981.

Franklin, Colin. *The Private Presses*. London: Studio Vista, 1969.

Hutner, M., and J. Kelly. *A Century for the Century: Fine Printed Books from 1900 to 1999*, rev. ed. Jaffrey, NH: David R. Godine, 2004.

Killy, W. *Literatur-Lexicon. Autoren und Werke deutscher Sprache*. Gütersloh: Bertelsmann, 1988–93.

Ransom, Will. *Private Presses and Their Books*. New York: R.R. Bowker, 1929.

Scholderer, Victor. *Greek Printing Types, 1465–1927*. London: British Museum, 1927.

Zapf, Hermann. "The Development of Greek Typefaces." In *Greek Letters: From Tablets to Pixels*. Edited by Michael S. Macrakis. New Castle, DE: Oak Knoll Press, 1996.

SECTION B

ENGLISH TRANSLATIONS

COMPLETE WORKS

B1

George Chapman (1559?–1634). *The Whole Works of Homer. . . .* London: Printed for Nathaniell Butter, [1616].

Folio.

The unsigned, engraved separate title page for the *Odyssey*, usually lacking, is present in this copy of the complete works.

ILIAD: Achilles banefull wrath resound, O Goddesse, that imposd,
Infinite sorrowes on the *Greekes*

ODYSSEY: The man (O Muse) informe, that many a way,
Wound with his wisedome to his wished stay.

George Chapman—playwright, poet, and translator—is one of the most important figures in the English Renaissance and in the history of the reception both of Homer and of Classical antiquity. This collected edition of Chapman's renditions of the *Iliad* (in rhyming fourteeners) and *Odyssey* (in rhyming decasyllables) contains the first complete translations of Homer's works into English. Chapman had previously published translations of books of the *Iliad* in several installments: *Seaven Bookes of the Iliades of Homere, Prince of Poets* (B6) and *Achilles Shield* (a partial translation of book 18) in 1598; the first twelve books in 1609; and the complete work around 1611 (Chapman claimed it took him "lesse than fifteene weekes" to render the last twelve books). He dedicated his *Iliad* to Henry, Prince of Wales, who had commissioned it with the promise of an annuity and the enormous sum of £300; however, Henry died in 1612. In search of a new patron, Chapman dedicated this volume to Robert Carr, Earl of Somerset; but Somerset was convicted of murder in 1616 and imprisoned in the Tower of London until 1622. Chapman's *Odyssey* was entered in the Stationers' Register on November 2, 1614, and may have been issued at that time.

In his verse preface, Chapman rejected Valla's Latin translation of the *Iliad* (C1) and Salel's version in French (C3) as not true to Homer: "they fail'd to search his deepe, and treasurous hart." Chapman described his own translation as a "Poeme of the mysteries / Reveal'd in *Homer*," and declared English the language best suited for Homeric translation: "no tongue hath the Muses utterance heyr'd /

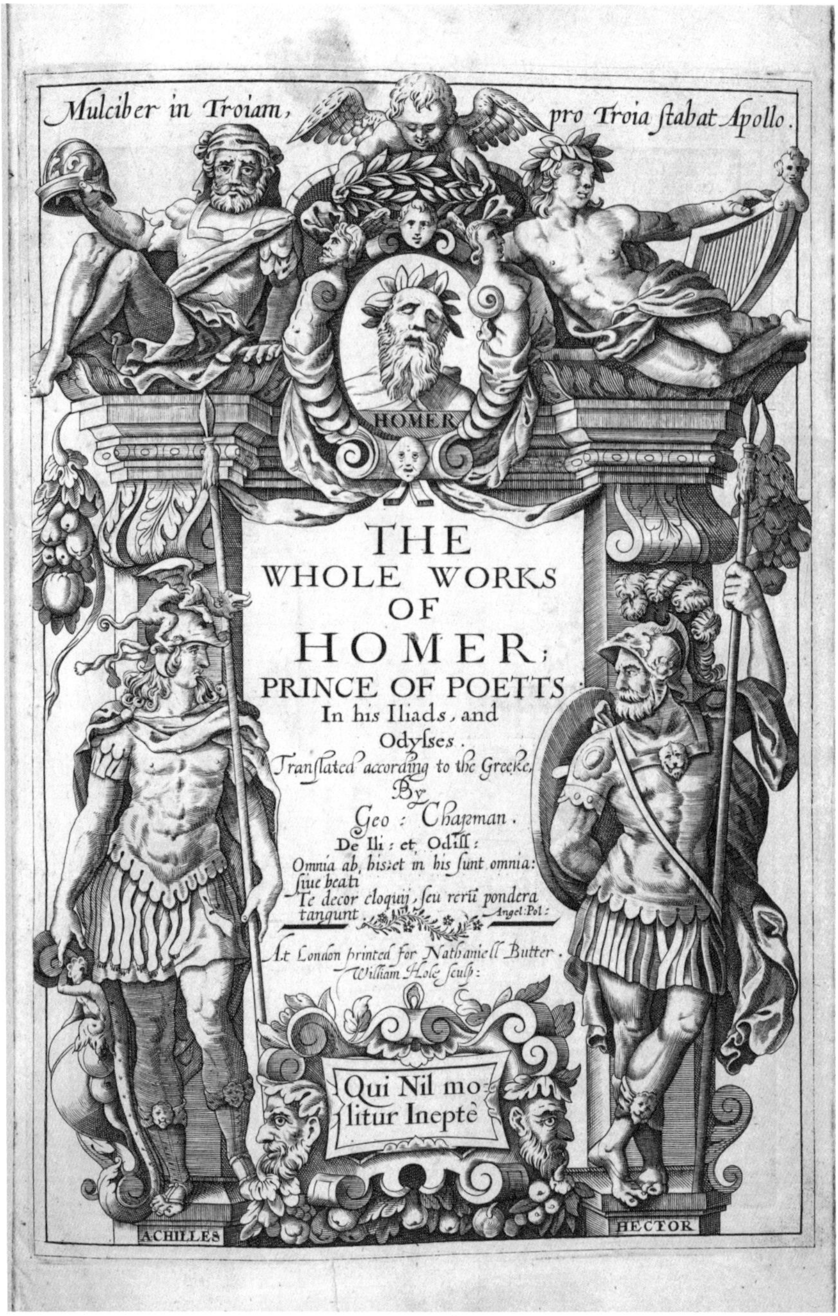
Mulciber in Troiam, pro Troia ſtabat Apollo.
HOMER
THE
WHOLE WORKS
OF
HOMER;
PRINCE OF POETTS
In his Iliads, and
Odyſses.
Tranſlated according to the Greeke,
By
Geo: Chapman.
De Ili: et Odiſſ:
Omnia ab, his et in his ſunt omnia:
ſiue beati
Te decor eloquij, ſeu rerū pondera
tangunt. Angel: Pol:
At London printed for Nathaniell Butter.
William Hole ſculp:
Qui Nil molitur Inepte
ACHILLES
HECTOR
B1

For verse, and that sweet Musique to the eare / Strooke out of time, so naturally as this." He disparaged word-for-word translations and attempted to justify his use of circumlocutions and "Needfull Periphrases," already defending his *Iliad* and *Odyssey* from the charges of poetic license that they have faced since their publication. The *Iliad*'s majestic fourteeners, which gave Chapman ample space to reproduce Homeric dactylic hexameters, also provided additional room for expansion on the Homeric text. Furthermore, despite his rejection of their accuracy, Chapman relied heavily on Latin translations, including Valla's and Divus's (C2), in addition to de Sponde's Greek text (A15). Chapman wanted to use poetry to illuminate Homer as a poet rather than to provide a verbatim translation of Homer's works. How successful he was in this is apparent from his numerous admirers, the most famous of whom perhaps was John Keats, who, in his poem "On First Looking Into Chapman's Homer," wrote: "Oft of one wide expanse have I been told / That deep-brow'd Homer ruled as his demesne; / Yet did I never breathe its pure serene / Till I heard CHAPMAN speak out loud and bold."

The title page by William Hole was enlarged and reengraved from earlier editions of Chapman's *Iliad*. Hole's numerous and diverse works include maps for the second edition of William Camden's *Britannia*, music plates for the *Parthenia* of 1612–13, and coinage for the Mint in London. The Latin epigrams on the title page are from Ovid's *Tristia* 1.2.5, Angelus Politianus's (Angelo Poliziano's) *Ambra* 481–2 (see A4), and Horace's *Ars Poetica* 140.

Baron, S. A. "Butter, Nathaniel (*bap.* 1583, *d.* 1664)." *Oxford Dictionary of National Biography* [Online edition]. Oxford: Oxford University Press, 2004.

Burnett, M. T. "Chapman, George (1559/60–1634)." *Oxford Dictionary of National Biography.*

Chapman, G. *Achilles Shield.* London: Imprinted by Iohn Windet, 1598.

———. *Homer Prince of Poets.* London: Printed for Samuel Macham, 1609.

———. *The Iliads of Homer, Prince of Poets.* London: Printed for Nathaniell Butter, 1611.

Corbett, M., and R. W. Lightbown. *The Comely Frontispiece: The Emblematic Title-Page in England, 1550–1660.* London: Routledge, 1979.

Fay, H. C. "Chapman's Materials for his Translation of Homer." *Review of English Studies* 2, no. 5 (1951): 121–28.

———. "George Chapman's Translation of Homer's *Iliad*," *Greece & Rome* 21, no. 63 (1952): 104–11.

Griffiths, A. "Hole, William (*d.* 1624)." *Oxford Dictionary of National Biography.*

Keats, J. *John Keats: The Major Works: Including Endymion, the Odes and Selected Letters.* Edited by E. Cook. New York: Oxford University Press, 2009.

Kent, H. W. *Bibliographical Notes on One Hundred Books Famous in English Literature,* 40–43. New York: Grolier Club, 1903.

Lord, G. d. F. *Homeric Renaissance: The Odyssey of George Chapman.* New Haven: Yale University Press, 1956.

Nicoll, A., ed. *Chapman's Homer: The Iliad.* Princeton: Princeton University Press, 1998.

———. *Chapman's Homer: The Odyssey.* Princeton: Princeton University Press, 2000.

Schoell, F. L. "George Chapman and the Italian Neo-Latinists of the Quattrocento." *Modern Philology* 13, no. 4 (August 1915): 215–38.

Snare, G. "George Chapman." *Dictionary of Literary Biography, Vol. 121: Seventeenth-Century British Nondramatic Poets, First Series.* Edited by M. Thomas Hester. Farmington Hills, MI: Gale Group, 1992.

B2

Thomas Hobbes (1588–1679). *The Iliads and Odysses of Homer. . . .* 2nd ed. London: Printed for Will. Crook, 1677.

Duodecimo.

ILIAD: O Goddess, sing what woe the discontent
Of *Thetis* Son brought to the *Greeks*

ODYSSEY: Tell me, O Muse, th'Adventures of the Man
That having sack'd the sacred Town of *Troy*

English philosopher Thomas Hobbes composed these verse renditions of the *Iliad* and *Odyssey* in rhyming pentameters in the last years of his life by dictation, because he was no longer able to write. Hobbes had been banned from publishing his controversial philosophical writings in England and was receiving an annual royal pension while he worked on his Homeric translations. He was familiar with Greek and had previously published a translation of Thucydides. Hobbes's first attempt at translating Homer was his 1673 *The Travels of Ulysses.* A full translation of *Homer's Odysses* (B48) appeared in 1675, and the first edition of the *Iliad* in 1676. By the time this second edition with the complete Homeric works appeared in 1677, Hobbes was eighty-nine years old.

Hobbes claimed that he had translated Homer "Because I had nothing else to do"; he published his translations "Because I thought it might take off my Adversaries from shewing their folly upon my more serious Writings, and set them upon my Verses to shew their wisdom"; he left out annotations "because I had no hope to do it better than it is already done by Mr. *Ogilby*" (B7, B47). Hobbes's Homeric translations have been largely ignored since their publication because they contain numerous errors, omissions, and deviations. In the preface to his 1715 *Iliad* (B9), Alexander Pope dismissed Hobbes's poetry as "too mean for Criticism," a sentiment that generations of literary critics echoed. Yet the simplicity of Hobbes's translations and their modest formats (all were published as duodecimos) provided for a Homer that was accessible to a much wider audience than Chapman's (B1) or Ogilby's lavish publications.

Hobbes, T. *Eight Bookes of the Peloponnesian Warre.* London: Imprinted for Hen. Seile, 1629.

———. *The Travels of Ulysses, as They Were Related by Himself in Homer's 9th, 10th, 11th, and 12th Books of his Odysses, to Alcinous King Phaeacia.* London: Printed for William Crook, 1673.

———. *Homer's Iliads in English.* London: Printed for William Crook, 1676.

Macdonald, H. and M. Hargreaves. *Thomas Hobbes; A Bibliography.* London: Bibliographical Society, 1952.

Malcolm, N. "Hobbes, Thomas (1588–1679)." *Oxford Dictionary of National Biography.*

McKenzie, A. T. "Thomas Hobbes." *Dictionary of Literary Biography, Vol. 151: British Prose Writers of the Early Seventeenth Century.* Edited by Clayton D. Lein. Farmington Hills, MI: Gale Research, 1995.

Molesworth, W., ed. *The English Works of Thomas Hobbes of Malmesbury.* Vol. 10. London: Longman etc., 1844.

Nelson, E. *Thomas Hobbes Translations of Homer: The Iliad and the Odyssey.* Oxford: Clarendon, 2008.

Riddehough, G. G. "Thomas Hobbes' Translations of Homer." *Phoenix* 12, no. 2 (Summer 1958): 58–62.

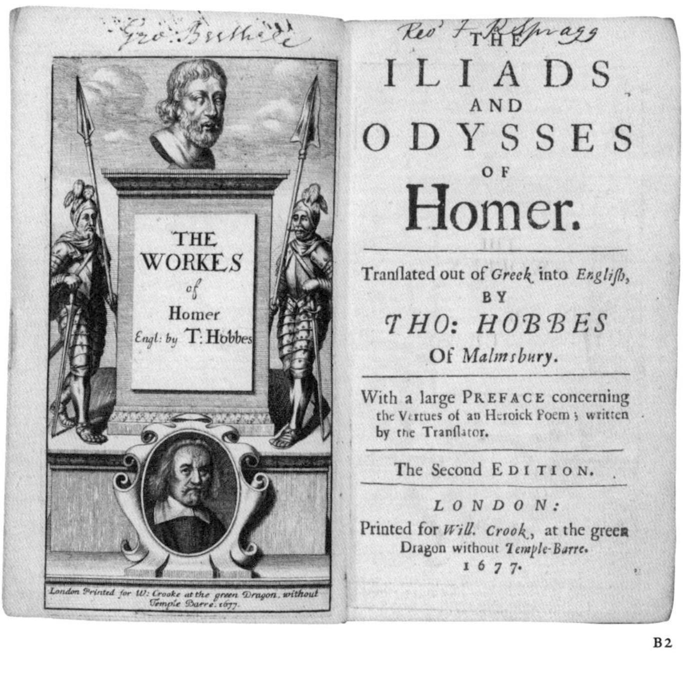
THE WORKES of Homer Engl: by T: Hobbes

London Printed for W: Crooke at the green Dragon, without Temple Barre. 1677.

THE ILIADS AND ODYSSES OF Homer.

Translated out of Greek into English, BY THO: HOBBES Of Malmsbury.

With a large PREFACE concerning the Vertues of an Heroick Poem; written by the Translator.

The Second EDITION.

LONDON: Printed for Will. Crook, at the green Dragon without Temple-Barre. 1677.

B2

THE

WORKS OF HOMER,

The Celebrated GRECIAN POET:

INCLUDING NEW AND COMPLETE EDITIONS OF

The ILIAD, and the ODYSSEY;

Thoſe very celebrated and univerſally-admired EPIC or HEROIC POEMS.

The ILIAD — in twenty-four Books — being compoſed on the Subject of the memorable SIEGE of TROY — interſperſed with the moſt beautiful ALLEGORIES, and containing a moſt ſublime Deſcription of the BATTLES between the GREEKS and TROJANS, during a Ten Years Siege, in which the Great and Valiant ACHILLES, the principal Hero of the War, after his Reconciliation with AGAMEMNON, ſlew HECTOR with his own Hand, and afterwards dragged the Corpſe at his Chariot-Wheels round the WALLS of TROY.

Comprizing a great Variety of valuable and uſeful Maxims on Military Diſcipline, Stratagem, Exploits in Civil Affairs, Politics, Virtue, Reſolution, Prudence, Œconomy, and, in ſhort, reſpecting all the various Offices and Duties of Human Life; and affording the moſt important, agreeable, and entertaining Inſtruction, conveyed in the moſt lively Manner, to Mankind in general.

The ODYSSEY — compoſed alſo in Twenty-four Books — and containing, among a Variety of other uſeful and entertaining Particulars, a moſt magnificent and delightful Deſcription of the VOYAGES and ADVENTURES of the wiſe and venerable ULYSSES, King of ITHACA, in GREECE, and one of the Princes who conducted the Siege of TROY, during his Abſence for Twenty Years from his Queen PENELOPE.

Exhibiting not only a juſt Picture of the Ancient Grecians, but a beautiful Syſtem of Morality, Wiſdom, Fortitude, Perſeverance, Moderation and Temperance, inſtructive to all Degrees of Men, and filled with ſtriking Images, Similies, Examples, and Precepts of Civil and Domeſtic Life. Including alſo that other excellent Piece of HOMER, entitled

The BATTLE of the FROGS and MICE—in THREE BOOKS—

A very beautiful, ingenious, ſatyrical, and intereſting Production, replete with Wit, Humour, and Entertainment, allegorically deſcribing the Valour and Intrepidity of thoſe ſagacious Animals.

Carefully Tranſlated from the ORIGINAL GREEK.

In the Execution of this New and Improved Edition, all former Editors and Commentators on HOMER will be carefully conſulted and attended to, viz. EUSTATHIUS, DACIER, OGILBY, CHAPMAN, DRYDEN, PARNEL, WARBURTON, &c. particularly that hitherto moſt eſteemed Tranſlation by ALEX. POPE, Eſq.

Illuſtrated with Large and Valuable NOTES,

Critical, Hiſtorical, Philoſophical, Allegorical, Poetical, Scholaſtic, Political, Moral, Entertaining, Philological, and Explanatory.

Comprehending the moſt ſalutary Reflections and uſeful Remarks, with many important References to Ancient Mythology, Geography, and Univerſal Hiſtory, &c. &c.——To which will be carefully added,

The ARGUMENTS at large to every Book or Chapter, and the moſt AUTHENTIC MEMOIRS of the LIFE of HOMER;

AS ALSO

A New ESSAY on HOMER's BATTLES, &c. and a Complete Geographical Table of the TOWNS, &c. in HOMER's Catalogue of GREECE.

Being the moſt perfect and beautiful Edition of HOMER ever publiſhed, and calculated to accommodate and pleaſe every Claſs of Readers.

The Whole embelliſhed with

A moſt SUPERB SET of GRAND QUARTO COPPER-PLATES,

Deſigned and engraved by the moſt Capital Artiſts; ſo that theſe Elegant Engravings will alone be worth more than the Purchaſe-Money of the whole Work.

The Whole Reviſed, Corrected, and Improved

By WILLIAM HENRY MELMOTH, ESQ.

Editor of the New and Beautiful Quarto Edition of TELEMACHUS,—The New ABRIDGMENT of the ROMAN HISTORY, &c. &c.

LONDON:

Printed for ALEX. HOGG, at the King's Arms, No. 16, Paternoſter-Row;
And Sold by all other Bookſellers and News-Carriers, in Town and Country.

B3

B3

William Melmoth (1710?–1799). *The Works of Homer, the Celebrated Grecian Poet. . . .* London: Printed for Alex. Hogg, [1785?].

Quarto.

ILIAD: Achilles' wrath, to *Greece* the direful spring
Of woes unnumber'd, heav'nly Goddess, sing!

ODYSSEY: The man, for wisdom's various arts renown'd,
Long exercis'd in woes, oh muse! resound

Writer and translator William Henry Melmoth published his *Works of Homer* in forty parts beginning around 1780. An advertisement in this volume announced, "Melmoth's New Quarto Edition of the Entertaining Adventures of Telemachus . . . being just printed off"; the *Telemachus* appeared with plates dated November 20, 1784 to April 30, 1785. The verse translations in this edition are from Alexander Pope's *Iliad* (B9) and *Odyssey* (B49), allegedly "revised and edited" by Melmoth, although it is difficult to find evidence of either revision or editing of Pope's text. The notes are gathered from various sources, including the commentaries of Eustathius (D4) and the editions of Dacier (C5, C7), Ogilby (B7, B47), and Chapman (B1). Melmoth wrote in his preface, "we have no doubt but an improved edition of the *Iliad* and *Odyssey*, &c. must prove agreeable to the taste of modern readers of every class." The title page identifies this volume as a "New and Improved Edition. . . . Being the most perfect and beautiful Edition of HOMER ever published."

Melmoth was a well-known translator of Pliny and the author of his own pseudonymous letters (published as *Letters on Several Subjects. By the Late Sir Thomas Fitzosborne, Bart.*). That collection included three letters on Pope's *Iliad*, in which Melmoth heaped praise on the translator whose work he would later use for this volume. Melmoth admired Pope not only for his preeminent Homeric translation but even for his embellishments on and improvements to the Homeric texts.

Amos, F. R. *Early Theories of Translation.* New York: Columbia University Press, 1920.

Cronin, G., and P. A. Doyle, eds. *Pope's Iliad: An Examination by William Melmoth.* Washington, DC: Catholic University of America Press, 1960.

Gillespie, S., P. France, D. Hopkins, and K. Haynes. *The Oxford History of Literary Translation in English.* Oxford: Oxford University Press, 2005.

Melmoth, W. *Letters on Several Subjects. By the Late Sir Thomas Fitzosborne, Bart.* Dublin: Printed for M. Owen and W. Brien, 1748–49.

Wilson, P. "Melmoth, William, the younger (*bap.* 1710, *d.* 1799)." *Oxford Dictionary of National Biography.*

B4

William Cowper (1731–1800). *The Iliad and Odyssey of Homer, Translated Into English Blank Verse.* London: Printed for J. Johnson, 1791.

Quarto. 2 vols.

Contains the bookplate of railway promoter and Member of Parliament Sir Edward W. Watkin.

ILIAD: Achilles sing, O Goddess! Peleus' son;
His wrath pernicious, who ten thousand woes
Caused to Achaia's host

ODYSSEY: Muse make the man thy theme, for shrewdness famed
And genius versatile, who far and wide
A Wand'rer, after Ilium overthrown

Poet William Cowper defended his decision to publish this blank-verse rendition of the works of Homer by arguing that "a just translation of any antient poet in rhime, is impossible" and that the resemblance of Homer's poetry to Milton's led to his choice of Miltonic blank verse for his translations. In his preface, Cowper criticized Alexander Pope extensively for "careless oversight" and "factitious embellishment" in his *Iliad* and *Odyssey* (B9, B49), but allowed that "Mr. Pope has surmounted all difficulties in his version of Homer that it was possible to surmount in rhime. But he was fettered, and his fetters were his choice." Cowper was kinder to Pope here than in his letters—one letter to a friend referred to Pope's "puerile conceits, extravagant metaphors, and the tinsel of modern embellishment," and a letter Cowper submitted to *The Gentleman's Magazine* in 1785 stated, "We have Homer in a straight waistcoat. . . . Pope resembles Homer just as Homer resembled himself when he was dead."

In his youth, Cowper had conducted a comparison between Pope's Homeric translations and the original texts; he was shocked by Pope's deviations, yet he did not attempt his own version of Homer until 1785, when he translated the first twelve lines of the *Iliad* to offset one of his frequent mental breakdowns. Working from commentaries and the original text, Cowper translated at least forty lines a day and finished his complete Homer in six years. He wrote of the translations, "My chief boast is that I have adhered closely to my original." His rendition was revised by the Swiss painter and writer Henry Fuseli before its publication. This subscriber's edition cost three guineas (half due on subscription and half on delivery), and the publisher Joseph Johnson, a relative of Cowper's, paid Cowper £1000 of the subscription money from the 498 subscribers listed. Johnson also allowed Cowper to retain the copyright.

Reviews were mixed: when this first edition appeared, the editors of *The Gentleman's Magazine* applauded Cowper for "having contributed to our delight, and promoted our instruction, by his chaste, moral, and animated Muse"; but they also regretted that he had focused more on his "commendable desire of retaining the strength of his original" than on Homer's "sweetness and melody," and they suggested revisions throughout. Cowper kept revising his Homeric translations for the rest of his life, resulting in a posthumously published second edition that *The Annual Review* called "a new rather than a revised work" that represented "a great, and, to a considerable extent, a successful undertaking, a more faithful exhibition" of Homer, "if not a more finished poem, than" Pope's rendition.

Aikin, A., ed. "*The Iliad and Odyssey of Homer, translated into English Blank-verse by the late William Cowper,* Esq. *The second Edition with copious Alterations and Notes.* 4 vols. 8vo." *Annual Review; and History of Literature; for 1802,* vol. 1, pp. 538–48. London: T. N. Longman and O. Rees, 1803.

Baird, J. D. "Cowper, William (1731–1800)." *Oxford Dictionary of National Biography.*

Cowper, W. *The Iliad of Homer, Translated into English Blank Verse by the Late William Cowper, Esq.* London: J. Johnson, 1802.

———. *The Odyssey of Homer, Translated into English Blank Verse by the Late William Cowper, Esq.* London: J. Johnson, 1802.

Hall, C. "Johnson, Joseph (1738–1809)." *Oxford Dictionary of National Biography.*

King, J. "An Unlikely Alliance: Fuseli as Revisor of Cowper's Homer." *Neophilogus* 67, no. 3 (July 1983): 468–79.

———. *William Cowper: A Biography.* Durham, NC: Duke University Press, 1986.

Newey, V. "William Cowper." *Dictionary of Literary Biography, Vol. 109: Eighteenth-Century British Poets, Second Series.* Edited by John Sitter. Farmington Hills, MI: Gale Group, 1991.

Rothschild, N. M. V. *The Rothschild Library; A Catalogue of the Collection of Eighteenth-century Printed Books and Manuscripts Formed by Lord Rothschild.* Nos. 685–87, pp. 156–61. Cambridge: 1954.

Southey, R. *The Life of William Cowper, Esq.* Vol. 2. Boston: Otis, Broaders, and Company, 1839.

Sutton, C. W. "Watkin, Sir Edward William, first baronet (1819–1901)." Rev. Philip S. Bagwell. *Oxford Dictionary of National Biography.*

Urban, S., ed. "*The Iliad and Odyssey of* Homer, *translated into Blank Verse, by* W. Cowper. *In Two Volumes. 4to.*" *The Gentleman's Magazine: and Historical Chronicle. For the Year MDCCXCI* 61, no. 2 (1791): 845–46, 929–30, 1034–36, 1133–34.

Walker, J., ed. *A Selection of Curious Articles from the Gentleman's Magazine.* Vol. 2. London: Longman, Hurst, Rees, etc., 1811.

Weinglass, D. H. "Fuseli, Henry (1741–1825)." *Oxford Dictionary of National Biography.*

B5

William Sotheby (1757–1833). *The Iliad and Odyssey of Homer. . . .* London: G. and W. Nicol; J. Murray, 1834.

Octavo. 4 vols.

ILIAD: Sing, Muse! Pelides' wrath, whence woes on woes
O'er the Achæans' gather'd host arose

ODYSSEY: Muse! sing the Man by long experience tried,
Who, fertile in resources, wander'd wide

This collection of the works of Homer in rhyming heroic couplets was published a year after writer and translator William Sotheby's death. Sotheby had previously published a partial translation of the *Iliad* in 1830 and a complete version in 1831. He completed his *Odyssey* in 1832, but it did not appear until the publication of this collection. The volume's outline illustrations by sculptor and illustrator John Flaxman also appear in E3. Sotheby was a central figure in the London literary and social circles of his time, and a friend and patron of many young Romantic writers. His translations from Latin and German works were received with great acclaim—poet Lord George Gordon Noel Byron wrote that Sotheby had "imitated everybody, and occasionally surpassed his models."

Contemporary reviews of Sotheby's Homeric translations offered similar praise: the editors of the *London Monthly Review* knew "of no book in any tongue but this single one of Sotheby's in which any thing like a just conception of Homer can be conveyed to an unlearned reader"; and, in a five-part series occasioned by the release of Sotheby's *Iliad*, *Blackwood's Edinburgh Magazine* declared Sotheby "entitled . . . to deal with that well-booted Grecian, even at this time of day, after all that has been done to, in, with, and by 'Him of the Iliad and the Odyssey,' by not a few of our prevailing Poets."

Blackwood's Edinburgh Magazine 29 (January–June 1831): 669.

Cooksey, "William Sotheby." *Dictionary of Literary Biography, Volume 93: British Romantic Poets, 1789–1832, First Series.* A Bruccoli Clark Layman Book. Edited by John R. Greenfield, McKendree College. The Gale Group, 1990.

Lee, S. "Sotheby, William (1757–1833)." *Oxford Dictionary of National Biography.*

London Monthly Review 2 (May–August 1831): 116.

Moore, T., ed. *Life of Lord Byron, With His Letters and Journals.* Vol. 5. London: John Murray, 1855.

Moulton, C. W. "William Sotheby." *The Library of Literary Criticism of English and American Authors.* Buffalo: Moulton, 1902.

Sotheby, W. *The First Book of the Iliad . . . Specimens of a New Version of Homer.* London: J. Murray, 1830.

———. *The Iliad of Homer.* London: J. Murray, 1831.

B6

George Chapman (1559?–1634). *Seaven Bookes of the Iliades of Homere, Prince of Poets. . . .* London: Printed by Iohn Windet, 1598.

Quarto.

The BHL copy contains a contemporary parchment manuscript wrapper relating to Thomas Barrington and his wife Lady Anne, daughter of Robert Rich, Third Earl of Warwick. An epigram from Horace, *Ars Poetica* 309, appears on the title page. The title page and preface are in facsimile.

> Achilles banefull wrath, resound great Goddesse of my verse
> That through th'afflicted host of *Greece* did worlds of woes disperse

This translation of *Iliad* books 1–2 and 7–11 in rhyming fourteeners represents not only George Chapman's first attempt at a Homeric rendition, but also the first English translation of a Homeric text—Arthur Hall's 1581 publication was a translation not of Homer's *Iliad*, but of Salel's version in French (C3). Chapman's translation was reprinted (with revisions) in his *Whole Works of Homer* (B1). In a brief preface, Chapman wrote, "The worth of a skillfull and worthy translator, is to observe the sentences, figures, and formes of Speech, proposed in his author . . . and to adorne them with figures and formes of oration fitted to the originall." In this first attempt, he aimed "to give you this Emperor of all wisedome . . . in your own language, which will more honor it (if my part bee worthily discharged) then any thing else can be translated." Chapman asked his reader to excuse the shortcomings and errors of "this first edition," and promised another volume with "the life of *Homer*, a table, a prettie coment, true printing, the praise of your mother tongue above all others, for Poesie."

Despite its faults, Chapman's translation had an immediate and dramatic impact on contemporary literature, because it made Homer more widely available to English speakers than he had ever been before. William Shakespeare almost certainly relied on Chapman's *Iliad* when he wrote his *Troilus and Cressida*.

Burnett, M. T. "Chapman, George (1559/60–1634)." *Oxford Dictionary of National Biography.*

The Carl H. Pforzheimer Library; English Literature 1475–1700, 167. New York: Privately Printed, 1940.

Fay, H. C. "Chapman's Materials for his Translation of Homer." *Review of English Studies* 2, no. 5 (1951): 121–28.

———. "George Chapman's Translation of Homer's 'iliad.' *Greece & Rome* 21, no. 63 (1952): 104–11.

THE SECOND BOOKE OF HOMERS ILIADES.

The Argument.

Ioue cals a vision vp from *Somnus* den,
To will *Atrides* muster vp his men:
The king to Greekes dissembling his desire
Perswades them to their Countrie to retire,
By *Pallace* will, *Vlisses* stayes their flight:
And prudent *Nestor* hartens them to ~~flight~~ fight
They take repast: which done, to armes they goe:
And marche in good aray, against the foe.
So those of *Troy*, when *Iris* from the skie,
Of frendlie *Ioue* performes the Ambasie.

An other Argument.

Beta, the dreame and synod cites,
And Catologues the Nauale knights.

THe other Gods and Knights at armes slept all the humorous night,
But Ioue *lay waking, and his thoughts kept in discursiue fight:*
How he might honor Thetis *Sonne, with slaughtering at their tents,*
Whole troupes of Greekes: this counsell then seemd best for these euents,
He instantlie would send a dreame to Atrius *eldest sonne:*
That with darke vowes might draw his powers to their confusion.
And calling him, he wingd these wordes; flie to the Grecian fleet,
Pernicious vision, and the king at our high summons greet,
Vttering the truth of all I charge: giue him command to arme,
His vniuersall faire-hayrd host, this is the last Alarme,

Hee

Kent, H. W. *Bibliographical Notes on One Hundred Books Famous in English Literature,* 40–43. New York: Grolier Club, 1903.

Knowles, R. "Review: *Shakespeare's Books: A Dictionary of Shakespeare Sources* by Stuart Gillespie." *Modern Language Review* 98, no. 2 (April 2003): 431–32.

Lord, G. d. F. *Homeric Renaissance: The Odyssey of George Chapman.* New Haven: Yale University Press, 1956.

Nicoll, A., ed. *Chapman's Homer: The Iliad.* Princeton: Princeton University Press, 1998.

Shakespeare, W. *The Historie of Troylus and Cresseida.* London: Imprinted for R. Bonian and H. Walley, 1609.

Snare, G. "George Chapman." *Dictionary of Literary Biography, Vol. 121: Seventeenth-Century British Nondramatic Poets, First Series.* Edited by M. Thomas Hester. Farmington Hills, MI: Gale Group, 1992.

B7

John Ogilby (1600–1676). *Homer His Iliads Translated, Adorn'd with Sculpture, and Illustrated with Annotations.* London: Printed by Thomas Roycroft, 1660.

Folio.

> Achilles *Peleus* Son's destructive Rage
> Great Goddess! sing, which did the *Greeks* engage
> In many woes

This sumptuous volume contains a translation of the *Iliad* in rhyming heroic couplets by the Scottish translator, publisher, and geographer John Ogilby. Ogilby had a diverse career in the arts: he began as a dance-master, but was injured; he opened the first Irish theater as Master of Revels in Ireland, but it was closed after the Irish Rebellion of 1641 and Ogilby relocated to England. He later wrote in the preface to his 1670 *Africa* that it was during the upheaval of the civil wars that "I betook myself to something of *Literature*, in which, till then, altogether a stranger." Ogilby most likely only began studying Latin and Greek at this time. In 1649 he published an octavo edition of his translation of Virgil's *Aeneid*, which he reprinted in 1654 in folio with splendid engraved illustrations that suggested the direction he would take in this volume and in his subsequent 1665 translation of the *Odyssey* (B47).

Homer was Ogilby's next project: "My next Expedition with Sails a Trip, and swoln with the Breath of a general Applause, was to discover *Greece* ... in which I had a double Design, not onely to bring over so Antient and Famous an Author, but to inable my self the better to carry on an *Epick Poem* of my own Composure." The expected cost of this venture was around £5000, but Ogilby (who acted as his own publisher) found an innovative strategy to pay for its

Honoratiss: Do: Dominæ Arabellæ Wentworth
Filiæ Honoratissimi Tho: Wentworth Comitis
Straffordiæ. Fabulam hanc. D. D. D. L. M. I. O.

B7

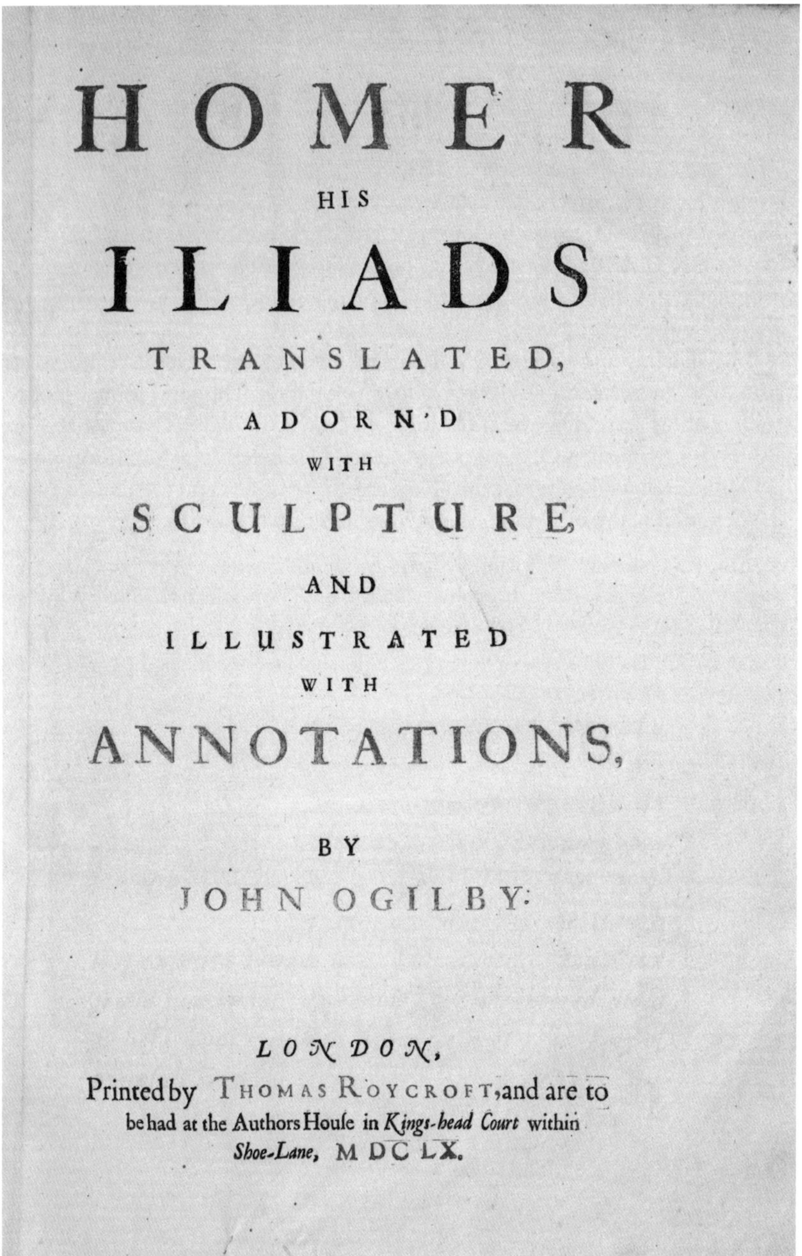
HOMER
HIS
ILIADS
TRANSLATED,
ADORN'D
WITH
SCULPTURE,
AND
ILLUSTRATED
WITH
ANNOTATIONS,

BY
JOHN OGILBY.

LONDON,
Printed by THOMAS ROYCROFT, and are to
be had at the Authors House in *Kings-head Court* within
Shoe-Lane, M DC LX.

B7

production: for a fee of £12 (£5 on subscription, £5 on receipt of the *Iliad*, and £2 on receipt of the *Odyssey*), subscribers could have their names, arms, and titles included on one of the full-page illustrations engraved by Wenceslaus Hollar, mapmaker, illustrator, and, later, royal "Scenographer"; other subscribers paid £6 for the two volumes, and anyone who brought in orders for five copies received a free set. Ogilby was one of the earliest English authors to use subscription publishing so extensively. To augment the funds brought in by this method, he disposed of unsold copies by lottery. Ogilby was extraordinarily successful in his publishing enterprise, and set up his own press in 1670. He then turned to geography, producing an exquisite series of atlases, including the *Britannia* road atlas, his most famous work.

The illustrations in Ogilby's *Iliad* and the volume's extensive notes and glosses are more acclaimed than Ogilby's translation. Thomas Hobbes referred readers of his own Homeric translations (B2, B48) to Ogilby's annotations; and, although he ridiculed Ogilby's poetic talent, Alexander Pope found inspiration in Ogilby's splendid editions when he was eight years old, and even incorporated the design of many of Ogilby's engravings in his own *Iliad* (B9).

Alvarez, P. "Collection Highlight: Homer. *His Iliads Translated, by John Ogilby.*" University of Rochester River Campus Libraries. http://www.library.rochester.edu/index.cfm?PAGE=4130 (accessed March 14, 2011).

Clapp, S. L. C. "The Subscription Enterprises of John Ogilby and Richard Blome." *Modern Philology* 30, no. 4 (May 1933): 365–79.

Foxon, D. *Pope and the Early Eighteenth-Century Book Trade.* Edited by J. McLaverty. Oxford: Clarendon Press, 1991.

Harding, R. J. D. "Hollar, Wenceslaus (1607–1677)." *Oxford Dictionary of National Biography.*

Johnson, S. *The Life of Pope.* Edited by J. Lynch. http://andromeda.rutgers.edu/~jlynch/Texts/pope.html (accessed March 14, 2011).

Ogilby, J. *Africa. . . .* London: Printed for the Author, 1670.

———. *Britannia. Volume the First.* London: Printed by the Author, 1675.

———. *The Works of Publius Virgilius Maro.* London: Printed for John Crook, 1649.

———. *The Works of Publius Virgilius Maro.* London: Printed for the Author, 1654.

Van Eerde, K. S. *John Ogilby and the Taste of His Times.* Folkestone, England: William Dawson, 1976.

Withers, C. W. J. "Ogilby, John (1600–1676)." *Oxford Dictionary of National Biography.*

B8

John Ozell (d. 1743), William Broome (1689–1745), and William Oldisworth (1680–1734). *The Iliad of Homer.* . . . London: Printed by G. James, for Bernard Lintott, 1712.

Duodecimo. 5 vols. in 2.

> Sing, Goddess, the Resentment of *Achilles*, the Son of *Peleus*; that accurs'd Resentment, which caus'd so many Mischiefs to the *Greeks*

John Ozell, William Broome, and William Oldisworth collaborated to publish this English blank-verse translation of Anne Dacier's 1711 *Iliad* in French prose (C5). Translator John Ozell (who translated books 1–8 and wrote this edition's preface) praised the scholarship and fidelity of Dacier's version, but judged that English was the most suitable language for Homer, and blank verse, the verse of "our English Homer, Milton," the most suitable vehicle for Homeric translation. Ozell dismissed rhyming verse as "affected finery" that is "too Effeminate" for Homer, singling out the rhyming couplets of Ogilby's *Iliad* (B7) in particular. Although Ozell admired the "sense" and "clearness" of Hobbes's

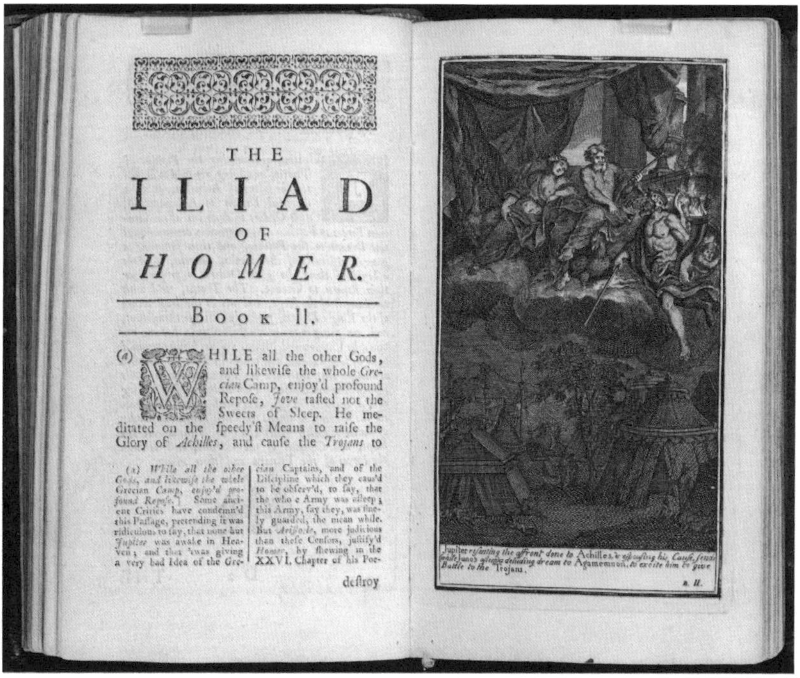

B8

Iliad (B2), he wished Hobbes had "aton'd for the Badness of his Poetry, by the Exactness of the Version." Ozell denied ever having looked at Chapman's translations (B1, B6). Ozell believed that Dacier's edition was by far the most learned and accurate; however, his own work was not "only a Translation of a Translation": "I have had a strict Regard to the Original Greek," and he mentioned Joshua Barnes's 1711 Greek edition (A18) specifically.

Thomas Johnson, the author of the notes, was a school headmaster and classical scholar known for his translations of Sophocles. William Oldisworth (who translated books 16–24) became a political figure and the main contributor to *The Examiner*. William Broome (books 9–15) also published his own blank-verse rendition of books 10 and 11 in Alexander Pope's 1712 *Miscellaneous Poems and Translations by Several Hands*, assisted Pope with the notes to his *Iliad* (B9), and wrote the notes and eight books of translation for Pope's *Odyssey* (B49). Although Pope ruthlessly mocked Ozell's skills as a translator, he borrowed heavily from this volume for his own rendition. In 1729, after being harshly satirized in Pope's *Dunciad*, Ozell retaliated by taking out an advertisement bragging that his *Iliad* had been called superior to Pope's and calling Pope an "envious wretch"; however, by 1779, Samuel Johnson wrote that the Ozell, Broome, and Oldisworth translation "has long since vanished, and is now in no danger from the criticks."

An engraved illustration designed by Antoine Coypel accompanies each book of translation.

Chahoud, A. "Broome, William (*bap.* 1689, *d.* 1745)." *Oxford Dictionary of National Biography.*

Cibber, T. *The Lives of the Poets of Great Britain and Ireland.* 1753. Vol. 4. Whitefish, MT: Kessinger, 2004.

Foxon, D. *Pope and the Early Eighteenth-Century Book Trade.* Edited by J. McLaverty. Oxford: Clarendon Press, 1991.

Gillespie, S., D. Hopkins, and P. France. *The Oxford History of Literary Translation in English: 1660–1790.* Oxford: Oxford University Press, 2006.

Goodwin, G. and P. Carter. "Johnson, Thomas (*d.* 1746)." *Oxford Dictionary of National Biography.*

Johnson, S. *The Lives of the Most Eminent English Poets.* Vol. 3. Edited by Roger H. Lonsdale. Oxford: Oxford University Press, 2006.

Pope, A. *Miscellaneous Poems and Translations by Several Hands.* London: Printed for Bernard Lintott, 1712.

———. *The Dunciad.* London: Reprinted for A. Dodd, 1728.

Williams, A. "Oldisworth, William (1680–1734)." *Oxford Dictionary of National Biography.*

———. "Ozell, John (*d.* 1743)." *Oxford Dictionary of National Biography.*

B9

Alexander Pope (1688–1744). *The Iliad of Homer.* . . . London: Printed by W. Bowyer, for Bernard Lintott, 1715–20.

Quarto. 6 vols.

With an engraved frontispiece portrait and the signature of Sir Samuel Young, Bart., created First Baronet of Formosa in 1813.

THE Wrath of *Peleus'* Son, the direful Spring
Of all the *Grecian* Woes, O Goddess, sing!

This edition of celebrated poet Alexander Pope's translation of the *Iliad* in rhyming heroic couplets was printed exclusively for subscribers. Ac-

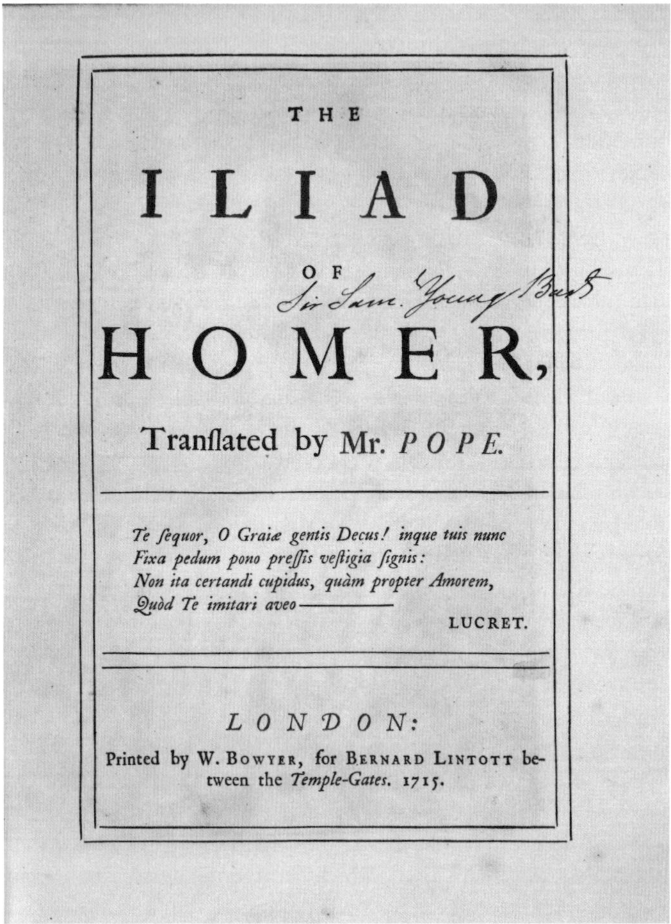
THE

ILIAD

OF

Sir Sam. Young Bart

HOMER,

Tranflated by Mr. *POPE.*

Te ſequor, O Graiæ gentis Decus! inque tuis nunc
Fixa pedum pono preſſis veſtigia ſignis:
Non ita certandi cupidus, quàm propter Amorem,
Quòd Te imitari aveo ———

LUCRET.

LONDON:

Printed by W. BOWYER, for BERNARD LINTOTT between the *Temple-Gates.* 1715.

cording to Samuel Johnson, only 660 sets were produced, and each volume was sold at a cost of one guinea. Pope received £1200 for the copyright (£200 from the publisher for each of the six volumes) plus all the proceeds from the sale of the subscriber's edition. Pope's total earnings were approximately £5000, a tremendous sum for an author at the time. Pope's *Iliad* had an immense influence both on English publishing and on the future of Homeric translation. Before 1715, luxury editions had been printed in folio and used engraved frontispieces merely as formal decoration, as in Ogilby's edition (B7). Pope's *Iliad* introduced the fashion of printing luxury editions in quarto and of using engraved frontispieces as illustrations. The design of many of the engravings in Pope's translation bears a striking similarity to the full-plate illustrations in the editions of Ogilby and of Ozell, Broome, and Oldisworth (B8). George Vertue engraved volume 1's exquisite frontispiece. Each volume includes a separate engraved title page with Latin epigram: vol. 1, Lucretius, *On the Nature of Things*, 3.3–6; vol. 2, Horace, *Odes* 1.6 13–16; vol. 3, Petronius, *Satyricon* 5; vol. 4, Horace, *Satires* 1.10 78–82; vol. 5, Virgil, *Georgics* 2.175; vol. 6, Horace, *Ars Poetica* 412–13.

Pope's *Iliad* earned immediate and enduring praise. Samuel Johnson called Pope's rendition "a performance which no age or nation could hope to equal," even though Pope humbly professed himself "utterly incapable of doing Justice to *Homer*" and claimed to "attempt him in no other Hope but that which one may entertain without much Vanity, of giving a more tolerable Copy of him than any entire Translation in Verse has yet done." Pope faulted Chapman's translation (B1, B6) for its "negligence" and "loose and rambling" style; he criticized Hobbes's edition (B2) for its omissions, "mistakes," and "carelesness"; and he dismissed both Hobbes's and Ogilby's poetry as "too mean for Criticism." Nevertheless, Pope frequently consulted his predecessors' translations, particularly those of Chapman and Dacier (C5), in crafting his own elevated and elaborate version. He used the Greek editions edited by Turnebus (A11) and Barnes (A18), and hired William Broome, who had collaborated with Ozell and Oldisworth for their *Iliad* (B8) and would later contribute eight books of translation to Pope's *Odyssey* (B49), to make extracts from the commentaries of Eustathius (D4) for the volume's notes. Although the accuracy of Pope's *Iliad* as a translation is subject to criticism—the classical scholar Richard Bentley wrote, "It is a pretty poem, Mr. Pope, but you must not call it Homer"—exuberant praise for Pope's version has continued long past Pope's own time. In his introduction to Robert Fagles's 1990 translation (B44), Bernard Knox called Pope's *Iliad* "the finest ever made."

The opening lines of Pope's translation exist in two versions. The lines printed above appear in this first edition, as well as the second edition (1720), and the 1729 printing. Beginning in the third edition (1731–32), the opening lines were revised to read "Achilles' Wrath, to *Greece* the direful spring/Of woes unnumber'd, heav'nly Goddess, sing!" (B3, B9A), which became the norm. The revision may have been a response to criticism of Pope's phrase, "all the *Grecian* woes," by John

Dennis, leading Pope to adopt a reading close to that of Thomas Tickell's translation of Book 1, which also appeared in 1715: "Achilles' fatal Wrath, whence Discord rose,/That brought the Sons of *Greece* unnumber'd Woes." Samuel Johnson, in his preface to the poems of Tickell, remarks, "To compare the two translations would be tedious; the palm is now given universally to Pope; but I think the first lines of Tickell's were rather to be preferred, and Pope seems to have since borrowed something from them in the correction of his own."

Chahoud, A. "Broome, William (*bap.* 1689, *d.* 1745)." *Oxford Dictionary of National Biography.*

de Quehen, H. "Bentley, Richard (1662–1742)." *Oxford Dictionary of National Biography.*

Debrett, J. *The Baronetage of England.* 7th ed. Edited by William Courthope. London: Rivington, 1839.

Erskine-Hill, H. "Pope, Alexander (1688–1744)." *Oxford Dictionary of National Biography.*

Foxon, D. *Pope and the Early Eighteenth-Century Book Trade.* Edited by J. McLaverty. Oxford: Clarendon Press, 1991.

Griffith, R. H. *Alexander Pope: A Bibliography.* Austin: University of Texas Press, 1922.

Homer. *The "Iliad" of Homer.* Translated by Alexander Pope. Edited by Steven Shankman. London: Penguin Books, 1996.

Johnson, S. *The Works of the English Poets,* Vol. 26: *The Poems of Rowe and Tickell.* London: Printed by H. Baldwin, for C. Bathurst, J. Buckland, W. Strahan, [etc.], 1779.

———. *The Lives of the Most Eminent English Poets.* Vols. 3–4. Edited by Roger H. Lonsdale. Oxford: Oxford University Press, 2006.

Rothschild, N. M. V. *The Rothschild Library; A Catalogue of the Collection of Eighteenth-century Printed Books and Manuscripts Formed by Lord Rothschild.* Nos. 1573–74, p. 421. Cambridge: 1954.

Williams, A. L. "Alexander Pope." *Dictionary of Literary Biography, Vol. 95: Eighteenth-Century British Poets, First Series.* Edited by John Sitter. Farmington Hills, MI: Gale Group, 1990.

WITH

B9A

Alexander Pope (1688–1744). *The Iliad of Homer.* . . . Philadelphia: Printed for J. Crukshank, W. Young, M. Carey, et al., 1795.

Duodecimo.

ACHILLES' wrath, to Greece the direful spring
Of woes unnumber'd, heav'nly goddess, sing!

This edition represents not only the first American publication of Alexander Pope's *Iliad,* but also the earliest American publication of any Homeric translation recorded in the *Evans Early American Imprint Collection.*

B10

James Macpherson (1736–1796). *The Iliad of Homer*. . . . London: Printed for T. Becket and P. A. de Hondt, 1773.

Quarto. 2 vols.

> The wrath of the son of Peleus,—O goddess of song, unfold! The deadly wrath of Achilles: To Greece the source of many woes!

Scottish poet James Macpherson wrote this prose translation at the request of a friend, "to please him, more than from any hopes of success." He attacked previous translators of Homer, although he mentioned none by name: "they have made him too much of a modern beau." Macpherson hoped his own translation "might preserve the simplicity and retain as much as possible of the gravity and dignity of the original." He "translated the Greek VERBATIM" into an English version he considered not "MERE PROSE," because he had "measured the whole in his ear." Macpherson believed his faithfulness to the Homeric text and freedom from strict meter would allow readers to study Homer himself "through an English medium."

This translation of the *Iliad* took Macpherson three months to produce and was poorly received. He had already gained notoriety for his claim that he discovered the ancient Gaelic manuscripts of the poems of Ossian, which were widely condemned as forgeries (most notably by Samuel Johnson). In a letter to Macpherson after his *Iliad*'s publication, Johnson wrote, "your abilities since your Homer are not so formidable." Johnson was not the only critic—David Hume remarked that he did not know "whether the attempt or the execution were the worse." And an anonymous epigram on Macpherson's *Iliad* offered even harsher judgment: "In *Ogilby's* dull Strains lay *Homer* dead; / *Hobbs* tried in vain to make him lift his Head; / He rose to live in *Pope's* immortal Verse, / And now lies buried in *Mac------son's* Erse."

Soon after the publication of his *Iliad*, Macpherson moved away from literary pursuits and devoted the rest of his career to politics and political writing.

Kraft, E. "James Macpherson." *Dictionary of Literary Biography, Vol. 109: Eighteenth-Century British Poets, Second Series*. Edited by John Sitter. Farmington Hills, MI: Gale Research, 1991.

Redford, B., ed. *The Letters of Samuel Johnson*. Vol. 2. Oxford: Oxford University Press, 1992.

Rothschild, N. M. V. *The Rothschild Library; A Catalogue of the Collection of Eighteenth-century Printed Books and Manuscripts Formed by Lord Rothschild*. No. 1351, p. 346. Cambridge: 1954.

Saunders, B. *The Life and Letters of James Macpherson*. New York: Macmillan & Co, 1894.

Thomson, D. S. "Macpherson, James (1736–1796)." *Oxford Dictionary of National Biography*.

B11

James Morrice (1739–1815). *The Iliad of Homer, Translated Into English Blank Verse.* London: Printed for John White by Richard Taylor and Co., 1809.

Octavo. 2 vols.

> Sing, Muse, the fatal wrath of Peleus' son,
> Which to the Greeks unnumb'red evils brought

The Rev. James Morrice published this rare blank-verse translation of the *Iliad* only eighteen years after William Cowper's own blank-verse rendition first appeared (B4). In his preface, Morrice apologized for adding "one to the versions which have been given in the English language"; his translation was "begun many years since, and continued . . . as an amusement rather than with any view to publication." Morrice attempted "to enter in some degree into the spirit of his author," and claimed he would be satisfied with the modest achievement of inciting others "to look into and study the original with more minute attention."

His *Iliad* suffered badly from comparisons with Cowper's work. A contemporary review in the *British Critic* stated, "A new translation in blank verse, appearing after Cowper's, ought either to be more poetical, or more exact, or both. That which is now before us, we must inevitably pronounce to be neither." The *Critical Review* echoed this sentiment: "Mr. Morrice has published another translation of the Iliad of Homer into blank verse, which has only added to our previous conviction of the fruitless labor of such attempts."

British Critic, and Quarterly Theological Review 35 (January–June 1810): 562–69.

Burke, J. *A Genealogical and Heraldic History of the Commoners of Great Britain and Ireland.* Vol. 3. London: Henry Colburn, 1836.

Critical Review: or Annals of Literature (Series the Third) 18 (1810): 420–29.

B12

Anonymous. *The Iliad of Homer, Translated Into English Prose. . . .* Oxford: Printed for Munday and Slatter, and G. and W. B. Whittaker, 1821.

Octavo. 2 vols. in 1.

> Sing, Goddess, the destructive wrath of Achilles, son of
> Peleus, which brought many disasters upon the Greeks

This literal prose translation of the *Iliad* was published anonymously by a graduate of the University of Oxford. The translator described his rendition as an aid for students of Homer. Addressing what he saw as a widespread concern that literal translation hinders students learning Greek, he argued that the "youth of good talents" would benefit from a literal translation until he no longer needed it, but would "never *trust* to it," whereas the "youth of modest talents" would be "greatly assisted" by a literal translation in learning what he otherwise could not. The translator compared his work to "a dead" rather than "a living tutor," adding that if his translation of the *Iliad* was "of the smallest use in furthering the views or prospects of any individual, the labour of the translator will be amply rewarded."

This translation went through multiple editions, and the preface to the 1833 third edition is signed "H. P." On the publication of the first American edition in 1847, the *American Whig Review* called the rendition "free, full, and spirited," and recommended it for exactly the kind of audience the translator had described: "Readers who wish to renew their acquaintance with the greatest of poets, but who have no leisure to review their Greek," and "the solitary student, whose means or opportunities do not afford him the aid of a private tutor."

American Whig Review 1–7 (1848): 649.

B13

William Munford (1775–1825). *Homer's Iliad. . . .* Boston: Charles C. Little and James Brown, 1846.

Octavo. 2 vols.

Of Peleus' son Achilles, sing, O Muse,
The direful wrath, which sorrows numberless
Brought on the Greeks

This blank-verse translation of the *Iliad* by poet, lawyer, and Virginia State Senator William Munford was published by the executors of Munford's estate twenty-one years after his death and is the first complete Homeric rendition by an American. The frontispiece portrait was engraved by D. C. Johnston, most likely Boston caricaturist and engraver David Claypoole Johnston. Munford finished his *Iliad* and its preface shortly before his death. He wrote of Pope (B9, B49) and Cowper's Homeric renditions (B4), "Pope has equipped him in the fashionable style of a modern fine gentleman; Cowper displays him . . . in 'rags unseemly,' or in the uncouth garb of a savage." Munford saw that there was "room for an effort to introduce him to the acquaintance of my countrymen in the simple yet graceful and venerable costume of his own heroic times." A translator's duty, he says, is "fidelity," but "in such language as is sanctioned by the use of the best writers and speakers of his own time and country." Munford chose Miltonic blank verse as "best adapted to the free and forcible expression of Homer's animated effusions of fancy and passion," but claimed that he had used his own style, rather than one that imitated "Milton or any other writer." Munford's extensive notes include his own scholarly contributions alongside those taken from the works of Eustathius (D4), Samuel Clarke (A19), Pope, and Cowper.

Contemporary reviews of Munford's *Iliad* celebrated the novelty of an American Homeric translation. The *Knickerbocker* wrote that a "new translation of Homer's Iliad, by a Virginian . . . is an event in literature" that "cannot fail to be a matter of pride and congratulation to our own country"; and the *Southern Quarterly Review* greeted the forthcoming publication by congratulating "the South, and the country generally, on the speedy appearance of a work which reflects much credit on Southern genius, and which will confer new honor on American literature."

Holliday, C. *A History of Southern Literature.* New York: Neale, 1906.

Knickerbocker; Or, New York Monthly Magazine 28 (1846): 248–51.

North American Review 63 (1846): 149–65.

Reinhold, M. *Classica Americana: The Greek and Roman Heritage in the United States.* Detroit: Wayne State University Press, 1984.

Southern Quarterly Review 9 (April 1846): 528; 10 (July 1846): 1–45.

Stauffer, D. M. *American Engravers upon Copper and Steel.* New York: Grolier Club, 1907.

B14

Theodore Alois Buckley (1825–1856). *The Iliad of Homer. . . .* London: Henry G. Bohn, 1853. *Bohn's Classical Library.*

Octavo.

> Sing, O goddess, the destructive wrath of Achilles, son of Peleus, which brought countless woes upon the Greeks

This is a reprint of the prose version of the *Iliad* translator and classical scholar Theodore Alois Buckley first published in 1851 alongside his translation of the *Odyssey* (B50). The engraved frontispiece was signed by "Hinchliff," most likely John Ely Hinchliff, assistant to John Flaxman (see E3). Buckley intended his *Iliad* "to convey, more accurately than any which has preceded it, the words and thoughts of the original." In his attempt to translate Homer as literally and as accurately as possible, Buckley consulted numerous sources, including the Greek editions of Barnes (A18), Clarke (A19), and Heyne (A23), and the commentaries of Eustathius (D4). Buckley also wrote the introduction and notes to new editions, also published in 1853, of Alexander Pope's translations of the *Iliad* (B9) and *Odyssey* (B49) with John Flaxman's illustrations (E3).

Buckley's translation of the *Iliad* was one of his many contributions to Bohn's Classical Library, a branch of the innovative series of modest and inexpensive volumes founded by Henry G. Bohn. *Gentleman's Magazine* credited Bohn's series with establishing "the habit in middle-class life, of purchasing books instead of obtaining them from a library." New York publishers Harper & Brothers sold reprints of many of the volumes at very low prices. When their edition of Buckley's *Iliad* appeared in 1856, *Hunt's Merchants' Magazine and Commercial Review* declared that Buckley had "done good service to literature" by producing a prose translation with "more of the force and spirit" of Homer than most verse renditions were able to convey.

"Bohn's Library and the Purchase of Books." *Gentleman's Magazine* 257 (July–December 1884): 413–14.

Cust, L. H. "Hinchliff, John Ely (1777–1867)." *Oxford Dictionary of National Biography.*

Hunt's Merchants' Magazine and Commercial Review 34 (January–June 1856): 782.

Mew, J. "Buckley, Theodore William Alois (1825–1856)." *Oxford Dictionary of National Biography.*

Mock, D. "H. G. Bohn." *British Literary Publishing Houses, 1820–1880.* Edited by P. J. Anderson and J. Rose. Detroit: Gale Research, 1991.

Pope, A. *The Iliad of Homer.* London: Ingram, Cooke, and Co., 1853.

———. *The Odyssey of Homer.* London: Ingram, Cooke, and Co., 1853.

B15

William George Thomas Barter (ca. 1807–1871). *The Iliad of Homer. . . .* London: Longman, Brown, Green, and Longmans, 1854.

Octavo.

The wrath of Peleus' son Achilles sing,
O Goddess, wrath destructive, that did on
Th' Achæans woes innumerable bring

Poet and barrister W. G. T. Barter proclaimed his translation of the *Iliad* in Spenserian stanzas "the most literal metrical English version of the Iliad hitherto published, and certainly the most literal in rhyme." He had published a translation of the first book of the *Iliad* (revised in this edition) in his 1850 *Poems, Original and Translated, Including the First Iliad of Homer.* Barter objected to previous translators' deviations from the Homeric text, as well as their efforts to "ungreek" or "Anglicize" Homer: Dacier (C5) attempted to elevate Homer's simple language; Chapman (B1, B6) was led by his own poetic talent into "repeatedly breaking off from his author" (Barter promised he had no "such poetic facility"); and translators using hexameters and pentameters "evince the indomitable reluctance of the material to be moulded into those forms." Barter saw the duties of the translator as "Great diligence, respect for his author, and oblivion of self."

He chose to use the Spenserian stanza because he found it "a noble instrument, complete and expressive beyond all others."

Barter's *Iliad* seems to have received little attention. Seven years after its publication, Philip Stanhope Worsley presented his *Odyssey* (B51) as the first Homeric translation in Spenserian stanzas (Barter pointed out Worsley's "ignorance" in his 1862 *Homer and the English Metre*). The attention Barter's *Iliad* did receive was overwhelmingly negative: *Putnam's Monthly Magazine* declared that "Mr. Barter's English is much harder to read than the original Greek"; and *Dublin Monthly Magazine* wrote: "Oh! Barter, Barter, in the circle of the currency the coin exists not minute enough to represent your value in the exchange."

Barter, W. G. T. *Poems, Original and Translated, Including the First Iliad of Homer*. London: W. Pickering, 1850.

———. *Homer and the English Metre*. London: Bell and Daldy, 1862.

Boase, F. "Barter, William George Thomas." *Modern English Biography*. Truro: Netherton and Worth, 1921.

Dublin Monthly Magazine 36 (July–December 1850): 570.

Putnam's Monthly Magazine 4 (July–December 1854): 225.

B16

Francis William Newman (1805–1897). *The Iliad of Homer Faithfully Translated Into Unrhymed English Metre....* London: Walton and Maberly, 1856.

Octavo.

> Of Peleus' son, Achilles, sing, oh goddess, the resentment
> Accursed, which with countless pangs Achaia's army wounded

Classical scholar and moral philosopher Francis William Newman composed this blank-verse translation of the *Iliad* to reflect what he saw as the poem's popular nature. Although Newman was the brother of Cardinal John Henry Newman, his philosophical tracts were anticlerical and focused on humanitarian causes, and his views on Homer were in line with his ethical concerns. Newman viewed Homer's style as "direct, popular, forcible, quaint, flowing, garrulous ... similar to the old English ballad, and ... in sharp contrast to the polished style of Pope [B9], Sotheby [B5], and Cowper [B4]." He found Chapman's translation (B1) "far more Homeric than these." Newman thought that a translation should be an accurate representation of the original text, "executed on the principles rather of a daguerreo-typist, than of a fashionable portrait-painter." Newman chose to represent Homer's dactylic hexameter with a meter "fundamentally musical and popular" that he adapted from the English ballad, dividing each line of his translation into a pair of three- or four-foot lines of unrhymed verse, as "the exigencies of rhyme positively forbid faithfulness." He intended his "sufficiently antiquated" and "Saxo-Norman" diction to match Homer's "essentially archaic" language. Newman's goal was to attain "a plausible aspect of moderate antiquity, while remaining easily intelligible."

Matthew Arnold launched a vicious attack on Newman's *Iliad* in his *On Translating Homer* (D12), rejecting its diction, style, and meter as "ignoble" and "grotesque." In his 1861 *Homeric Translation in Theory and Practice: A Reply to Matthew Arnold*, Newman defended his use of an archaic style and attempted to distinguish antiquity and popularity from ignobility. Unconvinced, Arnold reiterated his views on the translation's baseness in *On Translating Homer—Last Words* (D13). Critics seem to have agreed with Arnold's assessment: the *London Quarterly Review* wrote, "All Professor Newman's scholarship has not saved him from totally misrepresenting Homer's '*quaint and flowing*' style"; and the *British Quarterly Review* condemned Newman for misrepresenting Homer so badly "that the English reader would exclaim, 'Dear me, did those barbarian Greeks think this man a poet!'"

British Quarterly Review 55 (January & April 1872): 137–38.

Coulling, S. "Francis William Newman." *Dictionary of Literary Biography, Vol. 190: British Reform Writers, 1832–1914*. Edited by G. Kelly. Farmington Hills, MI Gale Group, 1998.

Ker, I. "Newman, John Henry (1801–1890)." *Oxford Dictionary of National Biography*.

London Quarterly Review 38 (April & June 1872): 261–62.

Newman, F. W. *Homeric Translation in Theory and Practice: A Reply to Matthew Arnold*. London: Williams and Norgate, 1861.

Sieveking, I. G., ed. *Memoir and Letters of Francis W. Newman*. London: K. Paul, Trench, and Trübner, 1909.

Stunt, T. C. F. "Newman, Francis William (1805–1897)." *Oxford Dictionary of National Biography*.

B17

J. Henry Dart (1817–1887). *The Iliad of Homer in English Hexameter Verse*. London: Longmans, Green, and Co., 1865.

Octavo.

> Sing, divine, Muse, sing the implacable wrath of Achilleus!
> Heavy with death and with woe to the banded sons of Achaia!

British lawyer Joseph Henry Dart published the first twelve books of his hexameter translation of the *Iliad* in 1862; this is the first complete edition, containing a revised version of books 1–12 and a new translation of 13–24. Dart began his rendition "undesignedly, and as a matter of experiment" after reading Charles Kingsley's hexameter *Andromeda.* (Dart's preface never mentioned Matthew Arnold's support for hexameter translations in his 1861 *On Translating Homer* [D12].) Dart continued to work on his translation "as an amusement, and without, in the first instance, any view to publication," relying on William Trollope's edition of the Greek text (based on the text of Heyne [A23]) to produce "a line-by-line translation." He chose to translate Homer into an English hexameter because "in it, and in it alone, is it possible ... to combine adequate fidelity to the original, with that vigor and rapidity of movement" the original contained. The Earl of Derby's 1864 blank-verse *Iliad* (B18) suffered from a lack of such rapidity, "a defect inherent in the English heroic blank verse."

Dart's use of an English hexameter was the subject of great debate among contemporary translators and critics: some applauded Dart's boldness in employing such an unfamiliar meter and defended the hexameter as appropriate for accurate representation of a Homeric epic. *The Times*, for example, noted that there was "a higher need of praise" for Dart, "who, despite all the difficulties and harshness of his metre, never flags in energy ... and at times harmonizes his rugged Northern consonants with a grace and ease not unworthy of the Homeric verse." Others rejected Dart's meter as un-English, agreeing with the Earl of Derby's condemnation of "that 'pestilent heresy' of the so-called English Hexameter." The *London Quarterly Review*, for example, wrote that Dart had chosen "a metrical form of presentation ... incapable of reproducing the measured ease and sweetness and strength of Homer."

Christian Remembrancer 51 (January–April 1866): 190–213.

Dart, J. H. *The Iliad of Homer, in English Hexameter Verse.* London: Longman, Green, Longman & Roberts, 1862.

"English Hexameters: Mr. Dart's Translation of the Iliad." *MacMillan's Magazine* 5 (1861–62): 487–96.

"Homer and his Translators." *Gentleman's Magazine and Historical Review* 1 (January–June 1866): 97–105.

"The Iliad of Homer in English." *The Times* (London), October 21, 1865, p. 6.

Kingsley, C. *Andromeda.* London: J. W. Parker and Son, 1858.

London Quarterly Review 43 (October 1874 & January 1875): 363–81.

Rigg, J. M. "Dart, Joseph Henry (1817–1887)." *Oxford Dictionary of National Biography.*

Ruutz-Rees, C. "A Neglected Translation of the 'Iliad.'" *Classical Journal* 29, no. 3 (December 1933): 206–12.

B18

Edward George Geoffrey Smith Stanley, Earl of Derby (1799–1869). *The Iliad of Homer Rendered Into English Blank Verse....* London: John Murray, 1864.

Octavo. 2 vols.

Of Peleus' son, Achilles, sing, O Muse,
The vengeance, deep and deadly; whence to Greece
Unnumber'd ills arose

Edward George Geoffrey Smith Stanley, the fourteenth Earl of Derby, Chancellor of the University of Oxford, Conservative leader, and three-time Prime Minister, published the first book of this blank-verse rendition of the *Iliad* for private circulation in *Translations of Poems Ancient and Modern* in 1862. In the preface to this first complete edition, Lord Derby wrote that translating Homer afforded him "in the intervals of more urgent business, an unfailing, and constantly increasing source of interest." His goal was "to produce a translation ... such as would fairly and honestly give the sense and spirit of every passage, and of every line," rather than "a happy adaptation of the Homeric story to the spirit of English poetry" like Pope's *Iliad* (B9).

Lord Derby viewed blank verse as the only meter capable of doing justice "to the easy flow and majestic simplicity" of Homer's work, and of "adapting itself to all the gradations ... of the Homeric style." Heroic couplets and rhyme were "trammels"; the Spenserian stanza Worsley had recently used in his *Odyssey* (B51) was inappropriate; and the hexameter verse Arnold recommended (see D12) and Dart used in his contemporary *Iliad* (B17) was "a metre wholly repugnant to the genius of our language."

Lord Derby's translation had gone through six editions by 1867. Contemporary reviewers loved it: the *Quarterly Review* praised its "forcible" diction, "easy and flowing" composition, and "cheerful vigour," and the *Edinburgh Review* wrote that Lord Derby had "crowned a career of daring if not successful statesmanship, of splendid eloquence, and of the highest social distinction, by no mean conquest for English literature."

Blackwood's Edinburgh Magazine 98 (January-June 1865): 439–60.

Derby, E. *Translations of Poems Ancient and Modern.* London: Printed for Hatchard & Co., 1862.

Edinburgh Review or Critical Journal 71 (January–April 1865): 136–51.

Hawkins, A. "Stanley, Edward George Geoffrey Smith, fourteenth earl of Derby (1799–1869)." *Oxford Dictionary of National Biography.*

"Homer and His Translators." *Gentleman's Magazine and Historical Review* 1 (January–June 1866): 97–105.

"The Iliad of Homer rendered into English Blank Verse." *Quarterly Review* 117 (January & April 1865): 93–113.

Kebbel, T. E. *Life of the Earl of Derby*. London: W. H. Allen & Co., 1893.

Vincent, J. R., ed. *Disraeli, Derby and the Conservative Party: Journals and Memoirs of Edward Henry, Lord Stanley, 1849–1869*. Brighton, Sussex: Harvester Press, 1978.

B19

John Stuart Blackie (1809–1895). *Homer and the Iliad*. Edinburgh: Edmonston and Douglas, 1866.

Octavo. 4 vols.

> The baneful wrath, O goddess, sing, of Peleus' son, the source
> Of sorrows dire, and countless woes to all the Grecian force

University of Edinburgh Greek Professor John Stuart Blackie intended this four-volume set—"Dissertations on Homer" (vol. 1), a translation of the *Iliad* in rhyming fourteeners (vols. 2 and 3), and notes and commentary to the poem (vol. 4)—to provide "such an exhibition of the great nation poem of the Greeks, and of the spirit of Greek life contained in it, as might place the English gentleman of culture and intelligence . . . on an equal platform with the professional scholar." Blackie's edition was aimed at a "popular" rather than "academical audience," with extensive notes and discussions to assist the reader. The translation, the "centre-piece" of Blackie's work, was written "to represent the special character of Homer as an . . . old Ionian minstrel." To achieve this, Blackie chose Chapman's (B1) fourteener as his meter, because it was "congenial" and "familiar" to the English reader, and had a "stately march" and "pleasant amplitude" that could reflect the Greek hexameter. Other translators had failed to accurately represent the Greek text because, "though they were good poets, they did not profess to be philologers."

Blackie consulted many works, including the *editio princeps* (A1), the later Greek texts of Aldus (A2 in this collection bears Blackie's signature), Turnebus (A11), Barnes (A18), Villoison (A21), Heyne (A23), and Knight (A25); the translations of Chapman (B1), Hobbes (B2), Pope (B9), Cowper (B4), Sotheby (B5), Newman (B16), Dart (B17), Lord Derby (B18), Dacier (C5), Voss (C13), and Monti (C12); and the scholarly works of Eustathius (D4) and Gladstone (D11). Despite this exhaustive scholarship, the *London Quarterly Review* wrote that "Professor Blackie's talents are those of a rhetorician rather than of a scholar. His translation, though rough and sometimes inaccurate, is not without a certain poetic ring. The critical part of his book is at least vigorous and entertaining."

Blackie, John Stuart. *Notes of a Life*. Edited by A. S. Walker. Edinburgh and London: W. Blackwood, 1910.

Borthwick, E. K. "Blackie, John Stuart (1809–1895)." *Oxford Dictionary of National Biography.*

"The Homeric Question." *London Quarterly Review* 125 (July–October 1868): 228–44.

Stoddart, A. M. *John Stuart Blackie.* Edinburgh and London: William Blackwood and Sons, 1895.

Turner, F. M. *The Greek Heritage in Victorian Britain.* New Haven: Yale University Press, 1984.

Wallace, S. *John Stuart Blackie: Scottish Scholar and Patriot.* Edinburgh: Edinburgh University Press, 2006.

B20

Sir John Frederick William Herschel (1792–1871). *The Iliad of Homer, Translated Into English Accentuated Hexameters.* London and Cambridge: Macmillan and Co., 1866.

Octavo.

> Sing, celestial Muse! the destroying wrath of Achilles,
> Peleus' son: which myriad mischiefs heaped on the Grecians

Mathematician and astronomer Sir John Frederick William Herschel published this hexameter translation of the *Iliad* when he was seventy-four years old. Herschel began his version in 1861 after reading a discussion on the English hexameter in a *London Times* review of Matthew Arnold's *On Translating Homer* (D12)—he claimed to have been unaware that another hexameter translation of the *Iliad* (B17) was then in progress. Herschel published an experimental translation of book 1 in *Cornhill Magazine* in 1862, four years before this first edition of the complete *Iliad* appeared.

While Herschel was working on his translation, the English hexameter became the subject of great debate among critics and translators: according to Herschel, "The hexameter metre is on its trial in this country. It is therefore entitled at all events to a fair hearing." As an "*addition to the rhythmical resources of our language*," it "will be found to afford an amount of variety such as none of the English metres in use possesses." The German hexameter translations of Johann Voss (C13) were "*fac similes*"; such literal translation is "impracticable" in English and would produce a poem that is "a task" rather than "a pleasure" to read. Herschel's version of the *Iliad* is "a careful interpretation of the Greek," although "it eschews altogether any attempt to clothe the simple and rude majesty of the great original in such amplitude of decorated working as to conceal its outlines."

Reviews were mixed. The *Illustrated London News* called Herschel's translation "admirable, not only for many intrinsic merits, but as a great man's tribute to Genius," whereas the *London Quarterly Review* objected that "Sir John's sins of omission and commission" were "literally legion in number."

Buttmann, G. *The Shadow of the Telescope: A Biography of John Herschel.* Cambridge: Lutterworth Press, 2001.

Crowe, M. J. "Herschel, Sir John Frederick William, first baronet (1792–1871)." *Oxford Dictionary of National Biography.*

Herschel, J. F. W. "Book I. of the Iliad, Translated in the Hexameter Meter." *Cornhill Magazine* 5 (January-June 1862): 590–609.

"Homer's Iliad in Translation." *London Quarterly Review* 43 (October 1874 & January 1875): 363–81.

Illustrated London News, cited in *Macmillan & Co.'s General Catalogue of Works in the Departments of History, Biography, Travels, and Belles Lettres, with Some Short Account or Critical Notice Concerning Each Book.* MacMillan & Co., 1869.

"On Translating Homer." *London Times,* October 28, 1861.

Warner, B., ed. *John Herschel 1792–1992: Bicentennial Symposium.* Cape Town: Royal Society of South Africa, 1994.

B21

Charles Merivale (1808–1893). *Homer's Iliad In English Rhymed Verse.* London: Strahan & Co., 1869.

Octavo. 2 vols. in 1.

> Peleïades Achilles his anger, Goddess, sing;
> Fell anger, fated on the Greeks ten thousand woes to bring

Charles Merivale—classical scholar, historian, and Dean of Ely Cathedral—prefaced his rhyming-verse translation of the *Iliad* with a dedicatory poem in Latin and English to his wife: "Who, link'd for ever to a letter'd life, / Has drawn the dubious lot of student's wife; / Kept hush around my desk, nor grudged me still / The long, dull, ceaseless rustling of my quill."

In his letters, Merivale wrote that the Homeric epics are full of "padding," and an English ballad meter is best suited to allow for "surplusage" in translation. Merivale's meter provided "more liberty" than Pope's couplets (B9), which Merivale viewed as "almost nauseous to modern taste." Merivale classified blank verse as "the worst imaginable vehicle for Homer, because it admits of no padding." Although he was fond of writing his own Latin poetry in dactylic hexameter, Merivale "utterly" rejected the meter for an English translation of Homer.

The *Contemporary Review* seems to have agreed with Merivale's assessment: its editors wrote that "the most bigoted of hexametrists could not deny his having established a strong case for the superiority of his measure to any other." Merivale had produced "a version of the immortal bard, the form of which is our nearest possible approximation to that of Homer and the rhapsodists."

"*Homer's Iliad.* In English Rhymed Verse. In Two Volumes. By Charles Merivale, B. D., D. C. L., Chaplain to the Speaker. London: Strahan & Co." *Contemporary Review* 11 (May–August 1869): 139–43.

Merivale, J. A., ed. *Autobiography of Dean Merivale with Selections from His Correspondence.* London: Edward Arnold, 1899.

Rigg, J. M. and J. D. Pickles. "Merivale, Charles (1808–1893)." *Oxford Dictionary of National Biography.*

B22

William Cullen Bryant (1794–1878). *The Iliad of Homer Translated Into English Blank Verse.* Boston: Fields, Osgood, & Co., 1870.

Quarto. 2 vols.

> Oh goddess! sing the wrath of Peleus' son,
> Achilles; sing the deadly wrath that brought
> Woes numberless upon the Greeks

American poet William Cullen Bryant published this blank-verse translation of the *Iliad* when he was seventy-six years old. Bryant had begun translating Homer in 1865 and, after the death of his wife, devoted himself to completing his version to "divert my mind from a great domestic sorrow." He hoped to be "strictly faithful" to Homer's text while transferring the epic "from his own grand and musical Greek to our less sonorous but still manly and flexible tongue." To match Homer's "simplicity of style" and "popular" language, Bryant used "such English as offers no violence to the ordinary usages and structures." Rhyming verse (like Pope's [B9]) entails an "inversion" and a "stiffening" of language; ballad meters (like Newman's [B16] or Merivale's [B21]) cannot capture Homer's "reach of thought" and "richness of phraseology"; and the English hexameter (like Dart's [B17], Herschel's [B20], or Cayley's [B23]) "cannot possibly render the Greek hexameter line for line," as Voss's German versions had (C13). Bryant considered blank verse, "the vehicle of some of the noblest poetry in our language," flexible enough to faithfully translate the Homeric epic.

Bryant's *Iliad* was the first translation of a Homeric epic by a major American poet; it was much-anticipated and so well received that Bryant began translating the *Odyssey* (B54) soon after its publication. The *London Quarterly* praised Bryant's "simplicity of style, his closeness of diction, his ease and elegance of movement," which made "his translation read with much of the naturalness of an original poem." The *Saturday Review* (London) congratulated "our American kinsfolk on having a poet among them who in his green old age has produced a translation of the 'Iliad' worthy to live amongst the best experiments of the kind in our common language." And *Harper's Magazine* wrote, "of all which we have seen . . . there is none to equal this work of our own poet. Nor can we conceive a medium more fitting for the rendition of the legends of the greatest of all bards."

Bradley, W. A. *William Cullen Bryant.* New York: The Macmillan Company, 1905.

Harper's Magazine 41 (June–November 1870): 141.

"Homer's Iliad in Translation." *London Quarterly Review* 43 (October 1874 & January 1875): 363–81.

Muller, G. H. *William Cullen Bryant: Author of America.* Albany: State University of New York Press, 2008.

Saturday Review, August 13, 1870. Cited in *Atlantic Monthly* 26 (1870): 2.

Tomlinson, D. "William Cullen Bryant." *Dictionary of Literary Biography, Vol. 3: Antebellum Writers in New York and the South.* Edited by Joel Myerson. Farmington Hills, MI: Gale Group, 1979.

B23

Charles Bagot Cayley (1823–1876). *The Iliad of Homer. Homometrically Translated.* London: Longmans & Co., 1877.

Octavo.

> Muse, of Pelidéan Achilles sing the resentment
> Ruinous, who brought down many thousand griefs on Achaians

Russian-born translator Charles Bagot Cayley termed his rendition of the *Iliad* "homometric," in that it replicated the hexameter of the Greek original. He dedicated his work to W. E. Gladstone (D11) "with permission." Cayley's preface to this edition, seven lines written in hexameter, mocked the hexametric poetry of German and English writers as "uproar": "Such measure I'd never hear! sooner blank-verse chloroform me, / Seesaw me couplets, gape for me sooner, immense Earth!"

Cayley aimed instead at a hexameter translation "true-tim'd." But his effort to compose a version of the *Iliad* in its original meter better than those of either Joseph Henry Dart (B17) or Sir John Herschel (B20) seems to have met with little appreciation: although the *Morning Post* granted Cayley's translation "archaic colouring," "animation," and a "bold . . . method of rendering the Homeric compound epithets," *Penn Monthly* wrote that had Cayley "deliberately tried to heap additional injury on the unfortunate English hexameter . . . he could not more certainly have effected that fell purpose." The title page bears an epigram from Ovid's *Amores* 1.1–2.

Elkin, S. "Cayley, Charles Bagot (1823–1883)." *Oxford Dictionary of National Biography.*

Marsh, J. *Christina Rossetti: A Literary Biography.* London: Jonathan Cape, 1994.

Morning Post, cited in *Fraser's Magazine* (New Series) 15 (January–June 1877): 26.

Omond, T. S. *English Metrists: Being a Sketch of English Prosodical Criticism from Elizabethan Times to the Present Day.* New York: Phaeton Press, 1968.

"Recent English 'Hexameters.'" *Penn Monthly* 9 (January–December 1878): 145–58.

B24

Andrew Lang (1844–1912), Walter Leaf (1852–1927), and Ernest Myers (1844–1921). *The Iliad of Homer Done Into English Prose.* London: Macmillan and Co., 1883.

Octavo.

> Sing, goddess, the wrath of Achilles Peleus' son, the ruinous
> wrath that brought on the Achaians woes innumerable

Andrew Lang, Walter Leaf, and Ernest Myers collaborated to publish this very successful prose translation of the *Iliad*, dividing the translating of the original text into three parts. This is the first edition; an American edition with an illustration from the *Odyssey* copyrighted 1882 is a reprint. Classical scholar and banker Leaf (books 1–9) would go on to publish his own edition of the Greek text (A30) along with numerous studies on Homer. Poet, anthropologist, and classicist Lang (books 10–16) was a student of anthropology and of folklore, of which he considered the Homeric works a specimen; Lang had coauthored a prose translation of the *Odyssey* with Samuel Henry Butcher in 1879 (B55) and would later translate the *Homeric Hymns* and produce three works of Homeric scholarship. Poet and translator Myers (books 17–24) wrote his own poetry as well as translations and adaptations of ancient texts. Poems by Lang and Myers appear at the beginning of this volume.

Lang, Leaf, and Myers's translation emphasized the archaic aspects of Homer's diction by drawing much of its language from the King James Bible. It was immediately popular and has been through many editions and reprints since its publication. Like Butcher and Lang's *Odyssey*, with which it has often been bound (for instance, in the 1905 *The Homeric Stories Iliad and Odyssey*), it became a standard classroom translation. *The Cambridge Companion to Homer* identifies the Lang, Leaf, and Myers translation as a "bridge to the modern period." At the time of its publication, the *British Quarterly Review* wrote of the "simplicity and rhythmic character," "sustained grace," and "faithfulness" that came from the collaboration of the three translators—with Leaf "conscientiously exact, clear, and graceful," Lang "vigorous, imaginative, and musical," and Myers "quaint and delicate." The *New York Tribune* could name no other translation "which persons unfamiliar with Greek can read with so much and such unflagging delight."

Bell, A. C. "Myers, Ernest James (1844–1921)." *Oxford Dictionary of National Biography.*

British Quarterly Review 77 (January & April 1883): 248.

Calkins, R. W. "Andrew Lang." *Dictionary of Literary Biography, Vol. 98: Modern British Essayists, First Series.* Edited by Robert Beum. Farmington Hills, MI: Gale Group, 1990.

Donaldson, W. "Lang, Andrew (1844–1912)." *Oxford Dictionary of National Biography.*

Fowler R. L. *The Cambridge Companion to Homer.* Cambridge: Cambridge University Press, 2004.

Green, R. L. *Andrew Lang: A Critical Biography with a Short-title Bibliography of the Works of Andrew Lang.* Leicester, England: Edmund Ward, 1946.

Lang, A. *Homer and the Epic.* London: Longmans, Green, and Co., 1893.

———. *Homeric Hymns.* London: G. Allen, 1899.

———. *Homer and His Age.* London: Longmans, Green, and Co., 1906.

———. *The World of Homer.* London: Longmans, Green, and Co., 1910.

Lang, A., S. Butcher, W. Leaf, et al. *The Homeric Stories Iliad and Odyssey.* Chautauqua, NY: Chautauqua Press, 1905.

Lubenow, W. C. "Leaf, Walter (1852–1927)." *Oxford Dictionary of National Biography.*

New York Tribune, May 19, 1883, p. 6.

B25

John Graham Cordery (1833–1900). *The Iliad of Homer . . . with Greek Text.* London: Kegan Paul, Trench, & Co., 1886.

Octavo. 2 vols.

> Sing, Goddess, of Achilles, Peleus' son,
> The Wrath that rose disastrous, and the cause
> Of woes unnumber'd to Achaia's host

John Graham Cordery of the Indian Civil Service published this revised edition of his blank-verse translation of the *Iliad* with facing Greek text fifteen years after the first edition (which contained only the English translation). Cordery would go on to publish a translation of the *Odyssey* (B60) in 1897. In his preface to this edition, he states his modest belief that his version "represents some features and characteristics of the original, which have been, more or less, lost sight of in many other translations." The most essential of these characteristics is the dramatic nature or "quality of vividness" that animates the Homeric text—Cordery considered "monotony" the "besetting sin of all poetical translations." He viewed translating the *Iliad* as the "converse" of the task he faced as British Resident at Hyderabad, India, where he depended "very largely on his faculty of so translating . . . the ideas and civilisation of the West to the Oriental mind as to remain in sympathetic contact with both."

Cordery's translation received moderate critical praise: The *British Quarterly Review* remarked on its "rapid and flowing" verse and "vivid pictures," and, comparing its first edition with Lord Derby's recent blank-verse translation (B18), called it "by no means inferior to that remarkable work in either faithfulness or animation." The *Academy* applauded the usefulness of this bilingual edition, but called the volume "bulky and unwieldy" and complained of a "certain inconvenience in being given too much at a time."

British Quarterly Review 59 (January & April 1874): 306.

Cordery, J. G. *The Iliad of Homer.* London: Rivingtons, 1871.

"Cordery, John Graham (1833–1900)." *Dictionary of Indian Biography.* London: Swan Sonnenschein & Co., 1906.

Morshead. E. D. A. "*The Iliad of Homer.* A Translation by J. G. Cordery. (Kegan Paul, Trench, & Co.)." *Academy* 30 (July–December 1886): 180–1.

B26

Arthur S. Way (1847–1930). *The Iliad of Homer Done Into English Verse.* London: Sampson Low, Marston, et al., 1886–88.

Quarto. 2 vols.

> The wrath of Achilles the Peleus-begotten, O Song-queen, sing,
> Fell wrath, that dealt the Achaians woes past numbering

Arthur Sanders Way, headmaster of Wesley College in Melbourne, Australia, published this translation of the *Iliad* in ballad meter following the success of his 1880 *Odyssey* (published under the pseudonym Avia—see B57). This first complete edition (books 1–6 having been previously published separately) includes selections from reviews of both works. Way adapted the translation's meter, a rhyming six-foot mixture of iambs and anapests, from William Morris's poetry before Morris used it in his own Homeric translation in 1887 (B59).

Contemporary critics greeted Way's skillful manipulation of the meter with great acclaim. The *Saturday Review* wrote that Way's translation "has advanced on all its predecessors" in metrical form—"his metre comes very near in length, volume, and movement, to being a genuine English equivalent for the Greek Hexameter." The *British Quarterly Review* agreed, noting that Way had mastered his meter since the publication of the first edition of his *Odyssey* (in which the meter sometimes faltered): "Mr. Way has, in a sense, constructed a new metre, by means of which he has been enabled to give a faithful line-for-line rendering of Homer"; he "has succeeded in imparting a swing and energy which leave most translators of Homer far behind."

"Belles Lettres." *Westminster Review* (July & October 1885): 292.

British Quarterly Review 83, no. 165 (January 1886): 472.

Browning, D. C., ed. "Way, Arthur Sanders." *Everyman's Dictionary of Literary Biography, English & American.* 3rd ed. London: Dent, 1962.

"Review: Way's Odyssey." *Classical Review* 20, no. 1 (February 1906): 60–1.

Saturday Review of Politics, Literature, Science, and Art 62 (August 21, 1886): 262–63.

B27

John Purves (1840–1890). *The Iliad of Homer Translated Into English Prose. . . .* London: Percival and Co., 1891.

Quarto.

> Sing, O goddess, the fatal wrath of Peleus' son Achilles,
> which brought ten thousand troubles on the Achæans

According to the introduction by classical scholar Evelyn Abbott, this prose translation of the *Iliad* "was the chief literary work of Mr. Purves's life." Purves, a classicist who produced *Selections from the Dialogues of Plato with Introductions and Notes*, worked on the translation between 1871 and 1884 but never published it. Abbott revised the manuscript of Purves's translation and published it in this limited edition of seventy-five copies with his own introduction the year after Purves's death. He was then working on a three-volume *History of Greece* that treated the Homeric epics as pure works of fiction rather than as historical texts. Purves based his translation on an 1870 edition of the Greek text by La Roche; Abbott used a text edited by Monro (see A31).

In its review of this translation, the *Times* wrote, "That so eminent a scholar and master of style as Mr. Abbott should stand sponsor for the work will be quite sufficient guarantee that the translation is of no common merit"; it is "worthy to rank in some respects" with Butcher and Lang's recent prose translation of the *Odyssey* (B55). The *Saturday Review* preferred Purves's translation to Lang, Leaf, and Myers's prose *Iliad* (B24), calling it "less archaic," "more rapid," and "more readable."

Abbott, E. *History of Greece.* New York: G. P. Putnam's Sons, 1888–1900.

Boase, F. "Purves, John." *Modern English Biography.* 6 vols. Truro: Netherton and Worth, 1892–1921.

"Books of the Week." *Times* (London), July 30, 1891, p. 4.

"Messrs. Pervical's List." In *The Victorian Age of English Literature.* Vol. 1, p. 25. Edited by M. Oliphant and F. R. Oliphant. London: Percival and Co., 1892.

Purves, J. *Selections from the Dialogues of Plato with Introductions and Notes.* Oxford: Clarendon, 1883.

The Saturday Review of Politics, Literature, Science, and Art, cited in *Messrs. Percival's List.* Quoted in G. Saintsbury, *Miscellaneous Essays*, London: Percival & Co., 1892.

Strachan-Davidson, J. L. "Abbott, Evelyn (1843–1901)." Rev. M. C. Curthoys. *Oxford Dictionary of National Biography.*

B28

Charles W. Bateman and Roscoe Mongan. *Homer's Iliad. . . .* London: James Cornish & Sons, [1895?]. *Kelly's Keys to the Classics.*

Octavo.

> Goddess, sing the destroying wrath of Achilles, Peleus' son, which brought woes unnumbered on the Achæans

This literal prose translation of the *Iliad* by Charles William Bateman and James Roscoe Mongan belongs to Kelly's Keys to the Classics, a series of inexpensive Latin and Greek cribs for schoolboys that was published in England from the mid-nineteenth to the early twentieth century. The publisher's catalogue in the back of this volume advertises two other educational series from James Cornish & Sons—Cornish's Interlinear Keys to the Classics and Kelly's Keys to the French Classics—and identifies this series as "Literal English Translations of the Latin and Greek Classics." This edition includes an introduction on Homeric language and meter, as well as scholarly notes and selections from the Greek text interspersed throughout the translation. Bateman composed books 1–8 (previously published by Kelly's Keys in three volumes as books 1–4, 5–8, and 1–8). Mongan, who rendered the rest of the *Iliad* (also previously published in installments as books 9–12, 13–16, 17–20, and 21–24), appears to have been a classical scholar and prolific translator, contributing numerous English versions of French, Latin, and Greek works to Cornish's different series. Mongan's contributions to Kelly's Keys to the Classics include a literal prose rendition of the *Odyssey* and a version of *Oedipus Tyrannus* that the Greekless poet William Butler Yeats, who consulted it while composing his *Sophocles' King Oedipus*, referred to as "a translation published at a few pence for dishonest schoolboys."

Clark, D. R., and J. B. McGuire. *W. B. Yeats: The Writing of Sophocles' King Oedipus.* Philadelphia: American Philosophical Society, 1989.

"Mongan, James Roscoe." *A Supplement to Allibone's Critical Dictionary of English Literature.* Philadelphia: J. B. Lippincott, 1891.

Mongan, R. *Oedipus Tyrannus.* London: J. Cornish, 1865.

———. *Homer's Odyssey, Complete.* London: J. Cornish, [n.d.].

Yeats, W. B. *Sophocles' King Oedipus, a Version for the Modern Stage.* London: Macmillan and Co., 1928.

B29

Samuel Butler (1835–1902). *The Iliad of Homer Rendered Into English Prose. . . .* London: Longmans, Green, and Co., 1898.

Octavo.

This copy bears a presentation by Butler.

> Sing, O goddess, the anger of Achilles son of Peleus, that brought countless ills upon the Achæans.

Artist and writer Samuel Butler published this first edition of his prose translation of the *Iliad* one year after his controversial *The Authoress of the "Odyssey"*; his translation of the *Odyssey* (B61) was already completed but not yet published. Butler acknowledged his debt to Lang, Leaf, and Myers's version of the *Iliad* (B24), which he considered "the best prose translation that has yet been made," but one whose literalness cost it the "spirit of the original." He preferred to allow translators a great deal of liberty to create "readable" versions in current "modes of speech." For example, Elizabethan translators (like Chapman [B1, B7]) were able to make "a dead author living" by transfusing "their blood into his cold veins" and giving him "their own livingness," and Butler sought to provide his generation with just such a translation of Homer's work. Whereas the *Journal of Education* called Butler's *Iliad* "a most readable romance" that conveyed "the thrilling story, the rhetoric, the dramatic presentment of characters in interaction" if not "the lilt, the large utterance, the epic grandeur" of the original, the *Literary World* condemned it as "an arbitrary mixture of Butler and Homer."

Breuer, H.-P. "Butler, Samuel." *Dictionary of Literary Biography, Vol. 57: Victorian Prose Writers After 1867*. Edited by William B. Thesing. Farmington Hills, MI: Gale Group, 1987.

Butler, S. *The Authoress of the "Odyssey."* London & New York: Longmans, Green, 1897.

Farrington, B. *Samuel Butler and the Odyssey*. London: Cape, 1929.

Hoppé, A. J. *A Bibliography of the Writings of Samuel Butler*. London: Bookman, 1925.

Jones, H. F. *Samuel Butler: Author of 'Erewhon' (1835–1902), a Memoir*. London: Macmillan, 1919.

Raby, P. *Samuel Butler: A Biography*. Iowa City: University of Iowa Press, 1991.

"Review." *Journal of Education*, February 1899, p. 122.

"Review." *Literary World* 30, no. 1 (January 7, 1899): 10.

Shaffer, E. "Butler, Samuel (1835–1902)." *Oxford Dictionary of National Biography*.

B30

Edward Henry Blakeney (1869–1955). *The Iliad of Homer Translated Into English Prose.* London: George Bell & Sons, 1909–13. *Bohn's Libraries.*

Octavo. 2 vols.

> Sing, O goddess, the accursèd wrath of Achilles, son of Peleus,
> the wrath which brought countless sorrows unto the Achaians

Headmaster and classicist E. H. Blakeney feared that the publication of another prose translation of the *Iliad* might be viewed as "another terror added to life." But Blakeney found translating Homer into "an English setting" "a consolation and a pleasure," and worked on his *Iliad* continuously for seven years. Beginning in 1905, Blakeney published his translation in several installments before issuing these complete volumes. He relied on a revised edition of Walter Leaf's Greek text (A30) and also consulted D. B. Munro's Greek edition (see A31) and Lord Derby's translation (B18). Blakeney intended his version for "those who know no Greek," not "scholars who can read Homer with ease." He viewed himself as a Homeric interpreter and reiterated J. W. Mackail's (see B62) theory that all poetry requires "perpetual reinterpretation." Blakeney chose to represent Homeric language in seventeenth-century English prose, which "precisely suits" Homer's style: "archaistic without preciosity, old-fashioned though without affectation." He hoped that he had "not seriously misrepresented the spirit of the original."

Reviewers in *Notes and Queries* treated Blakeney's translation as "a version of considerable literary merit . . . admirably calculated to give those who have no Greek a view of Homer's supremacy in the world of letters."

Notes and Queries: A Medium of Intercommunication for Literary Men, General Readers, Etc. (Eleventh Series) 1 (January–June 1910): 119.

B30.1 (addendum)

Arthur Gardner Lewis. *The Iliad of Homer Translated Into English Blank Verse.* New York: The Baker & Taylor Company, 1911.

Octavo. 2 vols.

> Sing thou the Wrath, O Muse! the baleful wrath
> Of Peleus' son, Achilles; wrath which heaped
> Unnumbered woes upon Achæa's band.

Boston lawyer Arthur Gardner Lewis spent twelve years composing this blank-verse translation of the *Iliad*, which provided him "amusement and relaxation for idle hours." Lewis sought to produce a translation that was "smooth, harmonious, and pleasing to the ear," while still representing an "adequate and literal interpretation of the poet's meaning" and complying with "the rules of simplicity, rapidity, and dignity" laid out in Matthew Arnold's *On Translating Homer* (D12). Acknowledging that publishing a new translation of the *Iliad* "may seem presumptuous to a degree," Lewis argued that "the possible English versions of a foreign author" are "innumerable"—no translation can be "wholly adequate" or "absolutely ideal," but every new version can contribute "a little new truth, a little added beauty, just a new felicitous touch here and there." In addition to the Greek text, Lewis consulted the prose translation of Buckley (B14) and the "noble version of Mr. Bryant" (B22) in producing his own rendition.

The *Outlook* determined that "Mr. Lewis has kept fairly close to the Homeric text, and the epic simplicity and energy are well preserved in his fluent rhythm"; and the *Harvard Graduates' Magazine* (the magazine of Lewis's alma mater) wrote that "Mr. Lewis succeeds in infusing some music into" his blank-verse translation.

Harvard College Class of 1896 Secretary's Fifth Report June, 1916. Norwood, MA: Plimpton, 1916.

Harvard Graduates' Magazine 20 (1911–12): 189–90.

Outlook 100 (January–April 1912): 98–99.

B31

A. T. Murray (1866–1940). *The Iliad. . . .* London: William Heinemann; New York: G. P. Putnam's Sons, 1924–25. *Loeb Classical Library.*

Duodecimo. 2 vols.

> The wrath do thou sing, O goddess, of Peleus' son, Achilles, that baneful wrath which brought countless woes upon the Achaeans, and sent forth to Hades many valiant souls of warriors

This prose translation of the *Iliad* with facing Greek text was A. T. Murray's second contribution to the Loeb Classical Library series, after his 1919 translation of the *Odyssey* (B64). Murray wrote that he was guided by the same principles as he had been in that earlier translation: he aspired to "the flowing ease and simple directness of Homer's style" while maintaining "due regard to the emphasis attaching to the arrangement of words in the original," and sought a level of diction that was "elevated" but "not stilted."

In a review for *Classical Philology*, S. E. Bassett compared the language and tone of Murray's *Iliad* with those of Lang, Leaf, and Myers's version (B24): "Murray's is perhaps a little closer to the Greek, and therefore a little farther from the English; but this is right for a bilingual edition of Homer."

Bassett, S. E. "Review." *Classical Philology* 20, no. 2 (April 1925): 190–91.

Hansen, H. D., J. P. Mitchell, W. D. Briggs, et al. "Memorial Resolution, Augustus Taber Murray (1866–1940)." *The Academic Council of Stanford University.* http://histsoc.stanford.edu/pdfmem/MurrayA.pdf (accessed March 18, 2011).

Misener, G. "Review." *Classical Philology* 16, no. 4 (October 1921): 402.

WITH

B31A

A. T. Murray (1866–1940) and William F. Wyatt (1932–). *Iliad. . . .* Cambridge: Harvard University Press, 1999. *Loeb Classical Library* 170–71.

Duodecimo. 2 vols.

> The wrath sing, goddess, of Peleus' son Achilles, the accursed
> wrath which brought countless sorrows upon the Achaeans,
> and sent down to Hades many valiant souls of warriors

The Loeb Classical Library commissioned classicist William F. Wyatt, grandnephew of A. T. Murray, to revise Murray's translation of the *Iliad* and bring it up to date. According to Wyatt, Murray's translation "has long set a standard for accuracy and style. But its archaic language no longer seems as appropriate as it did to earlier generations." Wyatt modernized the translation's diction but made few substantial alterations.

B32

Sir William Marris (1873–1945). *The Iliad of Homer. . . .* London: Oxford University Press, 1934.

Duodecimo.

> Sing, Goddess, of Achilles, Peleus' son,
> In his stark wrath, which brought upon the Greeks
> Infinite troubles

Sir William Marris prefaced this blank-verse translation by admitting, "I realize how doubtful are the chances that a new rendering of the ILIAD will find a welcome." But Marris saw "Homer's simplicity and nobleness" as "a tonic for some troubles of the present time." He was unaware of any recent translations of the *Iliad* for the Greekless, and found the older versions "generally too mannered or too slow" for modern readers. As in his 1925 *Odyssey* (B66), Marris maintained that blank verse was "the best form" for Homeric translation, despite Matthew Arnold's objections to this use of the meter (see D12, D13). Marris spent more than three decades holding increasingly senior positions in the Indian Civil Service, which perhaps explains why this volume, although published in London, was printed in India.

Reviews of Marris's translation were mixed. The *Journal of Hellenic Studies* called it "very readable," "on somewhat new lines," with "a charm of its own," a "freshness of style," and "many beauties"; but "Unfortunately it does no justice to the magnificence and dignity of Homer's diction." In the *Classical Review*, E. S. Forster regretted that Marris's blank verse did not have "more distinction," but conceded that "those who cannot read the original Greek will find in this attractive and handy little volume a good, plain, straightforward presentation of the *Iliad*, absolutely devoid of all pedantry and mannerisms."

Forster, E. S. "Review: Some Translations." *Classical Review* 49, no. 4 (September 1935): 129–30.

H., C. R. "Review: The Iliad of Homer. Translated by Sir William Marris. Pp. 566. Oxford University Press, 1934. 6s." *Journal of Hellenic Studies* 55, pt. 1 (1935): 104–5.

Haig, H. "Marris, Sir William Sinclair (1873–1945)." Rev. Philip Woods. *Oxford Dictionary of National Biography.*

B33

W. H. D. Rouse (1863–1950). *The Story of Achilles, a Translation of Homer's "Iliad" Into Plain English.* London: Thomas Nelson and Sons Ltd., 1938.

Octavo.

> An angry man—there is my story: the bitter rancour of Achillês, prince of the house of Peleus, which brought a thousand troubles upon the Achaian host

W. H. D. Rouse called his prose translation of the *Iliad* "a translation into plain English of the plain story of Homer, omitting the embellishments which were meant only to please the ear," in the style of his *Odyssey* (B70). Rouse saw no need "to augment" the *Iliad*, "a story naturally told," with "high-flown expressions." He emphasized the "comic background" to the tragedy in both Homeric tales, the "merriment," "open fun and delicate comedy, even farce." His translation of the *Iliad* is based on Walter Leaf's Greek text (A30).

In the *Classical Review*, W. G. Waddell noted details in Rouse's version at which "the critic will cavil," but accorded Rouse's rendition "vividness and power" and value as "a continuous commentary," with "the gist of Homer's meaning forcefully expressed in plain terms." When the New American Library published new editions of both of Rouse's Homeric translations in 1950, L. R. Lind wrote in the *Classical Weekly,* "Homer is not in the least pretentious; and this is the least pretentious of all translations of the *Iliad,*" with "a manly, often colloquial, but never cheap language" that should be "both refreshing and satisfactory" for those "who do not wish to feel uncomfortable as they read an English Homer."

D., R. M. "W. H. D. Rouse." *Folklore* 62, no. 1 (March 1951): 269–70.

Lind, L. R. "Review." *Classical Weekly* 44, no. 8 (January 22, 1951): 124–25.

"Loeb Classical Library: The History." Cambridge, MA: Harvard University Press. http://www.hup.harvard.edu/features/loeb/history.html (accessed March 18, 2011).

Rouse, W. H. D. "Machines or Mind?" *Classical Weekly* 6, no. 11 (January 11, 1913): 82–86.

Stray, C. "Rouse, William Henry Denham (1863–1950)." *Oxford Dictionary of National Biography.*

Waddell, W. G. "Review: The Iliad in Plain Prose." *Classical Review* 52, no. 6 (December 1938): 218–19.

B34

William Benjamin Smith (1850–1934) and Walter Miller (1864–1949). *The Iliad of Homer A Line for Line Translation in Dactylic Hexameters. . . .* New York: The Macmillan Company, 1944.

Octavo.

> Sing, O Goddess, the wrath of Achilles, scion of Peleus,
> Ruinous wrath, that afflicted with numberless woes the Achaeans,
> Hurling headlong to Hades souls many and brave ones

Mathematician and New Testament scholar William Benjamin Smith left the manuscript of his hexameter translation of the *Iliad* to classicist Walter Miller when he died. Smith and Miller were close friends and had worked together at Tulane University early in their careers. According to Miller, Smith had laid a "splendid basis" for the translation; however, there was a "drastic" need for revisions, and Miller left "scarcely a line" of Smith's original manuscript intact—he claimed to have "entirely rewritten" thousands of lines. In addition to revising the translation, Miller supplied the introduction and index. The distich at the head of each book is from Chapman's translation (B1), and the volume's illustrations are those of John Flaxman (see E3), to whom Miller attributed "unrivaled gifts of rhythmical design and penetrating feeling." Voss's German hexameter rendition (C13) had inspired Smith to try his own translation, and Miller called this version "the first attempt" to render the *Iliad* in English both "line for line" and "in the meter of the original," as older hexameter translations were "neither complete nor line for line."

Reviews were mostly positive, but they stressed the problem of translating Homer's Greek line for line while maintaining the same meter, necessitating wording to extend or save space in a line and devices to manipulate the rhythm, resulting in what W. E. Blake in the *American Journal of Philology* called only "the illusion of metrical equivalence." Still, Blake predicted Smith and Miller's *Iliad* would supplant the Lang, Leaf, and Myers version (B24), then "supreme in popular favor." In *Classical Philology*, W. P. Clark noted metrical problems and recognized that "we do not have Homer here any more than" in previous versions; but he found the translation "extraordinary," "fast enough," with "enough of Homer's fire and passion." Its publication during World War II was also timely: "Homer is a philosophic and sobering poet of war. A new rendering of his tragic war story at this time is therefore most fitting."

Arrowsmith, W. "Review: The Decade of Five Iliads." *Hudson Review* 5, no. 3 (Autumn 1952): 432–43.

Blake, W. E. "Review." *American Journal of Philology* 66, no. 2 (1945): 198–202.

Clark, W. P. "Review." *Classical Philology* 40 (October 1945): 260–62.

Gwatkin, Jr., W. E. "Walter Miller: 1864–1949." *Classical Journal* 45, no. 6 (March 1950): 285–87.

Larrabee, S. A. "Review." *College Art Journal* 5 (November 1945): 70–1.

Scott, J. A. "Review." *Classical Weekly* 38, no. 16 (February 26, 1945): 125–26.

"William Benjamin Smith." *The National Cyclopaedia of American Biography*. Vol. 9. New York: White, 1898.

B35

Alston Hurd Chase (1906–1994) and William G. Perry (1913–1998). *The Iliad. . . .* Boston: Little, Brown and Company, 1950. *Atlantic Monthly Press Book.*

Octavo.

> Sing, O goddess, of the wrath of Peleus' son Achilles, the deadly wrath that brought upon the Achaeans countless woes and sent many mighty souls of heroes down to the house of Death

Alston Hurd Chase, classicist at Andover, and William G. Perry, professor of education at Harvard, wrote this prose version of the *Iliad* for the "modern reader," who required a translation written "as faithfully as possible in a style appropriate to his own day." The volume's drawings are by American illustrator Steele Savage. Chase and Perry felt that contemporary readers generally neglected the *Iliad* for the "more immediately comprehensible *Odyssey*"; however, they had detected a recent revival of interest in the epic, which they attributed to "our refusal to shun any longer, through romanticism or cynicism, the facts of war." They sought to provide "a simpler and more direct transcription of the original" poem, one that avoided archaism's "artificial formality" and "slick colloquialism," and could convey "the sensation" of poetry through prose. Chase and Perry viewed Palmer's *Odyssey* (B58) as an ideal prose translation, but felt the "ease and grace" of Palmer's style were too far off from the style of the *Iliad*—which "moves in bone and muscle"—for imitation.

In the *Classical Weekly*, Preston H. Epps (B75) called Chase and Perry's *Iliad* "painstaking and well-rendered" and "about as close to the original wording, thought, and characteristics as clear and readable English will permit"; however, its attempt to reproduce the feeling of poetry through prose was "not even remotely realized." In the *Hudson Review*, on the other hand, William Arrowsmith characterized it as "prose with the flavor of poetry": "a fine, spirited and accurate translation, written in a rapid, lucid prose with a marked cadence."

Arrowsmith, W. "Review: The Decade of Five Iliads." *Hudson Review* 5, no. 3 (Autumn 1952): 432–43.

Chase, A. H. *Time Remembered.* San Antonio: Parker, 1994.

Epps, P. H. "Review." *Classical Weekly* 45, no. 3 (December 3, 1951): 42–43.

"Memorial Minute: William Graves Perry, Jr." *Harvard University Gazette,* May 27, 1999.

"Perry, William G., Jr." *New York Times,* January 18, 1998.

B36

E. V. Rieu (1887–1972). *The Iliad. . . .* Harmondsworth, Middlesex: Penguin Books, 1950. *Penguin Classics in Translation.*

Duodecimo.

> The Wrath of Achilles is my theme, that fatal wrath which, in fulfilment of the will of Zeus, brought the Achaeans so much suffering

Emile Victor Rieu published this prose translation of the *Iliad* as part of the popular Penguin Classics in Translation series initiated five years before with his enormously successful *Odyssey* (B71). He turned to the *Iliad* "with some trepidation," as "the *Odyssey*, with its happy ending, presents the romantic view of life: the *Iliad* is a tragedy." Rieu dismissed scholars who "tried to pick the *Iliad* to pieces" and discover multiple authors; in his introduction he explained inconsistencies and claimed to have "re-integrated Homer as one person, or at most two."

In the *Journal of Hellenic Studies*, R. D. Williams wrote that "Dr. Rieu's *Iliad* comes very near to repeating the great success of his *Odyssey*" and achieving the qualities of "rapidity" and "plainness and directness of style" called for by Matthew Arnold, "though often rather more colloquially than one would ideally wish." Rieu "presented the banquet of Homer to a wide public, and set before them many if not all of the dishes." In the *Hudson Review*, W. Arrowsmith praised Rieu's translation for its "rapidity, clarity and accuracy," but objected that it was "frequently colloquial, and often vulgar." And, in the *Classical Weekly*, Preston H. Epps (B75) found many faults with Rieu's version as a Homeric translation, but predicted that "many Greekless readers will bless him, as well as his publishers, for having made available such a readable and readily comprehended version of Homer's timeless story and achievement, and at so reasonable a price."

As with his *Odyssey*, the Penguin edition of Rieu's *Iliad* gained immediate popularity. A revised version by Peter V. Jones and D. C. H. Rieu (see B71B) remains in print today, despite Penguin's publication of Martin Hammond's 1987 prose rendition (B43).

Arrowsmith, W. "Review: The Decade of Five Iliads." *Hudson Review* 5, no. 3 (Autumn 1952): 432–43.

Connell, P. J. "Rieu, Emile Victor (1887–1972)." *Oxford Dictionary of National Biography.*

Epps, P. H. *Classical Weekly* 45, no. 2 (November 26, 1951): 25–26.

Williams, R. D. "Review." *Journal of Hellenic Studies* 72 (1952): 161.

WITH

B36A

E. V. Rieu (1887–1972). *The Iliad.* . . . London: Metheun & Co., Ltd., 1953.

Octavo.

The first hardcover edition of E. V. Rieu's prose translation of the *Iliad.*

B37

Richmond Alexander Lattimore (1906–1984). *The Iliad of Homer.* . . . Chicago: University of Chicago Press, 1951.

Octavo.

> Sing, goddess, the anger of Peleus' son Achilleus
> and its devastation, which put pains thousandfold upon the Achaians,
> hurled in their multitudes to the house of Hades strong souls
> of heroes

Poet and classicist Richmond Lattimore first published passages from this verse translation of the *Iliad* in the 1945 anthology *War and the Poet.* In 1946, Lattimore sent an experimental version of book 1 to the University of Chicago Press; their enthusiastic reaction encouraged him to complete his translation. According to Lattimore, friends refrained from asking why he would produce yet another English version of the *Iliad*—"a question which has no answer for those who do not know the answer already." Lattimore used the 1919 edition of Monro and Allen's Oxford text (A31), attempting to "convey the meaning of the Greek in a speed and rhythm analogous to the speed and rhythm" he found in Homer's original. He translated the epic in "a free six-beat line," which, because of its irregularity, he did not consider a true hexameter—he noted in particular that his meter was much less regular than the one Smith and Miller had recently used (B34). Although Lattimore actively strove to capture Homer's rapidity, plainness, and directness, he emphasized that nobility was a "result," not a "quality to be directly striven for." He rendered Homer in "the plainest language of contemporary prose."

Lattimore's *Iliad* met with immediate success and became a standard classroom translation within a year. Production of a cheaper, paperback edition was expedited, in part at the request of Columbia University, which wanted to use it for its required core Humanities course. All Columbia freshmen still read Lattimore's *Iliad* as their first college text, and their syllabus also includes his *Odyssey* (B77). Numerous commentaries for the aid of students have been based on Lattimore's translation. Lattimore's scholarly and poetic peers also greeted the translation with enthusiastic praise. Writing for the *Classical Weekly*, Preston H. Epps (B75) "congratulated" both Lattimore and the University of Chicago Press on "this distinguished piece of work," with its "outstanding" diction and "happy turns of phrase" (although Epps found its "metrical feeling" "very slight indeed"). In the *Kenyon Review*, Robert Fitzgerald (B41, B74) called the publication of Lattimore's *Iliad* "a big event"—"it brings Homer back from the prose where he has been getting submerged," restoring him to "poetry and magnificence." Fitzgerald found the translation "as solidly distinguished" as Pope's (B9) and likely "to survive at least as long." It was a "decisive feat," and Fitzgerald foresaw "a century or so in which nobody will try again to put the Iliad into English verse" (although he would publish his own poetic version [B41] only twenty-three years later): it "succeeds in its metric as well as otherwise," and "Lattimore has written a noble English for Homer to tell his story in."

Eberhard, R. and S. Rodman. *War and the Poet: An Anthology of Poetry Expressing Man's Attitudes to War from Ancient Times to the Present.* New York: Devin-Adair, 1945.

Epps, P. H. "Review." *Classical Weekly* 46, no. 2 (November 7, 1952).

Fitzgerald, R. "Review: Heroic Poems in English." *Kenyon Review* 14, no. 4 (Autumn 1952): 698–700, 702–6.

B37

Jones, P. V. *A Commentary on Three Translations.* London: Bristol Classical Press, 2003.

Lattimore, R. "On Classical and English Poetry." *Phoenix* 6, no. 3 (Autumn 1952): 84–91.

"Literature Humanities." New York: Columbia University. http://www.college.columbia.edu/core/content/iliad (accessed March 19, 2011).

Mitgang, H. "Richard Lattimore Dead; a Classical Scholar and Poet." *New York Times*, February 28, 1984.

B38

S. O. Andrew (1868–1952) and Michael J. Oakley. *Homer's Iliad. . . .* London: Dent; New York: Dutton, 1963. *Everyman's Library*, 453.

Duodecimo.

> Sing, Goddess, the wrath of Achilles Pelëides,
> The ruinous anger that woes on the Danaans brought
> Unnumber'd

Before he died in 1952, S. O. Andrew entrusted the manuscript of this verse translation of the *Iliad* to classicist M. J. Oakley. Andrew had published a translation of the *Odyssey* (B72) and a partial rendition of the *Iliad* (B93). Classicist John Warrington wrote the volume's introduction. In his preface, Oakley called this volume "the combined work of two translators," but not a collaboration, as Andrew and Oakley never corresponded. Oakley translated books 3, 6, and 13–15, and revised the rest from Andrew's draft. He first published the work in 1955. Oakley maintained that every age has "its own idea" about translation of the classics, and "the fluidity of language" necessitates occasional retranslation. He and Andrew both aimed to provide "a literal rendering" of the *Iliad*, and to avoid the failings of earlier translations: Chapman's (B1, B6) "Elizabethan quaintness" distracts readers; Pope's (B9, B49) eighteenth-century "prejudices" encouraged omissions; ballad meter is "far from the majestic onrush of the Homeric paragraph"; and blank verse, though rapid and "capable of infinite variations," is too closely associated with Milton. For an English reader "to get a glimpse of what Homer is like, he must read something which does not remind of Milton or Pope or Tennyson or Swinburne, because Homer does not do that." In language, a translator must "steer between the Scylla of modern banality and the Charybdis of Translator's English," thus this translation's diction is removed "a few degrees from that of everyday life." The meter is adapted, "capable of remarkable flexibility and variety."

In the *Classical Review*, J. A. Davison called the meter "the most interesting feature of the new translation." "Noticeable divergences" in style emerged from the combined work, and, despite their best efforts, Andrew and Oakley had produced an edition that included many forms of "Translator's English," and "inaccuracies of which even Pope would have been ashamed."

Davison, J. A. "Review." *Classical Review* (New Series) 6, no. 3/4 (December 1956): 299.

"Mr. Samuel Andrew." *Times* (London), April 14, 1952, p. 8.

B39

Robert Graves (1895–1985). *The Anger of Achilles Homer's Iliad. . . .* Garden City, NY: Doubleday & Company, 1959.

Octavo.

Sing, MOUNTAIN GODDESS, sing through me
That anger which most ruinously
Inflamed Achilles, Peleus' son,
And which, before the tale was done,
Had glutted Hell with champions—

Writer and classical scholar Robert Graves inserted verse passages into his prose translation of the *Iliad* to set apart moments he considered particularly dramatically or religiously significant, as in the invocation above. Graves considered himself a poet and regarded his successful prose works (which also include the historical novel *I, Claudius* and a biography of T. E. Lawrence [see B69]) "the show dogs I breed and sell to support my cat." His goal in this translation was to "rescue" the *Iliad* from its "classroom curse," and to restore its value as "entertainment," following the example of the ancient Irish and Welsh storytellers who mixed poetry with their prose. Graves approved of Homeric "cribs," such as Lattimore's recent translation of the *Iliad* (B37), but he disliked all previous Homeric "*translations*," which often failed to make Homer "immediately intelligible, and therefore readable" to a general audience, and rarely attempted to "save Homer's face" by disguising his "defects"—"Paradoxically the more accurate a rendering, the less justice it does Homer."

Graves viewed the original *Iliad* as cleverly concealed political satire composed by a family guild of bards called the Homeridae. In his attempt to restore the *Iliad*'s entertainment value, Graves also attempted to reconstitute the *Iliad*'s satirical features. The illustrations by artist and cartoonist Ronald Searle added to the comedic effect. In the *Hudson Review*, G. E. Dimock (see B64A) called Searle's drawings "extremely funny—and savage"; Searle's satire was "direct and brilliant," but Graves's was "pretty poor"—"Graves goes through the poem, making everything as ridiculous as he can while still preserving some show of translating the Greek," resulting in a "violent contrast" between Homer's original and Graves's own "naughty bits." J. E. Rexine disagreed in the *Classical Journal*, characterizing Graves's translation as "certainly great entertainment," even if it was based on "some provocative presuppositions," and not "the kind of translation that a Hellenist would write to convey the real essence of Homer." Graves's *Iliad* has been reprinted many times since its first publication, including most recently in a 2008 Penguin Classics edition.

Davies, R. *Ronald Searle, a Biography*. London: Sinclair-Stevenson, 1990.

Dimock, G. E., Jr. "Review: The Iliad Rescued: Or a Mustache for Mona Lisa." *Hudson Review* 13, no. 2 (Summer 1960): 293–97.

Graves, R. *I, Claudius*. New York: Modern Library, 1934.

——. *Lawrence and the Arabian Adventure*. Garden City, NJ: Doubleday, Doran & Co., 1928.

Rexine, J. E. "Review." *Classical Journal* 57, no. 6 (March 1962): 281–82.

Saxon, W. "Robert Graves, Poet and Scholar, Dies at 90." *New York Times*, December 8, 1985.

Steiner, G. "The Genius of Robert Graves." *Kenyon Review* 22, no. 3 (Summer 1960): 340–65.

B40

Ennis Rees (1925–2009). *The Iliad of Homer. . . .* New York: Random House, 1963.

Octavo.

> Sing, O Goddess, the ruinous wrath of Achilles,
> Son of Peleus, the terrible curse that brought
> Unnumbered woes upon the Achaeans and hurled
> To Hades so many heroic souls

As in his translation of the *Odyssey* (B73), Ennis Rees strove to make this verse rendition of the *Iliad* into an English poem: he believed that "Homer is first of all a poet, a singer," and that the *Iliad* is a song of "tragic joy." In the *Classical World*, G. E. Dimock (see B64A) questioned Rees's achievement: "Unfortunately, the verse seldom or never achieves poetry." In the *Modern Language Review*, however, O. L. Wilner found Rees's edition "a treat," both "merely as a book," and as an adequate translation of the *Iliad* "for the modern reader" in "straightforward narrative verse": the "language is very direct, in true English idiom, not marred by either artificial diction or vulgarity." Rees's *Iliad* has been reprinted at least three times since its first publication, most recently in 2005 by Barnes & Noble Classics.

Dimock, G. E. "Review." *Classical World* 57, no. 5 (February 1964): 188.

Holleman, J. "Ennis Rees: USC Professor, State Poet Dies." *The State*, March 26, 2009. http://www.thestate.com/local/story/727396.html (accessed May 27, 2009).

"In Memoriam: Ennis Rees." *University of South Carolina Times*, April 9, 2009, p. 7. http://www.sc.edu/usctimes/PDFs/2009/April_9_2009.pdf (accessed March 19, 2011).

Wilner, O. L. "Review." *Modern Language Journal* 47, no. 8 (December 1963): 382–83.

B41

Robert Fitzgerald (1910–1985). *The Iliad....* Garden City, NY: Anchor Press/Doubleday, 1974.

Octavo.

> Anger be now your song, immortal one,
> Akhilleus' anger, doomed and ruinous,
> that caused the Akhaians loss on bitter loss
> and crowded brave souls into the undergloom,
> leaving so many dead men—

Robert Fitzgerald composed this blank-verse version of the *Iliad* using the same principles of direct but free poetic translation he applied in his *Odyssey* (B74). Hans Erni provided the drawings for both editions. In an interview about his translations, Fitzgerald rejected Pope's rendition of the *Iliad* (B9) for its "Roman tinge," which prevented readers from discerning "anything like the narrative and dramatic life" of the Homeric original. Fitzgerald strove to minimize the Roman and neoclassical influences on his Homeric translations by working only from the Greek texts and using as much Anglo-Saxon vocabulary as possible. In his desire to give a living voice to the Homeric works, Fitzgerald also recorded selections from both of his translations read aloud, because both epics "were originally meant to be heard and were heard."

Reviewers praised Fitzgerald's *Iliad* highly, but stopped short of declaring it superior to Pope's: in the *Hudson Review*, V. Young wrote that "Professor Fitzgerald's verse translation is the best in English *since* Pope's"; and in the *Modern Language Review*, P. Merchant pronounced Fitzgerald's version "the first *Iliad* since Pope to respond to the poetic exuberance and virtuosity of the original." Fitzgerald's *Iliad* has been through many editions and reprints, and was popular enough in schools to prompt James C. Hogan's 1979 *Guide to the "Iliad,"* an aid for students based on Fitzgerald's translation.

Fitzgerald, P. L., ed. *The Third Kind of Knowledge: Memoirs and Selected Writings of Robert Fitzgerald.* New York: New Directions Books, 1993.

Fitzgerald, R. "Two Long Engagements with Homer." *Bulletin of the American Academy of Arts and Sciences* 30, no. 4 (January 1977): 21–30.

Hogan, J. C. *A Guide to the "Iliad."* Garden City, NY: Anchor Press/Doubleday, 1979.

Honig, E. "A Conversation with Robert Fitzgerald." *MLN* 91, no. 6 (December 1976): 1572–88.

Merchant, P. "Review." *Modern Language Review* 71, no. 3 (July 1976): 617–18.

Mitgang, H. "Robert Fitzgerald, 74, Poet Who Translated the Classics." *New York Times*, January 17, 1985.

Moos, S. v., and A. Kennington. "Hans Erni and the Streamline Decade." *Journal of Decorative and Propaganda Arts* 19, Swiss Theme Issue (1993): 129–49.

Young, V. "Review: On Looking into Several Homers." *Hudson Review* 28, no. 3 (Autumn 1975): 425–32.

B42

Denison Bingham Hull (1897–1988). *Homer's Iliad. . . .* Scottsdale, AZ: [s.n.], 1982.

Octavo.

> Sing, goddess, of Achilles' ruinous anger
> which brought ten thousand pains to the Achaeans,
> and cast the souls of many stalwart heroes
> to Hades'

Like his *Odyssey* (B78), Denison Bingham Hull's privately published blank-verse translation of the *Iliad* grew out of his readings to a seventh-grade poetry class. According to Hull, we have been cut off from "our classical heritage." Hull intended his rendition, based on Monro and Allen's Oxford text (A31), "to provide a connecting link with the great literature of English."

Although Hull's versions of Homer "won favor" when "tested competitively with young people," they seem to have found less favor with scholarly critics: in the *Classical World*, J. A. Dutra deemed Hull's *Iliad* a "rather weak link" to great English literature: although "fairly accurate," the translation had "too many instances where the critical blending of verse and meaning breaks down," "too much license," and a "myriad of mechanical errors"; Dutra advises relying "upon established translations pending a re-editing of this book." Hull, however, never produced a second edition.

Dutra, J. A. "Review." *Classical World* 77, no. 2 (November–December 1983): 131.

B43

Martin Hammond (1944–). *The Iliad. . . .* Harmondsworth, Middlesex: Penguin Books; New York: Viking Penguin, 1987.

Duodecimo.

> Sing, goddess, of the anger of Achilleus, son of Peleus, the accursed anger which brought uncounted anguish on the Achaians and hurled down to Hades many mighty souls of heroes

Penguin Books commissioned classicist and headmaster Martin Hammond to write an updated prose translation of the *Iliad* for the Penguin Classics series. Both Hammond's translation and a revised edition of E. V. Rieu's 1950 Penguin rendition (B36) remain in print today. Hammond based his version on a 1920 edition of Monro and Allen's Greek text (A31). He stressed the oral nature of the *Iliad*, which he identified as the "first substantial work of European literature," with a "fair claim to be the greatest": "it may fairly be described as the cornerstone of Western civilisation." And he believed that the *Odyssey* (which he would translate thirteen years later [B84]) could easily be the work of the same author.

In the *Classical Review*, J. G. Randall called Hammond's translation "outstandingly good. . . . [A] sensitive, scholarly version in authentic English accents; to read it is to be gripped by it." Despite "occasional oddities of dialect" and "inconcinnities," its "good vernacular English echoes the plain and direct language of Homer—simple, powerful and dignified." M. S. Silk's review in *The Journal of Hellenic Studies* is less complimentary: "Penguin books have, of course, commissioned H. to do better than his best-selling predecessor, Rieu. He does better." But Hammond "can neither draw on nor create" Homer's dramatic power, and his "competent, fairly readable crib" is filled with "that self-defeating no-man's language, translation-speak."

Howard, P. "Telling a Timeless Tale." *London Times*, August 22, 1987.

Randall, J. G. "Review." *Classical Review* (New Series) 38, no. 2 (1988): 391.

Silk, M. S. "Review." *Journal of Hellenic Studies* 110 (1990): 204–5.

B44

Robert Fagles (1933–2008). *The Iliad. . . .* New York: Viking, 1990.

Octavo.

> Rage—Goddess, sing the rage of Peleus' son Achilles,
> murderous, doomed, that cost the Achaeans countless losses

Poet and classicist Robert Fagles described his verse rendition of the *Iliad* as "not a line-for-line translation," but an attempt to produce a "modern English Homer"—one that was neither "literal" enough to "cramp and distort" his own language nor "literary" enough to obstruct Homer's "energy, his forward drive." Fagles aimed at a "middle ground," both between the features of Homer's original text (Fagles used Monro and Allen's Oxford *Iliad* [A31]) and modern readers' tastes, and between the Greek dactylic hexameter and "a tighter, native English line." He translated the *Iliad* into a "flexible" meter with a five- or six-beat base that he could expand or contract. Fagles acknowledged his debt to previous translators who had "trekked across the same territory," including

Rieu (B36), Lattimore (B37), Graves (B39), Rees (B40), Hammond (B43), Logue (B96, B98–B100), and, above all, Fitzgerald (B41). He viewed both Homer and his translator as performers and insisted that there would always be room for a new translation of the *Iliad*, because "no two performances of the same work ... will ever be the same."

In a sixty-page introduction that O. Taplin in the *New York Times* called "His Master's Voice, taking the best of contemporary scholarship and giving it special point and vividness," classicist Bernard Knox, who taught Fagles in graduate school at Yale, traces the history of Homeric reception from the printing of the *editio princeps* (A1) in 1488.

Fagles's translation was enormously successful: 22,000 copies of this $35 hardcover edition had been sold by the time Fagles's *Odyssey* (B83) was published in 1996, along with 140,000 of the paperback version (then in its eighth printing), and 35,000 copies of Penguin Audiobooks' recording of Derek Jacobi reading the translation—a trend P. Gray in *Time* referred to as "the Fagles phenomenon." In the *Classical World*, L. T. Pearcy called Fagles's version "the best modern *Iliad*," "a stark and terrible poem" with "the dramatic force we need to show us the possibilities of civilization in our most horrible endeavor." D. Mason in the *Hudson Review* called it "grittier, more fiery," than previous versions, conveying the *Iliad*'s "savage grandeur, its unalloyed bitterness at human mortality" with a "narrative drive" and an "almost unmitigated violence" that "speaks to the bloody history of our century." And, after praising Fagles's translation in Matthew Arnold's terms (see D12, D13) as "plain and direct, noble, above all rapid," Taplin summed up his review of this edition by reversing Richard Bentley's critique of Pope's version (B9): "It may not be such a pretty poem, but you might well call it Homer."

Gray, P. "Scoring a Homer." *Time* 148, no. 20 (October 28, 1996).

Mason, D. "Review: Achilles in the No Man's Land." *Hudson Review* 44, no. 1 (Spring 1991): 171–75.

McGrath, C. "Robert Fagles, Translator of the Classics, Dies at 74." *New York Times*, March 29, 2008.

Murnaghan, S. "Review." *Bryn Mawr Classical Review* 02.01.05.

Pearcy, L. T. "Review." *Classical World* 85, no. 1 (September–October 1991): 52–53.

Taplin, O. "Bringing Him Back Alive." *New York Times*, October 7, 1990.

B45

Michael Reck (1928–1993). *The Iliad.* . . . New York: Icon Editions, 1994.

Octavo.

Sing, Goddess, Achilles' maniac rage:
ruinous thing! it roused a thousand sorrows
and hurled many souls of mighty warriors
to Hades

Poet Michael Reck's line-for-line verse translation of the *Iliad* "for the spoken voice" was published posthumously in the United States. Reck had published the first book of his rendition in 1972, the whole translation in Germany in 1990 (under the title *The Iliad for Speaking*), and an audio recording of books 21–22 in 1991. Following Milman Parry (see D14), Reck stressed the oral nature of Homer's poetry and emphasized that literature in Homer's time was "*heard*, not read." Modern society, according to Reck, is also "oral and aural"; a new translation must therefore be "speakable," and Reck aimed his rendition at those wishing to "enjoy Homer as his contemporaries heard him." Because there was no English equivalent for the Greek dactylic hexameter, Reck chose to use a ten-syllable iambic meter that he felt best echoed the "tautness" of Homer's line. Reck's priority as a translator was to recreate Homer's "vivid, fluid" sound, and the "simplicity," the qualities that produced the "marvelous speed," "FLOW," and "kinetic energy" Matthew Arnold had noted (see D12, D13)—"Melody is all."

In the *New York Review of Books*, H. Lloyd-Jones evaluated the 1990 edition of Reck's translation according to Arnold's terms: it "certainly moves rapidly, though its often jerky movement is very different from the fluidity of Homer"; its "Plainness and directness" are "excessive," and entail "considerable simplification"; and its "colloquialism" and even "crudity" earn it "a C" for "nobility."

Haddas, R. "Reader's Notebook: New Iliads." *New England Review* 18, no. 3 (Summer 1987): 160–72.

Lloyd-Jones, H. "Welcome Homer!" *New York Review of Books* 38, no. 4 (February 14, 1991).

Reck, M. *The Iliad for Speaking*. Breitbrunn am Ammersee, West Germany: Porpentine, 1990.

B46

Stanley Lombardo (b. 1943). *Iliad*. . . . Indianapolis; Cambridge: Hackett Publishing Company, Inc., 1997.

Octavo.

Rage:
Sing, Goddess, Achilles' rage,
Black and murderous, that cost the Greeks
Incalculable pain, pitched countless souls
Of heroes into Hades' dark

Stanley Lombardo began writing portions of this verse translation of the *Iliad* as scripts for performance ten years before he published the entire work. He described his version as "a performance on the page for the silent reader," shaped, like Homer's original, by both the dramatic and the poetic aspects of its composition. Lombardo identified himself both as a poet who aimed to convey Homer's "energy" and as a classicist who was concerned with representing "the contours" of the Greek (he used Allen and Monro's Oxford text [A31], and a six-volume commentary by G. S. Kirk). Nevertheless, his primary goal was to render the *Iliad*'s "meaning," "nuance," and "overall poetic effect," rather than the "technical features" of Homer's verse. Lombardo's project entailed bringing Homer to life by finding his "tone, rhythm, and power," and replicating his "directness, immediacy, and effortless musicality." Because a poetic diction would "embalm Homer," Lombardo chose to employ a very colloquial "modern poetics based on natural language"—which he defended as "capable of great energy and beauty" rather than "prosaic"—while indenting and italicizing similes to set them off from the rest of the text.

In the *Bryn Mawr Review*, D. L. Burgess expressed "very serious concern for an excessive 'dumbing down' of Homer's poem" in language that is sometimes "as simple and as colloquial as that heard in a check-out line" and that "sacrifices the austere diction of Homer's verse"; yet Burgess found classicist Sheila Murnaghan's introduction "superb," and praised the "spare clarity," the "easy grace and the ever-vaunted rapidity" of Lombardo's verse. In the *New York Times Book Review*, D. Mendelsohn described the cover image of the D-Day landing at Normandy as "an apt symbol for what lies within": "a vivid and sometimes disarmingly hard-bitten reworking" of the *Iliad* that respects Homer's "dire spirit"; the italicized similes represent "the dreamlike reminders of a maddeningly distant peacetime world."

Lombardo published an abridged version of this translation in 2000 along with a volume containing selections from both his *Iliad* and *Odyssey* (B85); in 2006, Parmenides Audio released recordings of Lombardo reading each published version of his translations.

Burgess, D. L. "Review." *Bryn Mawr Classical Review* 97.7.20.

Kirk, G. S. et al. *The Iliad: A Commentary*. 6 vols. Cambridge and New York: Cambridge University Press, 1985–93.

Lombardo, S. *The Essential Homer: Selections from the Iliad and the Odyssey*. Indianapolis: Hackett, 2000.

———. *The Essential Iliad*. Indianapolis: Hackett, 2000.

Mendelsohn, D. "Yo, Achilles." *New York Times Book Review*, July 20, 1997.

B47

John Ogilby (1600–1676). *Homer his Odysses*. . . . London: Printed by Thomas Roycroft, for the Author, 1665.

Folio.

That Prudent *Hero's* wandring, Muse, rehearse,
Who (*Troy* being sack'd) coasting the Universe,
Saw many Cities, and their various Modes

This translation of the *Odyssey* in rhyming heroic couplets is the second volume of the set of subscriber editions John Ogilby initiated with his 1660 *Iliad* (B7). In the preface to his 1670 *Africa*, Ogilby described the effort and expense involved in his Homeric translations: "neither sparing Cost nor Pains, to dress and set forth my own Volumns with all the Splendor and Ostentation that could be." He recouped his expenses in part through his subscribers, who were required to pay £2 on receipt of this volume (their last payment for the collection). The names, arms, and titles of Ogilby's highest paying subscribers appear on the volume's full page plates designed by Abraham van Diepenbeeck and engraved by David Loggan, Cornelis van Caukercken, Jean Meyssens, and A. Hertochs.

Ogilby lost most of his stock and possessions in the Great Fire of London in 1666, but quickly rebuilt and set up his own press in 1670. He was enormously successful as a publisher, bringing in great sums of money from his translations of Homer and from the later geographical works for which he is most famous.

Alvarez, P. "Collection Highlight: Homer's *Iliads Translated, by John Ogilby*." Rochester, NY: University of Rochester River Campus Libraries. www.library.rochester.edu/index.cfm?PAGE=4130 (accessed March 14, 2011).

Clapp, S. L. C. "The Subscription Enterprises of John Ogilby and Richard Blome." *Modern Philology* 30, no. 4 (May 1933): 365–79.

Foxon, D. *Pope and the Early Eighteenth-Century Book Trade*. Edited by J. McLaverty. Oxford: Clarendon, 1991.

Harding, R. J. D. "Hollar, Wenceslaus (1607–1677)." *Oxford Dictionary of National Biography*.

Johnson, S. *The Life of Pope*. Edited by J. Lynch. http://andromeda.rutgers.edu/~jlynch/Texts/pope.html (accessed March 14, 2011).

Ogilby, J. *Africa*. London: Printed for the Author, 1670.

Van Eerde, K. S. *John Ogilby and the Taste of His Times*. Folkestone, England: William Dawson, 1976.

Withers, C. W. J. "Ogilby, John (1600–1676)." *Oxford Dictionary of National Biography*.

B48

Thomas Hobbes (1588–1679). *Homer's Odysses . . . With a Large Preface Concerning the Vertues of an Heroique Poem. . . .* London: Printed by J. C. for W. Crook, 1675.

Duodecimo.

> Tell me, O Muse, th'Adventures of the Man
> That having sack'd the sacred Town of *Troy*,
> Wandered so long at Sea

Thomas Hobbes published this verse translation of the *Odyssey* two years before reprinting it with his translation of the *Iliad* in his complete edition of Homer's works (B2). In his 1679 Latin autobiography, Hobbes wrote that he had published his *Odyssey* at the age of 87, "when his enemies at last were silent" (*silentibus tandem adversariis*).

Hobbes's straightforward language has earned him admirers even though his poetic talent has frequently been written off. Butcher and Lang, for example, reprinted the arguments from this edition's table of contents before each book of their prose translation of the *Odyssey* (B55), a translation intended to be plain and "without ornament." And, in a new critical edition of Hobbes's *Iliad* and *Odyssey* published in 2008, E. Nelson argues that many of the deviations and omissions for which Hobbes's translations have been frequently dismissed in fact represent significant aspects of Hobbes's work—they are, according to Nelson, features of Hobbes's attempt to continue circulating his banned philosophy by reinterpreting Homer to conform to his own philosophic views.

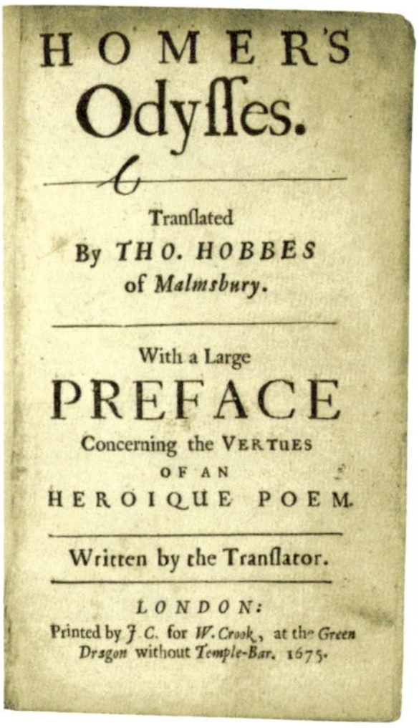
HOMERS
Odyſſes.
Tranſlated
By THO. HOBBES
of Malmsbury.
With a Large
PREFACE
Concerning the VERTUES
OF AN
HEROIQUE POEM.
Written by the Tranſlator.
LONDON:
Printed by J. C. for W. Crook, at the Green Dragon without Temple-Bar. 1675.

B48

Hobbes, T. *Thomae Hobbesii Malmesburiensis Vita.* London: By the author, 1679.

Macdonald, H., and M. Hargreaves. *Thomas Hobbes: A Bibliography.* London: Bibliographical Society, 1952.

Malcolm, N. "Hobbes, Thomas (1588–1679)." *Oxford Dictionary of National Biography.*

McKenzie, A. T. "Thomas Hobbes." *Dictionary of Literary Biography, Vol. 151: British Prose Writers of the Early Seventeenth Century.* Edited by Clayton D. Lein. Farmington Hills, MI: Gale Group, 1995.

Molesworth, W., ed. *The English Works of Thomas Hobbes of Malmesbury.* Vol. 10. London: Longman etc., 1844.

Nelson, E. *Thomas Hobbes Translations of Homer: The Iliad and the Odyssey.* Oxford: Clarendon Press, 2008.

Péti, M. *Bryn Mawr Classical Review* 2009.06.10.

Riddehough, G. G. "Thomas Hobbes' Translations of Homer." *Phoenix* 12, no. 2 (Summer 1958): 58–62.

B49

Alexander Pope (1688–1744). *The Odyssey of Homer.* London: Printed for Bernard Lintot, 1725–26.

Quarto. 5 vols.

This is a presentation copy, with *Donum Clarissimi Interpretis* (Gift of the Most Illustrious Translator) inscribed on the front free flyleaf of the first volume.

THE Man, for Wisdom's various
arts renown'd,
Long exercis'd in woes, oh Muse!
resound.

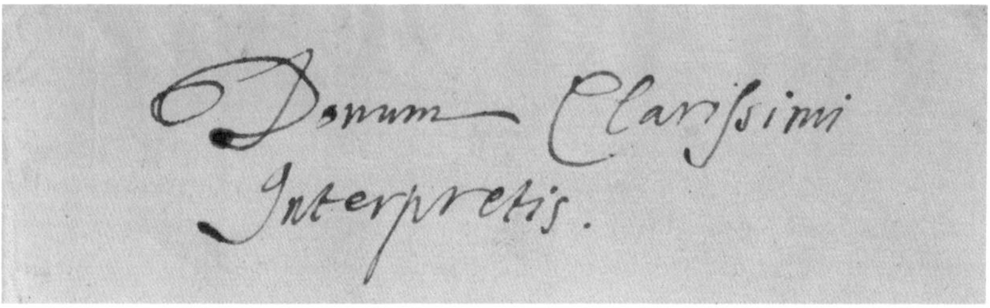

B49

Alexander Pope published his translation of the *Odyssey* in rhyming heroic couplets by subscription following the pattern of his enormously successful *Iliad* (B9). George Vertue engraved volume 1's frontispiece, and Pierre Fourdrinier engraved the numerous headpieces, tailpieces, and initial letters, which were designed by William Kent. Pope earned £4500 from the *Odyssey*'s publication. There were 610 subscribers for 1057 sets, with multiple subscriptions functioning as a kind of patronage. Pope retained some of the paid for but undelivered extra copies either to sell or to give as gifts. In his postscript, Pope warned his reader, "Whoever expects here the same pomp of verse, and the same ornaments of diction, as in the Iliad; he will, and ought to be disappointed." The *Odyssey* "is the reverse of the Iliad, in *Moral*, *Subject*, *Manner* and *Style*," a distinction Pope explored further in volume 1's introductory essay, which is based on the 1675 French exposition of René Le Bossu (D7). A large part of Pope's postscript is concerned with refuting the *Reflexions sur la Premiere Partie de la Preface de M. Pope* that the late Mme. Dacier had presented in her 1719 edition of the *Iliad* (C5), which accused Pope of striving to correct both Homer's poetry and his country's constitution. Pope responded with his firm belief that both were "the best that ever human wit invented": "Far therefore from the Genius for which Madam *Dacier* mistook me, my whole desire is but to preserve the humble character of a faithful Translator, and a quiet Subject."

Pope's *Odyssey* met with a more mixed reception than his *Iliad* had, in part because Pope had only written half of the translation himself: for the remainder he hired poets Elijah Fenton and William Broome, who had worked on the notes to Pope's *Iliad* and collaborated to produce the 1712 Ozell, Broome, and Oldisworth version (B8). Fenton translated books 1, 4, 19, and 20 for Pope's edition; Broome translated books 2, 6, 8, 11, 12, 16, 18, and 23, and wrote the notes to the whole edition. In his postscript, Pope mentioned the "assistance" "those Gentlemen who join'd with me" had provided, but Fenton and Broome's names appear nowhere in the five volumes. Fenton received £200 for his efforts; Broome received £570, which he viewed as unfair compensation for his enormous contribution to the translation. He severed connection with Pope, and their dispute resulted in public outrage. John Henley circulated an epigram on the subject: "Pope came off clean with Homer; but they say / Broome went before, and kindly swept the way."

An argument with Bernard Lintot over payment for this subscriber's edition of his *Odyssey* led Pope to switch publishers and never publish by subscription again. The translation received its own share of criticism: a debate between two characters in Joseph Spence's contemporary *Essay on Pope's Odyssey* (D8) reflects the contrasting estimations Pope's Homeric renditions have provoked ever since their publication. One character praises Pope's poetic skill and elevation, but the other observes, "Where we admire the Simplicity of *Homer* with Justice, we cannot avoid blaming the want of it in his Translator."

Barnard, J. *Alexander Pope: The Critical Heritage.* London: Routledge, 1995.

Chahoud, A. "Broome, William (*bap.* 1689, *d.* 1745)." *Oxford Dictionary of National Biography.*

Erskine-Hill, H. "Pope, Alexander (1688–1744)." *Oxford Dictionary of National Biography.*

Foxon, D. *Pope and the Early Eighteenth-Century Book Trade.* Edited by J. McLaverty. Oxford: Clarendon, 1991.

Griffith, R. H. *Alexander Pope: A Bibliography.* Austin: University of Texas Press, 1922.

Johnson, S. *The Lives of the Most Eminent English Poets.* Vols. 3–4. Edited by Roger H. Lonsdale. Oxford: Oxford University Press, 2006.

Levine, J. M. *The Battle of the Books: History and Literature in the Augustan Age.* Ithaca, NY: Cornell University Press, 1994.

Rothschild, N. M. V. *The Rothschild Library; A Catalogue of the Collection of Eighteenth-century Printed Books and Manuscripts Formed by Lord Rothschild.* No. 1588–91, p. 427. Cambridge: 1954.

Sherbo, A. "Fenton, Elijah (1683–1730)." *Oxford Dictionary of National Biography.*

Weinbrot, H. D. "Alexander Pope and Madame Dacier's *Homer*: Conjectures Concerning Cardinal Dubois, Sir Luke Schaub, and Samuel Buckley." *Huntington Library Quarterly* 62, no. 1/2 (1999): 1–23.

Williams, A. L. "Alexander Pope." *Dictionary of Literary Biography, Vol. 95: Eighteenth-Century British Poets, First Series.* Edited by John Sitter. Farmington Hills, MI: Gale Group, 1990.

B50

Theodore Alois Buckley (1825–1856). *The Odyssey of Homer, with the Hymns, Epigrams, and Battle of the Frogs and Mice....* London: Henry G. Bohn, 1851. *Bohn's Classical Library.*

Octavo.

> O Muse, sing to me of the man full of resources, who wandered very much after he had destroyed the sacred city of Troy

Theodore Alois Buckley composed this Bohn's Classical Library edition of his prose translation of the *Odyssey* "on the same plan as that of the *Iliad*, to which it forms the companion-volume." Buckley had presented his *Iliad* (B14), first published the same year, as an accurate and literal version of the Homeric epic. The *Knickerbocker* (reviewing Harper & Brothers's 1861 reprint) welcomed Buckley's literal prose rendition of the *Odyssey* as an additional resource for "intense scholarship" on Homer that demanded "something more than the standard metrical versions" that had previously been available.

"Bohn's Library and the Purchase of Books." *Gentleman's Magazine* 257 (July–December 1884): 413–14.

Knickerbocker, or New-York Monthly Magazine 57 (1861): 439.

Mew, J. "Buckley, Theodore William Alois (1825–1856)." *Oxford Dictionary of National Biography.*

B51

Philip Stanhope Worsley (1835–1866). *The Odyssey of Homer Translated Into English Verse in the Spenserian Stanza.* 3rd ed. Edinburgh and London: William Blackwood and Sons, 1877.

Octavo. 2 vols.

> Sing me, O Muse, that hero wandering,
> Who of men's minds did much experience reap,
> And knew the citied realms of many a king,
> Even from the hour he smote the Trojan keep.

This is the third edition of poet and translator Philip Stanhope Worsely's *Odyssey* in Spenserian stanzas, first published in 1861–62. Worsley aimed to convey to "the unprofessional reader" "something of what the classically educated feel in perusing Homer himself," and challenged Matthew Arnold's summary rejection of Spenser's meter for Homeric translation (see D12, D13): he saw the failure of blank-verse translations such as Cowper's (B4) as proof that unrhymed versions of epic poems could not "sustain the interest of the general reader," and argued that a rhyming meter like the Spenserian stanza, which could preserve "the charms, while veiling the blemishes of rhyme," might resemble the Homeric hexameter "in broad and general effect" and was, at any rate, "entitled to a trial." Worsley did not acknowledge that Barter had used the same meter seven years earlier in his *Iliad* (B15).

Worsley wrote his *Odyssey* "under the pressure of severe illness" and anticipated that critics would find many faults due to carelessness (he published a translation of the first twelve books of the *Iliad* in Spenserian stanzas in 1865, but died before completing the work). Contemporary critics, however, praised Worsley's translation: *Blackwood's Edinburgh Magazine* dismissed Arnold's objections to the Spenserian meter as "not warranted either in theory or by facts," and wrote that Worsley "has judged rightly ... to choose a metre familiar to the ears of all readers of the *Faery Queen* as already consecrated to the English Epic"; and, although it pointed out the "trammels of an intricate rhyming stanza," the *Edinburgh Review* applauded Worsley for having "produced a work which, having caught the spirit of the poem, can delight those to whom the original is a sealed book."

Garnett, R. "Worsley, Philip Stanhope (1835–1866)." *Oxford Dictionary of National Biography*.

The Odyssey of Homer, translated into English Verse in the Spenserian Stanza. By Philip Stanhope Worsley, M. A., Scholar of Corpus Christi College, Oxford. Two Volumes. Edinburgh and London: 1861–2." *Edinburgh Review* 117 (January–April 1863): 353–60.

"Translations of the Odyssey." *Blackwood's Edinburgh Magazine* 91 (January-June 1862): 345–59.

B52

George Musgrave (1798–1883). *The Odyssey of Homer Rendered Into English Blank Verse....* 2nd ed. London: Bell and Daldy, 1869.

Octavo. 2 vols.

Each volume contains a tipped-in slip reading "With the author's compliments."

Of that sagacious chief, in many a clime
A wanderer, when his victorious might
Had laid Troy's holy city in the dust,
Inform me, Muse

George Musgrave first published this blank-verse translation of the *Odyssey* in 1865, after he had retired from the clergy and turned to travel writing. Musgrave noted that the *Odyssey*, which he considered a "Nautical Romance," had suffered from particular neglect in the early part of nineteenth century, when the renditions of Chapman (B1), Pope (B49), and Cowper (B4) had been accepted as standard versions, and the "taste" for the classics in general had become "extinct."

The slew of new translations in the middle of the century demonstrated a revival of interest in the classics, which Musgrave attributed to the emergence of "a new Intellectual Fraternity" of "Middle-Class scholars," a "*novus ordo* in the literary commonwealth," seeking "to form familiar acquaintance, not only with the Philosopher but also with the Poets." Musgrave's translation offers an "introduction to primitive Greek Verse" that strives for "fidelity" and "usefulness." In his attempt "to construe the text honestly" and convey its "general spirit," Musgrave produced a translation of the *Odyssey* even more expansive than Chapman's lengthy edition.

In his preface to this second edition, Musgrave acknowledged the "judicious criticism" that had enabled him to emend his translation, much of which seems to have been focused on length: the *Gentleman's Magazine* ascribed Musgrave "very great credit on every score, except that of terseness. . . . He is simple and straightforward; is fond of plain sterling Saxon-English, and while using metaphors is always forcible and scholarlike." However, the *Fortnightly Review* found faults throughout that "disfigure" the translation—"a perversion of the natural order of the words, too great diffuseness, and a want of simplicity of expression."

Courtney, W. P. "Musgrave, George Musgrave (1798–1883)." Rev. Elizabeth Baigent. *Oxford Dictionary of National Biography*.

Havens, R. D. *The Influence of Milton on English Poetry*. Cambridge: Harvard University Press, 1922.

"Homer and His Translators." *Gentleman's Magazine* 220 (January-June 1866): 97–105.

Vardy, A. R. "Critical Notices." *Fortnightly Review* 3 (November 15, 1865-February 1, 1866): 521–24.

B53

George William Edginton. *The Odyssey of Homer: Translated Into Blank Verse. . . .* London: Longman, Green, Reader, & Dyer; Reading: Barcham & Beecroft, 1869.

Octavo. 2 vols. in 1.

The BHL copy contains a list of subscribers, including Edward, Earl of Derby (B18) and William Ewart Gladstone (D11), and a price list for the edition bound in either one or two volumes. It also reprints a letter with the Prince of Wales's acceptance of the translation.

> Sing, Muse, of that deep man, who wander'd much,
> When he had raz'd the walls of sacred Troy,
> And many towns saw, many customs learnt,
> And many griefs endur'd upon the sea

The title page of this blank-verse rendition of the *Odyssey* identifies the translator, George William Edginton, Esq., of Reading, as a "Licentiate in Medicine." Edginton published his translation with a dedication to Lord Derby (B18), as well as extracts from letters indicating Lord Derby's acceptance of the dedication and subscription for three copies of the volume. In "deference" to Lord Derby's *Iliad*, Edginton had "laid aside" his own English version of that epic (Lord Derby had no intention of translating the *Odyssey*, which he found "'not so well adapted to Blank Verse'"). Edginton sought to produce a rendition of the *Odyssey* that was "truthful to the original, rather than a poetical parody," and was composed with "a clearness of expression" that would make it "intelligible to all." He first translated Homer's text into English hexameters, and then "re-translated" it into blank verse, abridging his version to preserve it as a line-for-line translation without lengthening the total number of lines of English verse, "which would have diluted the spirit of the poetry."

In a review reprinted in this volume, the *Reading Mercury* praised Edginton for his "faithfulness in rendering"; and the *American Literary Gazette* called Edginton's *Odyssey* "a nearly literal version." The *Westminster Review*, however, found Edginton's translation unsuccessful: it is "a bald, spiritless, and monotonous version," with a "very wearisome" meter and a "pedestrian, and even slipshod" style. The present-day obscurity of both the translation and its author suggests that the editors of the *Westminster Review* may have presented the more widespread assessment.

Ditchfield, P. H. *The Literature and Writers of the Reading District.* Read at the Annual Meeting of the Library Association, Reading, 1890. http://library.oxfordjournals.org.proxy.uchicago.edu/cgi/reprint/s1-2/1/401 (accessed March 19, 2011).

"Notes on Books and Booksellers." *American Literary Gazette and Publishers' Circular* 13, no. 10 (Septemper 15, 1869): 296.

Reading Mercury, January 30, 1869.

Westminster Review (New Series) 36 (July & October 1869): 644.

B54

William Cullen Bryant (1794–1878). *The Odyssey of Homer Translated Into English Blank Verse.* Boston: James R. Osgood and Company, 1871.

Quarto. 2 vols.

Tell me, O Muse, of that sagacious man
Who, having overthrown the sacred town
Of Ilium, wandered far and visited
The capitals of many nations

William Cullen Bryant attributed his publication of this blank-verse rendition of the *Odyssey* to the "kind reception" his "countrymen" had accorded his *Iliad* (B22) one year before.

Bryant, who was seventy-seven when this translation was published, found translating Homer "a not unpleasing employment" for his old age, when he could not "many times more appear before the public in this or any other manner." According to Bryant, a translator is "spared the labor of invention": he expresses ideas but is not required to produce them.

Contemporary critics' praise for Bryant's *Odyssey* echoed his *Iliad*'s acclaim: the *Atlantic Monthly* applauded its "fidelity to the text; genuine simplicity of thought and style; successful transfusion of the heroic spirit; above all, a purity of language which is . . . a continual refreshment to the healthy-minded reader."

Bradley, W. A. *William Cullen Bryant.* New York: Macmillan, 1905.

Muller, G. H. *William Cullen Bryant: Author of America.* Albany: State University of New York Press, 2008.

"Recent Literature." *Atlantic Monthly* 29 (May 1872): 619–24.

Tomlinson, D. "William Cullen Bryant." *Dictionary of Literary Biography, Vol. 3: Antebellum Writers in New York and the South.* Edited by Joel Myerson. Farmington Hills, MI: Gale Group, 1979.

B55

S. H. Butcher (1850–1910) and Andrew Lang (1844–1912). *The Odyssey of Homer Done Into English Prose.* London: Macmillan and Co., 1879.

Octavo.

> Tell me, Muse, of that man, of many a shift, who wandered
> far and wide, after he had sacked the sacred citadel of Troy

This prose translation of the *Odyssey* by professor and classicist Samuel Henry Butcher and poet, anthropologist, and classicist Andrew Lang was such an immediate success that a second edition was published within a year. In their preface, Butcher and Lang argued that "of Homer there can be no final translation." Each rendition of the Homeric epics reflects the tastes and preferences of its times—"As transcripts of Homer they are like pictures drawn from a lost point of view." Chapman's translations (B1, B6) reveal the "daring and luxurious conceits" of his age; Pope's works (B9, B49) are filled with the "dazzling rhetoric . . . antitheses . . . *netteté* . . . artifice" that his contemporaries embraced; Gladstone's commentaries (D11) and many ballad-style renditions were written "when Europe woke to a sense . . . of the value of her songs of the people"; and Worsley's *Odyssey* (B51) betrays the "romantic style" of his times. No English version of

Homer can represent all that the original contains—Butcher and Lang's prose translation attempts to "transfer, not all the truth about the poem, but the historical truth," which is "the half of the truth" verse translators lose by constantly "adding" to the original tale. The *Odyssey*, according to Butcher and Lang, is an epic similar to the Nordic sagas, and, as such, it is a historical document. They tried to present it to the English reader that way, "without modern ornament, with nothing added or omitted," in a diction "old and plain." The arguments in their edition are taken from Hobbes's translation (B48).

Butcher and Lang's translation was extremely well received: the *American Journal of Philology* wrote that "for many years there will be no prose version that can rival this," and the *Contemporary Review* stated: "we cannot speak too highly of the great boon conferred" by "a work replete with matter for scholars, and yet calculated to simplify for English readers the perennial charm and fascination of the most delightful of maritime epics." The translation became a standard work in the classroom and was the version James Joyce read when he wrote his *Ulysses*. It was reprinted multiple times through the late twentieth century and often bound with Lang, Leaf, and Myers's translation of the *Iliad* (B24) in editions of Homer's complete works in prose.

American Journal of Philology 1 (1880): 466–68.

Calkins, R. W. "Andrew Lang." *Dictionary of Literary Biography, Vol. 98: Modern British Essayists, First Series.* Edited by Robert Beum. Farmington Hills, MI: Gale Group, 1990.

Contemporary Review 35 (April–August 1879): 943–53.

Green, R. L. *Andrew Lang: A Critical Biography with a Short-title Bibliography of the Works of Andrew Lang.* Leicester, England: Edmund Ward, 1946.

Lang, A., S. Butcher, W. Leaf, et al. *The Homeric Stories Iliad and Odyssey.* Chautauqua, NY: Chautauqua Press, 1905.

Quarterly Review 147 (January & April 1879): 533–51.

Schork, R. J. *Greek and Hellenic Culture in Joyce.* Gainesville: University Press of Florida, 1998.

B56

Sir George Augustus Schomberg (1821–1907). *The Odyssey of Homer, Rendered Into English Verse.* London: John Murray, 1879–82.

Octavo. 2 vols.

Sing Muse the hero versatile, who roved
So far, so long, after he overthrew
Troy's holy citadel; of many men
He saw the cities, and their manners learned

General George Augustus Schomberg, officer of the Marine Artillery, wrote this blank-verse translation of the *Odyssey* despite his awareness that "blank Iambics can hardly give the picturesque variety, and broken light and shadow of the Homeric Hexameter of the Odyssey." He attempted, though, "faithfulness to the original," which he believed "the additional burden of rhyme" would prevent in the translation of so long a poem. In his brief preface, General Schomberg gave no indication of his motives in undertaking this translation.

Contemporary reviewers were puzzled that he would devote his leisure time to such a task and attributed the work to the fascination that the *Odyssey* must hold for maritime men. Their reviews of General Schomberg's translation, however, were positive: the *Quarterly Review* praised its "explicit, simple, and withal spirited style," along with its "unvarnished and unexaggerated" rendering of the tale.

Contemporary Review 35 (April–August 1879): 943–53.

Quarterly Review 147 (January & April 1879): 533–51.

B57

Arthur S. Way (1847–1930). *The Odyssey of Homer in English Verse....* 3rd ed. London: Macmillan and Co., Limited, 1904.

Octavo.

This copy bears an embossed "Presentation Copy" stamp on its title page.

> The Hero of craft-renown, O Song-goddess, chant me his fame,
> Who, when low he had laid Troy-town, unto many a far land came
> And many a city beheld he, and knew the hearts of their folk

This is the third edition of Arthur S. Way's rhyming verse translation of the *Odyssey*, first published in 1880 under the pseudonym "Avia" (for A. Way). As in his *Iliad* (B26), Way used William Morris's six-foot iambic and anapestic meter (see B59). Way desired to "remove all traces of carelessness, and of undue licence in rhyme, and to bring the version closer to the original"—his "fire of enthusiasm," "intense concentration," and "great speed" had led to defects in the language and meter of his earlier versions.

Despite the faults Way was attempting to correct here, critics applauded his translation at its first publication: whereas the *British Quarterly Review* found "lapses into roughness and inversion—due in great part to the very nature of the metre," the *London Quarterly Review* wrote that "it shows power as well as grace and literalness. . . . [H]is work is not a paraphrase but a real translation, very literal and yet full of poetic beauty."

British Quarterly Review 82, no. 166 (April 1886): 472.

London Quarterly Review 55 (October 1880 & January 1881): 486–90.

"Review: Way's Odyssey." *Classical Review* 20, no. 1 (February 1906): 60–61.

"Way, Arthur Sanders." *Everyman's Dictionary of Literary Biography, English & American.* 3rd ed. Edited by D. C. Browning. New York: Dutton, 1962.

B58

George Herbert Palmer (1842–1933). *The Odyssey of Homer.* . . . Boston and New York: Houghton, Mifflin and Company, 1891.

Octavo.

This is a presentation copy inscribed "with kindest regards of G. H. Palmer."

> Speak to me, Muse, of the adventurous man who wandered long after he sacked the sacred citadel of Troy.

Harvard professor George Herbert Palmer wrote this translation of the *Odyssey* in "the veracious language" of prose instead of in "the dream language" of poetry. He strove to maintain "a simple rhythm," while achieving the following "alluring and impossible" aims: giving Homer's thought "a more direct and simple expression" than previous translators had; staying "minutely faithful" to the Greek and concealing "the fact that either an original or a translator exists"; presenting "the objective, unreflective, realistic, and non-literary features of the primitive story"; reporting "in all their delicacy the events which Homer reports"; and discarding "originality" in wording "to make free use of the fortunate phrases of preceding translators." Palmer had previously published the first twelve books of his translation (B58A); this first complete edition includes a revised version of that rendition.

Palmer's translation of the *Odyssey* was inevitably compared with Butcher and Lang's popular recent prose version (B55). M. L. D'Ooge in the *Dial* found the Butcher and Lang rendition "more picturesque," "more 'noble,'" and "more 'direct,'" but called Palmer's work "a true boon to English readers, who will not fail to get from his version a consciousness of the Homeric fire and spirit"—Palmer's translation was "eminently satisfactory" in its "rhythmic flow and cadence suggestive of the original effect of the poetry as recited," and "would enlarge the circle of admirers of the old Greek epic."

D'Ooge, M. L. "The Odyssey in English Prose." *Dial: A Monthly Journal of Current Literature* 12 (May 1891–April 1892) [September 1891 ed.]: 143–44.

Hocking, W. E. "George Herbert Palmer (1842–1933)." *Proceedings of the American Academy of Arts and Sciences* 69, no. 13 (February 1935): 533–35.

B58A

George Herbert Palmer (1842–1933). *The Odyssey of Homer Books I.–XII. The Text, and an English Version in Rhythmic Prose.* Boston: Houghton, Mifflin and Company, 1884.

Octavo.

> Tell me, O Muse, of an adventurous man who wandered
> far, when he had overthrown the sacred hold of Troy.

This edition contains George Herbert Palmer's first attempt at translating the first twelve books of the *Odyssey* into prose. The facing Greek text is edited by W. Walter Merry (A29). Palmer admired Homer's "peculiar psychology, his unique ethical attitude," and turned to Homer "to escape from our complicated and introspective world." He began this translation while he was teaching Greek twelve years earlier, with "no thought of publication"—he translated the first book to his students in one sitting in an attempt to give them a sense of the poem "as a piece of literature." Palmer sought to draw attention to Homer's "simplicity, his realism, his finding joy where a child finds it . . . his lack of self-consciousness," and to imitate the qualities of Homer "which characterize the speech of an eager, healthy, sensitive child." He was critical of his own skills as a translator, and did not intend to produce a translation of the second half of the poem: "I print these twelve Books (I have no intention of publishing more) in the hope of stimulating some one more skilful and scholarly than I to try what may be done here." But when this partial translation appeared, the *Critic* proclaimed that "Professor Palmer must abandon his idea of stopping at the twelfth book, and give us the whole."

Critic (New Series) 2, no. 46 (November 15, 1884): 231–32.

B59

William Morris (1834–1896). *The Odyssey of Homer Done Into English Verse.* London: Reeves & Turner, 1887.

Quarto. 2 vols.

This copy bears the the bookplate of Herbert John Gladstone, son of William Gladstone (see D11).

> Tell me, O Muse, of the Shifty, the man who wandered afar,
> After the Holy Burg, Troy-town, he had wasted with war

Before he published this translation of the *Odyssey* in rhyming anapaestic couplets, writer and designer William Morris wrote, "My translation is a real one so far, not a mere periphrase [sic] of the original as *all* the others are." Alongside his various artistic and literary pursuits, Morris was a student of Norse and Icelandic history and mythology. He based his own narrative poem about Norse wanderers at sea, *The Earthly Paradise*, on both classical and Norse literature. In the 1880s, Morris became involved in revolutionary socialist politics and joined the Democratic Federation. During this time of what Morris referred to as "the pernicious practice of what may be called professional agitation," he wrote this translation of the *Odyssey*, which he described in his letters as "very amusing: and a great rest from the other work." Morris began in 1886 and had published both volumes by the end of 1887. He frequently consulted Buckley's prose rendition (B50). Morris developed the translation's meter—which, like Chapman's fourteeners (B1), was long enough to accommodate the Homeric hexameter—for his narrative poem *The Story of Sigurd the Volsung and the Fall of the Niblungs*. Arthur Way had recently adapted it for his own Homeric translations (B26, B57).

Reviews of Morris's *Odyssey* were mixed: in two reviews for the *Academy*, E. D. A. Morshead wrote: "There are many translations of the *Odyssey*, and several good ones; but time has brought us the best, from Mr. Morris"; it has the "most of the matter and the manner of the original." But many critics felt that Morris's translation was too heavily influenced by his interest in Icelandic literature. *MacMillan's Magazine* wrote that Morris had "fallen back on translations or imitations of ancient Icelandic expressions," was "archaistic," and had used a meter that forced him "to fill out his lines often with uncalled-for words" ("An English Homer should not need notes explanatory of the English"). The *Standard* described Morris's translation as "the Odyssey as seen through Scandinavian spectacles. That is ... he gave us the poem as if it had reached him through the Eddas of the Viking age."

Faulkner, P., ed. *William Morris: The Critical Heritage*. London: Routledge, 1996.

Forman, H. B. *The Books of William Morris,* 126. London: Frank Hollings, 1897.

Goodwin, K. L. "William Morris." *Dictionary of Literary Biography, Vol. 35: Victorian Poets After 1850,* 138–57. Edited by William E. Fredeman and Ira B. Nadel. Farmington Hills, MI: Gale Group, 1985.

Lindsay, J. *William Morris: His Life and Work*. London: Constable, 1975.

MacCarthy, F. "Morris, William (1834–1896)." *Oxford Dictionary of National Biography*.

Mackail, J. W. *The Life of William Morris.* London & New York: Longmans, Green, and Co., 1898.

Morris, W. *The Earthly Paradise*. London: F. S. Ellis, 1868–70.

———. *Story of Sigurd the Volsung and the Fall of the Niblungs*. London: Ellis and White, 1876.

Morshead, E. D. A. *Academy* 31 (April 1887): 299.

———. *Academy* 33 (March 1888): 143–44.

"Mr. Morris's 'Odyssey.'" *MacMillan's Magazine* 56 (May–October 1887): 130–35.

Riddehough, G. "William Morris's Translation of the Odyssey." *Journal of English and Germanic Philology* 40 (1941): 558–61.

Scott, T. *A Bibliography of the Works of William Morris.* London: George Bell and Sons, 1897.

Standard, cited in A. Vallance. *William Morris, His Art, His Writings, and His Public Life*, p. 212. London: George Bell and Sons, 1897.

Vallance, A. *William Morris, His Art, His Writings, and His Public Life.* London: George Bell and Sons, 1897.

B60

John Graham Cordery (1833–1900). *The Odyssey of Homer.* London: Methuen & Co., 1897.

Octavo.

> Sing through my lips, O Goddess, sing the man
> Resourceful, who, storm-buffeted far and wide,
> After despoiling of Troy's sacred tower,
> Beheld the cities of mankind, and knew
> Their various temper!

John Graham Cordery published this blank-verse translation of the *Odyssey* twenty-seven years after the publication of his *Iliad* (B25). His preface, which analyses the plotlines of the *Odyssey* and identifies a main narrative framework interwoven by "consummate art" with elements that "belong to a very early stratum of folk-lore," shows the influence of Andrew Lang's scholarship (see B24 and B55). Cordery used the notes and commentaries of Henry Hayman and W. Walter Merry (A29). He believed that, despite its origins in folklore, the *Odyssey* was not a popular ballad, but "as remarkable an example of dramatic power as exists in the range of all literature." Cordery attempted to convey this dramatic power through "a spontaneous rhythm with sufficient rise and fall in it," and a translation "as literal and as close to the original as a thorough substitution of English for Greek grammar and idiom will allow." He rejected "mock-archaic diction" as antithetical to the spirit of the Greek text. Cordery hoped that his translation could extend "the knowledge of a noble poet amongst the ever-widening circle of English readers who have never acquired the Greek tongue."

The *Manchester Guardian* questioned whether there were any other translation "from which a more accurate knowledge of the original can be gathered with greater pleasure, at least of those that are in metre."

"Books of the Week." *Manchester Guardian*, December 11, 1897.

"Cordery, John Graham (1833–1900)." *Dictionary of Indian Biography*, 94. London: Swan Sonnenschein & Co., 1906.

Hayman, H. *The Odyssey of Homer*. London: D. Nutt, 1866.

Nation 66 (January-June 1898): 210.

B61

Samuel Butler (1835–1902). *The Odyssey Rendered Into English Prose. . . .* London: A. C. Fifield, [1900?].

Octavo.

The BHL copy contains the signature of the Irish classicist Benjamin Farrington.

> Tell me, oh Muse, of that ingenious hero who travelled
> far and wide after he had sacked the famous town of Troy.

Samuel Butler intended this prose translation of the *Odyssey*, first published in 1900 by Longmans, Green, and Co. in London, as a supplement to *The Authoress of the "Odyssey," Where and When She Wrote, Who She Was, the Use She Made of the "Iliad," and How the Poem Grew under Her Hands*. In his introduction to this edition, Butler reaffirmed that work's controversial theories: that the *Odyssey* was written by a young woman borrowing heavily from the *Iliad*; that this authoress introduced herself into the poem as the character Nausicaa; and that she lived in Trapani on the western coast of Sicily and situated the *Odyssey*'s events near that location. Butler followed the same principles of translation in this version of the *Odyssey* as he did in his *Iliad* (B29), defending the translator's liberty and aiming above all at modern, readable prose.

In the *Classical Review*, F. M. Cornford wrote that Butler's *Odyssey* had "no pretence to accuracy or to scholarship, and can hardly be called a translation." Cornford thought that Butler's scholarly views were not even worth disputing, and suggested that his theory of female authorship was nothing more than "a joke, a satire upon the sex." Thirty-four years later, J. W. Mackail (B62) summed up the fate of the *Odyssey* of "that distorted genius, Samuel Butler": "That version, or perversion, fell dead."

Breuer, H.-P. "Butler, Samuel." *Dictionary of Literary Biography, Vol. 57: Victorian Prose Writers After 1867*. Edited by William B. Thesing. Farmington Hills, MI: Gale Group, 1987.

Butler, S. *The Authoress of the "Odyssey."* London & New York: Longmans, Green, 1897.

Cornford, F. M. "Review: Butler's Translation of the Odyssey." *Classical Review* 15, no. 4 (May 1901): 221–22.

Farrington, B. *Samuel Butler and the Odyssey*. London: Cape, 1929.

Hoppé, A. J. *A Bibliography of the Writings of Samuel Butler*. London: Bookman, 1925.

Jones, H. F. *Samuel Butler: Author of 'Erewhon' (1835–1902), a Memoir.* London: Macmillan, 1919.

Mackail, J. W. "The Aircraftsman's Odyssey." *Classical Review* 49, no. 6 (December 1935): 219–20.

Raby, P. *Samuel Butler: A Biography.* Iowa City: University of Iowa Press, 1991.

Shaffer, E. "Butler, Samuel (1835–1902)." *Oxford Dictionary of National Biography.*

B62

J. W. Mackail (1859–1945). *The Odyssey Translated in Verse.* Oxford: Clarendon Press, 1932.

Octavo.

> O Muse, record for me the man who drew
> His changeful course through wanderings not a few
> After he sacked the holy town of Troy,
> And saw the cities and the counsel knew
> Of many men

Writer and classicist John William Mackail first published this translation of the *Odyssey* in a rhyming quatrain in three installments between 1903 and 1910; those editions were no longer in print when Mackail published this revised single-volume version. Mackail, who had been a student of Evelyn Abbott at Oxford (see B27), had written a biography of William Morris that questioned whether Morris's *Odyssey* (B59) was successful as a Homeric translation. He concluded that, if it "has not become the standard English version, it is only because that place still remains empty." For his own translation of the *Odyssey*, Mackail chose the Persian *Rubáiyát*, a quatrain meter made famous by Edward Fitzgerald in his 1859 *Rubáiyát of Omar Khayyám.* Mackail claimed he had not read Fitzgerald's work when he decided to use the meter, which he found best suited for translating Homer because it was "capable of the largest variation of pause and elasticity of musical phrasing," and able to reproduce both "the modulation of the Homeric verse" and its "combination of leisureliness and rapidity." The *Rubáiyát* could "carry the reader on, to some degree at least, as he is carried on by Homer himself."

A translation, according to Mackail, is "a continuous commentary" representing "so much of the total impression made by the original on the translator as he can succeed in conveying." Mackail intended his translation both for those who had never read the *Odyssey*—to introduce them to "one of the best stories in the world as well as one of the greatest achievements of human genius"—and for scholars—to reinforce "their appreciation of Homer, alike on broad lines of construction and in continuous quality of texture."

At the first publication of Mackail's *Odyssey*, the *Classical Review* wrote, "However improbable it may have seemed that the quatrain would prove a satisfactory form for a rendering of Homer, it must be admitted that this version is a success." At the appearance of this edition twenty years later, it declared that Mackail had placed "both the scholar and the general reader under a deep obligation." The *Classical Journal* called Mackail's translation "a notable achievement of classical scholarship combined with fine literary taste" that deserved "a place among the standard translations."

Bailey, C. "Mackail, John William (1859–1945)." Rev. Richard Smail. *Oxford Dictionary of National Biography.*

Clark, F. L. "Review." *Classical Journal* 28, no. 7 (April 1933): 544–46.

Fitzgerald, E. *Rubáiyát of Omar Khayyám.* London: B. Quaritch, 1859.

Forster, E. S. "Review." *Classical Review* 46, no. 5 (November 1932): 203–4.

Goldfarb, S. "FitzGerald , Edward (1809–1883)." *Oxford Dictionary of National Biography.*

Mackail, J. W. *The Life of William Morris.* London & New York: Longmans, Green, and Co., 1898.

"Review." *Classical Review* 26, no. 2 (March 1912): 67–68.

"Review." *Greece & Rome* 2, no. 6 (May 1933): 188–89.

B63

H. B. Cotterill (1846–1924). *Homer's Odyssey A Line-For-Line Translation in the Metre of the Original. . . .* London: George G. Harrap & Company, 1911.

Quarto.

This copy contains a tipped-in presentation inscription "To Her Royal Highness Princess Mary with most respectful congratulations from the Translator," dated February 15, 1922. It also contains the bookplate of Princess Mary, whose marriage to Viscount Lascelles took place thirteen days after the date of the inscription.

> Sing, O Muse, of the man so wary and so wise, who in far lands
> Wandered whenas he had wasted the sacred town of the Trojans.

Geographer Henry Bernard Cotterill first conceived of writing this hexameter translation of the *Odyssey* on an expedition to central Africa: "while exploring the unknown regions and navigating the storm waters of Nyasa I re-read the Wanderings of Odysseus with an interest very different." Cotterill longed to reproduce Homer's "simplicity," "directness," and "rapidity," which were "scarcely discernible" in other verse renditions. Frequently consulting Butcher and Lang's prose translation (B55), Cotterill wrote most of his *Odyssey* while wandering in the Swiss mountains. British illustrator Patten Wilson provided this sumptuous edition's full-page illustrations. Cotterill intended his *Odyssey* to act as "a good conductor for transmitting some of the vibration, the warmth and the impetuosity of the poem," so that the Greekless might be able to "experience something of the same pleasure as those feel who can read the original."

Cotterill's choice of diction and meter reflects this aim: he used "the most accurate imitation" of dactylic hexameter consistent with language that is "natural, simple, vigorous, direct" rather than "affected, quaint, archaic, 'literary,' 'poetical.'" He viewed rhyme as un-Greek and "essentially alien to Homer," necessitating "paraphrase," and ballad-meter as "still more alien," associated with what is "very prosaic, very banal." Blank verse, which has an "upward motion," contrasts with hexameter's "downward rush" and requires "wholesale recasting." Worsely's Spenserian stanzas (B51) grow "wearisome" in Homer's long narrative.

The *Quarterly Review* approved of Cotterill's choice of the English hexameter, observing "There is something 'catchy' about it"; and the *Classical Weekly* wrote that Cotterill "far surpassed in smoothness" both Dart (B17) and Herschel's (B20) hexameters, and called this edition "a truly sumptuous volume, superbly printed and charmingly illustrated"; the reviewer regretted only that it was "rather too costly to have the general circulation it deserves."

"Greek Poetry in English Verse." *Quarterly Review* 224 (July & October 1915): 297–327.

Haufe, S. "Patten Wilson." *The Dictionary of 19th Century British Book Illustrators and Caricaturists.* Woodbridge: Antique Collectors' Club, 1996.

Kirk, J. F. *A Supplement to Allibone's Critical Dictionary of English Literature.* 1891.

"Obituary." *Times*, July 28, 1924, p. 14.

"Obituary: H. B. Cotterill." *Geographical Journal* 65, no. 1 (January 1925): 86–87.

Omond, T. S. "Review." *Modern Language Review* 7, no. 2 (April 1912): 257–62.

Yeames, H. H. "Review." *Classical Weekly* 5, no. 18 (March 9, 1912): 142–43.

B64

A. T. Murray (1866–1940). *The Odyssey. . . .* London: William Heinemann; New York: G. P. Putnam's Sons, 1919. *Loeb Classical Library.*

Duodecimo. 2 vols.

> Tell me, O Muse, of the man of many devices, who wandered
> full many ways after he had sacked the sacred citadel of Troy.

Stanford University classics professor A. T. Murray published this prose translation of the *Odyssey* as part of the Loeb Classical Library, a series of classical translations with facing Greek and Latin texts founded by James Loeb in 1911 to revive interest in the classics in "an age when the humanities are being neglected more perhaps than at any other time since the Middle Ages and when men's minds are turning more than ever before to the practical and the material." W. H. D. Rouse (see B33, B70), one of the series' editors, wrote that the volumes were meant to provide "the right use of leisure" for those whose work was now being performed by newly invented machines: "They will not earn you one shilling of money, or build one electric tram; but they will fill your mind with wisdom and beauty." *Classical Weekly* greeted the forthcoming series as "a publication of magnificent promise for the higher things of the mind," and the *Classical Journal* wrote that "It will give the greatest impetus . . . to classical interests since the invention of printing and the spreading broadcast of classical texts in the late years of the fifteenth century."

Murray also contributed translations of the *Iliad* (B31) and the private orations of Demosthenes to the Loeb Classical Library. He viewed the *Odyssey* as "the work of one supreme artist"—modern "analytic and destructive" scholarship attacking the unity of the Homeric epics was "plainly without historic worth." Murray's aim was "to give a faithful rendering of the *Odyssey* that preserves in so far as possible certain traits of the style of the original"; such a translation should be "smooth and flowing . . . in elevated but not stilted language," and should retain all recurring lines and phrases. In *Classical Philology*, G. Misener praised Murray's translation for reflecting "the epic simplicity and dignity," "composure," "swiftness," "order," "conventional epithet," and "ease" of Homer's original.

Hansen, H. D., J. P. Mitchell, W. D. Briggs, et al. "Memorial Resolution, Augustus Taber Murray (1866-1940)." Stanford: Academic Council of Stanford University. http://histsoc.stanford.edu/pdfmem/MurrayA.pdf (accessed March 18, 2011).

"The Loeb Classical Library." *Classical Weekly* 5, no. 16 (February 17, 1912): 126–27.

"Loeb Classical Library: The History." Cambridge: Harvard University Press. http://www.hup.harvard.edu/features/loeb/history.html (accessed March 18, 2011).

Miller, J. "The Loeb Classical Library." *Classical Journal* 8, no. 6 (March 1913): 269–71.

Misener, G. "Review." *Classical Philology* 16, no. 4 (October 1921): 402.

Rouse, W. H. D. "Machines or Mind?" *Classical Weekly* 6, no. 11 (January 11, 1913): 82–86.

WITH

B64A

A. T. Murray (1866–1940). *The Odyssey. . . .* Cambridge: Harvard University Press, 1995. *Loeb Classical Library,* 104–5.

> Tell me, Muse, of the man of many devices, driven far astray
> after he had sacked the sacred citadel of Troy.

This revised Loeb Classical Library edition of A. T. Murray's prose version of the *Odyssey* includes a new introduction, notes, and index, and an updated translation. Classicist George E. Dimock wrote in his preface that although "no more faithful translation of Homer was ever made, and its elegance matched its fidelity," modern readers had "different expectations." Thus Dimock revised Murray's translation "to preserve its excellences while bringing all that sounds unnatural into line with today's canons of English." In the *Classical Review*, A. F. Garvie called Murray's translation more "consistently accurate" than many more modern renditions and praised Dimock for performing "a valuable service" by "translating M.'s translation into more modern English."

Garvie, A. F. "Review." *Classical Review* (New Series) 46, no. 2 (1996): 366.

B65

Francis Caulfeild (1843–1934). *The Odyssey . . . in the Original Metre.* . . . London: G. Bell and Sons, Ltd., 1923. *Bohn's Popular Library.*

Duodecimo.

> SING me, the RESTLESS MAN, O Muse, who roamed the world over,
> When, by his wondrous guile, he had sacked Troy's sacred fortress.

Bohn's Popular Library (see B14) reprinted Francis Caulfeild's hexameter translation of the *Odyssey*, which G. Bell & Sons had originally published in 1921. In his preface, Albert Augustus David, Bishop of Liverpool and headmaster of the Rugby School Caulfeild had attended, described every translator's twin goals: to "produce a faithful and accurate rendering of his text, such as will satisfy the scholar," and to "reproduce his author's spirit, so that new readers shall be held and moved." David was certain that Caulfeild's translation would "win the gratitude of many" if it "exercises but a shadow" of Matthew Arnold's "fourfold spell"—rapidity, simplicity, directness, and nobility (see D12, D13). According to David, readers of Caulfeild's version would "find that it does," and it was "a matter of pride" to David that Caulfeild, who "learnt to love the poems of Homer" at Rugby, achieved "such a labour of love."

Caulfeild included a note in the edition to assist his readers with the unfamiliar hexameters. The *Expository Times* wrote that "if these directions are followed ... the enjoyment obtained ... will be very great. It is a version in modern English. And that is good." The *London Mercury*, on the other hand, found Caulfeild's translation "fluent and easy to read, but hardly satisfactory from a metrical point of view."

"Entre Nous." *Expository Times* 32 (July 1921): 478–80.

Grimley, M. "David, Albert Augustus (1867–1950)." *Oxford Dictionary of National Biography.*

Rendall, V. "The Classics." *London Mercury* (October 1921), cited in *Classical Weekly* 15, no. 14 (January 30, 1922): 112.

B66

Sir William Sinclair Marris (1873–1945). *The Odyssey of Homer. . . .* London: Oxford University Press, 1925.

Duodecimo.

> Tell me, O Muse, of that Great Traveller
> Who wandered far and wide when he had sacked
> The sacred town of Troy.

Sir William Sinclair Marris, administrator in India and advisor in Transvaal, South Africa, used his leisure time to publish translations of the poems of Horace and Catullus in addition to this blank-verse version of the *Odyssey* and his 1934 *Iliad* (B32). Marris sought "conciseness" and insisted that blank verse "sacrifices no more than any other form of verse," because no English meter is capable of reproducing "the music of Homer's polysyllables." If the blank verse here "misses his qualities of simplicity, dignity and directness, that is at all events not the fault of the instrument."

Contemporary reviewers admired both the translation and Marris's use of his leisure time to produce it. J. A. Scott wrote in the *Classical Journal* that, despite his "great activity," Marris had managed to complete "the huge task of translating the entire *Odyssey*" into verses that "flow with melody and are written in simple and lucid language"; he had reproduced the poem's meaning in language "easily understood by those who are familiar with only ordinary English prose." A. B. Ramsay concurred in the *Classical Review*: readers "with no knowledge of Greek" can get from Marris's "plain tale of the *Odyssey*" "as fair an idea of the Homeric romance as is possible." The *Journal of Hellenic Studies* called the translation "very decidedly readable" with "a sense of Homer's limpidity and directness" and "the light-heartedness of a task carried through *con amore*." The volume itself "is very pleasant to look at and hold, and both type and press-work are far above the average of Indian-printed books."

Haig, H. "Marris, Sir William Sinclair (1873–1945)." Rev. Philip Woods. *Oxford Dictionary of National Biography.*

Ramsay, A. B. "Review: Some Translations." *Classical Review* 41, no. 2 (May 1927): 62–64.

S., V. "Review." *Journal of Hellenic Studies* 46, pt. 2 (1926): 261–62.

Scott, J. A. "Review." *Classical Journal* 22, no. 3 (December 1926): 234–35.

B67

Robert Henry Hiller (d. 1944). *The Odyssey of Homer Translated Into English Prose.* New York: The Book League of America, Inc., 1938.

Octavo.

> Tell me, O Muse, of that clever hero who wandered far after capturing the sacred city of Troy.

Professor and classicist Robert H. Hiller first published this prose translation of the *Odyssey* for students in 1927 at the instigation of his publishers, who asked him to produce a version in "present-day idiomatic English" for "readier comprehension." Hiller felt that "adequate comprehension of literature and art in general is impossible" without familiarity with both Homeric epics. It was therefore necessary for schools to teach the *Odyssey*, but "the modern youth" found the "archaic expressions" of the prose translations "dry and uninteresting," and no longer read the *Odyssey*'s "thrilling tales" "for the mere joy of reading." Hiller hoped that his modern version would appeal to students, and might even inspire some to study the original text, "which is really necessary for the full appreciation of the poem as literature."

C. H. Young in the *Classical Weekly* wrote that Hiller had "performed his task with discretion," creating "a thoroughly readable translation in plain, simple English, made without losing the dignity of the original," and presented in "an attractive little volume" to be used in schools, although it should "also be of interest to the general reader." J. A. Scott in the *Classical Journal* recommended it as "a very handsome little volume containing a translation of the *Odyssey* into modern conversational English" for "boys and girls," and for those "in spheres where the story and not the tone of the *Odyssey* is the thing desired."

Hiller, R. H. *The Odyssey of Homer.* Philadelphia, Chicago: John C. Winston, 1927.

Luce, S. B. "Archaeological News and Discussions." *American Journal of Archaeology* 48, no. 4 (October–December 1944): 368.

Scott, J. A. "Review." *Classical Journal* 23, no. 8 (May 1928): 638–39.

Young, C. H. "Review." *Classical Weekly* 22, no. 18 (March 11, 1929): 144.

B68

Herbert Bates (1868–1929). *The Odyssey of Homer Translated Into English Verse.* 2nd ed. New York and London: Harper & Brothers Publishers, 1929.

Octavo.

Tell me the tale, Muse, of that man
Of many changes, he who went
Wandering so far when he had
Plundered
Troy's sacred citadel.

Poet and educator Herbert Bates intended this "usually literal" abridged translation of the *Odyssey* in iambic tetrameter for use in high schools; the edition includes instructions for those teaching the epic, and the imprint identifies it as the "School Edition." Bates's omissions are mainly those recommended by the College Entrance Board in the United States. Bates was concerned that too few high-school students were reading the *Odyssey* and thought that translation of the poem was the best way to "bridge the gap" between their education and that of previous generations: "the more bridges we have, the more chance there is that every reader can find one to his taste." His version emphasized "certain qualities of mood and light narrative swiftness." He admired prose renditions, but Bates viewed the *Odyssey* as "essentially a poem" that should be represented in "poetic form." He regarded blank verse as difficult to keep "fluent and lyric," and the English hexameter as incompatible with "the spirit of the language." The iambic tetrameter was "simple to read, native to the spirit" of English, "varied" enough to fit "the wide Homeric range of expression," and capable of creating "a tune and movement that is to English what the original tune was to Greek—a light, rapid, lyric narrative form that lets the story show through."

The *English Journal*, a National Council of Teachers of English publication, found Bates's "emphasis upon light narrative" to be "the special value," and hailed Bates's translation as "An original, simplified conception of the *Odyssey* presenting a new opportunity for high-school reading of Homer in verse."

Dakin, D., et al. "News and Notes [Herbert Bates]." *English Journal* 18, no. 7 (September 1929): 600.

"In Brief Review." *English Journal* 18, no. 8 (October 1929): 703.

B69

T. E. Lawrence (1888–1935). *The Odyssey of Homer*. London: Printed and Published by Sir Emery Walker, Wilfred Merton, Bruce Rogers, 1932.

Folio.

O divine poesy
Goddess-daughter of Zeus
Sustain for me

THE ODYSSEY OF HOMER

PRINTED IN ENGLAND

1932

B69

This song of the various-minded man
Who after he had plundered
The innermost citadel of hallowed Troy
Was made to stray grievously
About the coasts of men

Thomas Edward Lawrence, more commonly known as Lawrence of Arabia, published this prose translation of the *Odyssey* under the name T. E. Shaw, a pseudonym he had used to enlist in the Royal Air Force without the notice of the press. Book designer Bruce Rogers commissioned Lawrence to write the translation for this edition of 530 copies after reading Lawrence's *Seven Pillars of Wisdom*, in which Lawrence recounted his role in the Arab revolt against the Turks. Lawrence had studied Greek and worked as an archaeologist at the Hittite city of Carchemish in Syria. In a letter to Bruce Rogers, he described the site as "a city of roughly the Odysseus period" that had given him "odd knowledges that qualify me to understand the *Odyssey*, and odd experiences that interpret it to me."

Lawrence intended his version of the *Odyssey* to be "essentially a straightforward translation" of what he described as "the first novel of Europe." He used "plain English" to match Homer's "Wardour-Street Greek." The *Odyssey*, according to Lawrence, is "Gay, fine, and vivid . . . never huge or terrible" like the *Iliad*: Homer, in an "apparently conscious" "limitation," "misses his every chance of greatness, as must all his faithful translators." Lawrence "uncritically" used the Oxford edition of the Greek text (A31).

His celebrity seems to have attracted at least as much attention to the work as his actual translation did. Although they praised the beautiful book, reviewers were highly critical of Lawrence's rendition and, in particular, of the views Lawrence presented in his Translator's Note. L. E. Lord wrote in the *Classical Journal*, "Mr. Shaw is certainly a competent killer of Turks. He is with equal certainty no literary critic"; however, Lord allowed the translation "a gripping power, a nervous energy that holds the reader." Writing for *Classical Philology*, A. T. Murray (see B31, B64) criticized the absence of a "spiritual kinship with the original" in which "the simplicity and the nobility of Homer" were retained. And, in the *Classical Review*, J. W. Mackail (see B62) wrote that "to an English reader who does not know Greek, the distinctive Homeric quality disappears," but blamed the translation's shortcomings on "faults of taste, not of scholarship."

The artistic success of the book, however, is not in dispute. American printer and book designer Joseph Blumenthal remarked, "I believe the Bruce Rogers *Odyssey* is indisputably among the most beautiful books ever produced. . . . In the *Odyssey*, with complete simplicity, without tricks or accessory decoration, with a classic austerity akin to the timeless proportions of the Parthenon, with only type and paper and ink, with consummate skill, Rogers created a masterpiece."

Aldington, R. *Lawrence of Arabia: A Biographical Enquiry*. London: Collins, 1955.

Blumenthal, Joseph. *Bruce Rogers: A Life in Letters, 1870–1958*. Austin, TX: W. Thomas Taylor, 1989.

Eason, R. and Rookledge, S. "Bruce Rogers 1870–1957." *Rookledge's International Handbook of Type Designers*. Carshalton Beeches, England: Sarema, 1991.

Garnett, D., ed. *The Letters of T. E. Lawrence*. London: Jonathan Cape, 1938.

Graves, R. *Lawrence and the Arabian Adventure*. Garden City: Doubleday, Doran & Co., 1928.

James, L. "Lawrence, Thomas Edward [Lawrence of Arabia] (1888–1935)." *Oxford Dictionary of National Biography*.

Knox, B. "Introduction." *The Odyssey of Homer: Translated by T. E. Lawrence*. New York: Oxford University Press, 1991.

Lord, L. E. "Review." *Classical Journal* 28, no. 7 (April 1933): 533–36.

Mackail, J. W. "The Aircraftsman's Odyssey." *Classical Review* 49, no. 6 (December 1935): 219–20.

Murray, A. T. "Review." *Classical Philology* 28, no. 3 (July 1933): 225–27.

O'Brien, P. *T. E. Lawrence—A Bibliography*. Boston: G. K. Hall, 1988.

"Review." *Greece & Rome* no. 14 (February 1936): 124–25.

"Scholar-Warrior." *Time*, November 28, 1932.

WITH

B69A

T. E. Lawrence (1888–1935). *The Odyssey of Homer Newly Translated Into English Prose.* New York: Oxford University Press, 1932.

Octavo.

Laid into the BHL copy is a signed letter from Bruce Rogers discussing the different editions of Lawrence's translation.

B70

W. H. D. Rouse (1863–1950). *The Story of Odysseus. . . .* New York: Modern Age Books, Inc., 1937.

Octavo.

> This is the story of a man, one who was never at a loss. He had travelled far in the world after the sack of Troy, the virgin fortress

Headmaster and classical scholar W. H. D. Rouse published the first four books of his prose rendition of the *Odyssey* in *New English Weekly* in 1935. The first complete edition came out in England in 1937 under the title *The Story of Odysseus: A Translation of Homer's "Odyssey" into Plain English*; this American edition, illustrated by American wood engraver Lynd Ward, appeared the same year, and Rouse's *Iliad* (B33) came out the following year. Rouse was coeditor of the Loeb Classical Library series from its foundation in 1911 until his retirement in 1947 (see B64). He wrote the introduction and notes for a 1905 edition of Matthew Arnold's *On Translating Homer* (D12). In the classroom, Rouse focused on teaching Latin and Greek as living, spoken languages. This edition attributes the origin of Rouse's translation of the *Odyssey* to Rouse's former students, who asked him to translate the story "for adults"; Rouse, however, asserted that the poet Ezra Pound was "the onlie begetter of this book. He suggested it, and he read the first part with Odyssean patience." Rouse also stressed that he had begun his *Odyssey* before Lawrence's prose version (B69) was published; he consulted the Greek text of Merry, Riddell, and Monro (A29) and the Loeb edition of A. T. Murray (B64).

According to Rouse, "it is a thousand pities that the new world should grow up without" the *Odyssey*. Existing translations were too full of un-Homeric "affectations and attempts at poetic language." Rouse aimed to provide "a readable story" that could "be read aloud and heard without boredom"; he compared his work to "thrillers and detective novels" and asked that his translation "be judged simply as a story."

It was as a story that contemporary reviewers seem to have accepted Rouse's version. In the *Classical Review* (which Rouse edited from 1911 to 1920), W. G. Waddell wrote that "This Homer in plain prose ... deserves welcome as a means of popularizing 'the best story ever written', and how skilfully [*sic*] Dr. Rouse brings out all the details!" As a translation, it "gives one many jars"; but, "as a running commentary ... it is most lively and illuminating, a book to read and enjoy."

Arnold, M. and W. H. D. Rouse. *On Translating Homer*. London: J. Murray, 1905.

D., R. M. "W. H. D. Rouse." *Folklore* 62, no. 1 (March 1951): 269–70.

Gilbert, O. "Lynd Ward: June 26, 1905-June 28, 1985." *Dictionary of Literary Biography, Vol. 22: American Writers for Children, 1900-1960*. Edited by John Cech. Farmington Hills, MI: Gale Group, 1983.

Kelly, L. "Pound, Ezra Loomis (1885–1972)." *Oxford Dictionary of National Biography*.

Lind, L. R. "Review." *Classical Weekly* 44, no. 8 (January 22, 1951): 124–25.

"Loeb Classical Library: The History." Cambridge: Harvard University Press. http://www.hup.harvard.edu/features/loeb/history.html (accessed March 18, 2011).

Rouse, W. H. D. "Machines or Mind?" *Classical Weekly* 6, no. 11 (January 11, 1913): 82–86.

———. *The Story of Odysseus: A Translation of Homer's "Odyssey" into Plain English*. London: Thomas Nelson and Sons, 1937.

Stray, C. "Rouse, William Henry Denham (1863–1950)." *Oxford Dictionary of National Biography.*

Waddell, W. G. "Review: The Odyssey in Plain Prose." *Classical Review* 52, no. 2 (May 1938): 61.

B71

E. V. Rieu (1887–1972). *The Odyssey. . . .* Harmondsworth, Middlesex; New York: Penguin Books, 1945. *Penguin Classics in Translation.*

Duodecimo.

> The hero of the tale which I beg the Muse to help me tell is that resourceful man who roamed the wide world after he had sacked the holy citadel of Troy.

Literary scholar and translator E. V. Rieu intended this prose version of the *Odyssey* as "a genuine translation," rather than "a paraphrase" or "a retold tale." Rieu's goal was to give the "modern reader" with no knowledge of Greek an *Odyssey* "he may understand with ease and read with appreciation." In such an endeavor, "too faithful a rendering defeats its own purpose." Rieu convinced Penguin Books founder Sir Allen Lane to launch a series of Penguin Classics in Translation that would publish inexpensive paperback versions of the classics for the general reader. This translation became the first volume of the series, which Rieu edited from 1944 to 1964. Rieu contributed his translation of the *Iliad* (B36) in 1950. By 1954, Penguin Books had published one thousand volumes, and Rieu's *Odyssey* was the best-selling book in all of Penguin's departments; by 1964, it had sold more than two million copies.

E. O'Neill in the *New York Times* greeted Rieu's twenty-five cent Penguin edition as "good news indeed, not only for lovers of Homer or of literature generally, but for anyone who enjoys a fine old story." The "style and tone" "are hopelessly un-Homeric," but "The important thing is that the wonderful story of the Odyssey is now available, in easily readable English, at a price which anyone can pay." In the *Classical Journal*, F. M. Combellack found it "surprising and pleasant" to see Homer's *Odyssey* "in the drugstore among the latest twenty-five cent mystery stories." Even more surprisingly, "it is a very good piece of work indeed," that, despite faults of accuracy, succeeds in making Homer available to "many for whom the *Odyssey* would otherwise be a closed book." And, in *Greece & Rome*, B. Newman called it a translation with "many merits: it is brisk, vigorous, never flat, and very readable." Newman hoped Rieu's version would "appeal to a generation which is impatient of tradition, suspicious of poetic diction."

Combellack, F. M. "Review: The Penguin 'Odyssey.'" *Classical Journal* 43, no. 2 (November 1947): 111–13.

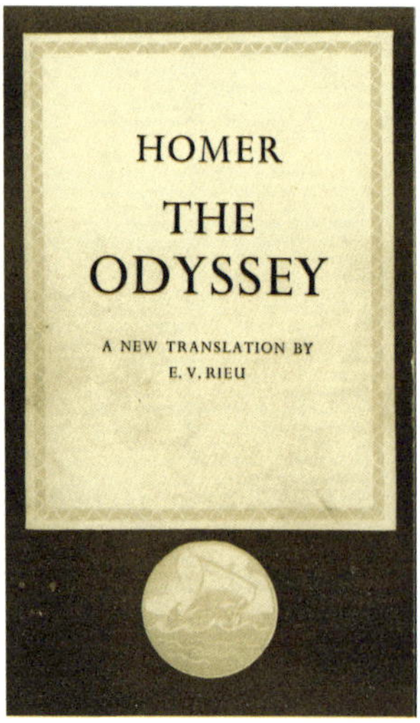

B71

Connell, P. J. "Rieu, Emile Victor (1887–1972)." *Oxford Dictionary of National Biography.*

Getty, M. "The Penguin Classics." *Phoenix* 9, no. 3 (Autumn 1955): 127–29.

MacKenzie, R. N. "Lane, Sir Allen (1902–1970)." *Oxford Dictionary of National Biography.*

Morpurgo, J. E. *Allen Lane, King Penguin: A Biography.* New York: Methuen Inc., 1980.

Neavill, G. B. "Review." *Library Quarterly* 51, no. 2 (April 1981): 223–25.

Newman, B. "The 'Penguin' 'Odyssey.'" *Greece & Rome* 15, no. 45 (October 1946): 119–24.

O'Neill, E. Jr. "Famous Voyage, Cut-Rate." *New York Times,* December 8, 1946.

WITH

B71A

E. V. Rieu (1887–1972). *The Odyssey.* . . . London: Methuen & Co., Ltd., 1952.

Octavo.

The first hardcover edition of E. V. Rieu's best-selling prose translation.

AND

B71B

E. V. Rieu (1887–1972). *The Odyssey.* . . . London; New York: Penguin Books, 1991.

Octavo.

> Tell me, Muse, the story of that resourceful man who was driven to wander far and wide after he had sacked the holy citadel of Troy.

Dominic Christopher Henry Rieu revised his father E. V. Rieu's translation of the *Odyssey* for Penguin with the help of classicist Peter V. Jones. D. C. H. Rieu had contributed an English version of *The Acts of the Apostles* to Penguin's Classics in Translation series in 1957. He and Peter V. Jones took up "the task of retaining the *joie de vivre* of E. V. R.'s version but being more accurate and faithful to Homer," excising E. V.'s "over-elaboration," "modernisms," and attempts "to add poetry to Homer's poetry," while restoring the "formulaic" aspects E. V. had left out.

According to S. Lowenstam in the *Classical World,* they achieved this goal, with almost every sentence "retranslated" to restore "faithfulness." What the new version lost in "smoothness," it made up for "in literalism": "E. V. Rieu often ignored the Greek to write what seemed appropriate, while his son is much more literal if sometimes interpretative." In 2003, D. C. H. Rieu and Jones produced a revised edition of E. V. Rieu's *Iliad* for Penguin; and Jones published a commentary on Rieu's *Iliad* as well as on Hammond (B43) and Lattimore's (B37) translations the same year. The revised editions of E. V. Rieu's *Iliad* and *Odyssey* are both still in print.

"Dominic Rieu." *Times* (London), May 24, 2008.

Jones, P. V. *A Commentary on Three Translations.* London: Bristol Classical Press, 2003.

Lowenstam, S. "Review." *Classical World* 88, no. 1 (September–October 1994): 70–71.

B72

S. O. Andrew (1868–1952). *Homer's Odyssey. . . .* London: J. M. Dent & Sons, Ltd., 1948.

Duodecimo.

> Tell me, O Muse, of the hero fated to roam
> So long and so far when Ilion's keep he had sack'd

In this verse translation of the *Odyssey*, headmaster and classicist S. O. Andrew sought to render Homer's "original as literally as English idiom permits." Andrew had published a partial translation of the *Iliad* in 1938 (B93) and left a draft of the whole poem to be revised and completed by Michael J. Oakley after his death (B38). Andrew saw no need "to *improve*" Homer, unlike Pope (see B9, B49), whose "sophisticated" eighteenth-century standards made Homer's simpler art too "remote" for him to understand. Andrew also rejected blank-verse and hexameter translations, choosing to employ a meter with "five stresses to the line separated from each other by one or two unstressed syllables."

In the *Classical Review*, E. S. Forster wrote that Andrew's meter has "the disadvantage of being unfamiliar, but it improves on acquaintance"; still, the translation contains lines that "do not run very easily." Forster saw the translation's language as "its chief merit": "it has the plainness and simplicity of the original and is free from far-fetched archaizing and elaborate constructions."

Forster, E. S. "Review." *Classical Review* 64, no. 1 (April 1950): 33.

"Mr. Samuel Andrew." *Times* (London), April 14, 1952, issue 52285, p. 8.

B73

Ennis Rees (1925–2009). *The Odyssey of Homer. . . .* New York: Random House, 1960.

Octavo.

> Of that versatile man, O Muse, tell me the story,
> How he wandered both long and far after sacking
> The city of holy Troy.

Poet, English professor, and children's author Ennis Rees attempted to make his verse translation of the *Odyssey* into "a readable English poem." He viewed it as essential for a translator to convey the poetic quality of Homer's work in addition to faithfully representing its "sentiments, ideas, and images." Rees felt that effectively translating poetry required frequent "re-creation" of the poem—a fact that modern translators of Homer, unlike Chapman (see B1, B6) and Pope (see B9, B49), had mostly ignored. He attributed the lasting appeal of the *Odyssey* and the *Iliad* (which he would later translate [B40]) to their "essentially and obviously metaphorical" character: the Homeric works portrayed life as a "battle" and a "journey," and reflected the "deepest and most enduring concerns" of all people.

Rees chose to use a diction that occupied "the large area between the stilted and the vulgar," and a "loose" five-beat meter to translate the *Odyssey* into a contemporary poem. His verse rendition seems to have had difficulty distinguishing itself from other contemporary Homeric translations, such as Lattimore's *Iliad* (B37) and Fitzgerald's *Odyssey* (B74). F. M. Combellack in *Classical Philology* even found that although there was "really nothing outstandingly wrong with Rees's version," and a reader could "discover with reasonable ease and comfort the story of the *Odyssey*," Rees's poetry was just prose printed as verse, and the $5 edition "is no whit more heroic and splendid, and hardly more poetical" than Rieu's cheap Penguin translation (B71). J. A. Davidson in the *Classical Review* objected that Rees had "no adequate knowledge either of Homeric Greek or what we still possessively regard as English." In the *Classical World*, however, S. Levin called Rees's rendition "accurate, smooth, and readable," and Rees's translation was popular enough to be reprinted more than once. Rees also published audio recordings of his translations of both Homeric works.

Combellack, F. M. "Review." *Classical Philology* 57, no. 1 (January 1962): 60–62.

Crossett, J. "Review." *Classical Journal* 57, no. 2 (November 1961): 89–90.

Davidson, J. A. "Review." *Classical Review* 12, no. 3 (December 1962): 303.

Holleman, J. "Ennis Rees: USC Professor, State Poet Dies." *The State*, March 26, 2009. http://www.thestate.com/local/story/727396.html (accessed May 27, 2009).

"In Memoriam: Ennis Rees." *University of South Carolina Times*, April 9, 2009, p. 7. http://www.sc.edu/usctimes/PDFs/2009/April_9_2009.pdf (accessed March 19, 2011).

Levin, S. "Review." *Classical World* 54, no. 5 (February 1961): 155.

B74

Robert Fitzgerald (1910–1985). *The Odyssey*. . . . Garden City, New York: Doubleday & Company, Inc., 1961.

Octavo.

> Sing in me, Muse, and through me tell the story
> of that man skilled in all ways of contending,
> the wanderer, harried for years on end,
> after he plundered the stronghold
> on the proud height of Troy.

Thirteen years before he published this blank-verse rendition of the *Odyssey*, poet and English professor Robert Fitzgerald began experimenting with poetic translation of the epic in a review of Rieu's prose version (B71). Fitzgerald later reiterated his objection to prose renderings of the *Odyssey*, "no novel but a narrative poem in Greek." In 1952, he received a Guggenheim Fellowship and moved to Europe to work on this translation. He noted that there was a "lack of a readable contemporary version of Homer," which universities in particular needed for the Humanities courses they were developing. Lattimore's 1951 verse translation of the *Iliad* (B37) was a "great achievement" that "had taken the poem out of the hands of the prose men." Fitzgerald's *Odyssey* would be "a poem" that had been "re-imagined," with each line "alive and in the rhythm of a living voice." Fitzgerald placed great emphasis on working directly from the Greek to "keep the Greekness of the poem" with "no reference to other translations . . . no Latinity between the Greek and the work in English verse." His "total apparatus" was the Oxford text (A31) and a Greek dictionary. Swiss artist Hans Erni provided the illustrations for this edition, as he would for Fitzgerald's *Iliad* thirteen years later (B41).

Fitzgerald saw Milman Parry's (see D14) explanation of the Homeric works as constantly improvised oral performances as a source of liberation: the translator's "obligation is to the originator, to the originating imagination," and "what we call free translation" fits with the improvisational character of the original poem. The *Odyssey* can therefore be translated "from one tradition into another, from one literature into another, from one life into another," rather than merely "from one dictionary into another dictionary."

Fitzgerald's *Odyssey* was very successful: it had sold almost 1.5 million copies when Vintage Books acquired the reprint rights in 1989. It was also critically acclaimed: S. Levin wrote in the *Classical World* that "The style is light and graceful, and urges the reader on," while Erni's drawings "capture the mood of the text." In the *Kenyon Review*, G. Steiner called Fitzgerald's *Odyssey* "marvellously submissive to the voice and intent of the Homeric text," and wrote that Fitzgerald was "taking his place beside Chapman and Pope in the unbroken lineage of English Homeric translations."

Fitzgerald, P. L., ed. *The Third Kind of Knowledge: Memoirs and Selected Writings of Robert Fitzgerald.* New York: New Directions, 1993.

Fitzgerald, R. "Two Long Engagements with Homer." *Bulletin of the American Academy of Arts and Sciences* 30, no. 4 (January 1977): 21–30.

———. "Homer: The Odyssey (Tr. by E. V. Rieu)." *Poetry* 72 (April 1948): 28.

Honig, E. "A Conversation with Robert Fitzgerald." *MLN* 91, no. 6 (December 1976): 1572–88.

Knox, B. "Review: Between Scylla and Charybdis." *Hudson Review* 14, no. 4 (Winter 1961–62): 618–21.

Levin, S. "Review." *Classical World* 54, no. 9 (June 1961): 291.

McDowell, E. "Book Notes." *New York Times,* April 19, 1989.

Mitgang, H. "Robert Fitzgerald, 74, Poet Who Translated the Classics." *New York Times,* January 17, 1985.

Moos, S. v., and A. Kennington. "Hans Erni and the Streamline Decade." *Journal of Decorative and Propaganda Arts* 19, Swiss Theme Issue (1993): 129–49.

Steiner, G. "Review: Two Translations." *Kenyon Review* 23, no. 4 (Autumn 1961): 714–21.

B75

Preston H. Epps (1888–1982). *The Odyssey of Homer. . . .* New York: The Macmillan Company, 1965. *Literary Heritage Series. Unabridged School Edition.*

Octavo.

> Recall for me, Muse, the toils of that man so ready of wit in every need, who wandered far and wide after he had sacked the sacred citadel of Troy.

Greek professor Preston H. Epps did not intend this prose translation "to improve" on the *Odyssey* or "to modernize" Homer's work, but "to put into clear and readable English what . . . Homer said" or "seems to have meant," basing his translation on Allen's Oxford text (A31). He retained much of "the Homeric flavor" of Butcher and Lang's version (B55), while making "evident . . . as many characteristics of Homeric epic as possible." Epps maintained that it was impossible for even a poetic English translation to either reproduce the "magic and grace of Homer's poetry" or satisfy those who can read the original Greek. Thus he created this school edition in prose "with the general reader . . . in mind."

In the *Classical World,* G. E. Dimock (see B64A) praised Epps's "translation of the *Odyssey* presented frankly as a schoolbook" for its binding, large print, and attractive typography. According to Dimock, "The translation itself is extremely literal and often awkward or discordant in tone," and teenagers found the book "hard" (Dimock preferred to use Palmer's 1891 edition [B58]). However, "The poetry is still there and the adolescent who does his assignments faithfully will learn a lot." Dimock worried that the "excellent" study questions, written by high-school teacher James J. Garvey, had "too easily satisfying answers" that might mislead a student into "feeling that he has seen to the bottom of Homer."

Dimock, G. E. Jr. "Review." *Classical World* 60, no. 1 (September 1966): 11.

B76

Albert Spaulding Cook (1925–1998). *The Odyssey A New Verse Translation.* New York: W. W. Norton, 1967.

Octavo.

> Tell me, Muse, about the man of many turns, who many
> Ways wandered when he had sacked Troy's holy citadel

This is the first paperback edition of English professor Albert Spaulding Cook's "literal" line-by-line verse translation of the *Odyssey*. Cook's main goal was "to preserve that crucial unit," the Homeric line, "while trying to catch some of Homer's flow." Cook thought the translator's duty was to "hear and re-create the sound and sense of his original." He used a metrical line with a syllabic base of varying syllables to match the Homeric hexameter, and aimed to replicate Homer's "words, lines, and phrases." Cook identified himself as a "literalist" rather than "impressionist" translator, who could assure his readers "that for the vast designative tapestry of the original a pink thread may sometimes do duty for a red one, or a blurred one for a blurred one—but never a blue one for a red one, and never a polychrome burst for a single color of the original." Although "Any rendering builds a wall," "One can only hope to build a translucent one."

Cook's translation of the *Odyssey* was well received and was published again in 1974 in a Norton Critical Edition containing scholarly articles and extracts. In the *Classical Review*'s piece on that edition, J. B. Hainsworth described Cook's translation as one "done into the fashionable plain and readable style, a sort of *sermo pedester* arranged as if by verse." In the *Classical World*, P. Vivante called the version "much more than might be expected" from a literal rendition: Cook has a "felicity of diction," and "the poetic burden delivers itself bit by bit" throughout the translation.

Hainsworth, J. B. "Review." *Classical Review* (New Series) 28, no. 1 (1978): 144–45.

Vivante, P. "Review." *Classical World* 69, no. 5 (February 1976): 338–39.

WITH

B76A

Albert Spaulding Cook (1925–1998). *Homer The Odyssey A New Verse Translation. . . .* New York: W. W. Norton, 1967.

Octavo.

This is a later printing of the hardcover edition.

B77

Richmond Alexander Lattimore (1906–1984). *The Odyssey of Homer.* . . . New York, Evanston, and London: Harper & Row, Publishers, 1967.

Octavo.

> Tell me, Muse, of the man of many ways, who was driven
> far journeys, after he had sacked Troy's sacred citadel.

Although he was pressed to produce a version of the *Odyssey* immediately following the enormous success of his 1951 *Iliad* (B37), Richmond Lattimore did not publish this verse translation until sixteen years later. His hesitation was due in part to the fact that Robert Fitzgerald, a friend whose scholarly and poetic skills he respected, had received a fellowship in 1952 to work on his blank-verse rendition of the epic (B74). The first book of Lattimore's six-beat version appeared in the journal *Arion* in 1964, three years after Fitzgerald's *Odyssey* had been published. By that time, Fred D. Wieck, the humanities editor for the University of Chicago Press who commissioned Lattimore's *Iliad*, had moved on to Harper & Row.

Lattimore composed his *Odyssey*—based on Allen's Oxford text (A31)—on "the principles stated and followed" in his *Iliad*, striving again to "render Homer into the best English verse" he could write, while avoiding any "mistranslation" that would result from inserting a word of his own choice rather than "the word which translates the Greek." Lattimore's version of the *Odyssey* was immediately incorporated into universities' humanities courses, and it is often still taught alongside his *Iliad* as the standard translation.

Critics heaped as much, if not more, praise on Lattimore's second Homeric rendition. In the *Hudson Review*, G. E. Dimock (B64A) called Lattimore's *Odyssey* "the best yet in English," because Lattimore "is a poet," but, unlike Fitzgerald, "lets the images speak for themselves." In the *Times Literary Supplement*, P. M. Green welcomed Lattimore's version as "a landmark in the history of modern translation," saying "Lattimore has achieved his *chef-d'oeuvre* as a translator" in this "dazzling and well-nigh flawless performance." In the *New York Times*, R. Warner identified Lattimore's "complete Homer" as "a splendid achievement," "the best translation there is of a great, perhaps the greatest, poet."

Dimock, G. "Review: The Best Yet: Lattimore's Odyssey." *Hudson Review* 20, no. 4 (Winter 1967–68): 702–6.

"Fred D. Wieck Dies; Penn Press Head, 62." *New York Times*, November 18, 1973, p. 77.

Green, P. M. "On Translating Homer." *Times Literary Supplement,* March 14, 1968.

Lattimore, R. "The Odyssey of Homer: Book I." *Arion* 3, no. 3 (Autumn 1964): 12–22.

Mitgang, H. "Richard Lattimore Dead; a Classical Scholar and Poet." *New York Times*, February 28, 1984.

Warner, R. "Out of the Greek." *New York Times*, October 22, 1967, p. 337.

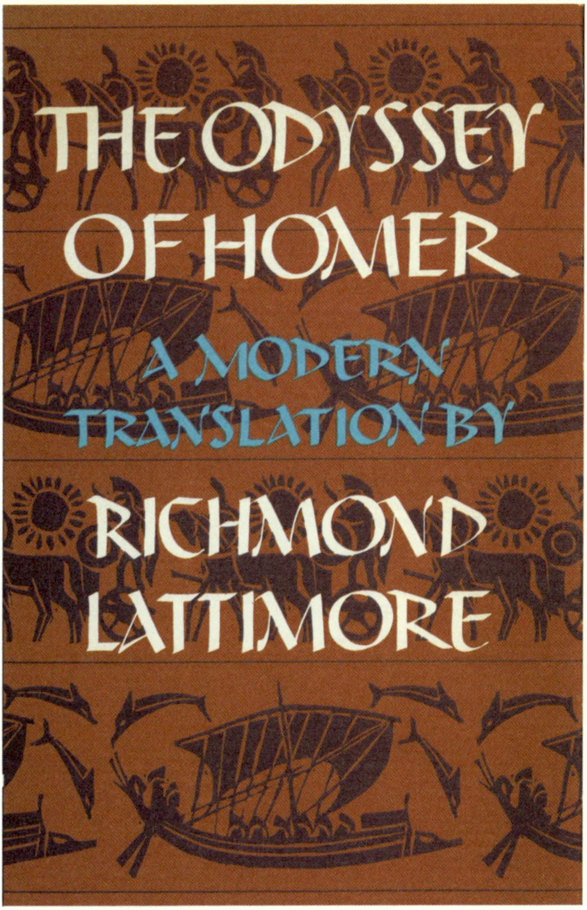

B77

B78

Denison Bingham Hull (1897–1988). *Homer's Odyssey*. . . . Greenwich, Connecticut: [Denison Bingham Hull], 1978.

Octavo.

> Tell, Muse, of that most devious man who wandered
> so far after he sacked Troy's sacred city

Architect Denison Bingham Hull privately published this blank-verse translation of the *Odyssey* when he was eighty-one years old, four years before his *Iliad* (B42). Hull began this version when was unable to find a suitable translation to read to a seventh-grade poetry class: the older translations, like Pope's (B49), "were almost unintelligible to the younger generation," whereas the more recent works were written either by classical scholars without a proper background in poetry or by poets who translated too freely. Hull had previously written *Hounds and Hunting in Ancient Greece*. Despite "knowing little English and less Greek," he decided to write his own line-for-line translation of the *Odyssey* in the "unrhymed five stress iambic line generally known as blank verse"—the English meter he believed comes closest to the Homeric hexameter. Working from Allen's Oxford text (A31), Hull translated the poem with "no stuffing" into "the English spoken by educated people," which he felt would convey the dignity and nobility that Matthew Arnold had underlined (see D12, D13).

Although Hull intended his translation "for a broad spectrum of readers," professional critics deplored it: reviewers in *Greece & Rome* wrote that, "At its best, the translator's English rises to a spare, direct nobility; at its worst it is betrayed by a lack of sensitivity to tone and nuance" approaching "bathos"; in addition, the translation was marred by "too many errors," frequent "obscurity," and "a clumsy roughness at times" in the meter.

Arnott, W. G. et al. "Brief Reviews." *Greece & Rome* (Second Series) 27, no. 2 (October 1980): 183–209.

Hull, D. B. *Hounds and Hunting in Ancient Greece*. Chicago: University of Chicago Press, 1964.

Richmond, J. A. "Review: *Laetae Venantibus Artes*." *Classical Review* (New Series) 16, no. 1 (March 1966): 110–12.

B79

Walter Shewring (1907–1990). *The Odyssey. . . .* Oxford; New York: Oxford University Press, 1980.

Octavo.

> Goddess of song, teach me the story of a hero.
> This was the man of wide-ranging spirit who had sacked the sacred town of Troy

Classical scholar Walter Hayward Shewring described his prose version of the *Odyssey* as his "diffident answer" to artist Eric Gill's question on Butcher and Lang (B55) and Lawrence's (B69) translations: "Can't they manage something better than that?" Classicist Geoffrey Stephen Kirk wrote the introduction. Shewring found fault with most verse renditions of the *Odyssey*: Chapman's meter (B1) lent itself to "rambling and monotony," and his style was "undisciplined and uneven"; Ogilby's version (B47) had too much "roughness and clumsiness"; Hobbes (B48) wrote at the "general level of contemporary tombstone poets" and included "absurdities" that made Shewring wonder: "Did he intend to satirise Homer?" (Shewring asked the same question of Samuel Butler [B61], who was "consumed by a bourgeois craving to shock the bourgeois"); Pope's (B49) version was the best: "sometimes magnificent, sometimes absurd, sometimes both at once"—but Pope "undertook to help Homer out" in achieving "the sublime"; Cowper (B4) was "more faithful," but was also "the most disappointing," because he was a better poet whose work on Homer was "opposed to his own genius"; Victorian translators using hexameter "cheated the reader or cheated themselves"; and Lattimore (B77) "insufficiently controlled" his six-beat meter.

Shewring mistrusted his own poetic abilities and chose to write his version in prose. Butcher and Lang were "archaisers," whereas Butler and those who followed him were "modernisers"—the twentieth-century prose translators "sing down" to their audience and present characters who suffer "only from such misfortunes as advertisements undertake to cure." Shewring's "rather free" prose translation used a contemporary diction, "but not the language of careless day-to-day talk and writing."

According to O. Taplin in the *Times Literary Supplement*, Shewring succeeded in creating such a diction: "it is Shewring's own prose—measured, plain and craftsmanlike. It is not the style of the past, nor is it straining to be the style of the future, it belongs to this one work"; Shewring's prose rendition of the *Odyssey* contains "the throb of blank verse," and is a work of "deft craftsmanship." More than 50,000 copies of the translation had been sold by the time of Shewring's death in 1990.

Easterling, P. E. "Kirk, Geoffrey Stephen (1921–2003)." *Oxford Dictionary of National Biography*.

MacCarthy, F. "Gill, (Arthur) Eric Rowton (1882–1940)." *Oxford Dictionary of National Biography.*

Taplin, O. "With an Eye on the Object." *Times Literary Supplement*, October 24, 1980, p. 1197.

"Walter Shewring." *Times* (London), August 6, 1990.

B80

Allen Mandelbaum (b. 1926). *The Odyssey of Homer A New Verse Translation. . . .* Berkeley: University of California Press, 1990.

Folio.

> Muse, tell me of the man of many wiles,
> the man who wandered many paths of exile
> after he sacked Troy's sacred citadel.

Poet and professor Allen Mandelbaum had published a highly successful English version of Dante's *Divine Comedy* and a National Book Award–winning rendition of Virgil's *Aeneid* before he wrote this translation of the *Odyssey* in iambic pentameter. He described his time spent translating as "many days in the burrows," and he hoped that the work that emerged would "be informed by—and shed—light." In rendering the *Odyssey*, Mandelbaum engaged in a "conversation with alternatives," consulting the texts and commentaries of Irish classicist and senator W. B. Stanford (revised from Allen's Oxford text [A31]) and the Valla Foundation's six-volume Italian edition (later translated into English and published by Oxford as *A Commentary on Homer's Odyssey*). Borrowing Stanford's term, Mandelbaum associated himself with the "unitarians": he viewed the *Odyssey* as essentially the work of one author, but detected later interpolations in the Greek text (which he left out of his translation). Mandelbaum attempted to capture Homer's "thought," which he considered "subtle, determined, measured, canny," and "committed to mortality"; and his "musicality"—he viewed poetry "as instigator of the voice and ear."

In the *New York Review of Books*, H. Lloyd-Jones called Mandelbaum's iambic pentameter "competent but uninspired," but in the *Classical World*, S. D. Olson found the meter "full of quiet but effective assonance and internal rhyme": Mandelbaum's *Odyssey* is "both a careful rendering of the original Greek and a new creation" that "can be read aloud" and "is pleasing to the ear." Both reviewers agreed that Italian artist Marialuisa de Romans's illustrations, which Lloyd-Jones called "gloomy and unsightly" and Olson "ugly and uninformative," marred the beauty of this expensive and otherwise lovely volume. A cheaper paperback edition was published in 1991, and an audio recording of Mandelbaum's translation read by English actor Sir Derek Jacobi followed in 1996.

"Biografia [of Marialuisa de Romans]." http://www.deromans.com/biografia.html (accessed March 24, 2011).

Fyten, D. "A Towering *Inferno*." *Window on Wake Forest*, May 2008. http://www.wfu.edu/wowf/2008/20080519.retiring.mandelbaum.html (accessed March 24, 2011).

Heubeck, A., ed. *Omero, Odissea*. Milan: Fondazione Lorenzo Valla, 1981–87.

Lloyd-Jones, H. "Welcome Homer!" *New York Review of Books* 38, no. 4 (February 14, 1991).

Mandelbaum, A. *The Aeneid of Virgil*. Berkeley: University of California Press, 1971.

———. *The Divine Comedy of Dante Alighieri*. Berkeley: University of California Press, 1980–82.

Olson, S. D. "Review." *Classical World* 85, no. 2 (November–December 1991): 119.

Stanford, W. B. *The Odyssey of Homer*. London: Macmillan, 1947–48.

B81

R. D. Dawe. *The Odyssey*. . . . Sussex, England: The Book Guild Ltd., 1993.

Octavo.

> Tell me, Muse, of the versatile man who was driven off course
> many times after he had sacked the holy citadel of Troy.

Classicist Roger Dawe received a grant from the Leverhulme Trust to write this "commentary with translation" in prose for readers "who are more concerned with what went into the cake than with the pretty ribbons on the box it comes in"; the commentary, which he describes as a "pretty grim affair," is extensive—sometimes leaving room for only one line of Homer on a page—and Dawe described the translation itself as "entirely devoid of literary merit." Dawe hoped to interest general readers in Homer, and to convey to them what "Homer actually said" rather than "what a rational man might suppose he must have meant" or "what we might wish he had said." He relied mainly on the Homeric scholia and on Eustathius (D4) to uncover "a text purged of alien elements." In his translation, he put words he deemed to be later insertions in italic or bold font. Dawe's desire to stay close to his Homeric text extended even to word order: his translation often echoed the order of the Greek to maintain "something of the flavour of the original." According to Dawe, the language of Butcher and Lang's version (B55) probably conveyed "a more authentic feel of the original" than the "more pellucid" modern translations.

Dawe suggested that Milman Parry's (see D14) deductions were "insecure"; he set out to show step by step that the *Odyssey* could not have been the work of one author, allowing his reader to "build up his own picture of Homer." His commentary concluded that "The enormous number of inconsistencies in style and content . . . far exceed anything which a rational man could attribute to a single author." In the *Classical Review*, M. J. Apthorp wrote that Dawe viewed the *Odyssey* as "essentially a botched job, a concatenation of contradictions and solecisms from beginning to end." Dawe's commentary was characterized by "exaggeration," "distortion," "rhetoric," "schoolmasterly attempt at humour," and "prolixity," thus "making of [*sic*] a mountain out of a mole-hill." Apthorp agreed with Dawe that the translation had no literary merit, and added that, at its best, it had "an almost Rieuan jauntiness" (see B71) and, at its worst, was "grotesque," but mostly just sounded "rather awkward and stilted." *Greece & Rome* gave Dawe's work a much more favorable review: it is "massive and exciting," "with considerable enlightenment," "massive scholarship and challenging insights"—Dawe is "the most entertaining writer on Classics of this day."

Ahl, F., and H. Roisman. *The Odyssey Re-Formed.* Ithaca: Cornell University Press, 1996.

Apthorp, M. J. "Review: Dawe's Odyssey." *Classical Review* (New Series) 45, no. 1 (1995): 1–2.

March, J. et al. "Subject Reviews." *Greece & Rome* (Second Series) 41, no. 2 (October 1994): 221.

B82

Brian Kemball-Cook (1912–2002). *The Odyssey Translated Into English Hexameter Verse.* Hitchin: Calliope Press, 1993.

Octavo.

Laid into this copy is a presentation letter signed by the author and an article written by him for *Friends of Classics.*

> Tell me, O Muse, of a man of resourceful spirit who wandered
> Far, having taken by storm Troy's sacred city and sacked it.

Classical scholar and headmaster Brian Kemball-Cook developed this hexameter translation of the *Odyssey* "in order to bring Homer alive" to adult students he was teaching. He described his version as "faithful to the original, neither omitting nor adding anything." In the article that accompanies this volume, Kemball-Cook wrote that the "crucial problem" of Homer's translator "is to reproduce his rapidity, which derives from the nature of the hexameter, with its forward impetus." In the introduction to this edition, Kemball-Cook cited Matthew Arnold's views on Homeric meter (see D12, D13), and defined his own rendition as an "attempt to reproduce the effect of Homer's *Odyssey* in English hexameters." Previous hexameter translations had "tended to come to grief, especially by shortening long syllables." Kemball-Cook tried to avoid these errors, and asked that his reader "remember that Homer's hexameters were composed for oral recitation" and read his version out loud "before passing final judgement."

Calliope Press, which is edited by Kemball-Cook's son and was established to publish Kemball-Cook's translation, calls this volume its "flagship publication."

"Calliope Press." http://www.calliopepress.co.uk/index.htm (accessed March 24, 2011).

"Lives in Brief." *Times* (London), October 23, 2002.

B83

Robert Fagles (1933–2008). *The Odyssey*. . . . New York: Viking, 1996.

Octavo.

> Sing to me of the man, Muse, the man of twists and turns
> driven time and again off course, once he had plundered
> the hallowed heights of Troy.

Although "modulating" his tone to fit the "more domestic, more intimate" "postwar world," Robert Fagles applied the same approach in this verse rendition of the *Odyssey* based on Allen's Oxford text (A31) as he had in his hugely successful *Iliad* (B44). Bernard Knox wrote the volume's introduction and notes and collaborated on drafts of the translation. Fagles learned from the "accuracy as well as grace" of the prose translations of Palmer (B58), Butler (B61), Murray (revised edition, B64A), Rouse (B70), Rieu (revised edition, B71B), Shewring (B79), and Dawe (B81); he got "inspiration" from the verse renditions of Rees (B73), Cook (B76), Lattimore (B77), Mandelbaum (B80), Oliver Taplin, and, especially, Fitzgerald (B74); and he gained insight from what he termed "the unapproachables"—those, like Chapman (B1) and Cowper (B4), "too remote" to attempt to follow, or those, like Pope (B49) and Lawrence (B69), "impossible to equal."

Fagles's *Odyssey* was an immediate success. Within six months of its publication, it was in its seventh printing and had sold 50,000 copies, and Penguin Audiobooks had sold 9,000 copies of its recording of actor Sir Ian McKellan reading the translation. In dual *New York Times* reviews, E. Rothstein called the translation "a phenomenon," praising Fagles's "swift prose" and ability to bring "plainness and poetry" together, and R. Jenkyns wrote that Fagles had found "a style that is of our time and yet timeless, dignified and yet animated by the vigor and energy essential to any good rendering of this poem." Jenkyns also celebrated the fact that "Homer thrives"—the enormous success of Fagles's Homeric translations along with NBC's 1997 broadcast of an *Odyssey* miniseries signaled to many contemporary observers that popular interest in the classics was reviving.

Gussow, M. "Finding the Right Words for the Father of Poetry." *New York Times*, April 15, 1997.

Jenkyns, R. "Heroic Enterprise." *New York Times*, December 22, 1996, Late Edition-Final.

Kinzer, S. "Adventures of a Man Who Defied the Gods: A Tale Retold with a New Goal of 'Reality.'" *New York Times*, May 18, 1997.

McGee, C. "The Classic Moment." *New York Times*, February 16, 1997.

McGrath, C. "Robert Fagles, Translator of the Classics, Dies at 74." *New York Times*, March 29, 2008.

Rothstein, E. "Fresh Light on the Wine-Dark Sea." *New York Times*, January 5, 1997.

Willett, S. J. "Review: New Homeric Studies." *Classical Journal* 93, no. 2 (December 1997–January 1998): 203–6.

B84

Martin Hammond (b. 1944). *The Odyssey....* London: Duckworth, 2000.

Octavo.

> Muse, tell me of a man: a man of much resource, who was made to wander far and long, after he had sacked the sacred city of Troy.

Martin Hammond published this prose translation of the *Odyssey* based on 1917 and 1919 editions of Allen's Oxford text (A31) thirteen years after his Penguin edition of the *Iliad* (B43) appeared. Jasper Griffin, classicist and author of many works of Homeric scholarship, wrote the introduction for this volume. Hammond attempted "to reproduce ... all that Homer actually *says*" while conveying "something of the *feel* of the *Odyssey*" and reflecting the poem's oral nature. "Fidelity ... to both matter and manner" was "cardinal" to Hammond's endeavor. Any translation, according to Hammond, is "an inevitable compromise," but translating the *Odyssey* in the style of "an Anglophone novelist (or poet) of the late twentieth century" might amount to "'treason.'" Too many recent translations of Homer sought to minimize the "alien" aspects of Homer's works. Although Lattimore's verse translations of the Homeric epics (B37, B77) had "a craggy integrity and a distinctive 'voice,'" they were difficult to read. Prose, which "can have both power and charm," had become "the natural medium for narrative."

In the *Classical Review*, A. F. Garvie wrote that "Hammond's admirable translation of the *Odyssey* complements his translation of the *Iliad*," as it is "remarkably successful in combining accuracy with a lively and highly readable style."

Garvie, A. F. "Review." *Classical Review* (New Series) 51, no. 2 (2001): 374.

Lloyd-Jones, H. "Navigating the Wine-Dark Sea." *Spectator*, March 11, 2000, p. 40.

B85

Stanley Lombardo (b. 1943). *Odyssey*. . . . Indianapolis: Hackett Publishing Company, Inc., 2000.

Octavo.

> Speak, Memory—
> Of the cunning hero,
> The wanderer, blown off course time and again
> After he plundered Troy's sacred heights.

Like his *Iliad* (B46), Stanley Lombardo's verse translation of the *Odyssey* started off as scripts for dramatic performances. Lombardo described his attempts to translate the Homeric epics as attempts to understand Homer by "locking eyebrows" with him. He based his version of the *Odyssey* on W. B. Stanford's Greek text and maintained the same poetic aims he had in his *Iliad*: reflecting the epic's oral nature while representing "the physicality, rapidity, and suppleness" of Homer's poetry in an English diction and rhythm "drawn from natural speech."

In the *New York Times Book Review*, C. Hedges envisioned classicists "blanching in horror" at Lombardo's colloquialisms, but found Lombardo's diction "real and convincing" for the general reader. In addition to his "laconic wit," "love of the ribald," and "clever use of idiomatic American slang," Hedges praised Lombardo's "carefully honed syntax," which gave "the narrative energy and a whirlwind pace," and his "rhythmic and clipped" poetic lines, which had "the tautness and force of Odysseus' bow." Lombardo published an abridged version of his translation in 2007.

Hedges, C. "The Humbling of Odysseus." *New York Times Book Review*, July 9, 2000.

Lombardo, S. *The Essential Odyssey*. Indianapolis: Hackett, 2007.

Stanford, W. B. *The Odyssey of Homer*. London: Macmillan, 1947–48.

Zwarg, C. "Review." *Bryn Mawr Classical Review* 2000.07.06.

B86

Randy Lee Eickhoff. *The Odyssey*. . . . New York: Forge, 2001.

Octavo.

> Sing, Muse, of that wanderer who sundered
> The sacred walls of Troy and traveled

In 2001, novelist Randy Lee Eickhoff published this prose translation of the *Odyssey* along with *Return to Ithaca*, a semiautobiographical novel about the Vietnam War that also incorporated elements of Homer's story. As a soldier in

Vietnam, Eickhoff had felt "a certain mystical camaraderie with Odysseus," a feeling that stayed with him when he returned to the United States and "stepped into a world I no longer recognized"—Odysseus was "if not my former life, at least a kindred one." Eickhoff, who earned a PhD in Classics, began writing novels: he observed that "all adventure novels have at their secret hearts a link to Homer." He "couldn't refuse" his publisher's request for this version of the *Odyssey*: the new millennium called for a new translation of the epic, because every generation "has a different lexicon reflecting its experiences and presenting them by major or minor changes in the meanings, both connotative and denotative, of its vocabulary." Eickhoff described his version as a "modern prose rendition" that narrated the *Odyssey*'s story but also explained the story's events.

In *Library Journal*, T. L. Cooksey referred to Eickhoff's version as a "novelized Odyssey," "more a close but highly embroidered paraphrase than a prose translation"; "both vigorized and readable," it was "enjoyable as a novel by Eickhoff," but "not suitable for those whose purpose is to read Homer."

Cooksey, T. L. "The Odyssey (Book Review)." *Library Journal* 126, no. 17 (October 15, 2001): 76.

Zaleski, Jeff. "Return to Ithaca (Book Review)." *Publishers Weekly* 248, no. 24 (June 11, 2001): 59.

B87

Rodney Merrill (b. 1940). *The Odyssey Homer*. . . . Ann Arbor: The University of Michigan Press, 2002.

Octavo.

> Tell me, Muse, of the man versatile and resourceful, who wandered
> many a sea-mile after he ransacked Troy's holy city.

After he retired from teaching English and Comparative Literature, Rodney Merrill published this hexameter translation of the *Odyssey* designed to reproduce Homer's "oral poetics" and to be performed aloud; an audio recording of Merrill reading his translation was released the same year. Merrill felt that archaeology and anthropology had increased the contemporary "taste for 'authenticity,'" and aimed to provide a more authentic experience of the *Odyssey* than previous Homeric translations had allowed. Twentieth-century translators like Fitzgerald (B74) and Fagles (B83) had focused more on modernizing Homer than on conveying the oral qualities Milman Parry (D14) had demonstrated. Writing in language from a "traditional stock," Merrill attempted to bring out Homer's "music, so crucial to the meaning and so implicated in the very existence of the epic," by emphasizing Homer's repetitive qualities and using "a fairly strict hexameter." He consulted many works of Homeric scholarship and acknowledged a deep debt to the *Odyssey's* previous translators, especially Cotterill (B63) and Kemball-Cook (B82), whose hexametric versions taught him what mistakes to avoid, and Murray (Merrill used the revised edition, B64A), Cook (B76), and Lattimore (B77). He admitted to having "freely plundered" his predecessors' renditions, because his aim was "fidelity" rather than "'originality.'"

Greece & Rome called Merrill's project "very bold and ambitious": the introduction by Merrill and Thomas R. Walsh, literary scholar and author of a book on anger in Homer, was "sensitive," Merrill's translation was "rewarding," and the reviewer's "only complaint" was the volume's high price. S. Evans in the *Bryn Mawr Classical Review* wrote that the "'music'" Merrill's hexameters produced would provide "fresh insight into the nature of Greek epic," although Merrill's "biblical vocabulary" "jars at times, upsetting this music." In 2007, Merrill published a translation of the *Iliad* in the same meter.

Evans, S. "Review." *Byrn Mawr Classical Review* 2003.06.42.

Halliwell, S. et al. "Subject Reviews." *Greece & Rome* (Second Series) 50, no. 2 (October 2003): 241–84.

Merrill, R. *The Iliad.* Ann Arbor: University of Michigan Press, 2007.

Walsh, T. R. *Fighting Words and Feuding Words: Anger and the Homeric Poems.* Lanham, MD: Lexington, 2005.

B88

Edward McCrorie. *The Odyssey.* . . . Baltimore: The Johns Hopkins University Press, 2004.

Octavo.

> The man, my Muse, resourceful, driven a long way
> after he sacked the holy city of Trojans

Poet and English professor Edward McCrorie sought both "vitality" and "fidelity" in this verse rendition of the *Odyssey*, attempting to unite the goals of what he saw as two distinct camps of Homeric translators: the "*free Homeric spirits*" like Chapman (B1) and Pope (B9), who "paid keen attention to color, drama, and vivacity of style" rather than to Homer's words, or Fitzgerald (B74) and Fagles (B83), who neglected "technicalities" in favor of "an inventive American style"; and the "*close followers of Homer*" like Murray and Dimock (B64, B64A) and Lattimore (B77), who were more concerned with "faithful" translation than with contemporary poetic style. McCrorie's goal was not "perfection," but "a good approximation" of Homer's words and poetic spirit. He consulted Stanford's text and the Oxford *Commentary on Homer's Odyssey*, translating the epic in a loose "'accentual'" line that "resembles Homer," which he adapted from a meter he had developed for his translation of Virgil's *Aeneid*. With a grant from Providence College (where he taught), McCrorie travelled to Greece to try to understand the *Odyssey*'s style, which he considered intrinsically connected to its author's experiences, and "deepest convictions and feelings."

In the *Bryn Mawr Classical Review*, G. S. Bowe wrote that McCrorie's translation had "much to recommend it," including "brisk, simple, ruddy verses," and "some marvelous turns of phrase that are true to Homer's Greek"; and classicist Richard P. Martin's notes were a "treasure trove of learned contextualization." In the *Bloomsbury Review*, J. Kenney recommended the translation "without reservation" to readers "who'd like to get as close to the original as is possible without reading the original Greek. It is refreshing, accurate, and direct." Johns Hopkins University Press reprinted McCrorie's translation in a less expensive paperback edition, and McCrorie is currently working on a new translation of the *Iliad*.

Bowe, G. S. "Review." *Bryn Mawr Classical Review* 2004.09.41.

"Edward McCrorie, Ph.D., Professor Emeritus." Providence College. http://www.providence.edu/Academics/Faculty/Humanities/McCrorie.htm (accessed March 24, 2011).

Heubeck, A. et al., eds. *A Commentary on Homer's Odyssey*. Oxford: Clarendon, 1988–92.

Kenney, J. "Review." *Bloomsbury Review* 24, no. 5 (2004).

McCrorie, E. *The Aeneid*. Ann Arbor: University of Michigan Press, 1995.

Stanford, W. B. *The Odyssey of Homer*. London: Macmillan, 1947–48.

B89

Charles Lloyd (1748–1828). *A Translation of the Twenty-Fourth Book of the Iliad of Homer.* Birmingham: Printed by Knott and Lloyd, 1807.

Octavo.

Inscribed by the translator to Professor Richard Porson, classical scholar.

> The games now clos'd, the people haste away,
> Each to the station where his vessel lay,
> Intent on supper, and the sweets of sleep

Banker and philanthropist Charles Lloyd published this translation of the last book of the *Iliad* in rhyming decasyllabic couplets for private circulation. Although Lloyd was "much occupied by public and private business"—he is identified in a penciled note as "Quaker, Philanthropist, Banker in Birmingham, a pioneer in the movement for the emancipation of slaves"—he enjoyed reading Latin and Greek and spent time translating the *Epistles* of Horace and the *Odyssey* in addition to producing this partial rendition of the *Iliad*, which "amused" his "leisure hours." Lloyd felt that Pope's "luxuriant and most elegant amplification and decoration" (B9) were more likely to please readers than his own "simple stile"; but he wanted "to keep near to Homer's meaning" (although not so near as Cowper had [B4]).

When Lloyd's son, the poet Charles Lloyd, showed the translation to Samuel Taylor Coleridge, he reported that Coleridge had remarked on "a *naturalness* ... and ease ... that very much delighted him." Charles Lamb (B105), another friend of Lloyd's son, wrote directly to Lloyd praising his translation's "manly versification": Lamb found Lloyd's version "plainer and more to the purpose than Pope's, though it may want some of his Splendour and some of his Sound."

Beer, J. "Coleridge, Samuel Taylor (1772–1834)." *Oxford Dictionary of National Biography.*

Fyfe, C. "Lloyd, Charles (1748–1828)." *Oxford Dictionary of National Biography.*

Garnett, R. "Lloyd, Charles (1775–1839)." Rev. Geoffrey Carnall. *Oxford Dictionary of National Biography.*

Lloyd, S. *The Lloyds of Birmingham.* Birmingham: Cornish Brothers, 1907.

Lucas, E. V. *Charles Lamb and the Lloyds.* Philadelphia: J. B. Lippincott, 1899.

Morson, G. V. "Porson, Richard (1759–1808)." *Oxford Dictionary of National Biography.*

Swaab, P. "Lamb, Charles (1775–1834)." *Oxford Dictionary of National Biography.*

B90

W. C. Green (1832–1914). *The Iliad of Homer with a Verse Translation.* London: Longmans and Co., 1884.

Octavo.

Sing, goddess Muse, the wrath of Peleus' son,
The wrath of Achileus with ruin fraught,
That to Achaians brought unnumbered woes,
And many mighty souls of heroes hurled
To Hades' home

Translator, teacher, and minister William Charles Green intended this blank-verse rendition of books 1–7 of the *Iliad* with facing Greek text as the first volume of a complete translation, but he published nothing further. Green, who had previously written a book on Homeric similes, had an "old-fashioned faith in verse" as the best form for translating poetry—he felt that not only the words but also the meter of the original poem conveyed "what the ancient poet thought and said." Blank verse, according to Green, "is compatible with great closeness of rendering"; prose, on the other hand, can never replicate the original's "whole effect."

The editors of the *Westminster Review* allowed that Green's version had "reproduced not a little of the music and dignity of the original," although they preferred Lord Derby's "freer and less pedantic" blank verse (B18), and denied that either Green's preface or translation had "put an end to the question as to whether Homer should be rendered in metre or in prose."

Green, W. C. *The Similes of Homer's Iliad.* London: Longmans, 1877.

Kirk, J. F. "Green, Rev. William Charles." *A Supplement to Allibone's Critical Dictionary of English Literature and British and American Authors.* Vol. 1. Philadelphia: J. B. Lippincott, 1897.

Westminster Review (New Series) 65 (January & April 1884): 600.

B91

Thomas Clark (1787–1860). *The Iliad of Homer with an Interlinear Translation, for the Use of Schools and Private Learners, on the Hamiltonian System, as Improved by Thomas Clark.* Philadelphia: David McKay, Publisher, 1888. *Hamilton, Locke and Clark Series.*

Octavo.

Sing, O - || Goddess (*Muse*), (the) || destroying [pernicious] anger
of-Achilles, son-of-Peleus, which || placed [*caused*] innumerable woes
[2]to (the) [1]Achæans

ENGLISH
PARTIAL

This interlinear translation of books 1–8 of the *Iliad* by Thomas Clark, editor for the Association of Philadelphia Booksellers for the Publication of the Latin and Greek Classics, was first published in 1860. The translation is on the "Hamiltonian System," developed by James Hamilton as a method for learning languages through word-for-word translation rather than through instruction in grammar. Hamilton wrote the first three books of this translation of the *Iliad*, and Clark supplied the rest. The English words in the edition are printed directly below the Greek words they represent, "the signification of each individual word being clearly given, and so combined as to form a clear and intelligible sentence." The Greek text of the *Iliad* had to be significantly rearranged to accommodate Hamilton and Clark's system, and symbols were necessary to guide the reader through the translation: multiple English words that express the meaning of one Greek word are connected by a dash (with "¹" before each of them when they are separated), English words not in the Greek are in parentheses, and substitutes for English words are in brackets ("||" marks where each substitution begins).

Hamilton and Clark each published numerous interlinear translations on the same system, although contemporary critics and educators seem to have been divided on their efficacy. In the *Edinburgh Review*, Sydney Smith published a defense of the Hamiltonian System (parts are reprinted in this volume), arguing that it would create "better scholars" by allowing students to acquire "the great art of understanding the sense" of another language in "cheerfulness and competition." A system that begins with grammar, on the other hand, "disgusts many . . . and is a less easy, and not more certain road to a profound skill in languages." Yet reviewers for the *National Quarterly Review* rejected the series for encouraging "indolence," doing "harm rather than good"—"the whole system is the veriest quackery, and we take it for granted that no respectable teacher would permit his pupils to have anything to with it." Despite such criticisms, this version of the *Iliad* went through many editions, and was most recently reprinted in 1952.

Clark, T. *The Iliad of Homer, with an Interlinear Translation.* Philadelphia: C. De Silver, 1860.

———. *The Iliad of Homer, with an Interlinear Translation.* New York: McKay, 1952.

"Notices and Criticisms." *National Quarterly Review* 2, no. 4 (March 1861): 179–81.

Smith, S. *Edinburgh Review* 44 (June 1826–September 1826): 47–69.

"Thomas Clark." *The Biographical Encyclopaedia of Pennsylvania.* Philadelphia: Galaxy, 1874.

Wroth, W. W. "Hamilton, James (1769–1829)." Rev. John D. Haigh. *Oxford Dictionary of National Biography.*

B92

George Ernle. *The Wrath of Achilleus Translated from the Iliad into Quantitative Hexameters.* London: Humphrey Milford; Oxford University Press, 1922.

Quarto.

> Sing me that Anger, Goddess, which blinding royal Achilleus
> Balefully, brought sufferings untold to the army of Argos

George Ernle, the author of this partial hexameter translation of the *Iliad*, appears to have been an English poet; he published an original poem, *Melusine*, in 1908, and his lengthy preface to this volume attests to his deep knowledge of English poetry and meter. In his rendition of the *Iliad*, Ernle strove "to naturalize" the Greek quantitative hexameter, the only meter he felt could reproduce "the swift, rolling, and magnificent music of Homer." Ernle viewed the English accentual hexameter used by Kingsley, Clough, and Longfellow as "clumsy, monotonous, and unworthy of its classical prototype." And, "however beautiful" he found Homeric translations in blank verse, couplets, or stanzas, he believed them incapable of accurately representing "the spirit" of Homer's original.

Despite Ernle's relative obscurity today, his *Wrath of Achilleus* seems to have earned some contemporary critical attention and praise. In a review for the *Measure*, Padraic Colum (B107) called Ernle "successful in his versification": his quantitative hexameters "give speed to the swiftly-moving story." In the *Classical Review*, T. F. Higham objected that Ernle sometimes "flaps indeterminately between verse and prose" when attempting to avoid monotony in his hexameters, but Higham still found the translation successful enough to hope that Ernle would "continue his experiments and find stronger wings."

Colum, P. "Heroic Poetry—The Wrath of Achilleus." *Measure: A Journal of Poetry* 25 (March 1923): 17–19.

Ernle, G. *Melusine*. London: Duckworth, 1908.

Higham, T. F. "Theory and Practice in Translation." *Classical Review* 36, no. 7/8 (November–December 1922): 149–54.

B93

S. O. Andrew (1868–1952). *The Wrath of Achilles Translated from Iliad I, XI, XVI–XXIV with a Note on the Metre. . . .* London: J. M. Dent and Sons Ltd., 1938.

Octavo.

Sing, Goddess, the wrath of Achilles Pelëides,
The ruinous anger that woes on the Danaans brought
Unnumber'd

S. O. Andrew published this partial translation of the *Iliad* in verse ten years before he published his *Odyssey* (B72); he continued working on the rendition after issuing this edition, and he left a draft of his work to be revised and published by Michael J. Oakley (B38) after his death. In this volume's preface, Sir Arthur Thomas Quiller-Couch, a writer and anthologist who often published under the pseudonym Q, affirmed that Andrew had "hit the nearest" to Homer, surpassing Chapman (B1, B6), Pope (B9), Cowper (B4), Lord Derby (B18), Lang, Leaf, and Myers (B24), and Butler (B29) in accuracy of both form and meaning. Andrew described his meter as a "new" form of verse, an accentual line with five stresses separated by one or two unstressed syllables.

In the *Classical Review*, F. R. Earp called Andrew's translation "a very interesting experiment" in a "simple and plain" diction and "entirely original metre" that is "light and rapid and free from stiffness and pomposity." Earp noted "disadvantages" to Andrew's meter—its shortness, for instance, sometimes led to a "bare bone" version of the Homeric line with "a loss of richness and sonority"—but hoped that Andrew would continue working on his rendition, since this partial version "deserves to be completed."

Earp, F. R. "Review: Homer in a New Metre." *Classical Review* 52, no. 4 (September 1938): 121–22.

"Mr. Samuel Andrew." *Times* (London), April 14, 1952, p. 8.

Smith, Michael Douglas. "Couch, Sir Arthur Thomas Quiller- (1863–1944)." *Oxford Dictionary of National Biography.*

B94

F. L. Lucas (1894–1967). *The Iliad Translated in Selection. . . .* London: The Folio Society, 1950.

Quarto.

Of the wrath of the son of Pēleus—of Achilles—Goddess, sing—
That ruinous wrath, that brought sorrows past numbering
Upon the host of Achaeans

This partial rhyming verse translation by classicist Frank Laurence Lucas contains selections from what Lucas described as the "five massive piers" of the *Iliad*'s narrative: book 1 (Achilles's quarrel with Agamemnon), book 9 (Achilles's refusal to reconcile), book 16 (Patroclus's death), book 22 (Hector's death), and book 24 (Achilles's return of Hector's body to Priam). The volume's copperplate engravings are by illustrator John Buckland Wright. According to Lucas, the "greatest poetry *is* translatable," even if its form is not. It is the "essential poetry" of Homer—his "vision" and his characters, rather than his meter and "golden" style—that an English translation of the *Iliad* is able to convey.

Still, contemporary critics found fault with the form that Lucas used to represent Homer. For example, G. S. Kirk (see B79) in the *Classical Review* found it "a pity" that Lucas included a great amount from this translation and from his *Odyssey* (B104) in his 1951 anthology, *Greek Poetry for Everyman*, "especially since Homeric hexameters are not adequately reproduced by the rhyming couplets to which the author tenaciously clings."

Cohen, R. H. L. "Lucas, Frank Laurence (1894–1967)." Rev. Mark Pottle. *Oxford Dictionary of National Biography*.

Horne, A. "Wright, John Buckland (1897–1954)." *Oxford Dictionary of National Biography*.

Kirk, G. S. "Review: Some Translations of Greek Poetry." *Classical Review* (New Series) 2, no. 3/4 (December 1952): 219–21.

Lucas, F. L. *Greek Poetry for Everyman*. London: Dent, 1951.

B95

I. A. Richards (1893–1979). *The Wrath of Achilles The Iliad of Homer, Shortened. . . .* New York: W. W. Norton & Company Inc., 1950.

Octavo.

> Sing, goddess, the anger of Achilles, the anger
> which caused so many sorrows to the Greeks.

Literary scholar and author Ivor Armstrong Richards intended this partial prose translation of the *Iliad* "in a moderately plain and fashion-free English" to be read aloud "without discomfort" and "grasped" by a general audience. Richards saw the invention of radio as a sign that we might be returning to an aural society; he presented selections from his version in eight radio broadcasts for the Lowell Institute Co-operative Broadcasting Council before this edition's publication. To hold the attention of his listeners, Richards was "appropriately ruthless" in shortening the Homeric text: he omitted books 2, 10, 13, and 17 entirely, and left out large parts of the rest "in the interest of the action." Richards also abandoned any attempt to represent Homer's language, which he viewed as "almost all hindrance" for the Greekless, and which he compared to the obstructive "noise" identified in communication theory. He described his version as a "simplification" that was "embarrassingly free"—freer even than Chapman's (B1, B6) or Pope's (B9) renditions.

In a review for the *New York Times*, G. Highet wrote that although Richards's

Iliad still contained "tushery" that would be "difficult to read aloud," and "some 'impediments to communication,'" "much of it sounds smooth and modern, and it is a long step toward the kind of translation we need." Richards continued to work with his rendition: he went on to present readings from it on educational television, and he wrote two unpublished dramatic plays based on the translation.

Highet, G. "The Gift of Tongues." *New York Times Book Review*, November 19, 1950.

Russo, J. P. *I. A. Richards: His Life and Work*. Baltimore: Johns Hopkins University Press, 1989.

Storer, R. "Richards, Ivor Armstrong (1893–1979)." *Oxford Dictionary of National Biography*.

B96

Christopher Logue (b. 1926). *Patrocleia* Book 16 of Homer's Iliad. . . . London: Scorpion Press, 1962.

Octavo.

> Now hear this:
> While they fought around the ship from Thessaly,
> Patroclus came crying to the Greek.

British poet Christopher Logue first published his translation of book 16 of the *Iliad* in the journal *Arion* in 1962, the same year it appeared in this volume designed by Germano Facetti, art director for Penguin Books from 1961 to 1972. Scorpion Press also issued an audio recording of Logue's translation called *The Death of Patroclus*, read in part by British actors Alan Dobie and Vanessa Redgrave. Logue reprinted the translation again in *War Music*, a version of books 16–19 (B98), where he described his Homeric renditions not as "translation in the accepted sense of the word," but as English poetry "dependent upon whatever, through reading and through conversation, I could guess about a small part of the *Iliad*." Logue knew no Greek: he read the translations of Chapman (B1), Pope (B9), Lord Derby (B18), Murray (B31), and Rieu (B36), as well as a literal version that classicist Donald Carne-Ross prepared for him, all of which gave him "a quite dissimilar impression" of Homer's work. Logue would "concoct a storyline" based on the translations he consulted, striving to make the voices of Homer's characters "come alive" and "keep the action on the move."

Carne-Ross, who first commissioned Logue to translate the *Iliad* for the BBC in 1959, identified Logue's method as "structural translation," focusing on what "is most truly Homeric: on the relation of incident and episode within a massively organised total action." Logue wrote that he did not hesitate "to cut or to amplify or to add to" those incidents, or to vary Homer's similes and omit his epithets.

Reviewing a 1963 edition of Logue's *Patrocleia* for the *Classical World*, F. M. Combellack objected that the rendition was "Homeric" only in so far as it "tells substantially the same story as Homer told"; it was otherwise "an original English poem . . . and a very good poem indeed" that "does not need to run for safety under Homer's mighty shield."

Carne-Ross, D. S. "Structural Translation: Notes on Logue's 'Patrokleia.'" *Arion* 1, no. 2 (Summer 1962): 27–38.

Combellack, F. M. "Review." *Classical World* 57, no. 2 (November 1963): 56.

Craven, P., and M. Heyward. "Christopher Logue." *Dictionary of Literary Biography, Vol. 27: Poets of Great Britain and Ireland, 1945–1960*. Edited by Vincent B. Sherry Jr. Farmington Hills, MI: Gale Group, 1984.

"Germano Facetti." *Times* (London), April 15, 2006.

Lewis, J. "24-Hour War: Is Christopher Logue a Genius or a Madman?" *Slate*, May 13, 2003.

Logue, C. "The Iliad: Book XVI. An English Version." *Arion* 1, no. 2 (Summer 1962): 3–26.

———. *Patrocleia of Homer*. Ann Arbor: University of Michigan Press, 1963.

———. *Prince Charming: A Memoir*. London: Faber and Faber, 1999.

Parotti, P. "Review: Homer Recast." *Sewanee Review* 96, no. 2 (Spring 1988): xli–xlii.

Wood, C. "Iliad with Sex, and a Plucked Chicken." *Times Higher Education*, December 21, 2001.

B97

M. L. West (b. 1937). *Sing Me, Goddess* Being the First Recitation of Homer's Iliad. . . . London: Duckworth, 1971.

Octavo.

Sing me, goddess, of the anger
of Achilles, son of Peleus,
bane that brought to the Achaeans
countless woe

Classicist and Homeric scholar Martin Litchfield West composed this verse rendition of book 1 of the *Iliad* in the unrhymed trochaic meter of the Finnish epic *Kalevala*. Translation, according to West, must reproduce not just the words, but also "the spirit and manner" of an original work. It is impossible to adequately translate the *Iliad* into prose because it is "rhythmical poetry, stylistically remote from any prose ever written." A verse translation of the epic, on the other hand, should not be an attempt "to contribute to modern English poetry"; instead, it should focus on conveying "an idea of" early Greek poetry. West found blank verse and other English meters with long lines "wearisome to read in any quantity." He felt that the short, four-stressed line of the *Kalevala* "has a rapidity that leads one on painlessly."

In the *Classical Review*, J. B. Hainsworth agreed that there was an "easiness" to the meter, "the essence of Dr. West's translation"; although there is "obviously no ideal English" verse for rendering the whole *Iliad*, "for parts and episodes West's experiment has very much to recommend it." West never published another Homeric translation, but he has produced many works of Homeric scholarship, including *Studies in the Text and Transmission of the Iliad* (2001) and a new edition of the Greek text for the Bibliotheca Scriptorum Graecorum et Romanorum Teubneriana (1998).

Hainsworth, J. B. "Review." *Classical Review* (New Series) 23, no. 2 (December 1973): 265.

West, M. L., ed. *Homeri Ilias.* Stuttgart and Leipzig: B. G. Teubner, 1998.

———. *Studies in the Text and Transmission of the Iliad.* München: K. G. Saur, 2001.

B98

Christopher Logue (b. 1926). *War Music an Account of Books 16 to 19 of Homer's* Iliad. New York: Farrar, Straus, Giroux, 1987.

Octavo.

> Now hear this:
> While they fought around the ship from Thessaly,
> Patroclus came crying to the Greek.

This first American edition of Logue's *War Music* contains reprints of Logue's *Patrocleia* (B96), *GBH* ("Grievous Bodily Harm," a combined version of *Iliad* 17 and 18 published in 1980), and *Pax* (a translation of *Iliad* 19 published in 1963). Logue first published *War Music* in 1981 in England, where he had also presented it as a dramatic performance.

In the *Sewanee Review*, P. Parotti called the appearance of this edition "an event to be greeted with enthusiasm": although it was "not a new 'version'" of Homer's work, and "more nearly a variation on the theme of *The Iliad* than anything like even a free translation," Logue's rendition of the epic was "an altogether new and exciting poem" in "language that is spare, often crisp, with sharp visual sensitivity." Parotti found "Account" an apt subtitle for Logue's work, which gives "a vivid echo of Troy in contemporary English." In *Erato*, W. Corbett described *War Music* as an "audacious risk," "a poem that is often as lurid and violent as Stephen King or a first-rate action movie" and preserves Homer's "grimness," if not his language. In 1997, Logue published a new, expanded edition of *War Music* that also included reprints of *Kings* (B99) and *The Husbands* (B100).

Corbett, W. "Review." *Erato* 5/6 (Summer–Fall 1987): 5.

Hadas, R. "Review: Watching from on High." *Threepenny Review* 32 (Winter 1988): 15–16.

Logue, C. "GBH: The Fight over the Body of Patroclus: An Account of Books 17 and 18 of the Iliad." *Kenyon Review* (New Series) 2, no. 1 (Winter 1980): 92–116.

———. "'*Pax*': Episodes from the 'Iliad', Book XIX." *Arion* 2, no. 4 (Winter 1963): 32–39.

———. *Pax: Book XIX of the Iliad.* London: Rapp & Carroll, 1967.

———. *War Music: An Account of Books 16 to 19 of Homer's Iliad.* London: Jonathan Cape, 1981.

———. *War Music: An Account of Books 1–4 and 16–19 of Homer's Iliad.* New York: Noonday, 1997.

Parotti, P. "Review: Homer Recast." *Sewanee Review* 96, no. 2 (Spring 1988): xli–xlii.

B99

Chrisopher Logue (b. 1926). *Kings an Account of Books 1 and 2 of Homer's* Iliad. New York: Farrar, Straus, Giroux, 1991.

Octavo.

Picture the east Aegean sea by night,
And in an open bay before that sea
Upwards of 30,000 men
Asleep like spoons among their fatal ships.

Christopher Logue approached this version of books 1 and 2 of the *Iliad* "in the same way" he had the translations in *War Music* (B98), this time basing his poem's storyline "on the main incidents of the *Iliad*'s first two books." *Kings* was published in England by Faber and Faber; this is the first American edition. Logue would later combine *Kings* with *War Music* and *The Husbands* (B100) to form 1997's *War Music: An Account of Books 1–4 and 16–19 of Homer's Iliad*, as he continued working on his Homeric renditions.

———. *War Music: An Account of Books 1–4 and 16–19 of Homer's Iliad.* New York: Noonday, 1997.

WITH

B99A

Chrisopher Logue (b. 1926). *Kings an Account of Books One and Two of Homer's* Iliad. London and Boston: Faber and Faber, 1991.

Octavo.

B100

Christopher Logue (b. 1926). *The Husbands an Account of Books 3 and 4 of Homer's* Iliad. New York: Farrar, Straus, Giroux, 1995.

Octavo.

A drink! A toast! *To those who must die.*

Logue first published this version of *Iliad* books 3 and 4 in England in 1994; it was reprinted in the 1997 edition of *War Music* (B98), which M. O'Leary in the *Chicago Review* praised for containing "some tremendous poetry and even a hint of that dread wrath," although O'Leary found *The Husbands* "more uneven" than the earlier accounts, representing "the downside of Logue's endeavor," with some "stilted jump cuts" and "groaners" produced by Logue's "interpretative leaps" in treating Homer's similes. A new edition of *War Music* was published in 2003 by the University of Chicago Press, and a drama based on Logue's work (adapted and directed by Lillian Groag) was performed at San Francisco's American Conservatory Theater in the spring of 2009. Logue did not stop translating the *Iliad* when he finished *The Husbands*: in 2003, he published *All Day Permanent Red: The First Battle Scenes of Homer's Iliad Rewritten*; and in 2005, *Cold Calls: War Music Continued.*

Bainbridge, C. "The War in Heaven." *Guardian*, October 8, 2005.

Hurwitt, R. "Theater Review: 'War Music.'" *SFGate*, April 3, 2009. http://www.sfgate.com/cgi-bin/article.cgi?f=/c/a/2009/04/02/DDO616PJMQ.DTL (accessed March 24, 2011).

Lewis, J. "24-Hour War: Is Christopher Logue a Genius or a Madman?" *Slate*, May 13, 2003.

Logue, C. *Cold Calls: War Music Continued.* London; New York: Faber and Faber, 2005.

———. *All Day Permanent Red: The First Battle Scenes of Homer's Iliad Rewritten.* New York: Farrar, Straus, and Giroux, 2003.

O'Leary, M. "Review." *Chicago Review* 43, no. 4, Contemporary Poets & Poetics (Fall 1997): 152–56.

B101

Henry Howard Molyneux Herbert, Earl of Carnarvon (1831–1890). *The Odyssey of Homer Books I–XII Translated Into English Verse.* London and New York: Macmillan and Co., 1886.

Octavo.

Tell me, O Muse, of that quick witted Chief,
Who, when the sacred citadel of Troy
Was wasted by his arms, wandered abroad

This blank-verse translation of the first half of the *Odyssey* was written by Henry Howard Molyneux Herbert, the Fourth Earl of Carnarvon, whose extensive political career included appointments as Colonial Secretary (first under the 1866–68 administration of Lord Derby [B18], then in 1874–78) and Lord Lieutenant of Ireland (1885–86). Lord Carnarvon offered "no excuse for another translation" of the *Odyssey*; his "best apology" was that its composition had afforded him "pleasure." He also found no fault with previous translations, praising the "great poet" Pope (B49) in addition to Chapman's "quaint Elizabethan conceits" (B1), Worsley's "musical verse" (B51), Way's "remarkable vigour" (B57), and Butcher and Lang's "mingled accuracy and spirit" (B55). Every generation, according to Carnarvon, "loves to tell the story in its own language." Carnarvon chose to tell it in blank verse, a compromise between "the inevitable redundancy of rhyme and the stricter accuracy of prose," and in a "language of great simplicity." For Carnarvon, book 12 was a natural place to stop, "a natural half-way-house in the story."

The *Classical Review* found Carnarvon's rendition "exact, and elegant, and readable," but "a very inadequate representation of Homer"—its "characteristic defect," in fact, was that it was "un-Homerically elegant."

Gordon, P. "Herbert, Henry Howard Molyneux, fourth earl of Carnarvon (1831–1890)." *Oxford Dictionary of National Biography.*

"Review." *Classical Review* 1, no. 5/6 (June 1887): 159–60.

B102

William Cudworth (1815–1906). *The Odyssey of Homer Books IX–XII. Rendered Into English Blank Verse.* Darlington: William Dresser, Printer, 1891.

Octavo.

Laid into this copy is a presentation card from the author, dated Christmas 1891.

Odysseus, man of many counsels spoke,
Answering Alkinous; 'O mighty prince
Renowned among all people, it is good
To listen to a minstrel such as this,
Whose song is like the gods'.

This blank-verse translation of books 9–12 of the *Odyssey* was privately printed for William John Cudworth, railway engineer and educator at the Friends' Adult School of Darlington. Cudworth retired after the death of his wife in 1883 and turned his attention to literature. His works (all printed privately) include translations of books 1, 6, and 9 of the *Iliad* (1895), Euripides's *Alcestis* (1888) and *Iphigenia of Aulus* (1889), and books 1 and 2 of the *Aeneid* (1901). Cudworth also continued working on the *Odyssey* after he issued this volume, producing a blank-verse rendition of books 5–8 in 1893.

Green, J. *Some Account of the Family of Cudworth of Yorkshire, Lancashire.* London: Headley Brothers, 1898.
http://members.tripod.com/holden_family/cudworth/cudworth_account.pdf

Minutes of the Proceedings [of the Institute of Civil Engineers] 166 (1906): 381–82.

B103

Cyril Arthington Pease (1868–1923). *The Toils and Travels of Odysseus.* ... Boston, New York, Chicago, et al.: Allyn and Bacon, 1926. *Academy Classics for Junior High Schools.*

Octavo.

Now Dawn arose from her couch to give light to gods and men, and the gods took their seats in council, and among them high-thundering Zeus, greatest of all in might.

Headmaster Cyril Arthington Pease first published his partial prose version of the *Odyssey* in England in 1916; Pease omitted books 1–4 and 24, as well as many passages from the remaining books. This school edition, "addressed to both the student and the general reader," was published after Pease's death. Charles W. Siedler, head of Classics at Walton High School in New York, supplied translations of book 24 and many of the passages Pease had left out. The volume's editor, Stella Stewart Center, head of English at Walton, also included poems on the *Odyssey* with the translation.

The *English Journal* called this edition's rendition of the epic "simple and melodious," "undoubtedly one that the average American student will find easier to understand than other translations now in use."

"Book Notices." *English Journal* 15, no. 2 (February 1927): 168.

Pease, C. A. *The Toils & Travels of Odysseus.* London: Wells Gardner, Darton & Co., 1916.

Townend, P., ed. *Burke's Genealogical and Heraldic History of the Landed Gentry, 18th edition.* London: Burke's Peerage, 1965–72.

B104

F. L. Lucas (1894–1967). *The Odyssey Translated in Selection. . . .* London: The Folio Society, 1948.

Octavo.

> But when came early Morning, with fingers rosy-red,
> Then the dear son of Odysseus started from his bed.

Frank Laurence Lucas hoped that this partial verse translation of some of the *Odyssey*'s "finest passages" would "bring home" the *Odyssey*'s "beauty" to modern readers who were put off by the length or repetitiveness of the Homeric epic. New Zealand born engraver John Buckland-Wright provided copperplate engravings. Lucas selected sections of the poem that were "full enough to give the heart of the story," and supplied an outline in prose of the rest. Lucas included much of this translation along with his *Iliad* (B94) in his 1951 *Greek Poetry for Everyman.*

Cohen, R. H. L. "Lucas, Frank Laurence (1894–1967)." Rev. Mark Pottle. *Oxford Dictionary of National Biography.*

Horne, A. "Wright, John Buckland (1897–1954)." *Oxford Dictionary of National Biography.*

Kirk, G. S. "Review: Some Translations of Greek Poetry." *Classical Review* (New Series) 2, no. 3/4 (December 1952): 219–21.

Lucas, F. L. *Greek Poetry for Everyman.* London: Dent, 1951.

B105

Charles Lamb (1775–1834). *The Adventures of Ulysses.* London: Groombridge and Sons, 1857.

Duodecimo.

> This history tells of the wanderings of Ulysses and his followers in their return from Troy, after the destruction of that famous city of Asia by the Grecians.

Essayist Charles Lamb first published this abbreviated prose version of the *Odyssey*, designed to convey "the air of a romance to young readers," in 1808. He intended it as "a supplement" to his 1805 *Adventures of Telemachus.* Lamb was very engaged in writing children's literature during the first decade of the nineteenth century, frequently collaborating with his sister, children's author Mary Anne Lamb. He felt that he had made the *Odyssey* "more attractive" to a young audience "by avoiding the prolixity" of its speeches and descriptive passages and adding "a rapidity" to its narrative. Lamb recognized, however, that his method entailed sacrificing "the manners to the passion, the subordinate characteristics to the essential interest of the story," and he insisted that this rendition be distinguished from the *Odyssey*'s "direct translations."

Lamb professed deep "obligations" to the *Odyssey* of Chapman (B1), and some editions of his work include the subtitle "Adapted from George Chapman's Translation of the Odyssey." Many contemporary reviewers felt that Lamb had borrowed too heavily from Chapman's rendition, resulting in a translation that the *Monthly Review* called frequently "harsh and obscure" and sometimes bordering "on vulgarity," and that the *Annual Review* criticized for its "unpleasing inconsistency of style . . . ingrafting antique phrases on modern diction." Despite these criticisms, Lamb's version of the *Odyssey* was extraordinarily popular: it has been translated into many different languages and gone through many editions, including one with an introduction by Andrew Lang (B24, B55) and one that accompanied John Flaxman's illustrations (E3). Lamb's *Adventures of Ulysses* was most recently reprinted in 2007 by Dodo Press in Gloucester.

Aaron, J. "Lamb, Mary Anne (1764–1847)." *Oxford Dictionary of National Biography.*

Annual Review and History of Literature; for 1808, vol. 7, p. 421.

Hayden, J. O. *The Romantic Reviewers, 1802–1824.* London: Routledge & Kegan Paul, 1969.

Lamb, C. *The Adventures of Telemachus, Son of Ulysses.* London: Printed for Tabart and Co., 1805.

———. *The Adventures of Ulysses.* London: Printed by T. Davison for the Juvenile Library, 1808.

Lamb, C., C. E. Atwood, and J. Flaxman. *The Adventures of Ulysses.* London: Society for Promoting Christian Knowledge, 1907.

Lamb, C., and G. Chapman. *The Adventures of Ulysses: Adapted from George Chapman's Translation of the Odyssey.* London: Horace Marshall, 1901.

Lamb, C., and A. Lang. *Lamb's Adventures of Ulysses.* London: Edward Arnold, 1890.

Lucas, E. V. *Charles Lamb and the Lloyds.* Philadelphia: J. B. Lippincott, 1899.

Monthly Review; or Literary Journal, Enlarged: From May to August, Inclusive 59 (May 1809): 105.

Swaab, P. "Lamb, Charles (1775–1834)." *Oxford Dictionary of National Biography.*

White, J. A. "Charles Lamb." *Dictionary of Literary Biography, Vol. 163: British Children's Writers, 1800–1880.* Edited by Meena Khorana. Farmington Hills, MI: Gale Group, 1996.

B106

Carl Witt (1815–1891). *The Wanderings of Ulysses (A Sequel to 'The Trojan War')*. . . . London: Longmans, Green, and Co., 1908.

Octavo.

> The long war against Troy had at last come to an end, and the Greek heroes were now preparing to return to their homes.

Professor Carl Witt, Headmaster of the Altstadt Gymnasium, Königsberg, originally published his German rendition of the *Odyssey* for young readers with his version of the *Iliad*, under the title *Der Trojanische Krieg und Die Heimkehr des Odysseus.* Witt rearranged each epic into a prose narrative that related the story's events in a chronological sequence. Frances Younghusband translated Witt's work into English in two separate volumes: *The Trojan War* (1884) and this sequel, *The Wanderings of Ulysses,* originally published in 1885. In her preface to this later edition, Younghusband noted the "kind reception" her rendering of *The Trojan War* had received, and she conveyed her hope that this volume would bring the story of the *Odyssey* within the English child's reach.

The *Saturday Review* predicted that children "would delight" in Witt's "bright and simple narratives" and praised Younghusband for "skillfully" preserving "the terse, expressive language, and admirable narrative style" of Witt's original. The *Scottish Review*, which could "conceive of nothing better" for children, went further in suggesting that *The Wanderings of Ulysses* might also "meet with the approval of those whose studies are long since passed."

Saturday Review, as cited in Longmans, Green, & Co.'s catalog in *Myths of Hellas, or, Greek Tales, Told in German by Professor C. Witt*, 5th ed. Translated by Frances Younghusband. London: Longmans, Green, and Co., 1891.

Scottish Review 6 (July & October 1885): 380–1.

Witt, C. *Der Trojanische Krieg und Die Heimkehr des Odysseus*. Augsburg, Germany: Lampart, 1883.

———. *The Trojan War*. Translated by F. Younghusband. London: Longmans, Green, and Co., 1884.

———. *The Wanderings of Ulysses*. Translated by F. Younghusband. London: Longmans, Green, and Co., 1885.

B107

Padraic Colum (1881–1972). *The Adventures of Odysseus and the Tale of Troy.* . . . New York: The Macmillan Company, 1918.

Octavo.

> This is the story of Odysseus, the most renowned of all the heroes the Greek poets have told us of—of Odysseus, his wars and his wanderings.

The spine-title identifies this prose retelling of the *Iliad* and *Odyssey* by Irish writer Padraic Colum as "The Children's Homer." The line drawings and color plates are by Hungarian illustrator Willy Pogany. Colum, who was born Patrick Collumb, adopted his Irish Gaelic name in 1901 when he joined the Gaelic League and the Irish Republican Brotherhood. He was also deeply involved in the Irish dramatic and poetic movements of that time. Financial concerns, however, prompted him to settle in New York after World War I, where he began writing works of Irish folklore for children. His first children's book, *The King of Ireland's Son* (1916), was well received and very profitable. Although he considered himself primarily a playwright and poet, Colum continued to support himself financially by producing children's books for the rest of his life.

The *Journal of Educational Philosophy* called his "Children's Homer" "at once intimate and spirited"—the "diction of the narration is simple, direct and dramatic," and the "charm of the tale is greatly enhanced by the splendid drawings of Willy Pogany." The volume has been reprinted many times, and Colum and Pogany renewed its copyright in 1946. In 1982, *Publishers Weekly* declared "Colum's stirring telling of the Greek epics" "still unequaled as an introduction to the classic myths for young readers." Recent editions of Colum's rendition of the *Iliad* and *Odyssey* include a 2001 audio recording by Sound Room Publishers and a 2004 printing by Aladdin Paperbacks.

Colum, P. *The King of Ireland's Son.* New York: Macmillan, 1916.

Journal of Educational Philosophy 11, no. 1 (1920): 178.

Publishers Weekly 222 (September 24, 1982): 73, cited in P. Colum, *The Children's Homer: The Adventures of Odysseus and the Tale of Troy.* New York: Aladdin, 1982.

Schirmer, G. A. "Padraic Colum." *Dictionary of Literary Biography, Vol. 19: British Poets, 1880–1914.* Edited by Donald E. Stanford. Farmington Hills, MI: Gale Group, 1983.

Sternlicht, S. "Colum, Padraic (1881–1972)." *Oxford Dictionary of National Biography.*

B108

Barbara Leonie Picard. *The Odyssey of Homer Retold. . . .* London: Oxford University Press, Geoffrey Cumberlege, 1952.

Octavo.

> After their ten-year-long war with the men of Troy was ended and the Trojan city had fallen in flames and smoke, the victorious Greeks gathered together their booty and their prisoners

Children's author Barbara Leonie Picard designed her prose version of the *Odyssey* "for young people" "to give the whole tale . . . as the exciting and wonderful adventure that it was." Only abridged or partial children's versions of the epic were available, and Picard found it "a pity" that girls and boys who couldn't yet read a standard translation were unable to experience Homer's entire story. She therefore set out to produce "a complete retelling" that altered the *Odyssey*'s language and narrative but omitted none of its story.

The *Peabody Journal of Education* praised Picard's "readable and exciting prose," and her "delightful telling of the story," which, together with British illustrator Joan Kiddell-Monroe's "imaginative" illustrations, rendered this volume "a book of distinction for young people." Picard's *Odyssey* has been reprinted in many editions, and now forms part of the Oxford Myths and Legends Series along with her *Iliad* (B109) and her numerous other retellings of fairy tales, myths, and legends.

Del Negro, J. M. "Barbara Leonie Picard." *Bulletin of the Center for Children's Books* [Online edition].http://bccb.lis.illinois.edu/0501true.html (accessed October 12, 2009).

Major Authors and Illustrators for Children and Young Adults: A Selection of Sketches from Something About the Author, 2nd ed. Detroit: Thomson/Gale, 2002.

"Peabody Bimonthly Booknotes." *Peabody Journal of Education* 30, no. 5 (March 1953): 315.

Picard, B. L. *The Odyssey of Homer.* Oxford: Oxford University Press, 1991.

B109

Barbara Leonie Picard. *The Iliad of Homer Retold. . . .* London: Oxford University Press, 1960.

Octavo.

> In the ninth year of the war against Troy a great disaster came upon the Greeks.

Barbara Leonie Picard retold Homer's complete story in this children's version of the *Iliad*, as she had in her *Odyssey* of eight years before (B108). Both volumes were illustrated by Joan Kiddell-Monroe. In the *Classical World*, E. F. Ridington recommended Picard's rendition not just to children, but "to almost anyone, young or old, who has been discouraged by the difficulties of Homer": Picard did "a very competent job" of presenting Homer's epic poem as "a smooth-flowing and easily understood story." Picard's *Iliad* was successful and went through many reprints; like her *Odyssey*, it was reissued in 1991 in the Oxford Myths and Legends Series.

Del Negro, J. M. "Barbara Leonie Picard." *Bulletin of the Center for Children's Books* [Online edition].http://bccb.lis.illinois.edu/0501true.html (accessed October 12, 2009).

Major Authors and Illustrators for Children and Young Adults: A Selection of Sketches from Something About the Author, 2nd ed. Detroit: Thomson/Gale, 2002.

Picard, B. L. *The Iliad of Homer.* Oxford: Oxford University Press, 1991.

Ridington, E. F. "Review: Some Recent Historical Fiction, III." *Classical World* 55, no. 1 (October 1961): 8.

SECTION C

TRANSLATIONS INTO OTHER LANGUAGES

LATIN TRANSLATIONS

C1

Lorenzo Valla (1407–1457). *Homeri Poetae Clarissimi Ilias per Laurentium Vallensem Romanum Latina Facta.* Cologne: Apud Heronem Alopecium, 1522.

Octavo.

Italian Renaissance humanist scholar Laurentius (Lorenzo) Valla wrote the first sixteen books of this Latin prose translation of the *Iliad* in the 1440s at the commission of King Alfonso V of Aragon (Alfonso the Magnanimous, ruler of Naples as Alfonso I), whom he served as private Latin secretary. Valla left the task of translating the remainder to Francesco Griffolini, one of his pupils. The earliest extant manuscript copy of the work recorded in WorldCat belonged to Pope Pius II and is preserved in the Vatican Library with the provisional dates of 1458–64, Pius II's papal tenure. The first printed edition was not published until 1474 in Brescia, after Alfonso and Valla's deaths. Amended editions had appeared in 1502 in Venice and 1512 in Leipzig before this Cologne publication by printer Hero Alopecius, dated June 1522 (*Mense Iunio Anni XXII*).

The prose medium that Valla chose reflected King Alfonso V's interest in obtaining the translation, which was primarily historical rather than literary. Alfonso explained his commission in a letter: "Since we so often find the poet Homer taken as a witness, an authority, an ornament by almost all writers . . . the desire seized us to know this great poet and to hear his account of the Trojan War, which among Italians is very celebrated, and yet no one really knows it" (*Cum sepenumero apud omnes fere scriptores inveniamus Homerum poetam in testimonium, in auctoritatem, in ornamentum assumi . . . cupido nobis incessit hunc tantum poetam cognoscendi et ab eo audiendi trojanum bellum, quod apud latinos etsi vulgatissimum tamen nulli pene est notum*). Although the *editio princeps* (A1) of Homer would not be printed until 1488, manuscript copies of the text of the *Iliad* and of commentaries like that of Eustathius (D4) were available. But knowledge of Greek, and especially Homeric Greek, was extraordinarily rare, and Homer was known in the west almost exclusively through two Latin works: the *Homerus Latinus* or epitome of the *Iliad*, a 1070-line Silver Age Latin hexametric poem based on Homer's story; and the *versio Latina*, a notoriously inelegant and inaccurate

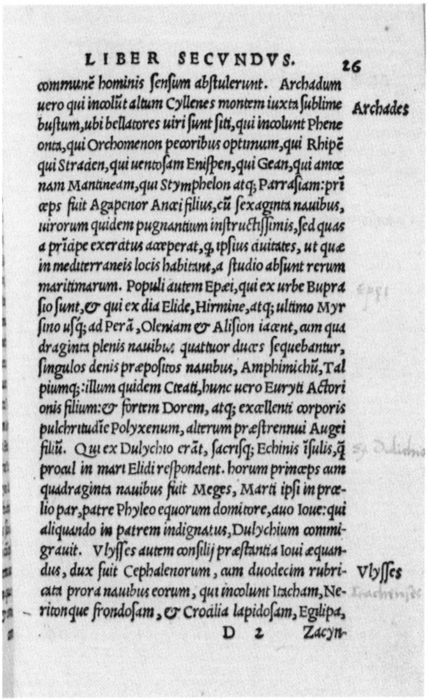

LIBER SECVNDVS. 26

communẽ hominis ſenſum abſtulerunt. Archadum uero qui incolũt altum Cyllenes montem iuxta ſublime buſtum, ubi bellatores uiri ſunt ſiti, qui incolunt Pheneonta, qui Orchomenon pecoribus optimum, qui Rhipẽ qui Stradien, qui uentoſam Eniſpen, qui Gean, qui amœnam Mantineam, qui Stymphelon atq; Parraſiam: prĩceps fuit Agapenor Ancæi filius, cũ ſexaginta nauibus, uirorum quidem pugnantium inſtructiſſimis, ſed quas a prĩcipe exercitus acceperat, q; ipſius ciuitates, ut quæ in mediterraneis locis habitant, a ſtudio abſunt rerum maritimarum. Populi autem Epæi, qui ex urbe Bupraſio ſunt, & qui ex dia Elide, Hirmine, atq; ultimo Myrſino uſq; ad Perã, Oleniam & Aliſion iacent, cum quadraginta plenis nauibus quattuor duces ſequebantur, ſingulos denis præpoſitos nauibus, Amphimichũ, Talpiumq;: illum quidem Cteati, hunc uero Euryti Actorionis filium: & fortem Dorem, atq; excellenti corporis pulchritudĩe Polyxenum, alterum præſtrennui Augei filiũ. Qui ex Dulychio erãt, ſacriſq; Echinis ĩſulis, q̃ procul in mari Elidi reſpondent. horum princeps cum quadraginta nauibus fuit Meges, Marti ipſi in prælio par, patre Phyleo equorum domitore, auo Ioue: qui aliquando in patrem indignatus, Dulychium commigrauit. Vlyſſes autem conſilij præſtantia Ioui æquandus, dux fuit Cephalenorum, cum duodecim rubricata prora nauibus eorum, qui incolunt Itacham, Neritonque frondoſam, & Croalia lapidoſam, Egilipa,

Archades

Vlyſſes

D 2 Zacyn-

C1

fourteenth-century verse rendition of the Homeric works written by the first professor of Greek at Florence, Leontius Pilatus, for Giovanni Boccaccio and annotated by Petrarch; this is the version that Andreas Divus would revise in the sixteenth century (C2).

Valla was renowned as a classical scholar, and his *de Elegantiis Latinae Linguae* was enormously influential in the reformation of Latin stylistics during the Renaissance. However, he was accused of basing his *Iliad* on Pilatus's Latin version rather than making a thorough examination of the original Homeric text. His work appears to reproduce neither the Greek original nor Pilatus's rendition, but instead to constitute a paraphrase of the *Iliad* in very elegant Latin, in line with the scholarly and linguistic priorities of Alfonso and Valla. As one of the earliest Latin representations of the epic, it was enormously important in the Renaissance transmission of Homer to the Greekless west. It was consulted extensively by Hugues Salel (C3), who was suspected of relying on it instead of the Greek text, and by George Chapman (B1, B6), who defended his own circumlocutions by challenging his critics to look at Valla, who was "ten parts more paraphrastical than I."

Allen, T. W. "Manuscripts of the Iliad in Rome." *Classical Review* 4, no. 7 (July 1890): 289–93.

Calonja, J. R. "Alfonso el Magnánimo y la Traducción de la '*Ilíada*' por Lorenzo Valla." *Boletín de la Real Academia de Buenas Letras de Barcelona* 23 (1950): 109–15.

Fay, H. C. "Chapman's Materials for his Translation of Homer." *Review of English Studies* 2, no. 5 (1951): 121–28.

———. "George Chapman's Translation of Homer's 'Iliad.'" *Greece & Rome* 21, no. 63 (1952): 104–11.

Kraye, J., ed. *The Cambridge Companion to Renaissance Humanism*. Cambridge: Cambridge University Press, 1996.

Rothstein, M. "Homer for the Court of François I." *Renaissance Quarterly* 59, no. 3 (Fall 2006): 732–67.

Sowerby, R. "Early Humanist Failure with Homer (I)." *International Journal of the Classical Tradition* 4, no. 1 (Summer 1997): 37–63.

———. "Early Humanist Failure with Homer (II)." *International Journal of the Classical Tradition* 4, no. 2 (Fall 1997): 165–94.

———. "The Homeric *Versio Latina*." *Illinois Classical Studies* 21 (1996): 161–202.

Warren, A. "Pope on the Translators of Homer." *Modern Philology* 29, no. 2 (November 1931): 229–32

C2

Andreas Divus (fl. 1535). *Homeri Poetarum Omnium Principis Ilias, Andrea Divo Iustinopolitao Interprete, ad Verbum Translata . . . Herodoti Halicarnassei Libellus, Homeri Vitam Fidelissime Continens, Conrado Heresbachio Interprete. . . .* Venice: Apud D. Iacob à Burgofrancho, 1537.

Octavo.

The BHL copy has an engraved title page, and a separate title for the *Odyssey*: *Homeri Poetae Clarissimi Odyssea, Andrea Divo Iustinopolitano Interprete, ad Verbum Translata . . . Batrachomyomachia . . . Aldo Manutio Romano Interpte . . . Hymni Deorum. XXXII Georgio Dartona Cretense Interprete.*

Little is known about the life of the Venetian Renaissance scholar Andreas Divus (Iustinopolitanus), the author of this *ad verbum* or literal Latin translation of the *Iliad* and *Odyssey*, as well as of literal Latin translations of Aristophanes and Theocritus that were printed in Venice in the two years following the publication of this edition (in 1538 and 1539, respectively). Divus's renditions of Homer were designed, as the preface to the *Odyssey* in this volume indicates, to be read in conjunction with the Aldine texts (A2, A6)—pages, line numbers, and lines corresponded to the Greek, "so that those reading this Greek poet can also have him in Latin, printed in such a way that with one glance they can see everything in both" (*ut qui Poetam hunc graecum legunt, eundem etiam habeant latinum ita excusum, ut uno intuitu omnia in utroque videre possint*). The Latin translation of the *Batrachomyomachia* in this edition is by Aldus Manutius; Ps.-Herodotus's *Life of Homer* (see A1) is translated by German Hellenist Conrad Heresbach and the *Hymns* by a (now obscure) Cretan scholar named Georgius Dartona.

Aside from the Aldine editions of the *Iliad* and *Odyssey*, Divus made extensive use of the fourteenth-century Latin translation by Leontius Pilatus that Valla had been accused of over-paraphrasing (C1), in many places copying it, but revising and correcting it by consulting the original Greek and the *scholia* attributed to Didymus (published in separate volumes by the Aldine Press in the 1520s [D1] and together with the Greek texts in Herwagen's 1535 Basel edition [A8]). A separate, improved but apparently unauthorized edition of Divus's translation

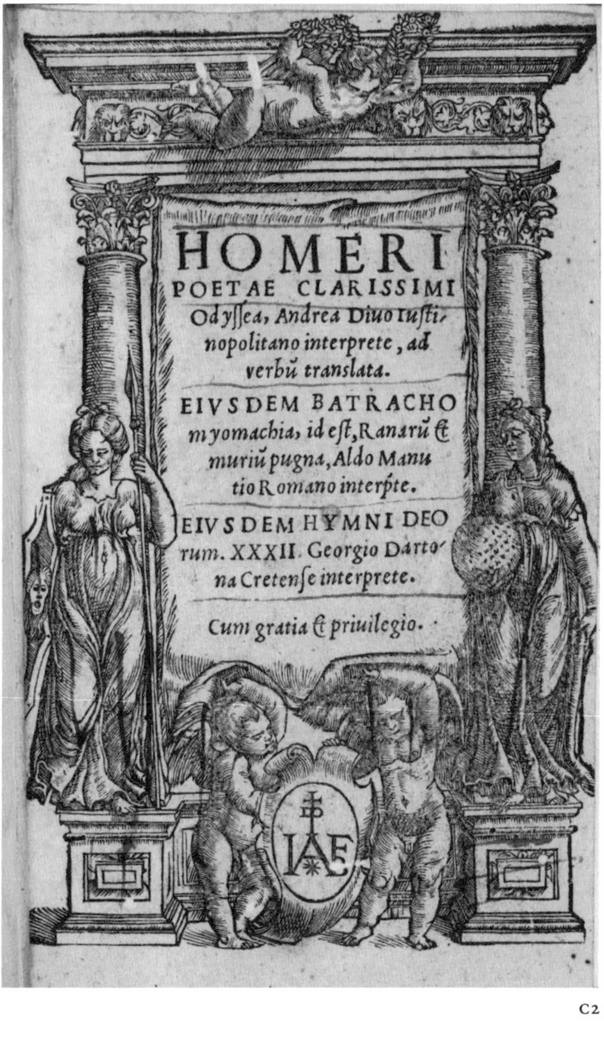
HOMERI
POETAE CLARISSIMI
Odyssea, Andrea Diuo Iustinopolitano interprete, ad
verbū translata.
EIVSDEM BATRACHO
myomachia, id est, Ranarū &
muriū pugna, Aldo Manu
tio Romano interpte.
EIVSDEM HYMNI DEO
rum. XXXII. Georgio Dartona Cretense interprete.
Cum gratia & priuilegio.

C2

also appeared in Venice in 1537; reprints in Paris, Lyons, and Solingen (1538–40), however, were based on this authorized edition, which has many more errors in its interpretation of the Greek. Divus's work was printed anonymously alongside the Greek text for the first time by Jean Crespin (A12, between 1560 and 1567), who published his bilingual editions of Homer as an aid to students trying to learn Greek (in the style adopted by James Loeb in the early twentieth century [B31, B64]). Divus's *Iliad* also appears in the 1561 bilingual Basel edition edited by Sebastien Castellion (A13), and both Divus's Homeric translations face Homer's text in Jean de Sponde's 1583 volume (A15).

Although Divus was rarely credited for his work, his *Iliad* and *Odyssey* became the standard Latin Homeric translations and were available to the Renaissance translators of Homer into French (like Salel and Jamyn [C3]), Spanish (like Pérez [C8]), Italian (like Baccelli [C9]), and English (like Chapman [B1, B6], who, without knowing Divus's identity, used Divus's version as it was printed in the Jean de Sponde edition so extensively that he sometimes translated directly from Divus's Latin, erring where Divus erred). Divus's *Iliad* and *Odyssey* continued to be printed and consulted long after modern-language translations of Homer had become common. Even in the twentieth century, Ezra Pound's first *Canto* included an English translation based on the first Paris edition of Divus's *Odyssey* rather than on Homer's text, as well as the invocation: "Lie quiet Divus. I mean, that Andreas Divus,/In officina Wecheli, 1538, out of Homer."

Fay, H. C. "Chapman's Materials for his Translation of Homer." *Review of English Studies* 2, no. 5 (1951): 121–28.

———. "George Chapman's Translation of Homer's 'Iliad.'" *Greece & Rome* 21, no. 63 (1952): 104–11.

Kenner, H. "Pound and Homer." *Ezra Pound among the Poets.* Edited by G. Bornstein. Chicago: University of Chicago Press, 1985.

Kraye, J., ed. *The Cambridge Companion to Renaissance Humanism.* Cambridge: Cambridge University Press, 1996.

Phinney, E. "Continental Humanists and Chapman's *Iliads.*" *Studies in the Renaissance* 12 (1965): 218–26.

Rothstein, M. "Homer for the Court of François I." *Renaissance Quarterly* 59, no. 3 (Fall 2006): 732–67.

Silver, I. *Ronsard and the Hellenic Renaissance in France.* Paris: Librairie Droz, 1961.

Sowerby, R. "Early Humanist Failure with Homer (I)." *International Journal of the Classical Tradition* 4, no. 1 (Summer 1997): 37–63.

———. "Early Humanist Failure with Homer (II)." *International Journal of the Classical Tradition* 4, no. 2 (Fall 1997): 165–94.

———. "The Homeric *Versio Latina.*" *Illinois Classical Studies* 21 (1996): 161–202.

C3

Hugues Salel (ca.1504–1553) and Amadis Jamyn (d. 1592 or 1593). *Les XXIIII Livres de L'Iliade D'Homere, Prince des Poëtes Grecs. Traduicts du Grec en Vers François. . . .* Paris: Pour Abel L'Angelier, 1584.

Duodecimo.

This edition contains a separate title page and text for *Les Trois Premiers Livres de L'Odyssee d'Homere. Mis du Grec en François, avec Certaines Notes sur les Principales Matieres.*

King François I commissioned poet and courtier Hugues Salel to translate the *Iliad* into French verse. In exchange for his efforts, Salel was appointed *valet du chambre* to the king and Abbé of Saint Cheron. In the *Privilege d'imprimer* for the first ten books (published in 1545), François wrote of "the usefulness, richness, and adornment that our French language receives today through this translation" (*l'utilité, richesse, & decoration que nostre langue Fran-*

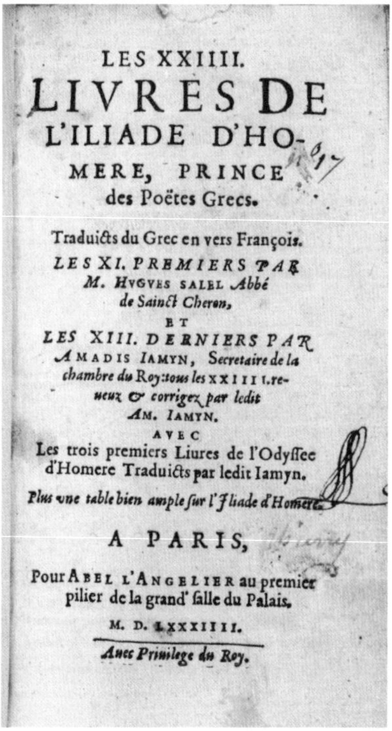

LES XXIIII.
LIVRES DE
L'ILIADE D'HOMERE, PRINCE
des Poëtes Grecs.

Traduicts du Grec en vers François.
LES XI. PREMIERS PAR M. HVGVES SALEL Abbé de Sainct Cheron,
ET
LES XIII. DERNIERS PAR AMADIS IAMYN, Secretaire de la chambre du Roy: tous les XXIIII. reueuz & corrigez par ledit AM. IAMYN.
AVEC
Les trois premiers Liures de l'Odyssee d'Homere Traduicts par ledit Iamyn.
Plus vne table bien ample sur l'Iliade d'Homere.

A PARIS,

Pour ABEL L'ANGELIER au premier pilier de la grand' salle du Palais.

M. D. LXXXIIII.

Auec Priuilege du Roy.

C3

coise recoit au iourdhuy, par ceste Traduction). Salel had completed only two more books by the time of his death eight years later. These were edited and published in 1554 by Salel's amanuensis, poet Olivier de Magny, who affirmed that Salel had worked from the original Greek, not, as some contemporaries alleged, solely from Valla's Latin translation (C1). In an epitaph first published in that edition, poet Pierre de Ronsard praised Salel, who, in first rendering Homer in French, "was among the first to draw our language out from its infancy, and whose wisdom well deserved being treated so kindly by so great a King" (*des premiers tira nostre langue d'enfance,/Et de qui le sçavoir avoit bien mérité/D'estre d'un si grand Roy si doucement traitté*).

Salel's translation was completed by poet Amadis Jamyn, friend and pupil of Ronsard, student of Adrianus Turnebus (A11), and Secrétaire et Lecteur Ordinaire to both Charles IX and Henri III. In 1577, Jamyn first published a complete French translation of the *Iliad* containing Salel's version of books 1–11 and his own of the remainder. This 1584 expanded edition also includes Jamyn's rendition of the first three books of the *Odyssey*. A 1581 translation of Salel's first ten books by British politician Arthur Hall represents the first English Homeric publication, preceding Chapman's *Seaven Bookes of the Iliades of Homere* (B6) by seventeen years. Although Chapman criticized "the Glose/Grave Salel makes in French as he translates," his remarks are a testament to the importance of Salel's *Iliade* in the history not only of French but also of English Homeric translation and reception.

Cary, H. *The Early French Poets: A Series of Notices and Translations*. London: Henry G. Bohn, 1846.

Ford, P. "Homer in the French Renaissance." *Renaissance Quarterly* 59, no. 1 (Spring 2006): 1–28.

Hall, A. *Ten Books of Homers Iliades, Translated out of the French*. London: Ralphe Newberie, 1581.

Harvitt, H. J. "Hugues Salel, Poet and Translator." *Modern Philology* 16, no. 11 (March 1919): 595–605.

Jamyn, A. and H. Salel. *Les XXIIII Livres de L'Iliade*. Paris: Lucas Breyer, 1577.

Kalwies, H. H. *Hugues Salel, His Life and Works*. Ann Arbor, MI: Applied Literature Press, 1979.

Rothstein, M. "Homer for the Court of François I." *Renaissance Quarterly* 59, no. 3 (Fall 2006): 732–67.

Salel, H. *Les Dix Premiers Livres de l'Iliade d'Homere traduits en Vers François*. Paris: Sertenas, 1545.

Silver, I. *Ronsard and the Hellenic Renaissance in France*. Paris: Librairie Droz, 1961.

C4

Claude Boitet de Frauville (1570–1625). *L'Odissee D'Homere. . . .* Paris: Chez la veusue Matthieu Guillemot, 1617.

Octavo.

The title page of this first French prose rendition of the *Odyssey* identifies the translator as Claude Boitel, Advocat au Parlement de Paris. The volume's dedicatory epistle to Cardinal de la Roche-Foucault is signed Cl. Boitet, and the translator is generally identified as Claude Boitet de Frauville, translator of Nonnus's Homeric *Dionysiaca* (1625) and author of *Les Tableaux d'Amour* (1618), *Le Fidelle Historien des Affaires de France* (1623), and *Le Prince des Princes, ou, l'Art de Regner* (1632). Although the obscurity surrounding Boitet's *Odyssey* suggests that it had little influence on Homeric scholarship or translation in France, a new, expanded edition of Boitet's version with a history of Troy appended did appear in 1619, and a revised edition was published posthumously in 1638.

Boitet, C. *Les Tableaux d'Amour.* Paris: Tiffaine, 1618.

———. *Le Fidelle Historien des Affaires de France.* Paris: T. Du Bray, 1623.

———. *Les Dionysiaques.* Paris: Fouet, 1625.

———. *Le Prince des Princes, ou, l'Art de Regner.* Paris: C. Besongne, 1632.

Goujet, C-P. *Bibliothèque Françoise, ou Histoire de la Littérature Françoise.* Vol. 4. Paris: P. J. Mariette & H.-L. Guerin, 1741.

Hoefer, J. C. F. "Boitet de Frauville (Claude)." *Nouvelle Biographie Générale.* 1852.

C4

C5

Madame Dacier (d. 1720). *L'Illiade d'Homere*. . . . Paris: Chez Rigaud, 1711.

Duodecimo. 3 vols.

From the Blenheim Library of Charles Spencer, Third Earl of Sunderland, with both the early (ink) and later (pencil) sets of shelfmarks (1675–1722).

Translator and classicist Anne Le Fèvre Dacier spent fifteen years rendering the *Iliad* and *Odyssey* (C7) into French prose, which she felt could best "follow all the ideas of the Poet, preserve the beauty of his images, and say all that he said" (*suivre toutes les idées du Poëte, conserver la beauté de ses images, dire tout ce qu'il a dit*)—a feat impossible in French verse, where a translator "must by necessity alter, subtract, and add" (*il faut necessairement qu'il change, qu'il retranche, qu'il ajoûte*). Following the original Greek text, the commentary of Eustathius (D4), and René le Bossu's rules of epic translation (D7), Mme. Dacier strove to present Greekless readers with a French version of Homer "much less altered than in previous translations, where he was so strangely disfigured as to be no longer recognizable" (*bien moins changé que dans les traductions qu'on en a faites, où on lá si étrangement défiguré, qu'il n'est plus reconnoissable*). Mme. Dacier had learned Greek and Latin at an early age from her father, professor of *belles lettres* Tanneguy le Fèvre. In the preface to her first publication, a 1675 bilingual Greek and Latin edition of the poems of Callimachus, she responded to those who questioned her father's decision to give her an education normally reserved for men: "he did it with the intention that there would one day be a woman who would serve as a reproach to [men] for their sloth and ignorance" (*hoc illum eo animo egisse, scilicet ut esset aliquando quae eis socordium & ignavium exprobraret*).

In 1683, Anne married André Dacier, a classicist and former student of her father; she continued editing and translating classical texts, occasionally working in collaboration with her husband. In the preface to this edition, Mme. Dacier refers to her earlier works as "amusements" but declares her ambition here "to give our age a translation of Homer, which, while preserving the principle traits of this great Poet, could reclaim the majority of cultured people from the disadvantageous prejudice given them by the deformed copies made of him" (*donner à nostre siecle une traduction d'Homere, qui, en conservant les principaux traits de ce grand Poëte, pust faire revenir la pluspart de gens du monde du préjugé desavantageux que leur en ont donné des copies difformes qu'on en a faites*). Her admiration for Homer and his poetry in opposition to the "false art" (*faux art*) of her own times, as well as her dedication to fidelity in her translation of Homer's works, placed Mme. Dacier firmly on the side of the Ancients in the *Querelle des Anciens et des Modernes*—a dispute that erupted in France in the late seventeenth century during the reign of Louis XIV between those who regarded the Greek and Latin classics as insuperable and perfect works and those who believed that modern society had come to surpass its classical models. In fact, Mme. Dacier's *Iliad* seems to have revived the quarrel both in France, where Houdar de la Motte soon afterward published his "modern" version of Homer's work (C6), and in England, where her principles continued in Ozell, Broome, and Oldisworth's translation of her work (B8)—Ozell wrote that she had "outdone herself, and given to her Name a Lustre which is capable of no further Addition"—and where her commentary and translation were indispensable to Alexander Pope in preparing his English version of the epic (B9).

This edition contains a frontispiece designed by Antoine Coypel and engraved by Charles Louis Simonneau, with illustrations engraved by Bernard Picart.

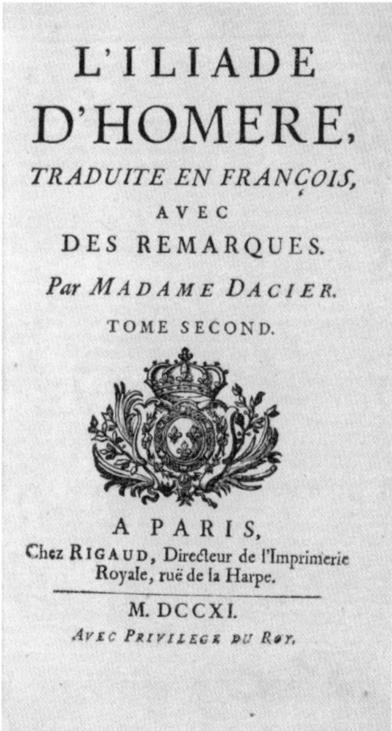

L'ILIADE
D'HOMERE,
TRADUITE EN FRANÇOIS,
AVEC
DES REMARQUES.
Par MADAME DACIER.
TOME SECOND.
A PARIS,
Chez RIGAUD, Directeur de l'Imprimerie
Royale, ruë de la Harpe.
M. DCCXI.
AVEC PRIVILEGE DU ROY.

C5

Barnard, J. *Alexander Pope: The Critical Heritage.* London: Routledge, 1995.

"Biographical Sketch of Madame Dacier (Extracted from Mary Hay's 'Female Biography')." *Belfast Monthly Magazine* 10, no. 57 (April 30, 1813): 288–93.

Dacier, A. *Des Causes de la Corruption du Goût.* Paris: Rigaud, 1715.

Farnham, F. *Madame Dacier: Scholar and Humanist.* Monterey, CA: Angel Press, 1976.

Levine, J. M. *The Battle of the Books: History and Literature in the Augustan Age.* Ithaca, NY: Cornell University Press, 1994.

Mazon, P. *Madame Dacier et les Traductions d'Homère en France.* Oxford: Clarendon Press, 1936.

Morton, R. *Examining Changes in the Eighteenth-century French Translations of Homer's* Iliad *by Anne Dacier and Houdar de la Motte.* Lewiston, NY: Edwin Mellen, 2003.

Patey, D. L. "Ancients and Moderns." *The Cambridge History of Literary Criticism, Vol. 4: The Eighteenth Century.* Edited by G. A. Kennedy, H. B. Nisbet, and C. Rawson. Cambridge: Cambridge University Press, 2005.

Pieretti, M.-P. "Women Writers and Translation in Eighteenth-Century France." *French Review* 75, no. 3 (February 2002): 474–88.

Rigault, H. *Histoire de la Querelle des Anciens et des Modernes.* Paris: s.n., 1856.

Weinbrot, H. D. "Alexander Pope and Madame Dacier's *Homer*: Conjectures Concerning Cardinal Dubois, Sir Luke Schaub, and Samuel Buckley." *Huntington Library Quarterly* 62, no.1/2 (1999): 1–23.

C6

Antoine Houdar de la Motte (1672–1731). *L'Iliade. Poëme. Avec un Discours sur Homere.* Paris: Chez Gregoire Dupuis, 1714.

Octavo.

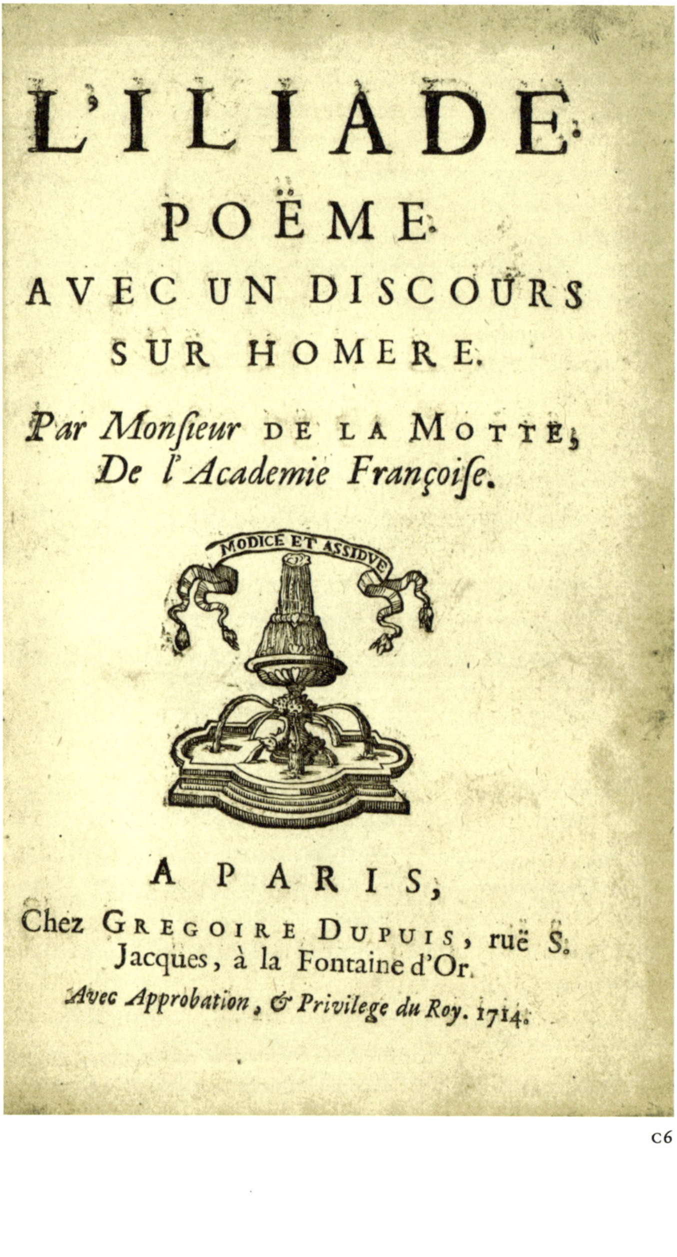

C6

FRENCH

Three years after the publication of Mme. Dacier's faithful prose translation of the *Iliad* (C5), poet Antoine Houdar de la Motte published this abridged French verse rendition, which he had been working on since 1701. The *Discours sur Homère* in this edition often responds directly to Mme. Dacier's work; it identifies La Motte as a *Moderne* who sees defects in Homer's poetry and adapts it to conform to the superior tastes and beliefs of his own times. He writes of his rendition: "I have followed those parts of the *Iliad* that seemed to me to deserve to be preserved, and I have taken the liberty of changing what I found disagreeable. I am a translator in many passages, and an original author in many others" (*j'ai suivi de l'Iliade, ce qui m'a paru devoir en être conservé, & j'ai pris la liberté de changer ce que j'ai crû désagréable. Je suis traducteur en beaucoup d'endroits, & original en beaucoup d'autres*). La Motte, who knew no Greek, altered, rearranged, rewrote, and cut out whole sections of Homer's epic in his attempt to compose a modern version in only twelve books: "I have contented myself with correcting, as far as it was possible, the defects that are shocking or boring; these cannot be excused" (*Je me suis donc contenté de remedier, autant qu'il m'a été possible, aux défauts qui choquent ou qui ennuyent; ceux-là ne se pardonent point*).

Mme. Dacier responded to M. de la Motte's rendition with *Des Causes de la Corruption du Goût* (1714), attacking both la Motte for having "disfigured" (*défiguré*) Homer beyond recognition and the delicate tastes of the contemporary readers his version found favor with. La Motte replied with three volumes of *Réflexions sur la Critique* (1715) that reiterated his views on Homer's epic and on Mme. Dacier's principles. Various translations carried their argument over to England, where, instead of taking sides in what he termed "the French dispute concerning Homer," Alexander Pope (B9, B49) concurred with his correspondent John Sheffield, Duke of Buckingham, in criticizing "the too great disposition of finding faults, in the one, and of confessing none in the other."

The illustrations were designed by Francois Roettier, Jean-Marc Nattier, and Ferdinand Delamonce, and engraved by Jean Chaufourier and Nicholas-Etienne Edelinck.

Dacier, A. *Des Causes de la Corruption du Goût.* Paris: Rigaud, 1715.

de la Motte, A. H. *Réflexions sur la Critique.* Paris: Du puis, 1715.

Levine, J. M. *The Battle of the Books: History and Literature in the Augustan Age.* Ithaca, NY: Cornell University Press, 1994.

Morton, R. E. *Examining Changes in the Eighteenth-Century French Translations of Homer's* Iliad *by Anne Dacier and Houdar de la Motte.* Lewiston, NY: Edwin Mellen, 2003.

Patey, D. L. "Ancients and Moderns." *The Cambridge History of Literary Criticism, Vol: 4: The Eighteenth Century.* Edited by G. A. Kennedy, H. B. Nisbet, and C. Rawson. Cambridge: Cambridge University Press, 2005.

Pope, A. *The Works of Alexander Pope, Esq.: With Notes and Illustrations.* Vol. 6, letters 6–7.

Edited by W. Roscoe. London: Longman, Brown, and Co., 1847.

Rigault, H. *Histoire de la Querelle des Anciens et des Modernes.* Paris: s.n., 1856.

Theobald. *A Critical Discourse upon Homer's* Iliad. *Translated from the French of Mr. de la Motte.* London: Bernard Lintott, 1714.

C7

Madame Dacier (d. 1720). *L'Odyssée D'Homere. . . .* Paris: Aux dépens de Rigaud, 1716.

Duodecimo. 3 vols.

From the Blenheim Library of Charles Spencer, Third Earl of Sunderland, with both the early (ink) and later (pencil) sets of shelfmarks (1675–1722).

As she stated in the preface to her 1711 *Iliad* (C5), Mme. Dacier delayed the completion and publication of this French prose version of the *Odyssey* after her daughter's death. Instead of continuing her defense of Homer against M. de la Motte (C6) and other *Moderne* critics, Mme. Dacier focused her preface here on outlining the art of epic poetry, illustrating for her readers "the difference between poems that are wise and useful, and poems that are ugly and dangerous" (*la difference qu'il y a entre des Poëmes sages & utiles, & des Poëmes informes & dangereux*). In the 1719 second edition of her *Iliad*, however, Mme. Dacier felt herself "obliged to defend him again" (*obligée de le défendre encore*), this time not against "those who have condemned him without knowing him" (*qui l'ont condamné sans le connoître*), but against Alexander Pope (B9, B49), a "more enlightened" (*plus éclairé*) man the better able "to harm him" (*lui nuire*) for appearing "to be filled with a greater admiration for him" (*rempli pour lui d'une admiration plus grand*). Mme. Dacier, who read a French version of the preface to Pope's *Iliad* (she read no English, and was unable to read Pope's translation), found fault with Pope for inadequately appreciating Homer's beauties, and for presenting himself as "Homer's reformer" (*reformateur d'Homere*), in addition to inadequately expressing the extent to which he had relied on her own work and notes in writing his translation. Pope, who had "fought under Madam *Dacier's* banner," waging "war in defence of the divine *Homer* against all the Hereticks of the age," responded in the Postscript to his *Odyssey* that he had been misunderstood: "How unhappy was it for me, that the knowledge of our *Island tongue* was as necessary to Madam *Dacier* in my case, as the knowledge of *Greek* was to Monsieur *de la Motte* in that of our great Author."

This edition contains a frontispiece designed by Antoine Coypel and engraved by Benoit Audran, and illustrations designed by C. Farret and engraved by Jonghe/Jongman and A. van Buysen/Buisen.

C8

Gonzalo Pérez (fl. 1533–1566). *La Ulyxea de Homero. . . .* Anvers: en Casa de Iuan Steelsio, 1556.

Octavo.

This verse rendition of the *Odyssey* by clergyman and courtier Gonzalo Pérez is the first Spanish Homeric translation. The work has sometimes been attributed to priest and Hellenist Juan Páez De Castro, who, along with Cardinal Francisco Mendoza de Bobadilla, appears to have helped Pérez work from the original Greek text. Pérez served as secretary of state in the courts of Holy Roman Emperor Charles V (ruler of Spain as Carlos I) and Philip II (King of Spain from 1556, when Charles V abdicated his Spanish kingdoms). He published the first thirteen books of his translation in 1550, dedicating the work to his pupil Philip and instructing the future ruler to look below the surface of Homer's words: Homer had written "many things, in which, once the outer crust was removed, one could discover very great secrets from which not only Your Highness with your excellent judgment, but also any other prince . . . could draw great benefit" (*muchas cosas, en que quitada la corteza se descubren muy grandes secretos de quo no sólo V. Alteza con su excellentíssimo juycio, mas aun otro qualquier príncipe . . . podría sacar mucho fructo*).

This first revised and complete edition of Pérez's *Ulyxea* is dedicated to Philip as the new King of Spain and, through his marriage to Mary I, King of England at the time of this volume's publication. Pérez's political prominence increased with Philip's ascension to the throne, and his illegitimate son, humanist Antonio Pérez, assumed the role of royal secretary from the time of his father's death until 1579, when Philip had him arrested for disloyalty. Gonzalo Pérez's *Odyssey* was reprinted in 1562 in Venice and in 1767 in Madrid. Although it has not been praised for beauty or accuracy, it has been celebrated for its importance in making Homer available for the first time in Spanish, and credited at least in part for the *Odyssey*'s influence on the romantic and picaresque literature of Golden Age Spain, particularly on the works of Miguel de Cervantes and Lope de Vega. Homer continued, however, to be read primarily in Latin in Spain through versions like Valla's (C1) and Divus's (C2), and this remained the only Spanish Homeric translation until Ignacio García Malo first published his *Iliada de Homero* in 1788, more than two hundred years later.

Guichard, L. A. "Un Autógrafo de la Traducción de Homero de Gonzalo Pérez (*Ulyxea XIV–XXIV*) Anotado por Juan Páez de Castro y el Cardenal Mendoza y Bovadilla." *International Journal of the Classical Tradition* 15, no. 4 (December 2008): 525–57.

Malo, Ignacio García. *La Iliada de Homero.* Madrid: Por Pantaleón Aznar, 1788.

Palencia, A. G. *Gonzalo Pérez Secretario de Felipe II.* Madrid: s.n., 1946.

Pérez, G. *De la Ulyxea de Homero XIII. Libros.* Antwerp: en Casa de Iuan Stelsio, 1550; Salamanca: en Casa de Andrea Portonariis, 1550.

———. *La Ulyxea.* Venice: en Casa de Francisco Rampazeto, 1562.

———. *La Ulyxea de Homero, Traducida de Griego en Lengua Castellana.* Madrid: F. Xavier, 1767.

Ricapito, J. V. "Classicity in the Spanish Golden Age: Gonzalo Pérez's Translation of *La Ulyxea* and the Origin of the Spanish Picaresque Novel." *The Picaresque: A Symposium on the Rogue's Tale.* Edited by C. Benito-Vessels and M. O. Zappala. Newark: University of Delaware Press, 1994.

Wright, E. R. *Pilgrimage to Patronage: Lope de Vega and the Court of Philip III, 1598–1621.* Lewisburg, PA: Bucknell University Press, 2001.

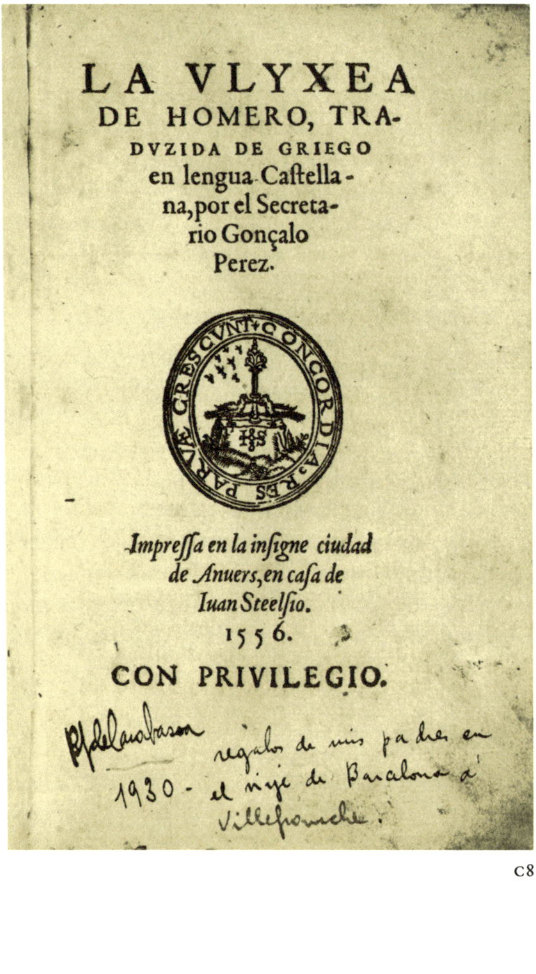
LA VLYXEA
DE HOMERO, TRA-
DVZIDA DE GRIEGO
en lengua Castella-
na, por el Secreta-
rio Gonçalo
Perez.

*Impressa en la insigne ciudad
de Anuers, en casa de
Iuan Steelsio.*
1556.
CON PRIVILEGIO.

regalo de mis padres en
1930 - el viaje de Barcelona à
Villefranche.

C8

C9

Girolamo Baccelli (ca. 1515–1581). *L'Odissea d'Homero Tradotta in Volgare Fiorentino*. Florence: Appresso il Sermartelli, 1582.

Octavo.

Florentine doctor and poet Girolamo Baccelli died before publishing this "*Homero Fiorentino*," his verse rendition of the *Odyssey* that broke with the tradition established by Renaissance translators in Italy like Valla (C1) and Divus (C2) and represents the first version of either Homeric epic in Italian instead of Latin. Baccelli was a member and (in 1551) *Consolo* of the *Accademia Fiorentina*, a state-sponsored institution fostered by first Grand Duke of Tuscany Cosimo I de'Medici to promote the use of the Tuscan vernacular rather than Latin in the arts. The manuscript of this *Odyssey* was prepared for publication by Baccio Baccelli, Girolamo's brother and fellow *Accademia Fiorentina* member. In the dedication of this edition to Francesco I de' Medici, second Grand Duke of Tuscany, Baccio praised his brother for first bringing "from Greece to Florence this, as it were, most precious joy of Homer's poetry" (*di Grecia in Firenze questa quasi preziosissima gioia delle Poesie d'Homero*). The translation's shortcomings, according to Baccio, should be attributed to his brother's untimely death rather than to his lack of skill as a translator: it would have been "more refined and cleaned up" (*piu affinata e tersa*) if Girolamo had lived long enough to revise it. In addition to his *Odyssey*, Girolamo had rendered the first seven books of the *Iliad* in Tuscan vernacular by the time he died. Baccio never published these, but he hoped that other writers would soon supply a complete Italian rendition, "tempted by his example" (*invitato dall'esempio di lui*). Nevertheless, an Italian version of the *Iliad*—Federico Malipiero's 1642 *l'Iliada d'Omero*—did not appear until sixty years later. This remained the only edition of Baccelli's *Odyssey* until 1805, when the translation was reprinted as part of a five-volume collection that also presented the work of many late eighteenth- and early nineteenth-century literary figures attempting to render Homer in Italian, including Ippolito Pindemonte (C11).

Davies, J. *Culture and Power: Tuscany and its Universities 1537–1609*. Leiden and Boston: Brill, 2009.

Inghirami, F. *Storia della Toscana*. Vol. 12. Florence: Dai Torchi dell'autore, 1843.

Malipiedo, F. *l'Iliada d'Omero Trapportata dall Greca nella Toscana Lingua*. Venice: Baglioni, 1642.

Poggiali, G., ed. *La Iliade di Omero Recata dal Testo Greco in Versi Toscani da G. Ceruti . . . L'Odissea Tradotta in Volgare Fiorentino da G. Baccelli*. Livorno: Presso Tommaso Masi e Comp., 1805.

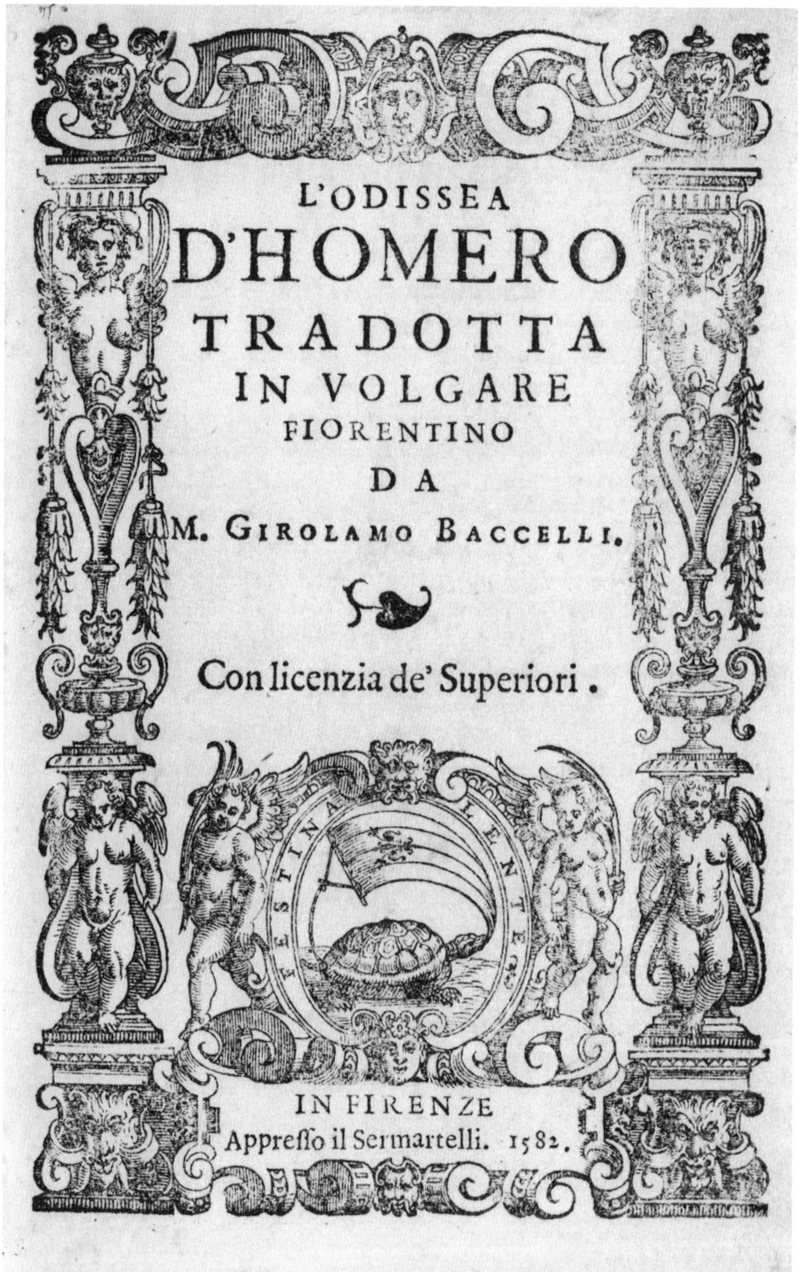

L'ODISSEA
D'HOMERO
TRADOTTA
IN VOLGARE
FIORENTINO
DA
M. GIROLAMO BACCELLI.

Con licenzia de' Superiori.

IN FIRENZE
Appresso il Sermartelli. 1582.

C9

C10

Francesco Velez e Bonanno (fl. 1661). *L'Iliade d'Homero, Tradotta in Verso Italiano*. Palermo: per il Bisagni, [1661].

Duodecimo.

Francesco Velez e Bonanno dedicated this verse translation of the *Iliad* in Sicilian dialect to Don Giovanni d'Austria (Don Juan José de Austria), the illegitimate son of Philip IV of Spain (King of Spain from 1621 to 1665). Don Juan José had formerly ruled Sicily as viceroy, but he was commanding troops against the Portuguese in western Spain at the time of this volume's publication (no date appears on the title page, but the dedication is signed D. Francesco Velez, e Bonanno, 1661). Velez e Bonanno offered his translation as a mark of his devotion, begging his patron to excuse Homer for his shortcomings, "since as a foreigner he cannot easily adapt to our ways" (*perche come forestiere, non può leggiermente ausarsi alle maniere nostrali*), and to excuse the fact that he could show his reverence "only with a few lines of verse" (*solo con poche righe*). He had no greater aspirations for his *Iliad*, which had been "undertaken as a private enjoyment, and as pure exercise in the two languages, Greek and Italian" (*intrapresa per un cotal privato diporto, e per mero esercitio delle due lingue, Greca, & Italiana*), than for it to "lie buried in dust, the prey of hungry moths" (*restarne sepolta di polvere, scherzo dell'ingorde tarme*)—a fate preferable to ending up in the "critical teeth of the spiteful" (*dente critico de'malevoli*), who would accuse him "either of audacity or of imprudence for trying to translate into the vernacular an author, who in his own native language has worn out admiration and applause" (*ò d'ardito, ò d'imprudente il tramettermi di volgarizzar un autore, che nella sua natia favella hà stancato l'anamiratione, e gli applausi*). The translation does not appear to have far exceeded its author's expectations at the time of its publication and is cloaked in obscurity now: this is the only copy recorded in WorldCat, and little seems to be known with certainty about Velez e Bonanno himself except that he was a Spaniard living in Palermo.

Mongitore, A. "Franciscus Velez, & Bonannus." *Bibliotheca Siculia*. Vol. 1. 1708.

C11

Ippolito Pindemonte (1753–1828). *Odissea d'Omero Tradotta*. Verona: Dalla Società Tipografica Editrice, 1822.

Octavo. 2 vols.

This is the first complete edition of poet Ippolito Pindemonte's verse translation of the *Odyssey*, which quickly became the standard Italian version of the epic. Pindemonte belonged to a wealthy and noble Veronese family, which afforded him the opportunity to receive an education in the classical languages, travel extensively, and become well versed in the European literature of his age. His earliest Homeric publications were a 1778 tragedy entitled *Ulisse* and a 1785 translation of the Hymn to Ceres (reprinted alongside Baccelli's *Odissea* [C9] in

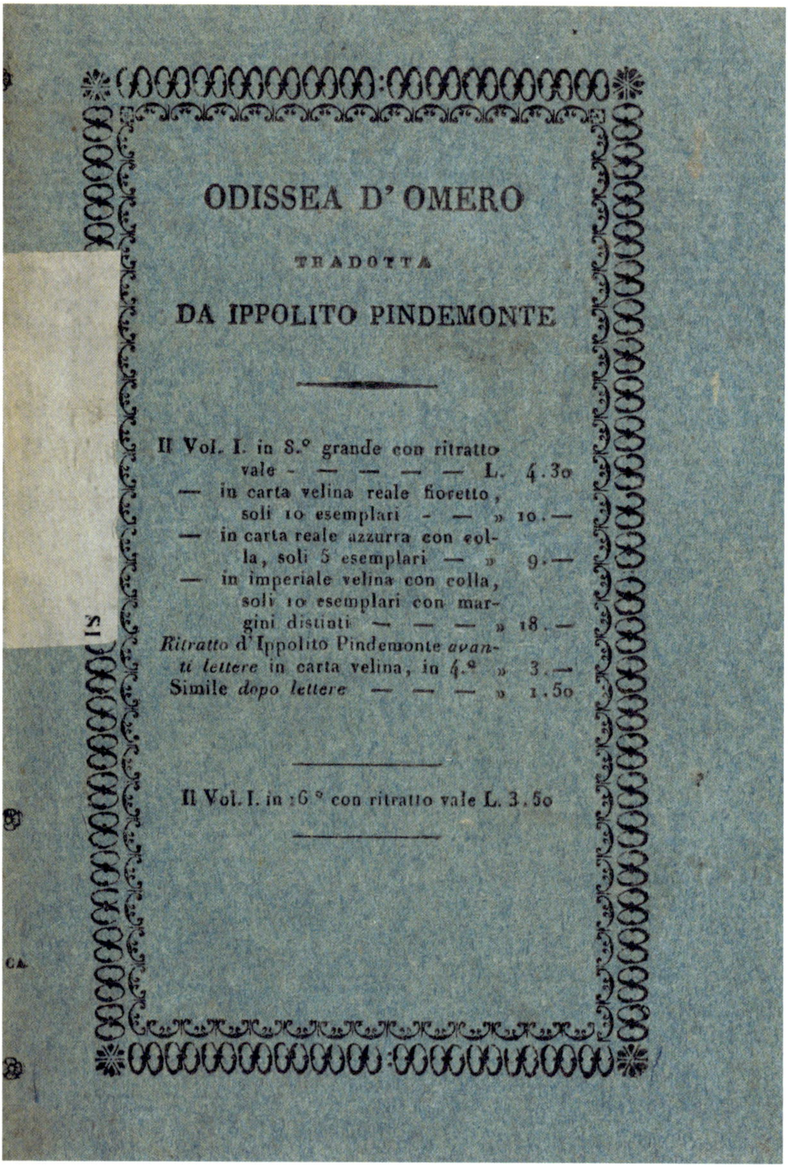

ODISSEA D' OMERO

TRADOTTA

DA IPPOLITO PINDEMONTE

Il Vol. I. in 8.° grande con ritratto vale - — — — — L. 4.30
— in carta velina reale fioretto, soli 10 esemplari - — » 10.—
— in carta reale azzurra con colla, soli 5 esemplari — » 9.—
— in imperiale velina con colla, soli 10 esemplari con margini distinti — — — » 18.—
Ritratto d'Ippolito Pindemonte *avanti lettere* in carta velina, in 4.° » 3.—
Simile *dopo lettere* — — — » 1.50

Il Vol. I. in 16.° con ritratto vale L. 3.50

CII

1805). Although surrounded by turmoil for much of his life—he was living in Paris when the French Revolution began in 1789, and in Italy throughout the Napoleonic wars of the 1790s and 1800s—Pindemonte refrained from becoming involved in the political events of his times. He patriotically remained in Verona when the Republic of Venice fell to Napoleon in 1797 but kept apart from public conflict and devoted himself instead to his private literary affairs. He was intimate with the leading contemporary literary figures in Italy, including Ugo Foscolo and Vincenzo Monti (C12), whose experiments with the *Iliad* (first published in 1807) inspired him to try translating the *Odyssey.*

In 1809, Pindemonte published his translation of the first two books, invoking the need for a balance between "fidelity" (*fedeltà*) and "license" (*lecito*) in translating the original Greek (Pindemonte consulted many texts, including Clarke's *Odyssey* [A19] and the commentaries of Eustathius [D4]) into Italian, a language he found inherently less capable of faithfully reproducing Homeric poetry than the English Alexander Pope had used (B9, B49). When he published this complete *Odyssey* thirteen years later, Pindemonte maintained that the beauty of Italian, "certainly the most beautiful language among the modern ones" (*lingua certo bellissima tra le moderne*), could never make up for the fact that "the Greeks had built their works in marble, and translators copy them in brick" (*avere i Greci innalzate le lor fabbriche in marmo, e i traduttori copiarle in mattoni*). He claimed that he had finished his version of the poem solely because of the pleasure it afforded him and the favor with which his translation of the first two books had been received. Despite Pindemonte's modest ambitions, his *Odyssey* was reprinted continuously in the years following this first publication, and it remained, alongside Monte's *Iliad* (C12), the standard Italian Homer through the early twentieth century.

This volume contains a frontispiece portrait of Pindemonte painted by Giacomo Fumicelli and engraved by Giovanni Boggi.

Bondanella, P. and J. C. Bondanella, eds. "Pindemonte, Ippolito (1753–1828)." *Cassell Dictionary of Italian Literature.* London: Cassell, 1996.

"Critical Sketches." *Foreign Quarterly Review* 5 (November 1829 & February 1830): 325–28.

Marrone, G., ed. "Ippolito Pindemonte." *Encyclopedia of Italian Literary Studies.* New York: Routledge, 2007.

Pindemonte, I. *Traduzione de'Due Primi Canti dell'Odissea e di Alcune Parti delle Georgiche.* Verona: Presso il Gambaretti, 1809.

———. *Ulisse: Tragedia: Si Aggiungono Alcune Osservazioni contro la Medesima.* Florence: s.n., 1778.

Poggiali, G., ed. *La Iliade di Omero Recata dal Testo Greco in Versi Toscani da G. Ceruti . . . L'Odissea Tradotta in Volgare Fiorentino da G. Baccelli.* Livorno: Presso Tommaso Masi e Comp., 1805.

Stebbing, H. "Ippolito Pindemonte." *Lives of the Italian Poets.* London: Richard Bentley, 1860.

C12

Vincenzo Monti (1754–1828). *Iliade di Omero. . . .* Milan: Dalla Società Tipogr. de'Classici Italiani, 1829.

Duodecmio. 2 vols.

This is a reprint of the 1825 fourth revised and corrected version of poet, translator, and dramatist Vincenzo Monti's Italian verse translation of the *Iliad.* It forms part of the Raccolta di Poeti Classici series, which published an edition of Pindemonte's *Odissea* (C11) the same year this volume appeared. Monti dedicated the 1810 first edition of his translation to Napoleon, who had named him poet and historiographer of the newly founded Kingdom of Italy. He began translating Homer in the late eighteenth century in response to a debate among contemporary literary figures over whether it was possible to render the Homeric epics both faithfully and elegantly in Italian. Monti's experiment first appeared in 1807, in a volume containing three Italian translations of *Iliad* book 1: a prose version by Melchiorre Cesarotti, whose other works include translations of the poems of Ossian (see B10) into Italian; and poet Ugo Foscolo's and Monti's verse renditions. Unlike Pindemonte, Monti knew little Greek. He composed his version with the assistance of Greek scholar Andrea Mustoxidi and of Latin translations, believing that "when one translates it is no longer the language of the work translated, to which the first attentions must be directed, but that of the translator" (*quando si traduce non è più la lingua del tradotto, a cui si debbano i primi riguardi, ma quella del traduttore*).

Monti's concentration on the Italian poetics of his version rather than on the original Greek earned him the ironic epithet from Foscolo: "grand translator of the translators of Homer" (*gran traduttor dei traduttor d'Omero*). William Cullen Bryant (B22, B54) cited Monti alongside Pope (B9, B49) as a poet capable of translating Homer without consulting Homer's own work: "one very good translation of the Iliad was made without knowing a word of the Greek original: The eminent Italian poet, Vincenzo Monti . . . translated the Iliad into excellent blank verse without any knowledge of Greek." Although far less faithful to Homer than Pindemonte's *Odyssey*, Monti's *Iliad* seems to have been more greatly admired in Italy, where the two translations were printed, read, and taught together for more than a hundred years after their first publications.

Brand, P., and L. Pertile. *The Cambridge History of Italian Literature.* Rev. ed. Cambridge: Cambridge University Press, 1999.

Bryant, W. C. "Translators of Homer." *Prose Writings of William Cullen Bryant.* Vol. 2, pp. 267–69. Edited by P. Godwin. New York: D. Appleton and Company, 1884.

Cesarotti, M., U. Foscolo, and V. Monti. *Esperimento di Traduzione della Iliade di Omero.* Brescia: Per Nicolo Bettoni, 1807.

Marrone, G., ed. "Vincenzo Monti." *Encyclopedia of Italian Literary Studies.* New York: Routledge, 2007.

Monti, V. *Prose Scelte Critiche e Letterarie di Vincenzo Monti.* Edited by R. Fornaciari. Florence: G. Barbèra, 1896.

Pindemonte, I. *Odissea di Omero.* Milan: Dalla Società Tipografica de'Classici Italiani, 1829.

GERMAN TRANSLATIONS

C13

Johann Heinrich Voss (1751–1826). *Homers Iliad / Odyssee.* Altona: J. F. Hammerich, 1793.

Octavo. 4 vols. (bound in 2).

Voss's translation of the *Iliad* and *Odyssey* was not the first translation of Homer into German. Johannes Spreng, a Meistersinger in Augsburg, published a version of the *Iliad* in rhyming couplets in 1610, and numerous other German writers projected, attempted, or published versions of their own in the following centuries. But Voss's translation was by far the most important one.

Voss was an intellectually vigorous, productive, and rather irascible poet, schoolteacher, and eventually Professor at the University of Heidelberg. Among his poems, the idyll "Luise" (1783, rev. 1795) is perhaps best known today, for its combination of ancient style with modern sentiment. Voss published lively and not always polite polemics against various classics professors; his *Mythologische Briefe* (1794, rev. 1827) attacked Christian Gottlob Heyne (see A23), and his *Antisymbolik* (1824–26) did the same for Georg Friedrich Creuzer. He translated Virgil's *Bucolics* and *Georgics* (1789) and his complete works (1799, rev. 1821), Ovid's *Metamorphoses* (1798), Horace (1806), Hesiod and the Orphic *Argonautica* (1806), the Greek bucolic poets (1808), Tibullus (1811), Aristophanes (1821), Aratus (1824), Aeschylus (1826, with his son), Propertius (1830), and Shakespeare (1818–29, with his sons). But it is his translations of Homer that have secured him a permanent and distinguished place in German literature and culture. His translation of the *Odyssey* appeared in 1781; this 1793 edition contains a revised version of his *Odyssey* translation and, for the first time, his translation of the *Iliad.*

For German readers, Voss's translation made Homer not only a Greek or Latin poet, but a German one. This was due partly to his intense study of the poem and of ancient and modern scholarship on it, and even more to his poetic language, elevated but not pompous, direct and only rarely padded. Voss's style reflected the current literary version of spoken German, although he did not hesitate to invent composite words in imitation of Homer's. But above all it was Voss's meter, German dactylic hexameters, that provided an astonishingly viable equivalent in the modern language for Homer's Greek dactylic hexameters. The long, spacious lines gave ample room for polysyllabic epithets; the supple rhythms varied from slow and stately to rapid and excited; and the varying number of syllables (anywhere from thirteen to seventeen) in each line gave the translator the freedom to find exactly one word for every important lexical item in the original. Voss perfected the German dactylic hexameter he had in-

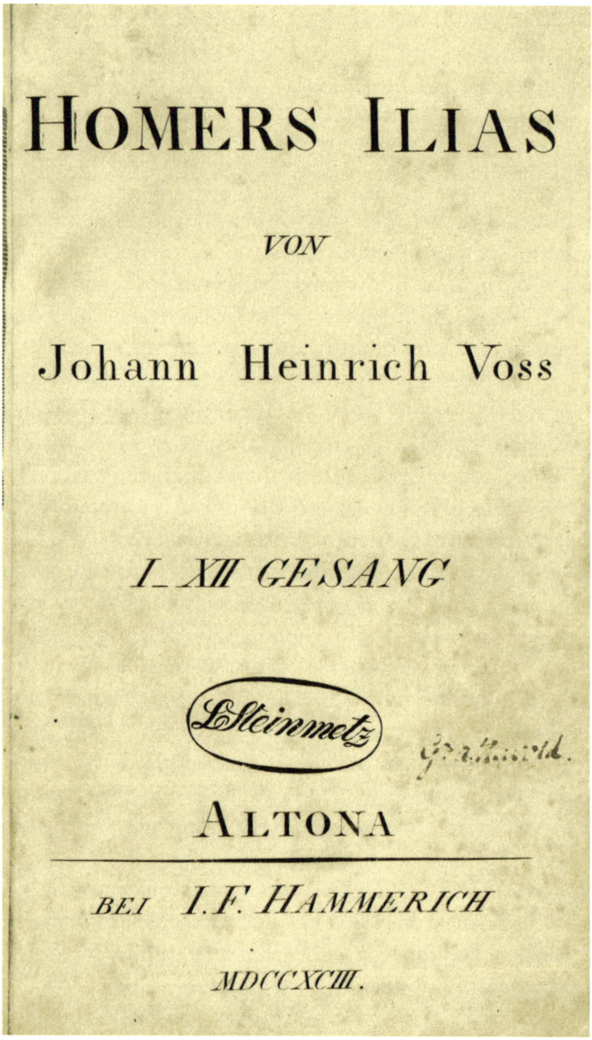
HOMERS ILIAS

VON

Johann Heinrich Voss

I_XII GESANG

L Steinmetz

ALTONA

BEI I.F. HAMMERICH

MDCCXCIII.

C13

herited from Friedrich Gottlieb Klopstock and bequeathed it to poets who were far greater than he was, including Johann Wolfgang Goethe, Friedrich Hölderlin, and Eduard Mörike.

Voss's translations had an enormous impact; they were read and discussed intensely by all German intellectuals of the time. For example, there is a lively description (reported in Humphrey Trevelyan's *Goethe and the Greeks* and elsewhere) of a visit Voss made on June 5, 1794, to the philosopher and writer Johann Gottfried Herder at his home in Weimar. Together with Goethe, the poet and novelist Christoph Martin Wieland, and local notables, they discussed the geography of the *Odyssey* and Voss read sections of his translation of the poem. During the following winter, at the meetings of the "Freitagsgesellschaft" ("Friday Society")—a group of about a dozen Weimar intellectuals including those named above, as well as Friedrich Schiller and Wilhelm von Humboldt, who met weekly at Goethe's house—Goethe read aloud a book of the *Iliad* in Voss's translation and the participants argued passionately about the meaning and beauty of both the Greek and the German texts. Many cultivated Germans think that Voss's Homer, like the Schlegel-Tieck translation of Shakespeare, rivals the original. Voss's translations are still in print today, revised and unrevised, in numerous inexpensive editions in Germany.

Häntzschel, Günter. *Johann Heinrich Voss. Seine Homer-Übersetzung als sprachschöpferische Leistung.* Munich: Beck, 1977.

Langenfeld, Klaus. *Johann Heinrich Voss: Mensch, Dichter, Übersetzer.* Eutin: Struve, 1990.

Linckenheld, Emil. *Der hexameter bei Klopstock und Voss.* Strassburg: C. J. Goeller, 1906.

Mittler, Elmar, and Inka Tappenbeck, eds. *Johann Heinrich Voss, 1751–1826: Idylle, Polemik und Wohllaut.* Göttingen: Niedersächsische Staats- und Universitätsbibliothek, 2001.

Most, Glenn W. "1805, Summer. Homer between Poets and Philologists." *A New History of German Literature,* 500–5. Edited by David Wellbery. Cambridge, MA: Harvard University Press, 2004.

Muncker, Franz. "Voß, Johann Heinrich." *Allgemeine Deutsche Biographie* 40 (1896): 334–49.

Riedel, Volker, ed. *Beiträge zu Werk und Wirken von Johann Heinrich Voss, 1751–1826.* Neubrandenburg: Literaturzentrum Neubrandenburg, 1989.

Rudolph, Andrea, ed. *Johann Heinrich Voss: Kulturräume in Dichtung und Wirkung.* Dettelbach: J. H. Röll, 1999.

Schroeter, Adalbert. *Geschichte der deutschen Homerübersetzung im XVIII. Jahrhundert.* Jena: H. Costenoble, 1882.

Trevelyan, Humphry. *Goethe and the Greeks.* Cambridge: Cambridge University Press, 1942, 1981; New York: Octagon Books, 1972.

C14

John MacHale (1791–1881). *Homer's Iliad, Translated Into Irish Verse. First Book.* Dublin: John Cumming and A. Milliken; London: Charles Dolman, 1844.

Octavo.

Irish nationalist and Roman Catholic Archbishop John MacHale composed this translation of the first book of the *Iliad* in Irish heroic couplets with facing Greek text "for the purpose of connecting the Father of classic poetry with the native language and literature of Ireland." MacHale was a strong supporter of Daniel O'Connell's campaigns for Irish liberation, lobbying for the political rights of Catholics in Ireland through Catholic emancipation in the 1820s and later for the political independence of Ireland from Great Britain through the repeal of the Acts of Union that had created the United Kingdom in 1800. His published works include letters calling for policy reform (sometimes under the pseudonym Hierophilos), political and doctrinal tracts in English and his native Irish, and Irish translations of scripture, songs, and poetry. MacHale's English-language preface to this Irish version of *Iliad* book 1 extols the benefits such a translation can accord a language, first by demonstrating that it is sufficiently "far advanced in strength and copiousness" to serve as an "adequate vehicle for conveying the thoughts of Homer," and then by providing it with "a reciprocal return in reflecting much of the richness and majesty of the great original."

The fact that no one before MacHale had attempted to render Homer in Irish was evidence not of the shortcomings of the Irish language—in fact "there is no European tongue better adapted than ours to a full and perfect version of Homer"—but of the oppression Ireland had endured for centuries. Religious and linguistic proscriptions had left Irish language and literature "almost a wreck, long abandoned without improvement to the humbler classes of society": the "necessities of life must be provided for before the introduction of foreign luxuries." In the relative freedom of mid-nineteenth-century Ireland, MacHale was able to compose his version of book 1 while "snatching some leisure intervals from weighty duties." Although his work on Homer lapsed during the Irish famine that began in 1845, MacHale continued publishing parts of his translation until he completed book 8 in 1871. He left off hoping "some other worthy hands" would pick up "the task of enriching our Irish literature with a translation of the remainder." The *Dublin Review* called MacHale's ambition to revive the Irish language "a noble one" and celebrated the publication of this first book of his *Iliad* as "a valuable addition to the literature of the country" that would also "contribute, in no ordinary degree, to facilitate the acquisition of the language, and recommend it to more general cultivation."

Andrews, H. *The Lion of the West: A Biography of John MacHale.* Dublin: Veritas Publications, 2001.

"Irish Language and Literature: Archbishop M'Hale." *Dublin Review* 16 (March & June 1844): 463–82.

Larkin, E. "MacHale, John (1791–1881)." *Oxford Dictionary of National Biography.*

O'Reilly, B. "The Irish Language. Labors for Restoring and Popularizing the Ancient Language and Literature of Ireland." *John MacHale, Archbishop of Tuam: His Life, Times and Correspondance.* New York and Cincinnati: F. Pustet & Co., 1890.

Stanford, W. B. "Towards a History of Classical Influences in Ireland." *Proceedings of the Royal Irish Academy, Section C: Archaeology, Celtic Studies, History, Linguistics, Literature* 70 (1979): 13–91.

Walshe, P. "Archbishop MacHale's Writings. A Defence of Creed and Country." *Irish Monthly* 59, no. 695 (May 1931): 308–18.

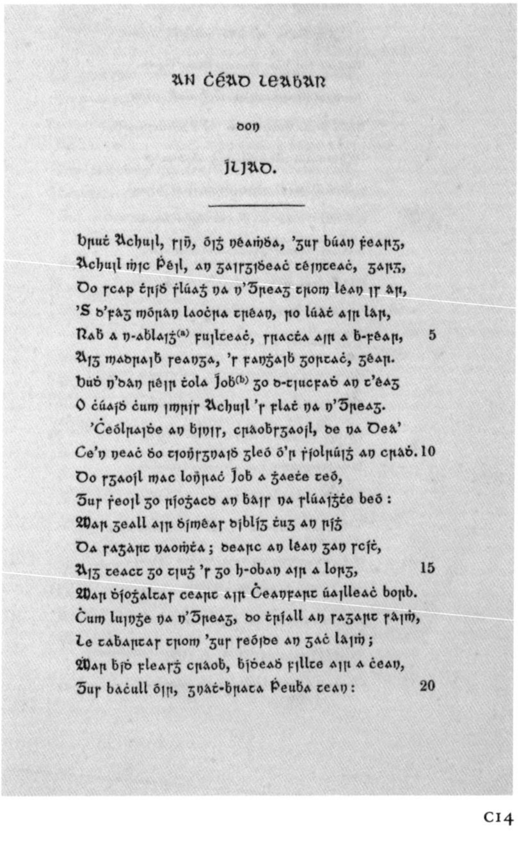

AN CÉAD LEABAR

DON

ILIAD.

Brúċ Achuil, sín, óiġ néaṁḋa, 'gur búan ḟearg,
Achuil ṁic Ṗéil, an gaisgiḋeaċ téinteaċ, garg,
Do scap ċríḋ ḟlúaġ na n'Greag trom léan is ár,
'S d'ḟág mórán laoċra tréan, ro lúaṫ air lár,
Raḃ a n-aḃlaiġ(a) fuilteaċ, sracṫa air a ḃ-ḟéar,
Aig madraiḃ seanga, 's fanġaiḃ gortaċ, géar.
Buḋ n'dán réir ṫola Iob(b) go d-tiucfaḋ an t'éag
O ċúaiḋ ċum imris Achuil 's flaṫ na n'Greag.
'Ċeólraiḋe an binis, craoḃsgaoil, de na Dea'
Ce'n neaċ do tioṁsgnaiḋ gleó ó'r ḟíolrúiġ an craḋ.
Do sgaoil mac loṁraċ Iob a ġaeṫe teó,
Gur ḟeoil go ríoġacd an báis na slúaiġṫe beó:
Mar geall air ḋímeas diblíg ṫug an ríġ
Da sagárt naoṁṫa; dearc an léan gan scíṫ,
Aig teacṫ go tiuġ 's go h-oban air a long,
Mar ḋíoġaltas ceart air Ċeanfart úailleaċ borb.
Ċum luinġe na n'Greag, do ṫríall an sagart sáiṁ,
Le taḃartas trom 'gur seóide an gaċ láiṁ;
Mar bíḋ flearg craoḃ, bíḋeaḋ fillte air a ċean,
Gur baċull óir, gnáṫ-ḃrata Peuḃa tean:

C14

SECTION D

SCHOLARLY WORKS

D1

[Didymus Chalcenterus (ca. 63 B.C.E.–10 C.E.)]. *Scholia palaia te, kai panu ōphelima eis tēn tou Omērou Iliada, kai eis tēn Odyssea / Interpretationes et Antiquae, et perquam Utiles in Homeri Iliada, nec non in Odyssea.* Venice: In aedibus Aldi, et Andreae soceri, 1521.

Octavo.

The Homeric scholia to the *Iliad* in this volume were first printed in Rome in 1517 and attributed to Alexandrian scholar Didymus Chalcenterus, but are no longer believed to have any connection with Didymus, and are now known as the "D Scholia" (after Didymus) or *scholia minora* (lesser scholia). The actual notes of Didymus can be found compiled with those of other Alexandrian critics and with parts of these "D Scholia" in the "A Scholia" from the manuscript known as Venetus A, which was first printed by Villoison in 1788 (A21). Although the title of this 1521 edition refers to both Homeric epics, the Aldine Press did not issue the companion volume containing the scholia to the *Odyssey* until their first printing in 1528. Both works were edited by Franciscus Asulanus, Aldus Manutius's brother-in-law. They present a series of notes to help the reader that were written in the margins of medieval manuscripts of the Homeric texts—especially vocabulary glosses, explanations, and paraphrases, many of which can be traced back to antiquity.

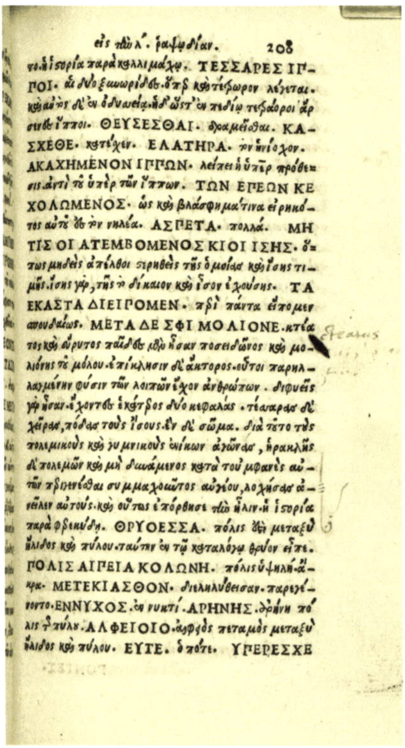

D1

The "D Scholia" were first reprinted alongside the text of the *Iliad* and *Odyssey* by Johann Herwagen in 1535 (A8), but they appear by themselves in the Aldine editions. Appended at the end of this volume (under the separate title page: *Porphyriou Philosophou Homerika Zetemata. Tou Autou Porphyriou peri tou, en Odysseia ton Nymphon, Antrou. Porphyrii Philosophi Homericarum Quaestionum Liber. Eiusdem de Nympharum Antroin Odyssea, Opusculum*) are two Homeric works by the Neoplatonist philosopher Porphyry: "Homeric Questions," a series of inquiries into the Homeric texts, and "On the Cave of the Nymphs," an allegorical explication along the same lines as the work of Heraclitus (D3). As the modern name *scholia minora* suggests, scholars have largely marginalized the "D Scholia" since Venetus A was published in 1788. Yet the manuscript evidence for these scholia is older (it dates back to the ninth century); they were the first scholia to be printed, and the only ones readily available to Homeric editors, translators, and commentators until the late eighteenth century. Heyne appended them to his *Iliad* in 1821 (A23), and online editions by H. van Thiel and N. Ernst have now made the "D Scholia" to the *Iliad* and *Odyssey* widely accessible once again.

Dickey, E. *American Philological Association: Ancient Greek Scholarship: A Guide to Finding, Reading, and Understanding Scholia, Commentaries, Lexica, and Grammatical Treatises, from their Beginnings to the Byzantine Period.* Oxford: Oxford University Press, 2007.

Ernst, N. *Die D-Scholien zur Odyssee.* PhD diss., Cologne, 2006. http://kups.ub.uni-koeln.de/volltexte/2006/1831/

Nagy, G. *Homer's Text and Language.* Urbana: University of Illinois Press, 2004.

"Review." *Bryn Mawr Classical Review* 94.09.18

van Thiel, H. *Scholia D in Iliadem Secundum Codices Manuscriptos*, 2000. http://www.kups.ub.uni-koeln.de/volltexte/2006/1810

West, M. L. *Studies in the Text and Transmission of the Iliad.* Munich: K. G. Saur, 2001.

D2

Johannes Hartung (1505–1579). *Prolegomena Ioannis Hartungi in Tres Priores Odysseae Homeri Rapsodias.* Frankfort: Christianus Egen, excudebat, 1539.

Octavo.

This Renaissance Latin commentary on the first three books of the *Odyssey* was written by Johannes Hartung, Professor of Greek and Hebrew at Heidelberg and Freiburg. Hartung developed his commentary in 1538 during a series of private lectures on Homer designed to keep his beginning students from forgetting their Greek over school holidays. It was issued the decade before the commentaries of Eustathius were first printed (D4) and consists of explanations of Homeric vocabulary (frequently following the "D Scholia" [D1]) and of passages from *Odyssey* books 1–3 (frequently in moral terms), as well as suggested corrections for the text. Although Hartung never completed his commentary or produced any additional Homeric scholarship, he published many other works

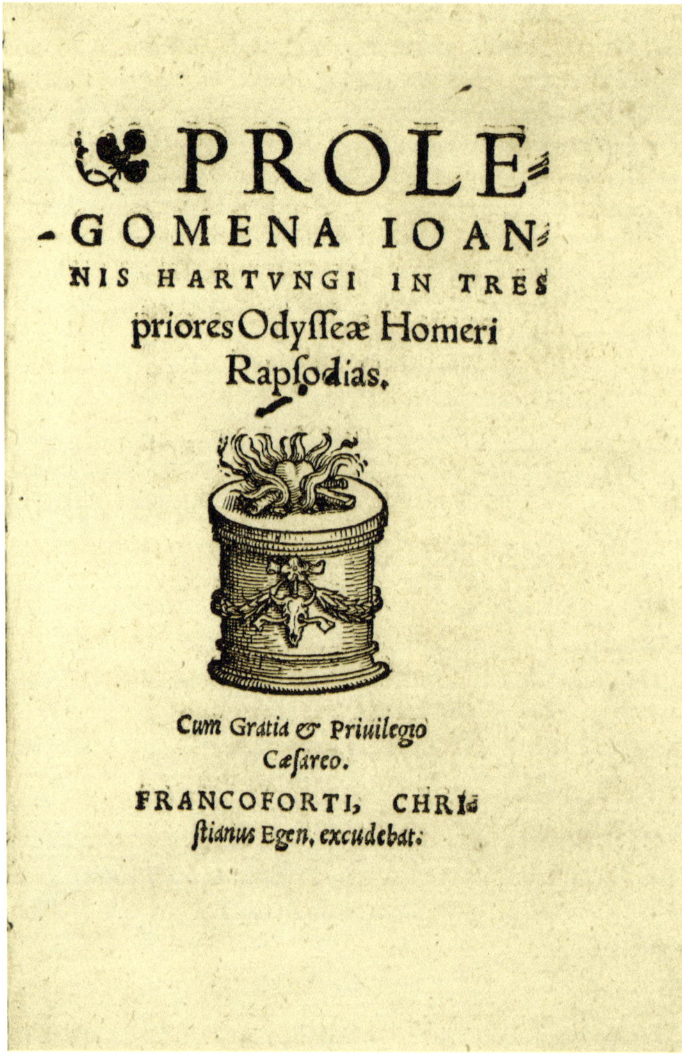

PROLE-
GOMENA IOAN-
NIS HARTVNGI IN TRES
priores Odyssææ Homeri
Rapsodias.

Cum Gratia & Priuilegio
Cæsareo.

FRANCOFORTI, CHRI-
stianus Egen, excudebat.

D2

for the aid of those studying the classical authors, including commentaries on Apollonius of Rhodes, Horace, and Virgil, and a Greek-Latin dictionary he coauthored with Swiss Hellenist Conrad Gesner (D3).

Ford, P. *De Troie à Ithaque: Réception des Épopéés Homériques à la Renaissance.* Geneva: Droz, 2007.

Gesner, C., and J. Hartung. *Lexikon sive Dictionarium Graecolatinum.* Basel: [Ex Officina Hieronymi Curionis], 1560.

D3

Konrad Gesner (1516–1565). *Heraclidis Pontici, Qui Aristotelis Aetate Vixit, Allegoriae in Homeri Fabulas de Dijs, nunc Primum è Graeco Sermone in Latinum Translatae.* Basel: ex officina Ioannis Oporini, 1544.

Octavo.

This volume contains the first Latin translation of Heraclitus's Homeric Allegories (by Swiss naturalist and professor of Greek Conrad Gesner), as well as the second printing of the Greek text—it had previously appeared in a 1505 collection from the Aldine Press. It was issued by Johannes Oporinus, who would go on to oversee the production of the earliest bilingual Greek and Latin editions of the Homeric texts (see A13). Although this volume's title page identifies Heraclitus as a contemporary of Aristotle, distinguishing him from the more famous pre-Socratic philosopher Heraclitus, it seems likely that this work was written during the first century AD. To defend Homer against the charges of impiety that critics like Plato had leveled against him for centuries, Heraclitus insisted that the treatment of the gods in the *Iliad* and *Odyssey* be read allegorically rather than literally: if the Homeric episodes showing the gods exhibiting human behavior, emotion, and weakness were taken at face value, there was no denying that Homer was impious; but those willing to look deeper into Homer's words would be able to penetrate "the hidden depths of his wisdom" (*tà múchia ths ekeínou sophías*). Homer's redemption lay in the allegorical explication of his seemingly blasphemous work. This use of allegory, common among the stoic philosophers of Heraclitus's time, was later applied to Homer by Neoplatonists like Porphyry (D1) and Christians like James Duport (D6) looking to bring the Greek and Latin classics into line with their views of morality and divinity.

Fletcher, H. "Milton's Copy of Gesner's 'Heraclides,' 1544." *Journal of English and German Philology* 47, no. 2 (April 1948): 182–87.

Lamberton, R. *Homer the Theologian: Neoplatonist Allegorical Reading and the Growth of the Epic Tradition.* Berkeley and Los Angeles: University of California Press, 1989.

Mazzeo, J. A. "Allegorical Interpretation and History." *Comparative Literature* 30, no. 1 (Winter 1978): 1–21.

Russell, D. A., and D. Konstan, eds. and trans. *Heraclitus: Homeric Problems.* Atlanta: Society of Biblical Literature, 2005.

D4

D4

Eustathius, Archbishop of Thessalonica (d. ca. 1194). *Eustathiou Archiepiskopou Thessalonikes Parekbolai eis ten Homerou Iliada kai Odysseian meta Euporotatou kai panu Ophelimou Pinakos.* Rome: [Apud Antonium Bladum Impressorem Cameralem], 1542–50.

Folio. 4 vols.

This edition of the massive twelfth-century Greek commentary on the *Iliad* and *Odyssey* by Archbishop of Thessalonica Eustathius is also known as the *editio Romana.* It was compiled from manuscripts dating back to the twelfth century, and issued alongside the Homeric texts in four volumes by Roman printer Antonio Blado. Cardinal Marcello Cervini (Pope Marcellus II from April to May 1555) initiated the project, and paid for the printing and production of the type. A total of 1275 copies of the first volume, edited by Greek-born scholar Nikolaos Sophianos, were printed in a sumptuous Greek type (Greek 1) with wide margins—a format abandoned (most likely due to cost) in the later volumes, which were edited by Niccolò Maiorano (Nicolaus Majoranus) and printed in a smaller type (Greek 2) between 1545 and 1550 (volume four contains the general title page, as well as the index provided by Matthaeus Devarius).

Eustathius's extant works also include religious writings, scholarship on Dionysius Periegeta and Pindar, and an eyewitness account of the 1185 sack of Thessalonica. His Homeric commentaries are considered to be immensely important works of Byzantine scholarship, not only for the aid they have provided students of Homer, their intended audience, but also for their references to and quotations from ancient texts that existed during Eustathius's time but had been lost by the beginning of the Renaissance. Much of Eustathius's commentary on the *Iliad*, for instance, is based on a lost set of Homeric scholia now known as Ap.H. and believed to be the archetype for the "A Scholia" found in Venetus A (A21). This Roman edition of Eustathius's work was reprinted in Basel (1559–60), in Florence (a partial reprint with Latin translation, 1730), and in Leipzig (1825–29), before it was finally superseded by a late-twentieth-century edition by Marchinus van der Valk based on a manuscript identified as Eustathius's autograph copy. Scholars and translators of Homer have consulted both of Eustathius's commentaries—and especially his commentary on the *Iliad*, which is longer and more thorough than his commentary on the *Odyssey*—since this first printing. Many volumes in the BHL reference or cite information from Eustathius's work on Homer, including those by Melmoth (B3), Pope (B9), Munford (B13), Buckley (B14), Blackie (B19), Dawe (B81), Valla (C1), Dacier (C5), and Pindemonte (C11).

Dickey, E. *American Philological Association: Ancient Greek Scholarship: A Guide to Finding, Reading, and Understanding Scholia, Commentaries, Lexica, and Grammatical Treatises, from their Beginnings to the Byzantine Period.* Oxford: Oxford University Press, 2007.

Layton, E. "The History of a Sixteenth-Century Greek Type Revised." *Historical Review, Institute for Neohellenic Research* 1 (2004): 35–50. http://www.historicalreview.org/index.php/historicalReview/article/view/169/65 (accessed November 16, 2010).

Makrinos, A. "Eustathius, Archbishop of Thessalonica, Commentary on the Odyssey: Codex Marcianus 460 and Parisinus 2702 Revisted." *Bulletin of the Institute of Classical Studies* 50, no. 1 (December 2007): 171–92.

Pettas, W. A. "Nikolaos Sophianós and Greek Printing in Rome." *Library* (Fifth Series) 29, no. 2 (1974): 206–13.

Tinto, A. "The History of a Sixteenth-Century Greek Type." *Library* (Fifth Series) 25, no. 4 (December 1970): 285–93.

van der Valk, M., ed. *Eustathii Archiepiscopi Thessalonicensis Commentarii ad Homeri Iliadem Pertinentes.* Leiden: Brill, 1971–87.

Wilson, N. G. "Review: Eustathius on Iliad I–IV." *Classical Review* (New Series) 24, no. 2 (November 1974): 188–90.

D5

Wolfgang Seber (1573–1634). *Index Vocabulorum in Homeri non tantum Iliade atque Odyssea sed Caeteris etiam quotquot extant Poëmatis, cum Rerum, Epithetorum, & Phrasium Insigniorum Annotatione, Catalogo item Graecolatino Vocabularum, quibus apud Homerum & ex eo in Indice Adjecta sunt Epitheta. . . .* [Heidelberg]: In Bibliopolio Commeliniano, 1604.

Quarto.

With the signature of J. Chelsum, most likely James Chelsum, English clergyman, scholar, and critic of Edward Gibbon's account of the spread of Christianity in his *History of the Decline and Fall of the Roman Empire* (1776).

German scholar Wolfgang Seber's Homeric index is the first printed concordance to Homer. It contains an alphabetical list of Greek words with reference to their corresponding line numbers in the *Iliad*, *Odyssey*, *Batrachomyomachia*, and hymns, compiled by Seber with the hope of providing "a not at all small benefit" (*haudquaquam exiguum . . . fructum*) to "those teaching, studying, or in some way making use of Greek poetry" (*qui Graecam Poësin vel docent, vel discunt, vel quoquo modo exercent*). The immediate value of Seber's work can be seen in the three celebratory Latin poems by contemporary clergymen, educators, and scholars from Seber's native Schleusingen included in this volume, which praise Seber for illuminating Homer and easing the study of his works. The utility of Seber's index was not confined to his own time or place: new editions appeared in 1649 in Amsterdam, in 1730–35 in Florence (in a set with a Latin translation

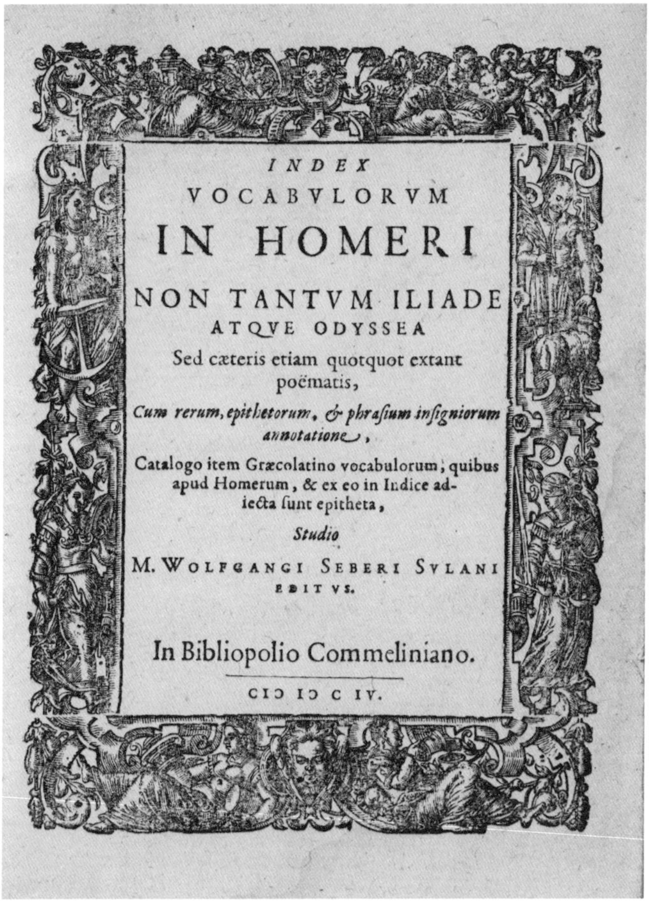

INDEX
VOCABVLORVM
IN HOMERI
NON TANTVM ILIADE
ATQVE ODYSSEA
Sed cæteris etiam quotquot extant
poëmatis,
*Cum rerum, epithetorum, & phrasium insigniorum
annotatione,*
Catalogo item Græcolatino vocabulorum, quibus
apud Homerum, & ex eo in Indice ad-
iecta sunt epitheta,
Studio
M. WOLFGANGI SEBERI SVLANI
EDITVS.

In Bibliopolio Commeliniano.

CIↃ IↃ C IV.

D5

of the commentary of Eustathius [D4]), and in 1780 in Oxford. The Oxford edition was still in use at least a hundred years later, when George Herbert Palmer (B58A) listed "the old *Index Homericus* of Seber" as an aid for those wishing to make a more detailed study of the *Odyssey*.

Politus, A. *Commentarii in Homeri Iliadem.* Florence: B. Paperinius, 1730–35.

Seber, W. *Argus Homericus, sive, Index Vocabulorum in Omnia Homeri Poemata.* Amsterdam: Joannes Janssonius, 1649.

———. *Index Vocabulorum in Homeri Iliade atque Odyssea Caeterisque quotquot extant Poematis.* Oxford: Ex Typographeo Clarendoniano, 1780.

Sorger, J. *Homerus Enucleatus, sive Phraseologia Homerica.* Frankfurt am Main: Kempfer, 1625.

D6

James Duport (1606–1679). *Homeri Poetarum Omnium Secularum Facile Principis Gnomologia, Duplici Parallelismo Illustrata. . . .* Cambridge: Excudebat Johannes Field, 1660.

Quarto.

The BHL copy includes a handwritten tipped-in list of errata signed by Duport.

Cambridge professor of Greek James Duport intended this massive collection of *Gnomologia Homerica*, Homeric *sententiae* or aphorisms, to fill the only void he perceived in the vast amount of ancient and contemporary Homeric scholarship he had surveyed, like the works of Porphyry and Didymus (D1), Heraclitus (D3), Eustathius (D4), and Seber (D5), as well as the more recent *Homerus Ebraizon* by Zachary Bogan, a 1658 comparison between the wording of the Homeric epics and the wording of the Hebrew Bible. Aligning himself both with the ancient tradition of allegorical interpretation exemplified by Porphyry and Heraclitus, and with contemporary Christian scholars like Bogan who saw a large scriptural influence in Homer's works, Duport affirmed that "there are certainly more than a few things in his poetry that are in the first place consistent with divine utterance, and that correspond to it almost exactly" (*sunt profectò in ejus poesi non pauca divinis eloquiis consona, & paenè ad amußin consentanea*). He focused his selection and explanation (in Latin) of Homeric passages on parallels with the Bible, seeking to underline the extent to which Homer had imported scriptural proverbs and adages into the *Iliad* and *Odyssey.*

Duport's work was highly influential on contemporary Homeric scholarship, and many seventeenth- and early eighteenth-century scholars and translators shared his views, including Joshua Barnes (A18), Mme. Dacier (C5, C7), and John Ozell (B8). By the end of the eighteenth century, however, Duport's work appears to have been valued mostly as a curiosity: in the 1790s, historian Edward Gibbon described the *Gnomologia Homeri* as "The moral sentences of Homer, with a copious and entertaining collection of imitations, allusions, applications, parodies, &c."; and, in the notes to his 1853 edition of Pope's *Iliad* (B9), Theodore Alois Buckley (B14, B50) cited "Old Jacob Duport, whose 'Gnomologia Homerica' is full of curious and useful things."

Allen, D. C. *Mysteriously Meant: The Rediscovery of Pagan Symbolism and Allegorical Interpretation in the Renaissance.* Baltimore: Johns Hopkins University Press, 1970.

Bogan, Z. *Homerus Ebraizon, sive, Comparatio Homeri cum Scriptoribus Sacris.* Oxford: Excudebat H. Hall, Impensis T. Robinson, 1658.

Gibbon, E. *The Miscellaneous Works of Edward Gibbon, Esq.* Vol. 5. Edited by John, Lord Sheffield. London: John Murray, 1814.

Levine, J. M. *The Battle of the Books: History and Literature in the Augustan Age.* Ithaca, NY: Cornell University Press, 1994.

Nelson, E. *Thomas Hobbes Translations of Homer: The Iliad and the Odyssey.* Oxford: Clarendon Press, 2008.

O'Day, R. "Duport, James (1606–1679)." *Oxford Dictionary of National Biography.*

Pope, A. *The Iliad of Homer.* London: Ingram, Cooke, and Co., 1853.

D7

René Le Bossu (1631–1680). *Monsieur Bossu's Treatise of the Epick Poem.* . . . London: Printed for Tho. Bennet, 1695.

Octavo.

This anonymous English translation of René Le Bossu's influential 1675 *Traité du Poëme Épique* is signed only with the initials W. J. The volume also includes the works of two other French critics: an essay on satire by André Dacier (see C5), and one on pastoral by Bernard le Bovier de Fontenelle (translated by Peter Anthony Motteux). In his preface, W. J. placed himself in the context of the French *Querelle des Anciens et des Modernes* (see C5–C7), aligning himself with the proponents of the classics against the "debouch'd World" of his day. He underlined the importance of Le Bossu's central principle, that the epic poem (as he translates) "'is a Discourse or Story invented by Art to form Mens Manners by such Instructions as are disguis'd under the Allegory of some one Important Action, which is related in Verse after a Probable, Diverting, and surprising manner.'" Although knowledge of French was common among contemporary educated Englishmen, the translator sought to make Le Bossu's rules of epic composition and explication of epic poetry into a vehicle for moral instruction—"too good to be confin'd to a Foreign Language"—more readily available, especially to those writing epic poetry who were uncomfortable with the language, or even "others who think they already understand it."

Le Bossu's work had a huge influence on both French and English epic translation in the late seventeenth and early eighteenth century. John Dryden, who published his translation of Virgil's works in 1697, called Le Bossu "the best of modern critics"; Mme. Dacier based her renditions of the *Iliad* (C5) and *Odyssey* (C7) on Le Bossu's rules for the nature and composition of epic, and Alexander Pope prefaced his *Odyssey* (B49) with an English summary of Bossu's treatise, "A General View of the Epic Poem, And of the *Iliad* and *Odyssey*. Extracted from *Bossu*."

Bossu, R. l. *Traité du Poëme Epique.* Paris: Michel Le Petit, 1675.

Kennedy, G. A., H. B. Nisbet, and C. Rawson. *The Cambridge History of Literary Criticism, Vol. 4: The Eighteenth Century.* Cambridge: Cambridge University Press, 2005.

Levine, J. M. *The Battle of the Books: History and Literature in the Augustan Age*. Ithaca, NY: Cornell University Press, 1994.

Ward, C. E. *The Life of John Dryden*. Chapel Hill: University of North Carolina Press, 1961.

D8

Joseph Spence (1699–1768). *An Essay on Pope's* Odyssey. . . . London: Printed for S. Wilmot, 1727.

Octavo.

This essay by literary critic, writer, clergyman, and Oxford professor Joseph Spence is composed in the style of a Platonic dialogue between two fictional characters debating the merits and flaws of Pope's *Odyssey* (B49): Antiphaus, an advocate of the simplicity of ancient poetry, with an "Aversion to Glitterings and Elevation," and Philypsus, an admirer of modern elaboration, of "fine Thoughts and warm Expressions" (for the Quarrel of the Ancients and Moderns, see C5–C7, D7). Their discussion takes place over the course of five evenings of conversation. Spence published the first part of the dialogue (the first three evenings) in 1726, after the first volume of Pope's *Odyssey* appeared. In his preface, Spence wrote that his dialogues were not "Invectives," or written out of "Self-love" or envy; instead, having observed "Many Beauties" and "some Faults" in Pope's work, Spence had "flung the Thoughts on both together," aiming at "Impartiality."

Philypsus opens the dialogue by admiring "the Flame and Spirit of a Writer, who is evidently Our present Laureat in Genius, and the most enliven'd Translator of the Age," to which Antiphaus responds "The aim of a translator is to give us the *Spirit* of the Original": Homer's "plain, and natural, and unadorn'd" manner is sometimes misrepresented by the "flourish, and ornament" of Pope's verse. By the end of their third conversation, Philypsus declares that he and Antiphaus can at least agree that Pope's *"faults are the faults of a Man, but his beauties are beauties of an Angel"* (by which he means only "a *Great and Uncommon Genius*"). Pope was pleased with the essay, and sought out Spence's acquaintance. He read and commented on the manuscript of the second part of the dialogue (written after Pope's whole *Odyssey* had been issued, and first published in this edition), which contained less criticism of Pope, and, some contemporaries alleged, less impartiality. Spence eventually became a close friend of Pope's, a leading figure in his intellectual and literary circle, and a patron of many young aspiring poets. This work appears to have been generally admired and went through numerous editions during his lifetime. Samuel Johnson begrudgingly wrote that Spence was "a man whose learning was not very great, and whose mind was not very powerful. His criticism, however, was commonly just; what he thought, he thought rightly; and his remarks were recommended by his coolness and candour."

Daniels, R. "Joseph Spence." *Dictionary of Literary Biography, Vol. 356: Eighteenth-Century British Literary Scholars and Critics*. Edited by Frans De Bruyn. Farmington Hills, MI: Gale Group, 2010.

Lynch, J., ed. *The Life of Pope by Samuel Johnson*. http://andromeda.rutgers.edu/~jlynch/Texts/pope.html

Sambrook, J. "Spence, Joseph (1699–1768)." *Oxford Dictionary of National Biography*.

Wright, A. "The Beginning of Pope's Friendship with Spence." *Modern Language Notes* 54, no. 5 (May 1939): 359–61.

———. *Joseph Spence: a Critical Biography*. Chicago: University of Chicago Press, 1950.

D9

Thomas Blackwell (1701–1757). *An Enquiry into the Life and Writings of Homer*. London: [s.n.], 1735.

Octavo.

This biographical study of Homer is by Greek scholar Thomas Blackwell, an important figure of the Scottish Enlightenment. Rejecting the traditional explanation of divine inspiration, Blackwell sought to understand the root of Homer's "Genius" and enduring poetic supremacy in rational or deterministic terms: "'*Homer's* Poems are of *Human Composition*; inspired by no other Power than his own natural Faculties, and the Chances of his Education . . . a *Concourse* of *natural* Causes, conspired to produce and cultivate that mighty Genius, and gave him the noblest Field to exercise it in, that ever fell to the share of a Poet.'" For Blackwell, the *Iliad* and *Odyssey* represented products of the "Circumstances" of Homer's life—factors like the climate and topography of his birthplace, the subjects and places Homer was exposed to in his education and profession, as well as the state of Greek political, social, and linguistic development of his times—acting upon Homer's "*Original* frame," his natural disposition and talents. Homer lived at the ideal time for the production of epic poetry, the precise interval between "Nakedness and Barbarity" and either "wide Policy and Peace" or "General Wars". The *Iliad* and *Odyssey*, the result of this specific confluence of natural, historical, and cultural forces, could never be reproduced.

Blackwell's work was an immediate success and went through many editions in the eighteenth century (the second only one year after this first publication). It exerted a great influence on contemporary ideas both about Homer and about the relationship between culture and genius. Blackwell is often credited as an inspiration for the Homeric work and Ossianic poems of James MacPherson (B10), one of his pupils at Aberdeen. As a historical biography, Blackwell's *Enquiry into the Life and Writings of Homer* has long been dismissed by modern scholars—Blackwell relied heavily on the details for Homer given in ancient sources like the "D Scholia" (D1), and the pseudo-Herodotian and pseudo-Plutarchian biographical works (found in A1). However, the theories Blackwell put forth about the relationship between natural and cultural forces in the formation of men and art represent very early examples of those adopted by modern anthropological thought.

This edition contains a frontispiece portrait of Homer engraved by Gerard Van der Gucht and a title page and vignettes designed by Hubert François Gravelot.

Donaldson, W. "Blackwell, Thomas (1701–1757)." *Oxford Dictionary of National Biography.*

Graver, B. "Romanticism." *A Companion to the Classical Tradition.* Edited by C. W. Kallendorf. Chichester, UK: Wiley-Blackwell, 2010.

Simonsuuri, K. *Homer's Original Genius: Eighteenth-Century Notions of the Early Greek Epic.* Cambridge: Cambridge University Press, 1979.

Webb, T. *English Romantic Hellenism: 1700–1824.* Manchester: Manchester University Press, 1982.

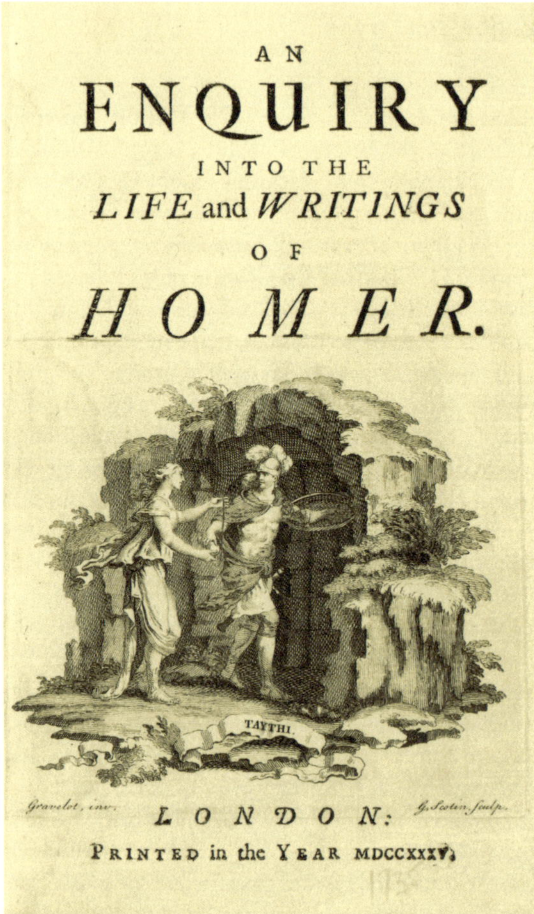

D9

D10

Robert Wood (1717?–1771). *An Essay on the Original Genius and Writings of Homer.* . . . London: Printed by H. Hughs; for T. Payne . . . and P. Elmsly, 1775.

Quarto.

Like Thomas Blackwell (D9), traveler, scholar, and politician Robert Wood sought to explain the *Iliad* and *Odyssey* as products of the natural and historical circumstances of Homer's place and time. Wood read the Homeric epics during his extensive travels around Greece and the Near East with antiquarians John Bouverie and James Dawkins and draughtsman Giovanni Borra (whose illustrations appear in this volume). This work began as a letter to Dawkins on their return; Wood expanded it into an essay at the instigation of Lord John Carteret, Earl of Granville, whom he served in the capacity of Under Secretary of State. Wood's essay was printed privately in 1767 and 1769, and appeared in a German translation in Frankfurt in 1773. This posthumous edition was the first published in English, and was revised and edited by Jacob Bryant, a classical scholar and Wood's friend.

Homer's "great merit," according to Wood, was "that of having transmitted to us a faithful transcript, or (which is, perhaps, more useful) a correct abstract of human nature, impartially exhibited under the circumstances, which belonged to his period of society, as far as his experience and observation went." Homer's topographical descriptions were based, as Wood verified in his travels, on the factual geography and nature of the regions he described. Wood's essay focuses on what he calls Homer's "Mimetic Powers," on the "Imitation" of fact produced by Homer as "Geographer, Traveller, Historian, or Chronologer." Homer was a truthful "Painter" of the natural and cultural circumstances that fell within his line of observation, and his work therefore serves as a window into the way of life of his society, which, Wood suggested, was illiterate. Wood placed great emphasis on the oral nature and primitiveness of the Homeric epics—the source of the naturalness of Homeric verse—rejecting the "modern dress" of the translations of Pope (B9, B49), which acts as a "disguise" that obscures the historical value of Homer's poems. His essay was very influential on contemporary Homeric scholarship, especially in Germany, where his theories on the oral composition of Homer's poetry were taken up by Heyne (A23) and by Friedrich August Wolf, whose seminal 1795 *Prolegomena* to Homer first questioned the unity of the Homeric poems and their authorship.

This edition contains a frontispiece portrait of Homer drawn by Giovanni Battista Cipriani and engraved by James Basire; a title-page vignette drawn by William Pars and engraved by Francesco Bartolozzi; and illustrations designed by Pars and Giovanni Battista Borra and engraved by Francesco Bartolozzi, Thomas Major, and Jacques-Philippe Lebas.

AN

ESSAY

ON THE

Original GENIUS and WRITINGS of HOMER:

WITH

A COMPARATIVE VIEW OF THE ANCIENT AND PRESENT STATE OF THE TROADE.

ILLUSTRATED WITH ENGRAVINGS.

By the late ROBERT WOOD, Esq;

AUTHOR OF THE DESCRIPTIONS OF PALMYRA AND BALBEC.

Drawn at Ephesus in 1764 by W. Pars — *Engraved by F. Bartolozzi*

LONDON:

PRINTED BY H. HUGHS;

For T. PAYNE, at the MEWS GATE, and P. ELMSLY, in the STRAND.

MDCCLXXV.

DIO

Butterworth, J. "Robert Wood and Troy: A Comparative Failure." *Bulletin of the Institute of Classical Studies* 32, no. 1 (1985): 147–54.

Graver, B. "Romanticism." *A Companion to the Classical Tradition,* 72–86. Edited by C. W. Kallendorf. Chichester, UK: Wiley-Blackwell, 2010.

"List of Books,—with Remarks." *Gentleman's Magazine, and Historical Chronicle* 45 (1775): 483–87.

Simonsuuri, K. *Homer's Original Genius: Eighteenth-Century Notions of the Early Greek Epic.* Cambridge: Cambridge University Press, 1979.

Webb, T. *English Romantic Hellenism: 1700–1824.* Manchester: Manchester University Press, 1982.

White, D. M. "Wood, Robert (1716/17–1771)." *Oxford Dictionary of National Biography.*

Woods, R. *Robert Woods Versuch über das Originalgenie des Homer.* Frankfurt am Main: in der Andreaischen Buchhandlung, 1773.

D11

W. E. Gladstone (1809–1898). *Studies on Homer and the Homeric Age.* Oxford: At the University Press, 1858.

Octavo. 3 vols.

Four-time Prime Minister and renowned orator William Ewart Gladstone composed this three-volume historical study of the Homeric works while he was out of political office. Although Gladstone held a minor position in Lord Derby's (B18) conservative government the year this work was published, he would later go on to become the leading figure of the liberal party in Victorian England. Gladstone's study appeared during a period of intense work on Homer in the 1850s and 1860s (see, for example, B14–B21, B50–B53, D12–D13), but diverged from much of the Homeric scholarship that had emerged since the publication of the Venetus A manuscript (A21) in 1788 and Friedrich August Wolf's 1795 *Prolegomena.* Gladstone affirmed the unity of the *Iliad* and *Odyssey*, arguing that the evidence for multiple versions of the epics in the "A Scholia" suggested the "restorative counter-agency" of the Alexandrian scholars rather than the fact that multiple authors were responsible for the modern texts, as Wolf had suggested. Gladstone also rejected the anthropological approach that explained Homer as a product of specific circumstances, exemplified in Blackwell's work (D9); in fact, he felt that contemporary scholarship would suffer no loss "if every copy of [Blackwell's treatise] could be burned," insisting that the *Iliad* and *Odyssey* were created by "design."

Although the presence of the Homeric epics in the curriculum at the University of Oxford (which Gladstone represented in Parliament) had been increased in 1850, Gladstone sought "to promote and extend" their further study, not only as poetry, but also "among the materials of historical inquiry." This work, which followed several articles on Homer Gladstone contributed to the *Quarterly Review*, approached Homer as a window into the "palaeozoic" "world of religion and ethics, of civil policy, of history and ethnology, of manners and arts, so widely severed from all following experience." Gladstone, a devout Christian, viewed the Homeric epics as a document of religion and morality.

His work was not well received among scholars: Benjamin Jowett, Regius Professor of Greek at Oxford, called it "'a mere nonsense,'" and Tennyson described Gladstone's views as "'hobby-horsical.'" Yet the *Gentleman's Magazine* welcomed Gladstone's Homeric study as a work of "scholarship in its widest sense . . . a contribution of unquestionable value to ancient history,—not the mere history of Greek literature, but to the national and political history of Greece," and the *North American Review* found that Gladstone had "infused a life and vigor" into subjects that, "having usually fallen into the hands of mere scholars, are by general readers considered as little better than the offal of literature, and left for these greedy vultures to prey upon undisturbed." While serving as Prime Minister eleven years later, Gladstone published an abridged version of his work, revised for a more general audience, and, undeterred by the lack of scholarly enthusiasm, continued to devote his leisure time to producing Homeric scholarship for the rest of his life.

Aldous, R. *The Lion and the Unicorn: Gladstone vs. Disraeli.* New York: W. W. Norton and Company, 2007.

Bebbington, D. "Gladstone and Homer." *Gladstone Centenary Essays.* Edited by D. Bebbington and R. Swift. Liverpool: Liverpool University Press, 2000.

———. *The Mind of Gladstone: Religion, Homer, and Politics.* Oxford and New York: Oxford University Press, 2004.

Gladstone, W. E. *Homeric Synchronism: An Enquiry into the Time and Place of Homer.* London: Macmillan and Co., 1876.

———. *Juventus Mundi: The Gods and Men of the Heroic Age.* London: Macmillan and Co., 1869.

"Gladstone on Homer and the Homeric Age." *Gentleman's Magazine* 204 (1858): 495–502, 613–20.

Matthew, H. C. G. "Gladstone, William Ewart (1809–1898)." *Oxford Dictionary of National Biography.*

McKelvy, W. R. III. "William Ewart Gladstone." *Dictionary of Literary Biography, Vol. 184: Nineteenth-Century British Book-Collectors and Bibliographers.* Edited by William Baker and Kenneth Womack. Farmington Hills, MI: Gale Group, 1997.

North American Review 91, no. 189 (October 1860): 301–26.

Smith, G. B. *The Life of the Right Honourable William Ewart Gladstone.* Glasgow: James Campbell, 1888.

D12

Matthew Arnold (1822–1888). *On Translating Homer: Three Lectures Given at Oxford.* London: Longman, Green, Longman, and Roberts, 1861.

Octavo.

This is a presentation copy inscribed "From the Author."

Poet and Oxford Professor of Poetry Matthew Arnold's hugely influential work on Homeric translation was originally delivered as three lectures in November and December 1860. Arnold's lectures, which coincided with a surge of Victorian interest in Homer (see, for example, B14–B21, B50–B53, D11), were prompted by Francis William Newman's translation of the *Iliad* into popular ballad meter (B16). Newman's version violated the fourth of Arnold's famous principles of Homeric translation, first outlined in these lectures: "Homer is rapid in his movement, Homer is plain in his words and style, Homer is simple in his ideas, Homer is noble in his manner." Arnold focused his examination of these qualities mainly on the failures of four translations of the *Iliad*: Cowper's (B4)—"between Cowper and Homer there is interposed the mist of Cowper's elaborate Miltonic manner, entirely alien to the flowing rapidity of Homer"; Pope's (B9)—"the mist of Pope's literary artificial manner" covered over the "plain naturalness of Homer's manner"; Chapman's (B1)—"the mist of the fancifulness of the Elizabethan age" covered over the "plain directness of Homer's thought and feeling"; and Newman's—which is "eminently ignoble, while Homer's manner is eminently noble."

Arnold sought to discover the qualities that translators should seek in translating Homer by identifying the flaws of previous Homeric translations—those that missed the defining characteristics of Homer's manner, which Arnold suggested could best be replicated by the English hexameter (as Voss had tried in German [C13]). He attempted a few passages of hexametric translation by way of illustration, but had "neither the time nor the courage" to render the *Iliad* or *Odyssey* himself. His lectures, however, spurred a great debate about the proper meter for Homeric translation among scholars, translators, and commentators, giving rise to numerous articles in British periodicals, experimental hexametric translations (like Dart's [B17], Herschel's [B20], and Cayley's [B23]), and translations that rejected the English hexameter outright, attempting instead to demonstrate a more traditional meter's unfulfilled potential (like Lord Derby's in blank verse [B18], Blackie's in fourteeners [B19], and Merivale's in rhymed verse [B21]). Arnold's lectures also gave rise to Newman's 1861 *Homeric Translation in Theory and Practice: A Reply to Matthew Arnold*, which Arnold responded to in turn with *On Translating Homer—Last Words* (D13).

Collini, S. "Arnold, Matthew (1822–1888)." *Oxford Dictionary of National Biography.*

Coulling, S. *Matthew Arnold and His Critics: A Study of Arnold's Controversies.* Athens: Ohio University Press, 1974.

Edwards, S. O. "Matthew Arnold." *Dictionary of Literary Biography, Vol. 57: Victorian Prose Writers After 1867.* Edited by William B. Thesing. Farmington Hills, MI: Gale Group, 1987.

"Homer and his Translators." *Gentleman's Magazine and Historical Review* 1 (January-June 1866): 97–105.

Newman, F. W. *Homeric Translation in Theory and Practice: A Reply to Matthew Arnold.* London: Williams and Norgate, 1861.

"On Translating Homer." *London Times,* October 28, 1861.

D13

Matthew Arnold (1822–1888). *On Translating Homer: Last Words: A Lecture Given at Oxford.* London: Longman, Green, Longman, and Roberts, 1862.

Octavo.

This is Matthew Arnold's response to Francis William Newman's (B16) *Homeric Translation in Theory and Practice: A Reply to Matthew Arnold.* Newman had taken great personal offense at Arnold's criticism in his first three lectures on Homer (D12), and Arnold sought to both further explain his critique of Newman's *Iliad* and further establish his theories on Homeric translation with this fourth lecture, originally delivered at Oxford on November 30, 1861. The lecture also responded to Arnold's own critics, who found his conclusions too vague to be useful. He could only clarify that Homer's "grand style," the defining feature of his manner, was "the last matter in the world for verbal definition to deal with adequately. One may say of it as is said of faith: 'One must feel it in order to know what it is.'" But Arnold reiterated his criteria for "the future translator of Homer" who would be able to grasp the qualities defining the Homeric works: Homer's poetry was "at once rapid in movement, plain in words and style, simple and direct in its ideas, and noble in its manner." These four qualities immediately became part of the terminology of Homeric scholarship and translation, and have been consistently referred to both by translators of Homer seeking to fulfill the scheme laid out by Arnold and literary critics evaluating the worth of published translations ever since these four lectures first appeared. There has been no consensus that a translation meeting all four of Arnold's criteria has ever been written, and translators were still trying to render the ideal *Iliad* and *Odyssey* in Arnold's terms at the end of the twentieth century (see, for instance, B44, B45, B82).

D14

Milman Parry (1902–1935). *L'Épithète Traditionnelle dans Homère: Essai sur un Problème de Style Homérique.* Paris: Société d'Éditions "Les Belles Lettres," 1928.

Quarto.

D14

This essay on the traditional epithet in Homer is the first of Homeric scholar and oral theorist Milman Parry's two University of Paris doctoral theses, and the first publication of what many consider to be the most important Homeric scholarship of the twentieth century. It appears in English translation in *The Making of Homeric Verse: The Collected Papers of Milman Parry* (D14A), alongside an English translation of Parry's second doctoral thesis on the relationship between Homeric formulae and meter, *Les Formules et la Métrique d'Homère*, as well as many articles Parry contributed to classical periodicals while serving as Professor of Greek at Harvard, and research from fieldwork Parry conducted on the oral tradition in Yugoslavia.

Homeric scholars had recognized the oral nature of the *Iliad* and *Odyssey* since the late-eighteenth-century work of Robert Wood (D10) and Friedrich August Wolf, which led to the great nineteenth-century debate over the "Homeric Question," or the unity of the Homeric poems. Parry examined the formulaic features of the epics—the repetitions of stock nouns, adjectives, and phrases—in relation to their oral composition, and concluded that the *Iliad* and *Odyssey* were not composed at one time, but gradually and through a continual process of improvisation as the poems were handed down orally until they reached their written form. The epics were based on specific themes and storylines, but each oral poet would create a new version as he selected from the traditional formulae of epic storytelling. Parry travelled twice to Yugoslavia, where he could verify his conclusions with evidence from a living tradition of oral heroic poetry. After his untimely death, his student and assistant Albert Bates Lord continued his research. Bates and Parry are generally regarded as the founders of modern oral-formulaic theory, since applied by anthropologists and linguists to many oral traditions. Parry's work had a profound effect on Homeric scholarship and translation, indisputably settling the Homeric question for many scholars, and giving rise to many twentieth- and twenty-first-century translations that emphasized the improvisational or performance aspects of oral poetry, such as the renditions of Fitzgerald (B41, B74) or of Lombardo (B46, B85), Merrill (B87), and Logue (B96, B98–B100).

Clark, M. "Formulas, Metre and Type-Scenes." *The Cambridge Companion to Homer*. Edited by R. Fowler. Cambridge and New York: Cambridge University Press, 2004.

Combellack, F. M. *Classical Philology* 67, no. 3 (July 1972): 203–4.

Foley, J. M. *The Theory of Oral Composition: History and Methodology*. Bloomington: Indiana University Press, 1988.

Kirk, G. S. *Homer and the Oral Tradition*. Cambridge: Cambridge University Press, 1976.

Trypanis, C. A. *American Journal of Philology* 94, no. 3 (Autumn 1973): 302–4.

Willcock, M. *Classical World* 65, no. 2 (October 1971): 60.

D14A

Milman Parry (1902–1935). *The Making of Homeric Verse: The Collected Papers of Milman Parry.* Edited by Adam Parry. Oxford: At the Clarendon Press, 1971.

Octavo.

Homeric scholar Adam Parry compiled, edited, and provided the introduction and English translations for this collected edition of the works of his father, Milman Parry (see D14), many of which either had never been published or were long out of print.

D15

Robinson Smith (1876–1954). *The Original Iliad: The Solution of the Homeric Question.* [s.l.: s.n., 1929–30].

Folio.

The BHL copy contains a tipped-in presentation slip "With the compliments of the author, 12 Rue de France, Nice, France."

This privately printed text by literary critic James Robinson Smith was an attempt to reconstruct the original version of the *Iliad* and was "presented in this provisional form in order that advantage may be taken of criticism and correction, which are seriously invited." Smith, whose wide-ranging written work also includes biblical scholarship, translations from Cervantes and Dante, and pamphlets on European food-rationing, later published this essay along with his other Homeric studies in 1938. Smith worked from the premise, first offered by Walter Leaf (A30, B24) and popularized in the late nineteenth century, that the *Iliad* and *Odyssey* were originally composed by Homer as short poems and that the repetitions in the modern editions are evidence of inferior later imitations, additions, and corruptions; for an alternate and ultimately much more influential contemporary explanation of the epics' repetitive elements, see the work of Milman Parry (D14, D14A). He developed twenty-five rules governing Homeric style and applied them to the *Iliad*, reducing the poem to 3423 uncorrupted and, he argued, original lines. This preliminary version of Smith's work contains a translation of those lines, as well as many tables analyzing the features of Homer's style.

Critics readily answered Smith's invitation to remark on his work, objecting both to his methodology in establishing his twenty-five rules and to his view of the modern *Iliad* as a flawed poem, a view that appeared to have become outdated. In the *Classical Journal*, S. E. Bassett wrote that Smith's "twenty-five major premises are mere hypotheses" that Smith never offered proof for; and, in *Classical Philology*, J. A. Scott summed up his view of Smith's amateur scholarship: "Mr. Smith is an itinerant higher critic who after demolishing the gospels of Matthew and Luke as well as the epistles of the New Testament takes the same tools and reduces the *Iliad* and the *Odyssey* to powder." Leaf, however, approved of the early versions of Smith's work he read before his death: in letters to Smith, Leaf called the principles he employed "'sound'" and his result "'in itself a justification of the methods by which it has been reached'"—"'It is for you and men like you to be champions of the good cause.'"

Bassett, S. E. *Classical Journal* 26, no. 7 (April 1931): 555–56.

MacLean, M. T. "Guide to the James Robinson Smith Papers." Yale University Library Manuscripts and Archives. http://drs.library.yale.edu:8083/fedora/get/mssa:ms.1634/PDF

Scott, J. A. *Classical Philology* 26, no. 1 (January 1931): 108–9.

Smith, R. "From the Editor's Mail." *Classical Weekly* 31, no. 13 (February 1938): 129.

Tate, J. "The Immaculate Iliad." *Classical Review* 53 (1939): 119–20.

W. F. W. *Greece & Rome* 8, no. 24 (May 1939): 187.

SECTION E

Illustrations, Facsimiles, & Manuscripts

E1

Antonio Maria Ceriani (1828–1907). *Ilias Ambrosiana, Cod. F. 205 P. inf., Bibliothecae Ambrosianae Mediolanensis.* Bern: In aedibus Urs Graf; New York: Published in the United States by Philip C. Duschnes, 1953. *Fontes ambrosiani,* 28.

Folio.

The *Ilias Ambrosiana* is a late fifth- or early sixth-century CE manuscript of the *Iliad* thought to have been produced in Constantinople and named for the Ambrosiana Library in Milan where it is housed. It consists of fifty-two fragments of parchment and a total of fifty-eight separate miniatures. All of the text that survives is written on the verso of the illustrations. The existing fragments are from books 1–2, 4–17, and 21–24. The original manuscript likely had approximately 380–390 leaves and about 240 illustrations.

The manuscript is the oldest surviving evidence of an illustrated manuscript of Homer and, together with two manuscripts of Virgil, one of only three manuscripts of classical literature to survive from antiquity. This first color facsimile reproduces all of the illustrations in color and the text in monochrome.

Cardinal Federico Borromeo purchased the manuscript in 1608 from the heirs of the humanist and bibliophile Gian Vincenzo Pinelli. In 1612, the manuscript was cataloged as a book of pictures without reference to the Homeric text. Cardinal Angelo Mai first identified it and published it with copy engravings in 1819; a second edition appeared in 1835. The text and illustrations were published together in 1905 in a black-and-white photographic edition with notes by Antonio Maria Ceriani. This fourth edition includes the introduction to the 1905 edition by Ceriani, an appendix of recent scholarship by Aristide Calderini, and the "Pictarum codicis Homerici descriptio historica" by Angelo Mai.

E2

Nikolaos Loukanēs. Ὁμήρου Ἰλιάς = *The Iliad of Homer.* Athens: Gennadeios Vivliothēkē, Amerikanikē Scholē Klasikōn Spoudōn, 1979. *Gennadeion Treasures,* 2.

Octavo.

This facsimile, published by the Gennadius Library of the American School of Classical Studies in Athens, reproduces the edition printed in Venice in 1526 by Stefano Nicolini da Sabio for Petros Kounadis with 138 woodcuts, three of them full-page. It is the first translation of *The Iliad* published in a modern language and the earliest surviving book printed in modern, or demotic, Greek.

In his introduction, Francis R. Walton describes an earlier reprinting of the edition, by Emile Legrand in 1870, part of which was destroyed before distribution, and demonstrates that Loukanēs based his verse translation on a fourteenth-century verse paraphrase by Kōnstantinos Hermoniakos.

E3

John Flaxman (1755–1826). *Flaxman's Classical Compositions, Iliad and Odyssey.* London: Printed for Longman, Hurst, Rees, et al., 1805.

Oblong.

John Flaxman's illustrations, said to be modeled after Greek vase painting, were inspired by a trip to Rome in 1787. Five years later, he was commissioned by British artist and patron Georgiana Hare-Naylor to illustrate *The Iliad* and *The Odyssey.* The designs for Homer spoke to the contemporary popular craze for Greek antiquity and were well-received and frequently reprinted. His drawings were based on the translation of Alexander Pope (B9 and B49); lines of the texts accompany each plate.

The 1805 Longman publication is the first English edition of the drawings from *The Iliad* and *The Odyssey.* This edition adds five drawings to the thirty-four drawings for *The Iliad* engraved by Thomas Piroli for the 1793 Rome edition. William Blake and James Parker engraved the five additional drawings for *The Iliad.* Blake also redid the thirty-four drawings for *The Odyssey* after the originals were lost en route from Rome.

Constable, W. G. *John Flaxman, 1755–1826.* London: University of London Press, 1927.

E4

Homeri Iliadis. Codex manuscript, 1708.

This is an unidentified translation of the *Iliad* into Latin, with a dated title page in the same hand as the manuscript. Notes on the first two flyleaves may indicate that the manuscript was purchased by "Andre Garcia Alvares Cabrol Soureiro" in 1757 and that the translation was done by Fr. Joaquim de Santa Clara, a Benedictine monk.

A SHAGGY-DOG STORY: THE LIFE, DEATH, AND AFTERLIVES OF ODYSSEUS'S TRUSTY DOG ARGUS[1]

One of the distinguishing features of the reception of Homer, in contrast with that of most other ancient authors, is that since antiquity almost every culture has considered his poems to be especially faithful to the truth and to be especially valuable precisely for that reason. Keats was not the first, or the only, reader who could claim that he felt the very same excitement at looking for the first time into Homer's poetry (even in translation) as he would have if he had been vouchsafed a glimpse not just into some book but instead into a hitherto unimagined but achingly real world beyond the narrow and conventional reality he had supposed was the only one.[2] So, too, when Goethe describes his own youthful enthusiasm for Homer, he celebrates his discovery of the ancient poet as the dawn of a new day, in which the bright sun suddenly revealed to him men and things for what they really were.[3]

But if we look more broadly at the various ways in which Homer has been read and understood in European culture over the centuries, we can see, far more clearly than Keats or Goethe could have, that their own experience was not only personal and individual but also traditional and almost commonplace. Throughout history, Homer has been celebrated as *the* poet of reality, and what varied from period to period was not the notion that his poems told an important truth about reality but rather the kind of reality that interpreters sought to connect with the poems and the kinds of connections they sought to establish.

The following pages detail the history of the reception of Homer as that of the changing understandings of a body of poetry to which an indisputable truth was always ascribed, however differently that truth was conceived. In the modern period, these variations are embodied in the works of Homer's editors and translators. For that reason, the Bibliotheca Homerica Langiana (BHL) provides a rich treasury of materials for research into the history of the understanding of his poetry. So vast and complex is this topic that I shall only be able to touch on it, illustrating it by the example of a single small but charming episode: the encounter between Odysseus and his dog Argus in book 17, lines 290–327 of the *Odyssey*. Reflecting on this subject from the perspective of the editions and translations in the BHL has provided new insights into how this small episode can illuminate the larger theme.

Even today, I suppose, this scene is well known. Odysseus, disguised as a beggar and accompanied by the swineherd Eumaeus, is about to cross the most dangerous of all thresholds, that of his very own palace, when suddenly Argus recognizes him. He had trained the dog before the Trojan War, but had to set sail before he could enjoy any of the fruits of his labors; in its master's absence, Argus gradually deteriorated and eventually fell into a state of total neglect. Now, twenty years later, the dog, infested with vermin and lying on a pile of manure in the courtyard, recognizes Odysseus despite its master's total disguise and desires to greet him, but the dog is too old and weak to do anything more than wag its tail and lower its ears. Odysseus secretly wipes away a tear and asks Eumaeus, who has noticed nothing, whether the dog had been good at hunting; the two men enter into the palace, and Argus dies.

The whole episode is constructed with the greatest artistry to produce an effect of deep pathos, the most obvious sign of which is Odysseus's tear, which comments on the event conclusively with silent eloquence and is surely intended to provoke a similar reaction on the part of at least some readers. One reason for its effectiveness is that Homer partially humanizes the dog. The movements of the animal's body become an expressive gestural language that Odysseus and we, but no one else, can interpret: when the dog first lifts its head and pricks up its ears, we know it has become attentive; when it it lowers its ears and wags its tail, we know that it has joyously recognized its master. Homer supplies no explicit interpretation of these signals but instead leaves them to our everyday experience to decipher, with two consequences: first, we understand that the dog is worthy not only of our attention but also of the effort of our interpretation, rendering it more significant, perhaps even noble; and second, we feel ourselves linked more closely with the shrewd Odysseus, who notices such matters and understands them, than with the congenial but far less attentive Eumaeus. In turn, Odysseus and Argus are linked closely with one another, but precisely by their simultaneous frustration. The dog wants to express its recognition of its master, but no longer has the strength to do so; by contrast, Odysseus could easily express recognition of his dog, but under these perilous circumstances dares not. As a result, only we and Odysseus notice the dog's excitement, and only we notice Odysseus's excitement. Here as always, Odysseus shows himself to be a human being who is able to suppress his natural impulse to react spontaneously to some stimulus; and for this reason he is all the more closely linked with this animal, which was not spoiled at the table like the suitors, but is a tough fighter, patient and long enduring, just like its master, who had trained it by instilling in it these same values (17.307–10, 313–17).

How can we explain the powerful effect of this episode? Its success certainly depends to some extent on its evident sentimentality, but we should not underestimate the contribution of the artistic mastery with which Homer has composed it and fitted it into the structure of the *Odyssey*. Odysseus's crossing of the threshold into his palace is far too fateful an act for it not to be marked in some way: but how? The scenes inside the house, beginning here, take the form of a sequence of recognitions, first with Argus, then with Eurycleia (19.386ff), then with the suitors (22.1ff), and finally with Penelope (23.153ff). But just as it is the most important condition for the success of Odysseus's return that he be recognized only at the right moment and under the right circumstances, so too it is the greatest possible danger for him that he might be recognized at the wrong moment and under the wrong circumstances. At the end of book 19 this danger will arise when Eurycleia recognizes him by his scar (19.467ff), and again at the beginning of book 20 when he sees the faithless serving maids and can scarcely control his anger (20.9ff). For Odysseus to be recognized here at the threshold would surely cost him his life, unless (and this was Homer's brilliant idea) Odysseus is recognized not by a human being but by a dog, no one except Odysseus notices it, and above all the dog dies immediately afterwards without making any noise, so that Argus will pose no further danger to Odysseus. Only in this way can this recognition be complete, but completely inconsequential.

Odysseus's tear reminds us of his hidden tears during the performance of the singer Demodocus at the court of Alcinous: in both cases one of the reasons he weeps is the evident contrast between his earlier splendor and his current misery.[4] For in twenty years Argus has declined no less than has his master Odysseus, who is about to enter his own house as a beggar. Odysseus weeps for himself but also for the dog, whose loyalty and keen senses stand the test of a separation of two decades. Odysseus had indeed trained it well, and in the very last moment of its life Argus succeeds in demonstrating for its master's practiced eye its surpassing natural capabilities and its excellent training as a hunting dog.

Other connections with different parts of the poem enrich this scene further. Because Odysseus in crossing the threshold is leaving the outside world behind and is entering the dangerous zone of the inner space of the house, it is significant that this is the last and most important in a series of episodes with guard dogs. Argus, portrayed with such affecting realism, is effectively contrasted with the gold and silver dogs placed before the palace of Alcinous, which, fairytale elements as they are, are "immortal and ageless for all days" (7.94), and with the dogs of Eumaeus, the first creatures that Odysseus meets on Ithaca, which prove themselves not less dangerous (although for opposite reasons), loyal, and keen-scented than Argus: they attack Odysseus immediately and would have torn him to pieces had Eumaeus not driven them away (14.29ff), but then they greet Telemachus joyously on his return (16.4) and are, together with Odysseus, the only creatures able to perceive Athena (16.162). On one other, very prominent occasion in the *Odyssey*, we find a dangerous hunting dog in connection with the question of Odysseus's identity: on the fibula that proves his identity in one of the lying tales he tells Penelope (19.226–31). And finally, Argus, the loyal dog, is contrasted implicitly with the many disloyal humans on Ithaca: with Melanthius, the wicked goatherd, who only a moment before had insulted Eumaeus by calling him a dog (17.248); with the disloyal servant Melantho, who rebukes the beggar Odysseus and whom first Melantho (18.338) and then Penelope call a dog (19.91); with the disloyal servingwomen, whom Eurycleia calls dogs (19.372) and whose shamelessness Odysseus describes as doggish (20.18); and finally with the suitors, whom Odysseus addresses as "you dogs" at the climactic moment when he finally reveals his identity to them (22.35). If Longinus could say that Homer made his gods into men and his men into gods,[5] then we might well add, thinking of Argus, that he makes this dog into a human and many humans into dogs.

This, more or less, is how we tend to read this episode today,[6] as a network of connections, of parallels and contrasts, backward and forward throughout the poem, raising and disappointing expectations, suggesting and correcting hypothetical interpretations. How then did readers in antiquity view it? Because Argus seems to have had astonishingly little effect on ancient readers—it is significant that not even one picture of this Homeric episode survives from all of ancient art[7]—we can try to collect and consider all the evidence.[8] Of course we must never forget that only a tiny fraction of the opinions actually expressed in antiquity (to say nothing of those thought but unexpressed) survives into our age. Nonetheless the picture that the surviving documentation provides is so coherent that the interpretative hypotheses we can derive from it may be plausible.

We can divide the ancient reception of the Argus episode roughly into two main streams, linked by numerous cross-references and points of contact, but easily distinguishable on the basis of clear differences in their fundamental interests and ways of reading. One is a nonphilological line of reception, represented by readers of Homer who were not experts on his life and poetry, the other a philological approach, consisting of readers who made their living by editing, commenting on, and teaching Homer's works.

Let us begin with the nonprofessional readers. What interested them about this episode? We might well suspect that many ancient readers, just like us, were struck by the Argus scene because of its pathos; but, strangely enough, not a single piece of evidence survives from all of antiquity to indicate that even one ancient reader ever felt such a reaction. Instead, with very few exceptions, only three things struck ancient nonphilological readers about this scene.

Some of these readers asked whether it was really possible for a dog like Argus to live more than twenty years. A passing reference in Aristotle proves that this question was already controversial in his own time: he says that male Laconian dogs live for ten years and females for twelve, whereas the females of most other races of dogs live fourteen or fifteen years, some of them as many as twenty. As he puts it, "and so some people[9] suppose that Homer was right when in his poem he had Odysseus's dog die at the age of twenty."[10] Aristotle does not explicitly indicate his own view on this subject (elsewhere he accepts that female dogs can give birth up to the age of twenty[11]), but it is not hard to guess his opinion: the phrase "some people suppose" in his scientific writings always refers to views he rejects as erroneous. In any case, for centuries Argus's longevity remained celebrated—and controversial. At the end of the first century C.E., Martial composed a poem in elegiac couplets for the tomb of a heroic dog, in which he compared the deceased favorably to various mythical canine celebrities, including Argus, whose long and useless life is devalued in comparison with this dead dog's precocious and heroic death in battle—almost, by implication, like the useless longevity of his patron Odysseus in comparison with Achilles's noble decision to die young.[12] And as late as the beginning of the third century C.E., Aelian set the maximal life expectancy of a dog at fourteen years and concluded that Homer's reference to Argus must therefore have been nothing more than a joke.[13]

A second group of ancient nonphilological readers were struck above all by the fact that Argus succeeded in recognizing his master even though Athena had disguised him. Varro, a Roman polymath of the first century B.C.E., and Lucillius, a Greek satirical epigrammatic poet contemporary with Nero, derive some clever literary witticisms from this observation. In a satire of mixed poetry and prose entitled "Sesqueulixes" (which means something like "An Odysseus and a Half"), Varro, away on a trip, claims that if he were delayed even further by adverse winds he would come home as a stumbling old man whom no one would recognize except his dog.[14] According to Lucillius, by contrast, it took twenty years to change Odysseus's appearance so much that only Argus could recognize him, but after only four hours in the ring the boxer Stratophon was beaten so severely that only dogs could recognize him, whereas his city and even he himself, when he saw himself in the mirror, had no idea who he was.[15] The elder Pliny, in the same century, sees in a dog's ability to recognize his master even when he arrives incognito and unexpected a typical trait of the species;[16] although he does not refer explicitly to the Argus episode, nevertheless the situation he presupposes is sufficiently precise and unusual for us to suspect that Pliny (or, likelier, his Greek source) was thinking of this particular Homeric scene.

Thereafter, the example of Argus became a fruitful topic for epistemological controversies in ancient philosophy until late antiquity. Around 200 C.E., Sextus Empiricus argues against the Stoics that, if we accept the Stoic principle that the possession of one virtue necessarily entails the possession of all of them, then we must accept the consequence that dogs who can demonstrate that they possess courage or (in the case of Argus) intelligence must be considered Stoic sages.[17] And approximately two hundred years later, Augustine asks in two philosophical dialogues whether dogs like Argus, which indisputably possess the faculty of memory, must also possess the faculty of reasoning; he answers in the negative with the argument that many animals are superior to humans in their sense perceptions but that God has granted reason only to human beings.[18]

The ancient texts belonging to the third group of nonphilological readers emphasize the loyalty of this dog that remained stubbornly faithful to its master even until its death. At the end of the second century C.E., the lexicographer Pollux made a catalogue of "illustrious dogs."[19] He recounts in great detail the stories of the dogs of Pyrrhus, Hesiod, Icarius, Alexander the Great, and others, in a colorful mixture of history, myth, and literature; in most cases the dogs became celebrated because they obeyed their masters with an extraordinary sense of duty even to the point of self-sacrifice. Only in the case of Argus does he mention this "miracle" without bothering to explain it in further detail, evidently because Homer is far too famous to have to be recapitulated in boring (and potentially offensive) specificity. He may be thinking too of Argus's loyalty to the point of death; the hint of skepticism connoted by the word "miracle" may be intended to remind us that this particular dog's loyalty was alleged to have lasted for twenty years. Aelian, whom we met in the first group, returns in this third one as well: a couple of decades after Pollux, he too tells a story about a dog's loyalty to his master and uses this historical event as an opportunity to defend the truthfulness of the Homeric episode.[20] He reports in detail how, during the course of a Colophonian merchant's business trip to Teos, his dog noticed that his master's servant had gone into the forest to answer the call of nature and had forgotten the moneybag there. The dog lay down on it and waited there without eating until the master and servant passed by on the return trip; only when the dog saw them again did it abandon its position, and at the very same moment it died. The contrast is instructive: whereas the Colophonian merchant's careless human servant is more obedient to nature than to his master, this devoted dog, though an animal, refrains from the most fundamental of all natural needs—eating—out of loyalty to his master, and thereby sacrifices its very life. (It would be interesting to know with exactly what words the merchant brought to the attention of his neglectful servant the virtues of his deceased dog.) Aelian takes over the Homeric contrast between canine loyalty and human disloyalty but exaggerates it; and so he can draw the conclusion from this edifying tale that Argus's loyalty was thereby proven to have been neither a "mere myth" nor a "poetic exaggeration."[21] And we may well identify a final ancient descendant of the Homeric Argus in the dog of Erigone, whose touching story is told by Nonnus, an epic poet who lived around 400 C.E. and composed a *Dionysiaca* in forty-eight books, the longest poem surviving from antiquity (and one of the very last ones).[22] To be sure, Nonnus is careful not to repeat even a single Homeric phrase exactly, and yet it is tempting to understand this episode in the penultimate book of his epic as a highly refined poetic elaboration on the Homeric model. Indeed, it may well be not only the only surviving ancient epic version of the story from the *Odyssey* but also the only significant one ever to have been composed—for poets later and more straight-laced than Homer, this episode's low, almost sordid realism seems to have disqualified it from imitation in the lofty genre of the epic.

These, then, are the three main lines of the ancient nonphilological reception of the Argus episode.[23] What evidence do these texts supply regarding the question how nonphilological readers understood this scene in antiquity? The answer may be surprising. Nowhere is there the slightest hint that it was prized because of its effect on the reader's emotions: apparently the earliest author who even mentions the pathos of this scene is Eustathius, in the late twelfth century.[24] Any claim that readers in antiquity appreciated it for the same reasons as we do today must contend with a monumental silence and explain why there is no surviving evidence whatsoever that this phenomenon even existed.

Instead, what we can say with certainty is that ancient readers took the Argus story as a serious contribution to scientific zoology. Where we see an affecting fiction that only achieves its full expressive power if it is seen as part of a complex poetic whole, ancient readers saw a collection of individual affirmations about the real world that one could test to determine the degree of their truth or falsehood. For us, Argus's longevity is the small and quite acceptable price that Homer must pay in order to have the dog recognize Odysseus (who left Ithaca twenty years before), and a welcome pretext for the dog's death and thus for the innocuousness of its recognition. For antiquity, by contrast, it was a factual claim that this particular dog lived for twenty years, and this not especially credible claim was one that could be, and needed to be, tested on the basis of other reports and observations about the life expectancy of dogs. For us, Argus's ability to recognize Odysseus despite his divine disguise is not a serious problem: at the very least, we know that dogs, unlike humans, rely for their knowledge of the world far more on their noses than on their eyes, and we recall that Athena had merely altered Odysseus's external appearance, not his other identifying features. If we have any difficulties accepting Argus's ability to recognize the disguised Odysseus, we can easily solve them by inferring that this excellent hunting dog used its superb sense of smell to recognize its master's characteristic scent, which in twenty years it had never forgotten. After all, had not Eumaeus's guard dogs alone, with Odysseus, been able to recognize Athena's presence (16.162)? For antiquity, by contrast, this dog's alleged sharpness of sense perception was striking in itself and could be used for scientific arguments, philosophical controversies, or literary points. Finally, for us, Argus's loyalty is an integral part of a dominant theme of the *Odyssey* and invites comparison with Odysseus, Penelope, the suitors, and the slaves; whereas for antiquity this dog's loyalty formed part of a series together with reports—historical, legendary, fictional, and otherwise—about other loyal dogs.

In short, at least this episode of Homer's poetry was understood as a collection of testable individual affirmations about specific phenomena of our real world, and its evaluation depended on whether these affirmations were true or false. If the poetry stood the test, then it was praised as true—as agreeing with other comparable reports or observations; if it failed, then it revealed itself to be merely a fiction and was demoted to the status of a false claim that adds nothing useful to our knowledge. At best, in this episode, Homer is the first, and perhaps the greatest, Greek zoologist; at worst, he is just wrong. And of course, as it turns out, for almost all ancient readers (with the notable exception of Aristotle) he is right, and what he says about Argus is justified as being true.

To be sure, the particular contents of this scene suggested scientific interpretations, and we must be cautious about generalizing our conclusions too broadly. But it is not surprising that ancient readers could often see Homer as a teacher, because every one of the writers we have encountered so far had studied the Homeric epics intensively in school during his childhood. Various sources, especially but not only school papyri,[25] give us an idea of the methods that ordinary ancient schoolteachers used when they taught Homer. They were most likely a somewhat coarser version of the very same methods whose traces are preserved in the surviving documents of ancient professional philology, which derive (admittedly only very incompletely) from an uninterrupted school tradition that lasted at least from the Hellenistic period in the third century B.C.E. until the collapse of the Byzantine empire in the fifteenth century C.E. Two surviving high points in this tradition are Porphyrius's fragmentarily transmitted *Homeric Investigations* from the late third century C.E. and Eustathius's voluminous and completely extant Homeric commentaries from the late twelfth century C.E. Let us turn to these texts in order to compare the ancient philological reception of the Argus episode with the other, nonphilological tradition.

To begin, some of the same questions that we already found in the nonphilological reception tradition—such as Argus's longevity[26] and ability to recognize Odysseus[27]—also occur in the philological one. But even when the question seems to be the same, these readers dealt with it differently. First of all, the attitude is entirely defensive for the philologists: Homer is not attacked, but defended; he is not even really tested, but immediately corroborated and justified; possible criticisms of his poetry are not justified but are nipped in the bud. And second, the main criterion for demonstrating Homer's truth comes far less from empirical observations or historical anecdotes and far more from a small number of canonical texts: Aristotle, later poets, and above all Homer himself. In this way, the poem is justified as a textbook of natural science, by reason of its demonstrated compatibility with other texts that are understood as being just such textbooks too.

This defensive approach appears in other discussions in the philological tradition that seem to be lacking in the nonphilological one, although perhaps the corresponding documentation has merely been lost. Why did Argus die so suddenly? The answer: because of his old age and the dangers of excessive joy.[28] How could Argus possibly have hunted hares on Ithaca, when Aristotle mentions once in passing that hares cannot survive on that island and, if imported onto it, die at once?[29] The answer: when Homer says the hunts took place "earlier" (17.294), the adverb *paroithen* is used not temporally but (in fact, impossibly) spatially, to mean "over there," on the mainland across from Ithaca.[30]

But the philological reception is characterized most distinctively by questions regarding the exact meaning of Homer's words. For example, when Homer wanted to denote the vermin that plagued Argus, he apparently (and unsurprisingly) found nothing ready to hand in the standard lexicon of the heroic epic tradition, so he simply coined the word *kynoraisteôn* ("dog-smashers") on the basis of the formulaic *thymoraisteôn* ("spirit-smashers"). He thereby invented a very elegant name for this very inelegant object on the basis of the effect it produced, but he also rendered forever futile any attempt to identify it exactly in terms of its genus and species. We have no idea whether Argus suffered from ticks, fleas, lice, gnats, mites, bugs, intestinal worms, or parasites. The question is evidently quite pointless, given that the poem in which Argus appears is a fiction, that Argus never existed, that *a fortiori* neither did its vermin, that there is no other evidence regarding its condition, and that the word in question is attested nowhere else in all of Greek literature except in a couple of passages in literary contexts in Aristotle that doubtless derive directly from this very line in Homer.[31]

But mere considerations of ordinary common sense have never stopped philologists from trying to answer unanswerable questions. Already around 100 C.E., Apollonius the Sophist, the earliest philologist whose explanation of this word is fully extant, reports that earlier scholars had proposed different solutions for its meaning;[32] and, even after and despite his own learned and detailed discussion, the controversy continued to rage for centuries without ever coming to a conclusion.[33] Evidently this particular word caused the philologists particularly intense headaches, because it seemed to denote a real object in the world but did not indicate exactly what it was; but the ancient and medieval commentaries and dictionaries are full of many other lexical explanations that suggest just how difficult much of Homer's language was for later Greeks.[34]

If we consider the practice of schoolteachers, it is easy enough to explain all these features of the philological reception of Homer as measures designed to secure authority. A school author must never be shown to have made a mistake—for if he makes mistakes, why should one take such trouble to study him, and how can one justify correcting pupils' mistakes? We can also see why one school author's credibility tends to be proved by his agreement with others: for the authority of each single school author reinforces that of all the others in a system of values declared to be coherent and valid, and any pupil who submits to one thereby acknowledges his consent to all. The predominance of linguistic explanations indicates that Homer served above all as a textbook for instruction in a foreign language, the Attic literary idiom, in which demonstrable competence was for many centuries the indispensable premise for a career as an orator or a functionary in ancient and mediaeval public administration. Alas, in point of fact Homer's language is not at all Attic but instead an artificial mixture of various dialects and invented forms that as such was never spoken except by Homeric rhapsodes—so Eustathius, like many another Byzantine scholar, finds himself obliged sometimes to claim, bizarrely, that some recalcitrant Homeric word is in fact "early Attic."[35] If Homer makes an appearance in the philological tradition not only as a poet or linguist or historian but as a zoologist as well, this is especially useful, for elementary instruction is thereby revealed to be justified by the fact that it transmits many other kinds of useful knowledge. After all, most pupils were not likely to have gone very far if at all beyond Homer in their studies, and few if any ever read much of Aristotle, Ptolemy, or Galen. But this might not be such a bad thing, could Homer be shown to provide basic information in fields such as zoology, astronomy, and medicine, especially if the claim could be made that Aristotle and the others had derived everything they themselves had known about these sciences from Homer. Thus, the pupil who read only Homer's poetry could console himself and his parents by reflecting that he had drunk out of the earliest source. Ancient philological texts such as Heraclitus's *Homeric Allegories* and Pseudo-Plutarch's *Life and Poetry of Homer* already claim that all sciences ultimately derive from Homer[36]; and Eustathius still begins his Homeric commentary with the commonplace that, just as all rivers have their origin in the sea, so too all the sciences have their source in Homer.[37] Eustathius is being entirely consistent with this tradition when at certain points in his explanation of the Argus scene he asserts that Homer is giving lessons in agriculture and zoology in it,[38] and he happily swells the already ample volume of his interpretation by inserting further bits of information that are only marginally relevant to the Homeric text, such as a reference to the large number of hares in Carpathia or a catalogue of the most famous races of dogs.[39] Homer seems to function as a kind of cultural life preserver, to ensure that anything worth knowing is linked to his immortal name and thereby protected from being swallowed up in the floodwaters of oblivion.

But even so, the claim that Homer can teach us much that is worth knowing and useful about our world is not self-evidently correct. After all, is it not the case that his poetry often offends against good manners, moral virtue, philosophical doctrine, Roman and Byzantine Imperial values, and even Christian belief? Homer's secure and central place in the school curriculum over many hundreds of years had to be secured by a method of reading that could prove to suspicious religious and secular functionaries and above all to worried parents that even in those passages where the poet seemed to have nothing whatsoever to contribute to the pupil's future success, he was transmitting, at a deeper, hidden level, vital knowledge about the moral or physical nature of our world.

In this way too Homer's poetry is rescued as truth, but now the truth is not straightforward scientific information about everyday experience communicated directly and explicitly, but esoteric doctrines about fundamental natural or religious entities, which are only hinted at on the surface level of the poetry and must be extracted from it by the convoluted procedures of allegorical interpretation. It is not surprising that, through all of antiquity and the Middle Ages, allegorical interpretation flourished so strongly, and even today its legacy is everywhere. For allegoresis was an indispensable support for the practice of school instruction: it made it possible to find every science in one text; it disarmed any possible objection of irrelevance or vice; and it managed even to find an explanation for the fact that in his sublime poem Homer introduced an old, dirty, vermin-infested dog. We are lucky to still possess Eustathius's allegorical interpretation of Argus[40]: maybe the dog was white (Eustathius is unsure about this, and in fact Homer says nothing at all about Argus's color), and everything white is a positive omen; its old age and its death at the sight of Odysseus point to the fate of the suitors, who are shameless like dogs but weak in comparison to Odysseus and therefore will die soon—although they have hitherto been flattering themselves with doggishly deceptive hopes. Eustathius's allegory is patently absurd (although not untypically so), but at least it insulates not only Homer but also Eustathius himself, and those schoolteachers who read and apply him, against the unruly pupil (and his distrustful parents) who want to know the point of studying this apparently banal episode.

When Homer emigrated in the early Renaissance from Constantinople to Italy, he brought with him this scholarly combination of truth claims and allegorical interpretations. The Italians and then other Europeans who welcomed the poet did not at first question the value of the late ancient and Byzantine exegetical materials that accompanied him.[41] This mode of interpretation continued uninterrupted for the first two centuries of the Renaissance: Politian and Erasmus repeated the commonplace of Homer as the sea from which all knowledge flows[42]; and until the late seventeenth century the ancient allegorical handbooks, often in Latin translation, and their Renaissance continuations were frequently reprinted.[43] George Chapman and the other seventeenth-century translators of Homer into English made ample use of the traditional moral and physical allegorical interpretations[44]; indeed, Keats's vision of Chapman's Homer as the vast and hitherto undiscovered Pacific Ocean is indebted at least as much to Chapman's traditional allegorical claim that Homer is the ocean from which all knowledge draws its origin as it is to Renaissance accounts of the voyages of exploration.

The BHL provides strong evidence that early modern translators showed no trace of embarrassment about the Argus episode and made no attempt to prettify the text. Here is Chapman's version (B1):

But, his King gone, and he now past his parts,
Lay all abjectly on the Stable's store,
Before the Oxe-stall and Mules' stable dore,
To keepe the clothes, cast from Pessants hands,
While they laide compasse on *Ulysses'* Lands,
The Dog with Tickes (unlook'd to) over-growne.

Here is John Ogilby's (B47):

But now he lay in a dejected state,
Upon a Dunghill just before the Gate,
That Mules and Steeds congested with their Dung,
Which Swains on the improving past'rage flung,
There lay poor *Argus* full of Ticks.

And here is Thomas Hobbes's (B48):

But all the while his Master was away,
The Servants of his keeping took no care,
But on the Dung before the Door he lay,
Which there was heap'd to manure Fields and Leas,
From many Mules and Cattle faln away.
There lay the old Dog *Argus* full of Fleas.

Evidently Homer's description was simply enjoyed as being true to nature or justified as being allegorically meaningful.

It was not until the end of the seventeenth century that poor Argus was first exposed to serious attacks. This happened in France during the controversies between the partisans of antiquity and the advocates of modernity known as the *Querelle des anciens et des modernes.* Charles Perrault's celebrated polemic was not the first time in European culture that older poets were played off against newer ones, but it was the first time that allegorical interpretation failed to protect their favorite authors from attack. For during the course of the sixteenth and especially the seventeenth centuries it had become ever more difficult to take allegory seriously as an exegetical tool.[45] There were a variety of reasons for this general development: the gradual emancipation of European classical philology from its Byzantine heritage, for example in questions of pronunciation or chronology; new philosophies that greatly reduced the appeal of Stoic or Neoplatonic interpretations of Homer; new scientific discoveries that deprived the notion that Homer had anticipated Aristotelian physics or Hippocratic medicine of interest; and above all the general critique of allegorical interpretation associated with the Reformation.

It had always been allegorical interpretation that insulated Homer against any attack, and the almost complete neglect of this kind of exegesis among any of the participants in Perrault's treatise is a significant signal of an epochal change. Only once does the President, the defender of the ancients in Perrault's book, invoke allegorical interpretation to defend Homer. When the modernist Abbé attacks the scene in the first book of the *Iliad* in which Hephaestus expresses his concern that Zeus might beat Hera,[46] the Chevalier, the mediator in the discussion, remarks that peasants would be pleased to learn about this passage, because they could justify their own marital abuse by pointing to the example of Zeus. The President replies cautiously, "Do you not know, Monsieur l'Abbé, that there is a mystery in these words?" He is alluding to the ancient tradition of allegorical interpretations of such passages in terms of the identification of the Homeric gods with meteorological phenomena and the elements of nature. The Abbé then explains the mystery and simultaneously makes it ridiculous: because Zeus is the god of thunder and Hera is the goddess of the air, Zeus beating her means that the thunder beats the air and violently shakes it. The Chevalier comments scornfully that for him such an interpretation is not to be taken any more seriously than the childish belief that when the sun shines during a rainstorm the devil is beating his wife, and he suggests that they move on to a different topic. Embarrassed, the President immediately agrees—and that moment marks the death of allegorical interpretation.

But without allegory, Homer's readers could no longer ignore the fact that there were fundamental differences between Homer's time and their own. These had been dissimulated as long as the poet had been conceived as the promulgator of a timeless wisdom that could anticipate the knowledge of later times. But once the veil of allegory had been rent, it became inescapably evident that there were oddities in Homer's text that could no longer be explained away as concealed references to conditions in our own world, and could only be understood as characteristic features of Homer's. This is exactly what happens in the course of Perrault's discussion of the Argus episode.[47] First the age-old question of the dog's longevity is raised once again and discussed inconclusively. But then the Abbé delivers a mortal blow: "This dog," goes his accusation, "was lying on a dunghill in front of the entrance of Odysseus's palace," whereupon the Chevalier cries out in horror, "A dunghill in front of a palace!" Perhaps for the very first time in the history of the reception of Homer, it is not Argus that is considered problematic, but the dunghill on which he is lying. Evidently the criterion is no longer the relatively unchanging, naturally given physiological constitution of dogs, but instead historically developed and socially contingent ideas of taste and hygiene. A French dog at the end of the seventeenth century probably lived about as long as a Greek dog 2500 years earlier, but in the meantime the public character of dung, especially in front of a splendid public building, had changed fundamentally. In Perrault's text, both the partisans of the ancients and the advocates of the moderns are of one mind in recognizing the force and necessity of this historical development. The President declares that in the age of Homer, "*ce temps-là*," wealth consisted principally of land and cattle, presumably in contrast to his own time; and the Chevalier concludes the discussion by remarking that the princes of Homer's time, "*ce temps-là*," were apparently similar to the peasants of his own time, "*ce temps-cy*."

As a result, it becomes possible to correlate conditions in the Homeric age ("*ce temps-là*") with primitive phenomena in a modern world that prides itself on having developed far beyond antiquity in its own time ("*ce temps-cy*"). For the moderns, Homer thereby becomes less valuable, for he depicts obsolete conditions from which we have finally succeeded in emancipating ourselves. But Homer's defenders too were able to use this same idea by simply inverting this conclusion. For them, Homer's poetry could be considered beautiful precisely because it was full of allusions to primitive conditions that we can scarcely find in today's world, and only in simple and remote cultures. This is how the defenders of the ancients argued in direct response to Perrault, for example Madame Dacier and Alexander Pope in the notes to their translations of Homer. First Madame Dacier (C7):

> Pendant qu'ils parloient ainsi,[54] un chien nommé Argus … mais alors accablé de vieillesse & n'étant plus sous les yeux de son maître, il étoit abandonné sur un tas de fumier qu'on avoit mis devant la porte,[55] en attendant que les laboureurs d'Ulysse vinssent l'enlever pour fumer les terres.[56] Ce chien étoit donc couché sur ce fumier & tout couvert d'ordure …
>
> [54] Voici une nouvelle espece d'épisode qu'Homere n'auroit pû employer dans l'Iliade, & qu'il employe heureusement dans l'Odyssée, qui est sur

un autre ton; c'est la reconnoisance d'Ulysse par son chien. Cet episode, très-different de tout ce qui a precedé, jette dans cette poësie une varieté charmante. Le Poëte en faisant l'éloge d'Argus, enrichit l'histoire naturelle & marque le caractèristique d'Ulysse.

[55] Les narrations d'Homere sont ordinariement mêlées de preceptes indirects, soit pour les moeurs, soit pour le ménage. En voici un pour l'oeconomie rustique. Le fumier devoit être fort precieux à Ithaque, car comme les terres y éstoient fort maigres, elles avoient grand besoin d'être fumes, & c'est ce qu'Homere n'a pas oublié. Virgile en a fait un précepte, *Ne saturare fimo pingui pudeat sola.* Lib. I. Georg. *Un tas de fumier devant la porte d'un palais!* s'écrie l'auteur du *Parallele. Demeurez d'accord que les princes de ce tems-là ressembloient bien aux paysans de ce tems-ci.* Voilà comme ce critique étoit bien instruit de l'antiquité.

[56] Le grec dit, *& tout plein de vermine.* Mais le mot de l'original est beau & harmonieux, au lieu que celui de *vermine* est desagréable & bas. L'auteur du *Parallele* abuse encore de cet endroit: *Homere di que ce chien étoit tout mangé de tics.*[48] Il ne sent pas combien les termes bas qu'il employe flêtrissent la diction & deshonorent la poësie.

While they were speaking in this way,[54] a dog named Argus ... but then, exhausted by old age and no longer under its master's eyes, it had been abandoned on a dunghill that had been placed in front of the door,[55] waiting until Odysseus's workmen would come and carry it away to manure the fields.[56] So this dog was lying on this dung and was completely covered with filth ...

[54] Here is a new kind of episode that Homer could not have used in the *Iliad* and that he uses successfully in the *Odyssey*, which has a different tone; it is the recognition of Odysseus by his dog. This episode, very different from everything that has preceded, adds a charming variety to this poetry. In praising Argus, the poet enriches natural history and indicates the personality of Odysseus.

[55] Homer's narratives are ordinarily interspersed with indirect precepts for morals or for housekeeping. Here is one for running a farm. Dung must have been very precious in Ithaca, since the land there was very barren and greatly needed to be fertilized, and this is something that Homer has not forgotten. Virgil turns this into a rule, *Ne saturare fimo pingui pudeat sola* (*Georgics* I.80). "A dunghill in front of the door of a palace!" exclaims the author of the *Parallèle.* "Let us agree that the princes of that time were very similar to the peasants of this time." You can see how much this critic knew about antiquity.

[56]The Greek says, "and all full of vermin." But the word in the original is beautiful and harmonious, while the word "vermin" is unpleasant and coarse. The author of the *Parallèle* misuses this passage too: "Homer says that this dog was completely devoured by ticks." He does not perceive how the coarse words he uses ruin the diction and dishonor the poetry.

And now Alexander Pope (B49, pp. 126–27):

> Now left to man's ingratitude he lay,
> Un-hous'd, neglected, in the publick way;
> And where on heaps the rich manure was spread,
> Obscene with Reptiles, took his sordid bed.

... This whole Episode has fallen under the ridicule of the Critics; Monsieur *Perrault* in particular: 'The Dunghill before the Palace (says that Author) is more proper for a Peasant than a King; and it is beneath the dignity of Poetry to describe the Dog *Argus* almost devour'd with vermin.' It must be allow'd, that such a familiar Episode could not have been properly introduced into the *Iliad*: It is writ in a nobler style, and distinguish'd by a boldness of sentiments and diction; whereas the *Odyssey* descends to the Familiar, and is calculated more for common than heroic life. What *Homer* says of *Argus* is very natural, and I do not know anything more beautiful or more affecting in the whole Poem: I dare appeal to every person's judgment, if *Argus* be not as justly and properly represented, as the noblest figure in it. It is certain that the vermin which *Homer* mentions would debase our Poetry, but in the *Greek* that very word is noble and sonorous, Κυνοραιστέων: But how is the objection concerning the Dunghill to be answer'd? We must have recourse to the simplicity of manners amongst the Antients, who thought nothing mean, that was of use to life. *Ithaca* was a barren Country, full of Rocks and Mountains, and ow'd its fertility chiefly to cultivation, and for this reason such circumstantial cares were necessary. 'Tis true such a description now is more proper for a Peasant than a King, but antiently it was no disgrace for a King to perform with his own hands, what is now left only to Peasants. We read of a Dictator taken from the plough, and why may not a King as well manure his field as plough it, without receding from his dignity? *Virgil* has put the same thing into a Precept: *Ne saturare fimo pingui pudeat sola.*

To be sure, both Madame Dacier and Pope also have recourse to various older arguments.[49] But their emphasis on the specific agricultural conditions that they can claim to have prevailed on Ithaca, their reference to Virgil's *Georgics*, and above all Pope's eulogy of ancient simplicity and naturalness are novel. They are the harbingers of a largely new approach to Homer's ancient text.

Once again Homer's poetry is being rescued because of its alleged truth: but now that truth resides neither in its faithful representation of the natural world nor in its revelation of the timeless principles of moral or physical reality, but instead in the traces it has preserved of an almost completely vanished time. Pope's drastic judgment in favor of Argus, "I do not know anything more beautiful or more affecting in the whole Poem," did not remain uncontroversial.[50] But it stands paradigmatically at the beginning of a century that continued with the positive revaluation of Homer by Johann Jakob Bodmer and Johann Jakob Breitinger,[51] the travels of discovery of Robert Wood,[52] and the rise of the Homeric sun described by Goethe, and concluded with the historicization of the Homeric text by Friedrich August Wolf[53] and the new, realistic, yet elevated Homer translation by Johann Heinrich Voss (C13). It is with Voss's precise, unembarrassed, yet elegant version that this survey of the afterlife of Argus may fittingly close:

> Aber jetzt, da sein Herr entfernt war, lag er verachtet
> Auf dem großem Haufen vom Miste der Mäuler und Rinder,
> Welcher am Tore des Hofes gehäuft war, daß ihn Odysseus'
> Knechte von dannen führen, das Königs Äcker zu düngen;
> Hier lag Argos, der Hund, von Ungeziefer zerfressen.

> But now that his master was gone he lay despised
> on the big pile of dung of mules and cattle
> that was piled up at the palace door so that Odysseus'
> workmen could carry it off to manure the king's fields;
> here lay Argus, the dog, devoured by vermin.

GLENN W. MOST

NOTES

1. An earlier version of this article was published in German as "Ansichten über einen Hund: Zu einigen Strukturen der Homerrezeption zwischen Antike und Neuzeit," *Antike und Abendland* 37 (1991): 144–68. Unless otherwise noted, the translations are mine.

2. John Keats, "On First Looking into Chapman's Homer."

3. J.W. Goethe, *Dichtung und Wahrheit = Gesamtausgabe der Werke, Briefe und Gespräche*, ed. Ernst Beutler (Zürich: Artemis, 1948–64), vol. 10, pp. 588–89. Cf. especially Kirsti Simonsuuri, *Homer's Original Genius. Eighteenth-Century Notions of the Early Greek Epic* (Cambridge: Cambridge University Press, 1979) and Joachim Wohlleben, *Die Sonne Homers. Zehn Kapitel deutscher Homer-Begeisterung: Von Winckelmann bis Schliemann* (Göttingen: Vandenhoeck & Ruprecht, 1990).

4. Cf. W.-H. Friedrich, "Odysseus weint. Zum Gefüge der homerischen Epen," in *Dauer im Wechsel. Aufsätze*, ed. C. J. Classen and U. Schindel (Göttingen: Vandenhoeck & Ruprecht, 1977), pp. 63–85, especially 65f.

5. Longinus, *On the Sublime* 9.7.

6. Some modern discussion of this scene: L.A. Stella, *Il poema d'Ulisse* (Firenze: Nuova Italia, 1955), pp. 365 ff.; G. S. Schwartz, "The Kopros Motif. Variations of a Theme in the *Odyssey*," *Rivista di studi classici* 23 (1975): 177–95; G.P. Rose, "Odysseus' Barking Heart," *Transactions of the American Philological Association* 109 (1979): 215–30; H. Rohdich, "Der Hund Argos und die Anfänge des bürgerlichen Selbstbewusstseins," *Antike und Abendland* 26 (1980): 33–50; E. Wirshbo, "The Argus Scene in the *Odyssey*," *Classical Bulletin* 59 (1983): 12–15.

7. Images of Odysseus together with a dog are found only in Etruscan and Roman art. In all these artworks, the dog is still alive, and in most of them it appears in the company of Odysseus and Penelope. Most likely such images simply express a vague notion that a hero like Odysseus, whose exploits included hunting, must under normal domestic circumstances be shown to have not only a wife but also a hunting dog. But some scholars have thought them to be—and it is not quite impossible that they might be—evidence for a specifically Etruscan version of the legend, different from the Greek ones. In any case, it is impossible to interpret these images as illustrations of the Argus episode as we know it. On this material see E.H. Richardson, "A Mirror in the Duke University Classical Collection and the Etruscan Versions of Odysseus' Return," *MDAI (Rom)* 89 (1982): 27–34 with Tables 8–13; F. Brommer, *Odysseus. Die Taten und Leiden des Helden in antiker Kunst und Literatur* (Darmstadt: Wissenschaftliche Buchgesellschaft, 1983), pp. 99, 102–4.

8. J. Perfahl, ed., *Wiedersehen mit Argos und andere Nachrichten über Hunde in der Antike = Kulturgeschichte der Antiken Welt* 15 (Mainz: Philipp von Zabern, 1983), provides little help.

9. Perhaps he means Antisthenes, who wrote a book, now lost, *On the Dog*; in the list of the works of this author transmitted by Diogenes Laertius, *Lives and*

Opinions of Eminent Philosophers 6.18, this title follows *On Odysseus and Penelope.*

10. Aristotle, *Historia animalium* 6.20.574b29–575a1.

11. *Historia animalium* 5.14.546a30–-32.

12. Martial, *Epigrams* 11.69.

13. Aelian, *De natura animalium* 4.40.

14. Varro, *Saturae Menippeae,* "Sesqueulixes," Frag. 471 Astbury.

15. Lucillius, *Anthologia Palatina* 11.77.

16. Pliny, *Naturalis historia* 8.61.146.

17. Sextus Empiricus, *Pyrrhoneioi Hypotyposeis* 1.14.68.

18. Augustine, *De quantitate animae* 26.50, 28.54; *De musica* 1.4.8. Augustine uses the example of Argus in the same argumentative context twice in these dialogues, which are almost exactly contemporary with one another, and then never mentions the dog again; this is probably to be explained by his having taken the story from some philosophical source and not having had detailed direct knowledge of the *Odyssey* himself.

19. Pollux, *Onomasticon* 5.44.

20. Aelian, *De natura animalium* 7.29.

21. In his moralizing conclusion to the story, Aelian makes a slip and says the Colophonian merchant lived in Teos.

22. Nonnus, *Dionysiaca* 47.219–45.

23. Apart from the texts indicated hitherto, I have found only two further certain references to the episode in ancient nonphilological texts: Plutarch, *De tranquillitate animi* 16.475A, and Libanius, *Epistle* 1155.3–4 Foerster. But in both cases the reference is not so much to the dog Argus as to its master Odysseus. Two other ancient texts are most probably not to be understood as references to this episode at all: Horace, *Epistle* 1.2.23–28 and Artemidorus, *Oneirocritica* 2.11.

24. Eustatius 1820.15–21 on *Odyssey* 17.290.

25. See especially R. Cribiore, *Writing, Teachers, and Students in Graeco-Roman Egypt* (Atlanta, GA: Scholars Press, 1996) and *Gymnastics of the Mind* (Princeton, Oxford: Princeton University Press, 2001), and R. Nünlist, *The Ancient Critic at Work* (Cambridge: Cambridge University Press, 2009).

26. Porphyrius, *Quaestiones homericae* on *Odyssey* 17.291ff. (123.19–20 Schrader); Eustathius 1821.5–6 on *Odyssey* 17.327.

27. Porphyrius, *Quaestiones homericae* on *Odyssey* 17.291ff. (123.13–19 Schrader); Eustathius 1820.29–46 on *Odyssey* 17.294.

28. Porphyrius, *Quaestiones homericae* on *Odyssey* 17.291ff. (124.1–4 Schrader); Eustathius 1821.7–9 on *Odyssey* 17.327. Here one seems to hear the voice of the tired schoolteacher, irritated by years of trying in vain to dampen the boyish high spirits of his pupils.

29. Aristotle, *Historia animalium* 8.28.606a2–5.

30. *Scholia* on *Odyssey* 17.294 (644.23–25 Dindorf); Eustathius 1821.28–32 on *Odyssey* 17.295.

31. Aristotle, *Historia animalium* 5.31.557a17–18, *Rhetoric* 2.20.1393b23–28.

32. Apollonius Sophista, *Lexicon Homericum* 105.14–17 Bekker.

33. Hesychius, *Lexicon* K 4605–6; *Suda* K 2718; *Scholia* on *Odyssey* 17.300 (645.4–8 Dindorf); *Etymologicum magnum* 546.10–11; Eustathius 1821.45–46 on *Odyssey* 17.300.

34. E.g., *Scholia* on *Odyssey* 17.296 (644.29 Dindorf), 17.299 (645.1–3 Dindorf); Eustathius 1821.39–40 on *Odyssey* 17.296, 1821.41–45 on *Od.* 17.298.

35. E.g., Eustathius 1821.19 on *Odyssey* 17.298.

36. Heraclitus, *Homeric Allegories* 4.4, 22.2, 76; Ps.-Plutarch, *De vita et poesi Homeri* 6.

37. Eustathius, *Commentarii ad Homeri Iliadem* 1.7f.

38. Eustathius 1821.41–45 on *Odyssey* 17.298, 1820.15–21 on *Odyssey* 17.290.

39. Eustathius 1821.31–33 on *Odyssey* 17.295, 1822.4–6 on *Odyssey* 17.315.

40. Eustathius 1821.9–13 on *Odyssey* 17.327.

41. On various aspects of the early modern reception of Homer and the allegorical interpretation of myths, cf. G. Finsler, *Homer in der Neuzeit von Dante bis Goethe* (Leipzig, Berlin: B. G. Teubner, 1912); J. Seznec, *La survivance des dieux antiques = Studies of the Warburg Institute* 11 (London: Warburg Institute, 1940, English trans. New York: Pantheon Books, 1953); T. Bleicher, *Homer in der deutschen Literatur (1450-1740). Zur Rezeption der Antike und zur Poetologie der Neuzeit* (Stuttgart: J. B. Metzler, 1972); M. Murrin, *The Allegorical Epic: Essays in its Rise and Decline* (Chicago, London: University of Chicago Press, 1980); and G. Baldassarri, *Il Sonno di Zeus. Sperimentazione narrative del poema rinascimentale e tradizione omerica* (Rome: Bulzoni, 1982).

42. A.L. Rubinstein, "The Notes to Polizian's 'Iliad,'" *Italia medioevale e umanistica* 25 (1982): 205–39, here 223; Bleicher, p. 60.

43. So for example T. Gale, ed., *Opuscula Mythologica, Ethica et Physica. Graece & Latine* (Cambridge: Joann. Creed, 1671, Amsterdam: Henricum Wetstenium, 1688 [2nd ed.]). Natalis Comes' *Mythologiae* was published for the first time in 1568 and was reprinted at least twenty-four times until 1653 in the original language or in various translations.

44. E.g. A. Nicoll, ed., *Chapman's Homer: The Iliad, the Odyssey, and the Lesser Homerica* (Princeton: Princeton University Press, 1956), vol. 1, p. 44 (Commentarius on *Iliad* 1.197), 2.5f.

45. I have discussed the general question of the decline of allegorical interpretation in this period in "The Second Homeric Renaissance: Allegoresis and Genius in Early Modern Poetics," in Penelope Murray, ed., *Genius: The History of an Idea* (Oxford: Basil Blackwell, 1989), pp. 54–75.

46. C. Perrault, *Parallèle des anciens et des modernes en ce qui regarde les arts et les*

sciences (Paris: J. B. Coignard, 1688), vol. 3, pp. 55–56; I cite from the edition of H.R. Jauss (München: Eidos, 1964), pp. 297–98.

47. Perrault, vol. 3, pp. 96–99.

48. The handwritten French gloss on this word in the margin next to this line in item A2 of the BHL translates it just as Perrault does: "tiques."

49. Thus Madame Dacier derives her note 54 directly from Eustathius 1820.15–21 on *Odyssey* 17.290.

50. E.g., J.B. Dugas-Montbel, *Observations sur l'Odyssée d'Homère* (Paris: F. Didot, 1833).

51. Johann Jakob Bodmer and Johann Jakob Breitinger, *Schriften zur Literatur*, ed. Volker Meid (Stuttgart: Reclam, 1980): see most recently Annegret Pfalzgraf, *Eine Deutsche Ilias? Homer und das "Nibelungenlied" bei Johann Jakob Bodmer. Zu den Anfängen der nationalen Nibelungenrezeption im 18. Jahrhundert* (Marburg: Tectum, 2003) and Anett Lütteken und Barbara Mahlmann-Bauer, ed., *Bodmer und Breitinger im Netzwerk der europäischen Aufklärung* (Göttingen: Wallstein Verlag, 2009).

52. Robert Wood, *An Essay on the Original Genius of Homer* (1769 and 1775) (repr. Hildesheim/New York: Georg Olms, 1976); see especially David Constantine, *Early Greek Travellers and the Hellenic Ideal* (Cambridge/New York: Cambridge University Press, 1984).

53. Friedrich August Wolf, *Prolegomena to Homer, 1795*, translated with introduction and notes by Anthony Grafton, Glenn W. Most, and James E.G. Zetzel (Princeton: Princeton University Press, 1985).

QUARRELING OVER HOMER IN FRANCE AND ENGLAND, 1711–1715

Montesquieu's 1721 epistolary novel *Persian Letters* invited its contemporary European readers to view their own culture through the foreign eyes of two traveling Persian noblemen, Rica and Usbek, whose letters home detail their impressions of the manners and customs of their hosts. In a letter dated 1713, Usbek recounts his initiation into Parisian café culture. The latest subject of very hot debate among its fashion-conscious, novelty-hungry clientele has obviously left him in a state somewhere between disgust and wonderment:

> Le café est très en usage à Paris: il y a un grand nombre de maisons publiques où on le distribue. Dans quelques-unes de ces maisons, on dit des nouvelles; dans d'autres, on joue aux échecs. Il y en a une où l'on apprête le café de telle manière qu'il donne de l'esprit à ceux qui en prennent: au moins, de tous ceux qui en sortent, il n'y a personne qui ne croie qu'il en a quatre fois plus que lorsqu'il y est entré.
>
> Mais ce qui me choque de ces beaux esprits, c'est qu'ils ne se rendent pas utiles à leur patrie, et qu'ils amusent leurs talents à des choses puériles. Par exemple, lorsque j'arrivai à Paris, je les trouvai échauffés sur une dispute la plus mince qu'il se puisse imaginer: il s'agissoit de la réputation d'un vieux poète grec dont, depuis deux mille ans, on ignore la patrie, aussi bien que le temps de sa mort. Les deux partis avouoient que c'étoit un poète excellent: il n'étoit question que du plus ou du moins de mérite qu'il falloit lui attribuer. Chacun en vouloit donner le taux; mais, parmi ces distributeurs de réputation, les uns faisoient meilleur poids que les autres: voilà la querelle. Elle étoit bien vive, car on se disoit cordialement de part et d'autre des injures si grossières, on faisoit des plaisanteries si amères, que je n'admirois pas moins la manière de disputer que le sujet de la dispute. Si quelqu'un, disois-je en moi-même, étoit assez étourdi pour aller devant l'un de ces défenseurs du poète grec attaquer la réputation de quelque honnête citoyen, il ne seroit pas mal relevé; et je crois que ce zèle si délicat sur la réputation des morts s'embraseroit bien pour défendre celle des vivants! Mais, quoi qu'il

en soit, ajoutois-je, Dieu me garde de m'attirer jamais l'inimitié des censeurs de ce poète, que le séjour de deux mille ans dans le tombeau n'a pu garantir d'une haine si implacable! Ils frappent à présent des coups en l'air: mais que seroit-ce si leur fureur étoit animée par la présence d'un ennemi? (pp. 182–83)[1]

Coffee is very popular in Paris; there are a lot of public establishments where it is distributed. In some of these people report the news; in others they play chess. There is one where they prepare the coffee in such a way that it gives wit to those who drink it; at any rate, of those exiting there is no one who does not think himself at least four times smarter than he was on entering.

But what shocks me about these fine wits is that they do not make themselves useful to their country, but amuse their talents with childish things. For example, when I arrived in Paris I found them all heatedly debating the most trivial of subjects imaginable. It had to do with the reputation of an old Greek poet whose place of birth, like the date of his death, has been unknown for two thousand years. Both sides agreed that he was an excellent poet; the only thing in question was the greater or lesser degree of worth to be assigned to him. Everyone wanted to pronounce on his rating; but among these distributors of reputation, some gave a higher mark than others. And that was the whole quarrel! A lively one, too: for they uttered such rude insults in all heartfelt seriousness, and made at each other's expense such bitter jokes, that I wondered at their manner of debating no less than at the subject of their debate. If anyone were so foolish (I said to myself) as to stand before one of those defenders of the Greek poet and attack the reputation of some honorable citizen, he would be in for a pretty sharp rebuff! I do believe that their zeal, being so prickly about the reputation of the dead, would mount to red hot fury in defense of the reputation of the living! But be that as it may (I added to myself), may God preserve me from drawing down on myself the hostility of that poet's critics, since two thousand years in the tomb has not managed to protect him from their implacable hatred! At present their blows land in the air. But what would happen if their passions were roused by the actual presence of an enemy?

The object of Usbek's naïve misrecognition (and Montesquieu's sly critique) is a set of events known as the *Querelle d'Homère*, an intellectual battle that in its day was as fashionable as coffee, and no less addictive. Montesquieu's wit may have a double edge here, but his Persian persona is not at all exaggerating the intensity of this war of words or the ferocity of its combatants. If anything, the novel understates both the bounds and the duration of this fight over a dead Greek poet's reputation. Paris was the geographic epicenter, the "Greenwich meridian" of this and every other literary cultural phenomenon during the century of enlightenment and revolution, but the debate over Homer was an event of pan-European significance and was quickly recognized as such.[2] And in 1713, the fictional date of Usbek's letter, the Quarrel he claims to remember in the past was in fact still picking up speed, as was the production of treatises, essays, articles, and letters about a poet who, his detractors had been arguing for some time now, may have never existed. Above all, and fortunately for us, the years of the Homer Quarrel saw an unparalleled spike in the proliferation of modern vernacular versions of the Homeric epic poems. Here, I describe and compare the texts and authors of four very different early modern *Iliads* that were published in France and England between 1711 and 1715, by Anne Dacier, John Ozell and collaborators, Antoine Houdar de la Motte, and Alexander Pope. Each of these is now magnificently represented in the Bibliotheca Homerica Langiana.

However easy it was for satirists and wags of the day to mock it, and for historians of literature and culture to trivialize it ever since, the Homer Quarrel has a significance that perdures. It still has things to teach us about Homer. Less obviously, it has things to teach us about our relations to the past, to the powers of language, to the kinds of truth we impute to poetry, to prose written about it, and to ourselves as cognitive, affective, and ethical beings. It represents, among other things, a very late moment in the history of Western culture in which Homer's poetry could be taken seriously enough to be held up as an ethical guide, and even seriously enough to be attacked as morally repellent and dangerous. Homer's detractors in the fight sometimes turn out to have read him more astutely, more sympathetically, than some of his adulators. The blindnesses of the combatants on both sides are sometimes more instructive than their insights. Then too, it may be that a fight, simply by virtue of being a fight, opens up access to a unique and still relatively unexplored set of hermeneutic potentials that more peaceable modes of intellectual discourse about literature cannot attain. If this is true anywhere, it is likely to be true in the case of the Homeric epics. Monumental celebrations of fierce and archaic ways of being in the world, verbal artifacts at once primitive and intricately sophisticated, foundational and radically strange, these poetic wellsprings of European culture possess a terrible beauty that, as Plato already saw, threatens to frustrate every attempt to organize human life and human communities solely in accord with the sweetness and light of reason.

What, precisely, was the Homer Quarrel a quarrel about? In part, it continued and renewed hostilities that the earlier *Querelle des Anciens et des Modernes* ("Quarrel of the Ancients and Moderns") had left to smolder unresolved. This more famous culture war, sometimes known in English as the Battle of the Books after the title of Jonathan Swift's satirical intervention in it, was still a fresh memory in the second decade of the eighteenth century.[3] In France, at least, it had the narrative structure of a proper war, arcing from an opening skirmish to an uneasy peace agreement. On January 27, 1687, at a meeting of the Académie française celebrating the king's recovery from a serious illness, Charles Perrault had read aloud a poem, *Le Siècle de Louis le Grand* ("The Age of Louis the Great"), that he had composed for the occasion. This lionizing of modern progress in the arts and sciences was at the same time a bold declaration of independence from the tyranny of the ancients. Antiquity, Perrault asserted, deserves our respect but not our worship. History's greatest achievements in conquest and governance have now been equaled or surpassed by the reigning monarch. In the realm of knowledge of the world, Aristotle's authority, like that of every other long-unquestioned author, has been upended by the progress of modern science. And in the realm of culture, Perrault continued, even Homer, known for millennia as the inimitable "father of all the arts," for all his "vast and mighty genius," can no longer stand unscathed under the scrutiny of a modern taste conformable to enlightened reason in its ethics as well as its aesthetics:

> Cependant si le ciel favorable à la France
> Au siècle où nous vivons eût remis ta naissance,
> Cent défauts qu'on impute au siècle où tu naquis
> Ne profaneroient pas tes ouvrages exquis.
> Tes superbes guerriers, prodiges de vaillance,
> Prêts de s'entrepercer du long fer de leur lance,
> N'auroient pas si longtemps tenu le bras levé,
> Et lorsque le combat devroit être achevé,

Ennuyé les lecteurs d'une longue préface
Sur les faits éclatants des héros de leur race.
Ta verve auroit formé ces vaillants demi-dieux
Moins brutaux, moins cruels, et moins capricieux.[4]

Still, if Heaven, for a blessing to France,
had postponed your birth to the age we live in now,
a hundred flaws (chalk them up to the age you were born into)
would not profane your exquisite works.
Your haughty warriors, those prodigies of valor,
when ready to pierce each other with their lances' long points,
would not have held their arms up for so long,
and when the fight should have been over and done with,
would not have bored their readers with a long preamble
on the stunning deeds of the heroes of their bloodlines.
Your verve would have fashioned those valiant demigods
less brutal, less cruel, and less capricious.

Among the Academicians present that day was Nicolas Boileau, the translator of Longinus's essay on the sublime and author of verse treatises, satires, and epistles in imitation of Horace. As Perrault read, Boileau's scandalized indignation mounted visibly and audibly. When he gave vent to it at the poem's conclusion, accusing Perrault of bringing shame on the Academy by attacking what it ought most to honor, his Iliadic passion opened a personal rift between the two men that, drawing the lines of engagement, set each of them up as the chieftain of an embattled camp. Perrault led the charge for his party, known henceforth as the Moderns, with a rapidly produced (1688–92) four-volume set of *Parallèle des anciens et des modernes en ce qui concerne les arts et les sciences* ("Ancients and Moderns Compared in Regard to the Arts and Sciences") in which his dialogue mouthpiece asserted his own age's superiority over its predecessors in every human endeavor. Ranged on Boileau's side, the party of the Ancients, were the tragedian Jean Racine, the fabulist Jean de la Fontaine, and virtually every other literary great of France's classical golden age. All the most illustrious names a Modern might have wished to cite as evidence that the Greeks and Romans had now been definitively surpassed in the production of literature were names whose owners had (in the eyes of the Moderns) betrayed their own age, by publicly declaring allegiance to the ancient models that, they insisted, had nourished, instructed, chastened, and enabled their own writing lives in a way that nothing could replace. The Quarrel of the Ancients and Moderns ended as publicly as it had begun, through an engineered piece of theatre in which Boileau and Perrault publicly sealed their reconciliation with a kiss before the Academy on August 30, 1694. This outcome was sufficiently inconclusive that both parties could walk away simultaneously claiming victory and nursing the sting of defeat.[5]

Five years later, by 1699, Anne Dacier had apparently completed a first version of her *Iliad* translated literally into French prose. But it was the complete edition she published in 1711, copiously annotated and introduced with a lengthy preface, that would make a dead Greek poet's reputation into a new *casus belli.* Raised in the Calvinist intellectual community at Saumur, Madame Dacier (née Le Fèvre) had received a thorough schooling in the classical languages from her father Tanneguy Le Fèvre, a Saumur academician whose enlightened methods of childhood pedagogy in the Renaissance humanist tradition, as recorded in his *Méthode pour commencer les humanités grecques et latines* (1670), would exercise wide influence through the eighteenth century in England as well as France. After her father's death in 1672 she moved to Paris. There she had published an edition of Callimachus and translated several Greek and Latin authors by the time of her 1683 marriage to André Dacier, a former student of her father's who had also made his way to the capital for a career as a classical scholar. In the year of the revocation of the Edict of Nantes, 1685, the couple announced their conversion to Catholicism at the end of a spiritual and studious retreat, and were granted a royal pension. Ten years later, André Dacier was received into the French Academy as its perpetual secretary, having produced a series of workmanlike translations of classical texts that included Aristotle's *Poetics*, and having served as general editor of the series of bilingual editions *ad usum Delphini.*

It is probably no accident that the three elegant volumes of Madame Dacier's 1711 *Iliad* are easily mistaken for a novel of her time. Her entire project in translating the epic, as she believed Homer's had been in composing it, was one of moral improvement. For her this meant, among other things, putting something better than the corrupting stuff of gallant romance—Scudéry and the like—into worldly hands. What had long held her back from publishing her translation, she claims, was a sorrowful awareness that most readers of her time, "spoiled by having read scads of vain and frivolous books" (*gâtés par la lecture de quantité de livres vains et frivoles*) would have but meager appetite for "these austere poems that deliver useful instructions packaged in an ingeniously devised plot, feeding our curiosity none of those intrigues that we call 'touching' and 'interesting' only to the degree that they revolve around love" (*ces poèmes austères, qui sous l'enveloppe d'une fable ingénieusement inventée, renferment des instructions utiles, et qui n'offrent à notre curiosité aucune de ces aventures que nous n'appelons touchantes et intéressantes qu'autant qu'elles roulent sur l'amour*, pp. v–vi).[6] Homer, she reasoned, was a teacher of virtue *ex hypothesi*, because epic poetry had obviously been invented for no other reason than instruction and improvement. From this certainty she derived a further one: even Plato, by granting Homer the great name of poet, had thereby proved his own censure unfounded. Besides, she continued, what Plato had chiefly faulted in Homer was his depiction of divinity doing things like succumbing to the passions of anger and grief, waging battle in heaven, and inflicting pestilential ills on humankind. What Plato did not know, but the Hebrew scriptures assure us, is that precisely those things turn out to be predicable of the one true God, who punishes wrongdoing as vigorously as Zeus. From this guarantee of revealed truth, she concluded triumphantly, we can see that Homer was right, and Plato wrong, on these and many other counts.

The world according to Anne Dacier, as this brief foray into it shows, is decidedly its own place. Peopled with an idiosyncratic mix of humanist philology and Christian theology, an amalgam whose cohesion she defended and championed with tireless rhetorical aggression, it is a world situated at some remove from the urbane discursive climate of early eighteenth-century Paris, as foreign in that setting, in a way, as Montesquieu's Persians were. But what made it impossible for her contemporaries to dismiss Madame Dacier as merely an eccentric—as much as they would have liked to, and as much as they mocked her as a *femme savante*, an Amazon, more "vigorous" than her husband, passionately in love with the ghost of Homer, and so on—was the fact that she seemed to know more Greek, and to have read more of it, than just about any of her contemporaries.[7]

For us, what makes Anne Dacier's *Iliad* so important as a literary historical event is that hers is the first modern vernacular rendering of the entire poem intended as a fully literal translation, in the late modern sense of the term. She offered two chief justifications for a model of literary translating practice now widely thought to require none. First, Homer's music is an effect of resources and powers of the Greek language that the French language lacks and therefore cannot reproduce. And second, Homer's poetic beauties, however remarkable, are less valuable than what the poems convey: historical knowledge about antiquity, stylistic models of eloquence in every genre, powerful variety in character depiction, maxims of sound philosophy, and an amazing affinity with the inspired words of the Hebrew scriptures in both style and thought (pp. xxiii–xxv). On both these counts, her thinking is hard to position in regard to her tradition(s), her own time, and our reception. At one moment her discussion of the differences between Greek and French can seem to be moving toward a formulation remarkably close to the late modern theorized preference for "alienizing" over "familiarizing" translation.[8] The moment passes, and her claims for the unrivaled and transcendent expressiveness of the Greek tongue go back to sounding like a less amusing version of lines spoken by one of Molière's comic learned ladies. Her insistence that the translator's principal task is the accurate conveyance of content implies some version of the belief that an ancient poem is most importantly a "document" like any other, an information delivery system. Familiar on its face, that view sounds less like the credo of a historicist practitioner of the modern discipline of philology once we learn where she thinks the usefulness of said information lies.

Anne Dacier occupies a unique position on the threshold between early and late modernity. Her certainty about the right way to translate Homer into a modern language, and the arguments by which she justifies it, are liable to shake our comfort to just the degree that we dislike entertaining the thought that late modernity's overwhelming preference (on ethical grounds, among others) for what we call literal translation might turn out to be based on a set of naturalized propositions whose genealogy we prefer to leave uninvestigated. We will not be surprised, for example, to see Dacier pushing back hard against a charge that late modern translators have not had to fear for a long time—that verbatim translation is a servile thing—if we remember that Horace's *Ars Poetica* could still be cited as a normative authority in her own community of readers (pp. xlii–xliii). Rather more surprising, if easily recognizable as characteristic of her vigor in argument, is her very strong and paradoxical claim that "poets translated into verse cease to be poets" (*les poètes traduits en vers cessent d'être poètes,* p. xxxix). Still more surprising than this positive assertion, and discomfiting for reasons that go beyond physical queasiness, is her apparently strategic concession that her French prose *Iliad* stands in relation to Homer's Greek poem as the embalmed corpse of Helen of Troy, if available for display in eighteenth-century France, would stand in relation to the living woman who bore that name. Just as Helen's mummy would show its viewers the beautiful proportions of her features and figure but nothing of her grace and charm, so likewise what Dacier claims to offer her readers "is not Homer living and breathing, I admit, but it is Homer" (*n'est pas Homère vivant et animé, je l'avoue, mais c'est Homère*, p. xxxvii). It is impossible not to wonder what motivates this more than striking image: A scholar's sober commitment to scientific accuracy at all cost? An antiquarian's nostalgic hunger to experience the past as real (albeit dead, decomposed, and preserved) presence? A cryptosectarian's cruel delight in the mortification of the senses? The invitation to confront the possibility that those impulses might be inextricably interentailed in the history of our modernity is among the bracing fascinations of reading Dacier's translation, commentary, and treatises on Homer.

For a taste of Madame Dacier's work, and for comparison, here is the seven-verse proem to the *Iliad* in a number of different versions: (1) the Greek original, (2) Richmond Lattimore's 1951 line-by-line American English literal-and-literary modernist verse translation (B37), (3) Dacier's 1711 French prose version (with my Englishing of the same), and (4) John Ozell's 1712 rendering of Dacier into English blank verse (B8), together with two of her notes on the passage as translated by Ozell or one of his collaborators:

Homer, *Iliad* 1.1–7:[9]

μῆνιν ἄειδε θεὰ Πηληϊάδεω Ἀχιλῆος
οὐλομένην, ἣ μυρί᾽ Ἀχαιοῖς ἄλγε᾽ ἔθηκε,
πολλὰς δ᾽ ἰφθίμους ψυχὰς Ἄϊδι προΐαψεν
ἡρώων, αὐτοὺς δὲ ἑλώρια τεῦχε κύνεσσιν
οἰωνοῖσί τε πᾶσι, Διὸς δ᾽ ἐτελείετο βουλή,
ἐξ οὗ δὴ τὰ πρῶτα διαστήτην ἐρίσαντε
Ἀτρεΐδης τε ἄναξ ἀνδρῶν καὶ δῖος Ἀχιλλεύς.

Lattimore:[10]

Sing, goddess, the anger of Peleus' son Achilleus
and its devastation, which put pains thousandfold upon the Achaians,
hurled in their multitudes to the house of Hades strong souls
of heroes, but gave their bodies to be the delicate feasting

> of dogs, of all birds, and the will of Zeus was accomplished
> since that time when first there stood in division of conflict
> Atreus' son the lord of men and brilliant Achilleus. (p. 59)

Dacier:

> Déesse, chantez la colère d'Achille fils de Pélée; cette colère pernicieuse, qui causa tant de malheurs aux Grecs, et qui précipita dans le sombre royaume de Pluton les âmes généreuses de tant de Héros, & livra leurs corps en proie aux chiens & aux vautours, depuis le jour fatal qu'une querelle d'éclat eut divisé le fils d'Atrée & le divin Achille; ainsi les décrets de Jupiter s'accomplissoient. (p. 1)

> Goddess, sing the wrath of Achilles son of Peleus; that destructive wrath which caused so many woes to the Greeks and precipitated into the somber realm of Pluto the noble souls of so many heroes, and rendered their bodies prey to dogs and vultures, from the fateful day when a momentous quarrel had divided the son of Atreus and the divine Achilles; so the decrees of Jupiter were being fulfilled.

Ozell, with Broome and Oldsworth:[11]

> Sing, Goddess, the Resentment of *Achilles*,
> The Son of *Peleus*, that accurs'd Resentment,
> Which caus'd so many mischiefs to the *Greeks*,
> And immaturely sent to *Pluto*'s Realm
> So many Heroes gen'rous Souls, and gave
> Their Bodies as a Prey to Dogs *(d)* and Vulturs,
> From that dire Day, when a momentous Quarrel
> First set at variance the Divine *Achilles*,
> And *Atreus*' Son: *(e)* so were *Jove*'s Laws fulfill'd. (pp. 1–3)

Dacier's notes, as translated in Ozell:

(a) *And Vulturs.*] In the *Greek* it is *all Birds*, and it has been made a Question, to what the Word πᾶσι, *all*, refers, whether it agreed with οἰωνοῖσί, or ought to be join'd with what comes after. This Question seems to me to be very frivolous. *Homer* says in this Place, *every Dog and every Bird*, as *Moses* said to those who did not obey his Law, *Sit cadaver tuum in escam cunctis volatilibus caeli, & bestiis terrae*, Deut xxviii 26, *Thy Carcass shall be Meat unto all Fowls of the Air, and unto the Beasts of the Earth.*

(*b*) *So were* Jove's *Laws fulfill'd.*] The *Epic* Poem is designed for Instruction, and therefore ought to be full of Religious and Moral Maxims, this is what *Homer* practices to Admiration. At the very first, he shews that nothing happens without the secret Appointment of *Jupiter*, who conducts all Things, by his Providence. *Plutarch* was in the wrong, to pretend to have *Fate* understood by *Jupiter*, alledging, that it was impious to say, God was the Author of humane Misfortunes. That unenlightened Philosopher did not comprehend this Truth, That God inflicts Punishments on Mankind, and, That out of the greatest Evils, with which he chastises them, he knows how to draw the greatest Good (p. 3).

The proem opens the *Iliad* with a masterful synoptic view of its plot that forces us at once to confront what is most paradoxical and unsettling in the dire unfolding of its action. We can see Dacier very clearly in her notes to these lines, and more subtly in her translation of them, already pressing the Homeric text very hard into conformity with a rationalized, scriptural, and enthusiastically fire-and-brimstone theodicy recognizable at once as belonging to a version of reformed Christianity. As a set of philosophical and religious views, her position is utterly familiar. What is utterly remarkable and strange is her eagerness to impute a large measure of those same views to Homer, and a quasi-scriptural veridical authority to his text. If, for example, she is quick to foreclose the long allegorizing tradition (here represented by Plutarch) that justified Homer to a philosophically inflected late ancient pagan readership, it is clear that her defense of the archaic Greek bard and his many-minded Olympian skyfather against figurational strategies of reading has, by its conclusion, become seamlessly indistinguishable from a brief for the literal truth of the Pentateuch of Moses and a theological justification for the harsh punishments inflicted by the God of Israel.

In her earlier note, on the birds of prey shown feasting on the victims of Achilles's anger and (the poem seems to say) Zeus's design, Dacier had already explicitly brought the authority of the Mosaic text to bear on a question of Homeric syntax. By a characteristic move, she had quietly (but not without a slap on the wrist for those who put frivolous questions to serious texts) assimilated the stout-souled Greek heroes whose corpses litter the *Iliad*'s proem to the justly punished commandment-breakers of Deuteronomy. But her boldest bit of hermeneutic revisionism here is also her subtlest, and it appears in her translation of the text itself, where Ozell and even Pope would follow her. The Greek original places the fulfillment of Zeus's plan in a clause directly following the grisly depiction of animal predation on human warriors who have died what was supposed to be a beautiful and glorious death. However we interpret Zeus's plan and construe the clause's syntax, the juxtaposition is so stark, and the questions it raises so complex, that it is hard not to believe that these superbly wrought lines were carefully engineered to provoke all the ethical and aesthetic disorientation they have engendered.[12] Here, Dacier has restored order to a dangerously unstable poetic moment by spiriting Zeus away from the rotting carcasses where Homer had left him, and setting him back down—without comment and by the exercise of even the most strictly "literal" translator's right to reorder syntactic units—at the end of the poetic paragraph. From there, the fulfillment of Zeus's "decrees" can look far more unambiguously like a providential will mysteriously working the good, and the proem can resolve itself on a reassuring note of pious sonority very far from the tone of Homer, who instead rounds out the period by showing the quarrel's two parties faced off and brandishing, as epithets, their rival claims to precedence.

All that said, it should also be said that no translator can escape the charge of having imposed prejudicial views on her original text in the process of translating, for the simple reason that the act of translating is also always an act of interpreting, and interpretation entails resolving the unknown into what is, at the moment of translating, taken as known and therefore exempted from questioning. Dacier's was the first translation of the *Iliad* to intend to give the clearest possible account of Homer's discursive sense in a modern tongue, and thereby to give direct and ready access to a set of experiences of the poem that had previously required abstruse learning. Nor are those experiences limited to cognitive mental processes. The noble austerity of her prose bespeaks an intimate appreciation of Homer's epic, rendering its diction with a high degree of adequation relative to the constraints and resources native to the speech of her own linguistic community.

Dacier's achievement as a translator of the *Iliad*, on the view of a contemporary and colleague in the profession, had "given to her name a lustre which is capable of no further addition." It was with that ringing accolade that John Ozell opened his preface to the English version of Dacier's 1711 *Iliad* that he had managed, with help from William Broome (who would later do several books of Pope's *Odyssey*) and William Oldsworth, to complete in time to hit the shelves of London booksellers before the end of 1712. This translation of a translation and hot commodity on a booming market (it would go on to a third printing in 1734) sparkled with the luster of both members of the pair of cultural artifacts, archaic Greek and contemporary Parisian, that it had brought impressively over into the Anglophone world. Ozell and his workshop had not only translated the quarrel of Achilles and Agamemnon from the plains of Troy, the festivals of Athens, and the Museum of Alexandria into English blank verse and Queen Anne armchairs. They had effected at the same time another brilliant translation—of the heated debate provoked by Madame Dacier's fresh reconstruction of a dead Greek poet's ammoniated symmetries—from the chess tables of the Procope in Paris to places like Daniel Button's newly opened Coffee House in London's Covent Garden.

It was in that same year, 1712, that Joseph Addison relocated his circle of Whig literary conversationalists there, and Ozell was among the frequenters of the Button Club, as the society came to be known. A Londoner by choice, he had learned Latin and Greek at free school as a boy in Leicestershire and, a talented linguist, had gone on to teach himself French and other modern European languages. While pursuing a career in accountancy that led to a position as Auditor-General of the City of London, he produced a series of literary translations of major contemporary French authors that included, among others, Boileau's *Lutrin*, some tragedies of Racine, Fénelon's *Télémaque*, and Montesquieu's *Persian Letters*, in addition to Dacier's *Iliad*.[13]

Ozell is quick to qualify the note of high praise for Dacier's translation on which his preface opens. If it is safe to say that her *Iliad* "will never have its fellow in the French tongue," it is also the case that "of all the European languages that pretend to any politeness, the French is certainly the unfittest for heroic subjects, as Madam Dacier in several places of this work pretty plainly confesses; and on the contrary, the English tongue the fittest for such subjects, as Father Rapin, in his reflections upon Aristotle's *Poetics*, does as good as allow" (l. A3 verso). The French language, Ozell explains, bars the formation of new compound words, and suffers from so extreme a poverty of simple ones that when, for example, Homer shows the Olympian giving his awesome assent to Thetis—

> And that thou mayst not doubt of what I promise,
> I will confirm it to thee with a Nod,
> The surest Seal among th'immortal Gods,
> With which I ratify the Grants I make.

Whate'er this Sanction of the Head enacts,
It nor deceives, nor is to be recall'd,
Nor does it ever fail to come to pass.
This said, with his black Brows the Son of *Saturn* nodded:
Th'Ambrosial Locks of his immortal Head
Were strongly shook, and whole *Olympus* trembled. (pp. 47–48)

—Dacier, in rendering the same lines—

> et afin que vous n'en puissiez douter, je vais vous le confirmer par un signe de tête, qui est la marque la plus sûre dont je scelle la vérité des promesses que je fais aux Immortels. Car tout ce que j'ai autorisé par la majesté de ce signe, ne trompe point, est irrévocable, et ne manque jamais d'arriver ». En même temps il fit un signe de ses noirs sourcils, les sacrés cheveux furent agités sur la tête immortelle du Dieu, et il ébranla tout l'Olympe. (p. 34)

—must resort to a flat periphrasis, designating the solemn act that shakes Olympus as a "sign of the head," for the simple reason that French lacks a word for what English and Greek call a nod (l. A4).

As to the question of form, Ozell responds implicitly to Dacier's strong claim for prose as the only fit conveyance for translating poets, first by voicing the doubt "whether an English translation of Homer, any otherwise than in verse, can be made so as to please an English reader" and later with a more positive assertion: "in all translations, regard ought to [be] had, not only to the sense of the original, but to the very manner of the composition, which ought to be resembled as near as possible, and not a new one introduced" (l. A5). The real issue Dacier was up against, Ozell clearly thinks, was the unsuitability of French prosody (he likens the *alexandrin* to "the drone of a bagpipe") and rigid couplet form (what he calls "the affected finery of rhyme") as a channel for the sweeping tide of heroic narrative (l. A4 verso). If we dislike the overplayed Francophobic machismo of Ozell's comparisons, we can still admit the very great advantage that the blank verse meter of "our English Homer, Milton" enjoys in rendering "that divine simplicity which is the peculiar character of this poet" (l. A4 verso). And we can prize the result for what it represents in the history of English poetry and the reception of Homer.

The two short samples I already offered are enough to give a taste of just what Ozell achieved as a poetic translator of Homer's epic poem, or rather of Dacier's literal prose version of it. If Dacier could liken her *Iliad* to a mummy—a kind of foretaste of the gothic romance of high modern philology, presenting to its viewers' senses only those chaste and somber beauties that supervene on the preservation of decay—then Ozell can be said to have found the resuscitating charm to breathe back life into Homer's rendered words by setting them to the measure that poets like Shakespeare, Marlowe, and Milton had trained into an instrument of stately grace, pithy verve, and nimble freedom like no other. This English blank verse *Iliad* gives a sustained poetic experience that is everywhere recognizably Homeric, and everywhere beholden both to Anne Dacier's protophilological reverence for the letter and also to the power of a native poetic tradition that allows passably good poets, if steeped in it and trusting it enough, to fashion words into a music that strains toward greatness. Take, for example, the lines that round off Zeus's response to Thetis (1.525–27). A clanging triplet of rare descriptors, two of them appearing nowhere else in Homer, iconizes the holdfast fixity of what his nod ordains:

> τοῦτο γὰρ ἐξ ἐμέθεν γε μετ' ἀθανάτοισι μέγιστον
> τέκμωρ· οὐ γὰρ ἐμὸν (1) παλινάγρετον οὐδ' (2) ἀπατηλὸν
> οὐδ' (3) ἀτελεύτητον ὅ τί κεν κεφαλῇ κατανεύσω.

Lattimore translates it as:

> For this among the immortal gods is the mightiest witness
> I can give, and nothing I do shall be (2) vain or (1) revocable
> nor a thing (3) unfulfilled when I bend my head in assent to it.

Dacier's studious care had resolved each negated epithet into the unsung paraphrase of a full predicate (while quietly rationalizing their order of appearance), giving (2) *ne trompe point* ("does not deceive") for οὐδ' ἀπατηλὸν ("not deceiving"), (1) *est irrévocable* ("is irrevocable") for οὐ... παλινάγρετον ("not revocable"), and (3) *ne manque jamais d'arriver* ("never fails to happen") for οὐδ' ἀτελεύτητον ("not able-to-go-unfulfilled").[14] The effect of reading Dacier's prose version is (to translate and update her mummy image) not unlike that of reading a supertitle without being able to see or hear the opera happening on stage. The "useful information" thereby conveyed, a faithful but dead letter, looks as if the actual experience it records would be impressive and significant, if only it could be experienced through a live medium.

A full and fully satisfying enactment of (imagined) live utterance and lived experience is precisely what Ozell's *Iliad* in very large measure achieves. It presses toward this goal of restoring Homer's text to poetic life not so much by going around and behind Dacier (although Ozell and his team all had enough Greek to check her literal accuracy, and did so at least sometimes) as by pressing forward into the poetic. In the present passage, rather than trying to unwrite Dacier's periphrastical literal glosses back into a series of adjectives, as Pope would later do—"The faithful, fix'd, irrevocable Sign" (p. 35)—Ozell instead takes up Dacier's version and, as if letting his form and its tradition do his work for him, spins it into the fine thread of a tricolon crescendo that swells over a pair of verses (a pattern Virgil had perfected in Latin and Milton in English) and rides to its close on a line whose words, all but one, are solemn monosyllables: "It not deceives; nor is to be recalled: / Nor does it ever fail to come to pass."

The result is a poetic translation that accounts not only for the letter of Homer's Greek but also that letter's passage through Dacier's French. As literal a rendering as any, Ozell's is in fact truer, here at least, to the rhetorical tone and dictional register of the original than the late modern unrhymed verse *Iliads* of Lattimore and his successors. Ozell's Whig *Iliad*, although eventually overshadowed by Pope's Tory version, deserves to be remembered. Better yet, it deserves a modern edition, one that rescues it from the indignity of its original presentation—Bernard Lintot chose to cut publishing costs by typesetting it on the page as if it were prose, with verse beginnings marked only by capitals—and puts it in the hands of readers who have a care for poetry.

Another reworking of Dacier's prose *Iliad* into verse was underway in those same years, this one in her own language and produced with a different, sharply polemical, intent. Antoine Houdar de la Motte published in 1714 what might best be called an abridged adaptation (C6)—La Motte himself called it more an imitation than a translation—of the *Iliad*, cut down to twelve books from Homer's twenty-four, and set to the classic French poetic form of rhymed alexandrine couplets. This was the event that launched the *Querelle* proper, and Montesquieu's satirical Persian letter seems to owe a few of its choicest phrases to the polite and delicious malice of the *Discours sur Homère* that La Motte appended in preface to his work. A member of the Académie française and sometime author of some notably unsuccessful drama followed by some very popular opera libretti and ballet texts, La Motte was thoroughly of the party of the Moderns in the spirit of Perrault. To the study of Homer he brought no Greek at all, a cordial irreverence toward ancient authority based on enlightened confidence in the power of reason and progress, and a combination of intellectual honesty and wickedly understated wit that made him an appealing figure to most of his contemporaries—and would make Madame Dacier want to administer very stern correction.

The reader who opens the elegant single volume of this *Iliad* is greeted by a surprising image. The frontispiece shows, in a vaulted chamber, La Motte himself rising from his armchair and boldly extending a hand to receive the lyre proffered by an apparition of Homer. The latter, floating on a dignified cloud, is flanked by a rather comically upended Mercury about to touch La Motte with his caduceus. The caption, understood to be spoken by the Greek blind bard to the French one (La Motte had lost his sight in 1710), reads *Choisis, tout n'est pas prétieux* ("Choose, not all is precious.") The line turns out to be self-quoted from La Motte's prefatory ode, *L'Ombre d'Homère,* in which Homer's shade entrusts the poet-translator with a sacred task: [15]

Homme, j'eus l'humaine faiblesse ;
Un encens superstitieux,
Au lieu de m'honorer, me blesse ;
Choisis, tout n'est pas précieux
Prends mes hardiesses sensées,
Et du fonds vif de mes pensées
Songe toujours à t'appuyer ;
Du reste je te rends le maître.
À quelque prix que ce puisse être,
Sauve-moi l'affront d'ennuyer.

Mon siècle eut des Dieux trop bizarres,
Des héros d'orgueil infectés,
Des rois indignement avares ;
Défauts autrefois respectés.
Adoucis tout avec prudence ;
Que de l'exacte bienséance
Ton ouvrage soit revêtu,
Respecte le goût de ton âge
Qui sans la suivre davantage,
Connaît pourtant mieux la vertu.

Ne borne pas la ressemblance
À des traits stériles et secs ;
Rends ce nombre, cette cadence
Dont jadis je charmai les Grecs.
Sois fidèle au stile héroique,
Au grand sens, au tour pathétique,
Enfants d'un travail assidu.
Qu'en ce choix la raison t'éclaire ;
Je plaisois, si tu ne sais plaire
Crois que tu ne m'as pas rendu. (pp. clxxvii–clxxviii)

A human, I had human weaknesses.
A superstitious adoration,
instead of honoring me, does me violence.
Choose! Not all is precious.
Take on my bold moves where they make sense,
And take care always to stand firm
Upon the living soil of my thoughts;
Of the rest I make you master.
At whatever the cost may be,
Save me from the affront of being boring.

My age possessed gods too bizarre,
heroes infected with pride,
kings unbefittingly greedy:
flaws that used to be respected.
Sweeten all things with prudence;
let strict adherence to decorum
clothe your work in every part.
Respect the taste of your age
which, though following it no better,
has better knowledge of what virtue is.

Do not limit your resemblance
to features that are dry and barren;
Render that number, that cadence
with which I once enthralled the Greeks.
Be faithful to the style heroic,
the great-souled thought, the touch of pathos,

engendered by a tireless labor.
In this choice let reason light your way.
I gave men pleasure. If you do not achieve this,
Consider that you have not rendered me.

What this poem ventriloquizes through Homer merits close study. If he believes in cultural and social progress toward the telos of reason, La Motte also believes in the seriousness of poetry. This he conceives, implicitly, as an art through which one human being, situated in the actuality of his own culture and society, but in potential relation with all other human beings, makes linguistic artifacts out of rhythmed word chains laden with beauty and significance. To these poetic artifacts he attributes, at least when they are as strong as those of Homer, the potential to give a characteristically human kind of pleasurable experience, one that is cognitive and ethical as well as aesthetic, and resilient enough to persist authentically in all those perceptual modes, through an act of poetic translation, into the poetic medium of a foreign place and time. But if La Motte thinks that Homer's ancient significances are translatable into modern poetic experience by way of a new form that successfully reembodies a measure of the *charme*—the power to enthrall—of Homer's original "number" and "cadence" while still standing firm on the "living soil" of his original thoughts, he also acknowledges that those significances are intimately bound up with the specific cultural norms and social practices that constituted, in part, the conditions of the ancient poem's production. And these conditions are in his view such that right-thinking citizens of enlightened modernity must often find them not only aesthetically ugly or boring but morally repellent. On this last point, La Motte stands historically near the head of an intellectual line that includes, for example, Simone Weil's profound (if less critically alert) modern moral response to the *Iliad*.[16] We are not likely to applaud La Motte's attempt to respond to the problem he sees by recalibrating the text of the *Iliad* to the sensibilities of a modern bourgeois readership. But we deceive ourselves if we fail to recognize the problem he takes himself to be confronting as an early version of a familiar and still productive late modern literary critical stance.

Sharp everywhere, the point of La Motte's critical wit never thrusts deeper than when he finds the way to combine what he sees as Homer's flaws and the *encens superstitieux* of Madame Dacier's Homerolatry into a single target. On one particularly choice page he develops what starts as a riposte to Dacier's strongest claim against verse translation into the most impertinent of animadversions on the unflattering light to which Homer finds himself exposed when viewed through the crisply focused lens of literal prose. After conceding to Dacier a series of advantages that prose translations enjoy, he continues:

> Mais avec tout cela, l'on n'a pas raison de prétendre que la versification ne puisse suivre par des équivalents les pensées d'Homère, et que les *poètes cessent d'être poètes,* quand ils sont traduits en vers.
>
> Que prétend-on dire par ce paradoxe ? Entend-on que le poète traducteur ne puisse rendre le fonds, la substance des pensées du poète original ? Il n'y a pas d'apparence qu'on le veuille dire, cela est trop évidemment faux. Entend-on seulement que, pour peu qu'on change l'original, on le défigure ? c'est ce que Madame Dacier paroît penser à l'égard d'Homère, et si le principe qu'elle pose est vrai, elle a raison d'en tirer cette conséquence, *Ce qu'Homère a pensé et dit,* ce sont ces termes, *quoique rendu plus simplement et moins poétiquement qu'il ne l'a dit, vaut certainement mieux que tout ce qu'on est forcé de lui prêter en le traduisant en vers.* Voilà la traduction d'Homère formellement interdite aux poètes ; mais j'appelle ce principe, et j'en pose un tout opposé. Homère est quelquefois si défectueux en ce qu'il a pensé et dit, que le traducteur prosaïque, et le plus déterminé à être fidèle, est souvent contraint de le corriger en beaucoup d'endroits. Je le prouverois aisément par l'exemple même de Madame Dacier. Ce n'est donc pas un si grand malheur à un poète qui traduit Homère de ne pouvoir être aussi littéral qu'on peut l'être en prose. (pp. cl–cli)

> But for all that, it is not correct to claim that verse writing can never follow Homer's thoughts equivalently and that "poets cease to be poets" when they are translated in verse.
>
> What can be the claim asserted by this paradox? Does it mean that the poet-translator can never render the foundation ("soil") and substance of the original poet's thoughts? Apparently not, for this is too obviously false. Does it merely mean that however little one changes the original one disfigures it? This is what Madame Dacier seems to think in regard to Homer, and if the principle she posits is true, then she is right to draw from it this consequence: "What Homer thought and said"—these are her words—"although rendered more simply and less poetically than he said it, is surely worth more than all that one is forced to put into his mouth when

translating him into verse." By this logic, poets do turn out to be strictly forbidden to translate Homer. But I appeal against this principle, and I posit an altogether contrary one. Homer is sometimes so flawed in what he thought and said that even the prose translator who is most determined to be faithful is often forced to correct him in many places. I could prove this easily by the example of Madame Dacier herself. So, for a poet translating Homer, it is not such a great misfortune to be unable to be as literal as one can be in prose.

His closing observation, that even Dacier herself has felt Homer's need for a cosmetic touchup here and there, and has quietly "corrected" him, scores a point we have already seen confirmed more than once.

La Motte's own versified rendition of the lines that open the *Iliad* not only enacts a polemical reading of Dacier's translation of the passage, which he must have compared to some other version, probably in Latin:

Muse, raconte-moi la colère d'Achille,
Pour les Grecs, pour lui-même, en malheurs si fertile ;
Et qui le retenant dans un cruel repos
Fit, aux Champs Phrygiens, périr tant de Héros.
Tel fut de Jupiter le décret homicide ;
Depuis qu'aux cœurs d'Achille & du puissant Atride
La discorde insolente eut versé son poison,
Et dans ces cœurs aigris eut éteint la raison. (p. 1)

Muse, tell me of the wrath of Achilles,
for the Greeks, <u>for himself</u>, so fertile in ills,
and which, <u>restraining him in a cruel repose</u>,
made to perish, on the Phrygian fields, so many heroes.
Such was Jupiter's <u>homicidal</u> decree,
from when into the hearts of Achilles and the mighty Atrides
<u>insolent</u> discord had poured her <u>poison</u>,
and in those <u>embittered</u> hearts had <u>snuffed out reason</u>.

It also bears witness to an engaged reading of the whole poem informed by a sharply felt sense of what we might call, to borrow a pair of terms from La Motte's ode, the pathos of heroism. By his additions (underlined in my English version) to the letter of Homer's text as well as his subtractions from it, La Motte is, at least here at the outset, doing poetic translation as an act of critical reading. None of his departures from the literal sense of these lines is a mere plug or embellishment, and not all his differences from Dacier are moves away from the literal. While he has politely spared modern readers the graphic image of rotting corpses and carrion birds that Dacier had found so easy to naturalize by quoting Holy Writ, he has not followed her reordering of Homer's clauses to set the Will of Heaven at the farthest possible remove from the stench of what it wrought on earth. La Motte leaves the sky god's *décret* where Homer put it, in stark juxtaposition with its grisly fulfillment. He removes the soft-pedal effect of her generalizing plural (*décrets*) and restores the troubling clarity of Homer's singular, because he understands, as Dacier pretends not to, that one of the referents of this multivalent word in this saturated context is the "plan" (βουλή) through which Zeus will make good on his nod to Thetis when he tricks Agamemnon into a disastrous attack and makes Greek warriors pay with their lives for an unbefittingly greedy king's affront to a pride-infected hero's honor.[17]

Tel fut de Jupiter le décret homicide: the epithet's raw indictment shocks, and is meant to. Clearly a polemical flick in the face of Dacier and every appearance-saving partisan of ancient authority, this denunciation of a divinity (albeit a "bizarre" pagan one) as murderous feels hot with the revolutionary indignation of the dawning century of lights. Does La Motte think he is improving Homer here by correcting a flaw, or joining forces with him by rendering his sense and telling the *Iliad*'s truth? He might not have been able honestly to say, and probably would have claimed on some level to be doing both. In the case of at least one of his poetic choices in translating the proem—the phrase *pour lui-même* in verse 2 that adds Achilles himself, along with the other Greeks, to the list of parties injured by his wrath—we have La Motte's own stated reasons for the alteration:

> Le Père Le Bossu, dans son *Traité du poème épique*, ouvrage le plus méthodique et le plus judicieux que le préjugé ait produit, prétend que tout le dessein de l'Iliade n'est que de faire voir combien la discorde est fatale à ceux qu'elle divise. Il n'est pas bien sûr qu'Homère y ait pensé ; mais quoiqu'il en soit, j'ai tâché que cette vérité se sentît dans mon ouvrage ; je l'ai même établie dès la proposition, en disant que la colère d'Achille lui fut funeste à lui-même, aussi bien qu'aux Grecs (ce qu'Homère auroit dû faire, si'il avoit eu le dessein qu'on lui suppose) et après avoir ainsi préparé l'esprit à la vérité morale dont il doit s'instruire, j'ai dégagé le poème de ce qui pourroit l'en distraire dans la suite : en un mot, je n'ai été plus

court, qu'afin de dire plus nettement ce qu'on prétend qu'Homère a voulu dire. (pp. clviii–clix).

Fr. Le Bossu, in his *Treatise on the Epic Poem*, the most methodical and judicious work prejudice ever produced, claims that the entire design of the *Iliad* is but to show how fatal discord is to those it divides. It is not obvious that Homer had this in mind, but be that as it may, I have tried in my work to make this truth perceptible. I have even established it from the opening statement of purpose, by saying that the wrath of Achilles was baneful to himself as well as to the Greeks (what Homer ought to have said if he had had the design imputed to him), and having thus prepared the readers' minds for the moral truth in which they are to be edified, I have relieved the poem of what subsequently might distract them from that truth: in a word, I have been briefer than Homer only in order to say more plainly what Homer is claimed to have meant.

It is hard to disentangle the coyly ironic from the merely disingenuous in this staking out of a highly unstable position. Polemically, La Motte seems to be arguing that his alterations and omissions serve the purpose of making his *Iliad* a better delivery system for the message his adversaries—the party of Le Bossu and the Daciers—claim Homer meant to send. If he wins this point, he can then say that when they attack his translation (as he knows they can be counted on to do), they are attacking the morally edifying principles they themselves impute to Homer, and which he claims to have followed as a guide in making a new *Iliad* for his own age.

What queers La Motte's game here, as well as the reader's attempt to count his moves, is his implicit assertion that only a prejudiced reader of the *Iliad* as we have it could take it for a morality tale with a plainly statable *moralité*. I am convinced of both the sincerity of this assertion and its correctness as a characterization of Homer's epic, but I am less persuaded by his claim to have had Le Bossu's doctrinaire pronouncements in mind while composing what turns out to be a surprisingly strong rendition of the *Iliad*'s proem into the poetic form Corneille and Racine had perfected. In fact, his changes to the letter of these seven Greek verses suggest that the only authoritative text he had in mind while making them was the *Iliad* itself. The embassy in book 9 and Patroclus in book 16, speaking for all the Greeks, would agree with the characterization of Achilles's withdrawal from the fight as a *cruel repos*; Agamemnon in book 19 as much as allows that insolent discord had snuffed out his reason; and Achilles, rolling in the dirt for dead Patroclus in book 24, would think it no exaggeration to call his own anger baneful to himself.

No accident, then, and little wonder, that La Motte's argument, for all his commitment to reason, got away from him when he tried to justify the response he had made as a poet-translator to the intensely freighted lines that introduce the poem. His allegiance to his own living neoclassical cultural models and the vision of human life those models encode rendered the whole *Iliad*, in the full force of its archaic and turgid splendor, quite indigestible to his sensibilities. And his critical intelligence rejected every attempt to make it palatable to modern tastes by ameliorating and edulcorating its terrible sublimity through Christianizing, neo-Aristotelianizing, and moralizing interpretive practices that asserted claims to authentic fidelity to ancient truth buttressed by relentless erudition. And yet, for all that, his translation suggests that La Motte had enough poetry in him—if only just enough—to feel the pull of Homer, and to be troubled by the feeling.

For a poet of the highest ambition and strength to realize it, the task of translating the *Iliad* consists in achieving adequate responsiveness to the dictional vigor and narrative sweep of the original monument while authentically meeting—and thereby transforming, elevating, and enriching—the expectations and possibilities of poetic experience in the language of translation. No poet has been credited by his contemporaries and his posterity with a higher measure of success at answering that set of challenges than Alexander Pope. Samuel Johnson described Pope's *Iliad* in heroic couplets as "the noblest version of poetry which the world has ever seen."[18] To Coleridge's eyes it was "an astonishing product of matchless talent and ingenuity."[19] And Gerard Manley Hopkins, writing at a time when "artificial" poetry had few admirers (and Pope fewer), asserted that "when one reads Pope's Homer with a critical eye, one sees, artificial as it is, in every couplet that he is a great man."[20]

The six sumptuous quarto volumes of his translation with commentary, sold by subscription in its first edition, were published between 1715 and 1720 by Bernard Lintot, under a contract that gave Pope full control over paper quality, type design, and engravings—and would make him a rich man.[21] Barred as a Catholic from attending an English university and therefore lacking the formal credentials of a classical scholar, he seems to have acquired (although his enemies would never concede it) enough Greek, from his Jesuit tutor and on his own, to parse it adequately, with the help of Joshua Barnes's 1711 edition with Latin translation and, of course, the French prose of Madame Dacier, along with other commentaries. His observations on each book, the "chief design" of which was "to comment upon Homer as a poet," show a translator steeped not only in his original text but also in the long tradition of its exegesis from Eustathius to his own time (p. 49). They also show a remarkable generosity of spirit, intellectual curiosity, and critical honesty, in a man better known for the biting sting of his satiric wit.

Here is Pope's translation of the proem to the *Iliad*:

> Achilles' Wrath, to Greece the direful Spring
> Of Woes unnumber'd, heav'nly Goddess, sing!
> That Wrath which hurl'd to *Pluto*'s gloomy Reign
> The Souls of mighty Chiefs untimely slain;
> Whose Limbs unbury'd on the naked Shore
> Devouring Dogs and hungry Vultures tore.
> Since Great *Achilles* and *Atrides* strove,
> Such was the Sov'reign Doom, and such the Will of *Jove*.[22]

Along with the majesty, liquid fire, and palpable sonic witchery of these saturated verses, we can also already see Pope's clear indebtedness to Dacier at several points: the epanalepsis of "Wrath" (an effect he enhances by placing the repeated word after the invocation); the epithet "gloomy" applied to the underworld (absent from the original, but perhaps suggested by the traditional etymology of *Hades* as "sightless" (*A-idēs*); and the delay of the clause featuring the "Will of Jove" to the end of the passage.[23] Pope, unlike Dacier, discloses in a note that he has made this alteration to the original order, adding his judgment that the proem seems thereby to end "more nobly" (p. 52–53). His comments on the phrase make clear that he sees and acknowledges the ethical stakes of interpretation on this point. They also make clear his interest, which neither Dacier nor most of his contemporaries shared, in thinking through the whole poem, philosophically as well as poetically, to get to the fullest possible account of the kind of world it imaginatively inhabits:

> *Will of Jove.*] *Plutarch* in his Treatise of reading Poets interprets Διός in this Place to signify *Fate*, not imagining it consistent with the Goodness of the supreme Being, or *Jupiter*, to contrive or practise any Evil against Men. *Eustathius* makes [*Will*] here to refer to the Promise which *Jupiter* gave to *Thetis*, that he would honour her Son

by siding with *Troy* while he should be absent. But to reconcile these two Opinions, perhaps the Meaning may be that when *Fate* had decreed the Destruction of *Troy*, *Jupiter* having the power of Incidents to bring it to pass, fulfill'd that Decree by providing Means for it. So that the Words may thus specify the Time of Action, from the beginning of the Poem, in which those Incidents work'd, 'till the Promise to *Thetis* was fulfill'd, and the Destruction of *Troy* ascertain'd to the *Greeks* by the Death of *Hector*. However it is certain that this Poet was not an absolute *Fatalist*, but still suppos'd the Power of *Jove* superior: For in the sixteenth *Iliad* we see him designing to save *Sarpedon* tho' the Fates had decreed his Death, if *Juno* had not interposed. Neither does he exclude *Free-will* in Men; for as he attributes the Destruction of the Heroes to the *Will* of *Jove* in the beginning of the *Iliad*, so he attributes the Destruction of *Ulysses*'s Friends to their *own* folly in the beginning of the *Odysseis*,

αὐτῶν γὰρ σφετέρῃσιν ἀτασθαλίῃσιν ὄλοντο.

Pope's *Iliad* is one of the small handful of poetic translations to have won a place in world literature, and not only for the strength of its claim to have responded to the Homeric monument with poetic adequacy. As a kind of touchstone and shibboleth, this is the text that has, in a sense, kept the Homer Quarrel alive. Your opinion of it, whether based on reading or on authoritative hearsay, is a fair diagnostic sign of your imagined relation to modernity as well as classical antiquity, and this has been the case from Pope's time into our own. Richard Bentley, whose status as a principal English champion of the party of the Moderns is now less well remembered than his foundational role in the modern discipline of classical philology, is said to have told Pope to his face that his English *Iliad* was "miserable stuff," possibly in the same brief conversation in which he tossed off the remark that some classicists still like to quote about it being a "pretty poem, Mr. Pope, but you must not call it Homer."[24]

A partisan of Pope eager to rush to his rescue can easily discount Bentley's judgment of poetry by pointing to the "emendations" he made to the text of Milton's *Paradise Lost*, more damning than any satire Pope's wit could ever devise.[25] But even if Pope did need vindicating against Bentley, doing so misses the point. Bentley's allergic reaction to Pope's *Iliad* and what it represents has bigger stakes than any question of literary taste. Very many late moderns, including not just classical philologists but poet-critics of the highest caliber, seem to have shared the motivating principle of his disgust. Chief among the latter is Matthew Arnold, whose appreciative care for poetry and devotion to Homer are hard to fault, and who found that "between Pope and Homer there is interposed the mist of Pope's literary artificial manner, entirely alien to the plain naturalness of Homer's manner."[26] By this, Arnold does not mean to say that Pope's artifice is at a far remove from Homer's, but that Homer is never artificial. In the same paragraph he asserts implicitly, by similar logic, a series of similarly wild claims: Homer is never elaborate like Cowper's Miltonic translation, never fanciful like Chapman's Elizabethan translation, and never ignoble like Newman's contemporary translation. A reader who remembers the speeches of Nestor, the simile likening Menelaus's bleeding thigh to ivory tinged with crimson, and the moment when Priam rolls in dung and kneads it in his fingers like dough, will wonder just what Arnold thinks a poet would have to do to count as occasionally elaborate, fanciful, or ignoble. As for artifice, even a reader who never went to the twentieth century's school of formulaic epithet will wonder, after reading the first seven lines of the *Iliad*, just what aspect of the poem Arnold has in mind when he claims that "Homer presents his thought to you just as it wells from the source of his mind." His intent here, if not his picture of Homer, becomes clearer on reading the second half of the antithesis: "Mr. Tennyson carefully distils his thought before he will part with it" (p. 55).

The fundamental belief that Arnold holds, or wants to hold, about Homer, seems to go something like this: Homer is, on every count, not just superior to all modern poets—and for Arnold this means all English poets—but utterly, transcendently different and distant from them, in his every verse, in his every quality. Every page of his Homer criticism shows him implicitly defending this belief, with all the vigor of his rhetoric, against all evidence to the contrary, as if his life depended on it. Perhaps on some level he thought it did. As H. A. Mason has suggested, Arnold occupied the late modern position of a subject alienated from his own modernity, experiencing it as uninhabitably brutal, and averting his gaze from it to contemplate a vision of "the Greek classics fixed in godlike calm, like the statues under glass cases of which the Victorians were so fond" (p. 91).[27] Literary antiquarianism is a familiar enough late modern position. Arnold's strong statement of it as analyzed by Mason gives us a view into what lies at the heart of at least some versions of it. On this view, it becomes clearer and easier to name what it is about Pope's translation that irritates the antiquarian sensibility, whether philological like Bentley's or poetic and literary critical like Arnold's, and provokes so emphatic a rejection of its claim to have rendered the *Iliad* with adequacy by making a strong new poem in English. The image of antiquity as a world apart, whether taken as an object of scientific study or an oasis of bliss, is threatened at its core by Pope's model of translation, founded as it is on a confidence in the possibility of adequate translation, across the gap of centuries from one human context to another, not just of cognitively apprehended linguistic meaning, but of the set of sensuous, affective, psychological, and even cultural responses that pass through a human organism in an experience of the kind called poetic. Pope, to put it simply, aims at rendering not just words and meanings but what he calls the "unequal'd fire and rapture" of Homer's poetry (l. B2). Whatever the measure of his success, the mere fact of his entertaining that bold aim implies a vision of human life in which "Homer" and "Pope," as names of poetic experiences, can be simultaneous and juxtaposed. That vision does not, as some might immediately complain, turn out to entail the erasure of cultural difference. But it does entail the negation of a set of late modern beliefs about the specialness of what it calls classical antiquity.

By embodying an early version of those beliefs in her literal translation of Homer, and by mounting a fierce defense of them that kept the Homer Quarrel, while it lasted, as hot and lively as the brew served up in French and English coffeehouses, Dacier played a foundational role in the early history of late modern relations to Greco-Roman antiquity. Studying her work and how her contemporaries responded to it, like reading Homer, has the potential to show us new things about ourselves. Between the image of Homer as a statue under glass that Mason attributes to Arnold and Dacier's likening of her Homeric translation to a mummified Helen of Troy, there obtains a more than coincidental kinship. Her armor-clad preservationist model of translating Homer, and therefore ultimately of reading him and relating to him, resembles that of Arnold and the Victorians, and that of the historicist classical scholarship of our own time, more closely than we might readily acknowledge. Her version of *odium philologicum*, it should be said, was more teacherly and less specialized than most scholarly production in the high modern mode, and more aimed at persuading an educated general public—which, by all accounts, including Montesquieu's, seems to have come away more entertained than edified. Her publication, in 1715, of a massive volume aimed chiefly at demolishing La Motte's preface sentence by sentence inspired the comic playwright Pierre de Marivaux to spring to his fellow Modern's defense with a parodic travesty of the *Iliad* based on La Motte's. In his preface to this version of Homer at a third remove, Marivaux permits himself the following quip at the expense of Dacier and the model of erudition she represented:

> Il a paru un livre intitulé *Des causes de la corruption du goût*, où la préface de M. de la Motte et son ouvrage sont fort vilipendés; je me sais bon gré de n'avoir jamais lu l'ancienne *Iliade* dans son original, car après la lecture *des causes de la corruption du goût*, livre fait par Madame Dacier, je commence à croire que l'ancienne *Iliade* est pernicieuse à qui peut la lire. Je ne puis penser qu'une dame s'irrite assez pour ménager aussi peu qu'elle l'a fait le plus doux de tous les hommes. Ne seroit-ce pas qu'en lisant Homère on respire cet esprit de ferocité qu'il a donné à ses personnages?[28]

> A book has appeared bearing the title *On the Causes of the Corruption of Taste*, in which Monsieur de la Motte's preface and work are utterly vilified. I am grateful never to have read the *Iliad* in the original, because after reading *On the Causes of the Corruption of Taste*, the work of Madame Dacier, I begin to think that the old *Iliad* is pernicious to anyone who can read it. I cannot imagine a *lady* being stirred to such a pitch of anger as to treat the gentlest of all men with as little kindness as she did. Might it be that by reading Homer one breathes in that spirit of ferocity he gave to his characters?

That a six-hundred-page attack on La Motte had left Dacier's polemical fire undiminished is unsurprising. It is no more surprising that Pope, although nominally her ally in the cause, managed to draw some of that fire on himself by calling Homer's work a "wild paradise" in his 1715 *Iliad* preface (l. B1 verso). This minor skirmish in the ranks of the Ancients is generally regarded as a mere unfortunate misunderstanding, based in part (this was Pope's polite suggestion) on the bad French translation in which she had read it, and scholars have been eager to offer formulations like this recent one from Emmanuel Schwartz: "Madame Dacier failed to perceive all that the sensibility of Alexander Pope could bring to her own defense of Homer."[29]

To speak as if these two great partisans of Homer could have come to an easy agreement is to underestimate the fundamental differences in their theories of translation, models of reading, and notions of just what defending Homer would amount to. Pope owed a very great debt to Dacier's learning, and would probably have never achieved his *Iliad* translation without the help of hers. Pope's sensibility could indeed have made Dacier some return, but it would have involved a radical change to her vision of Homer's poems and the imagined heroic world they depict. It would have involved deidealizing the nostalgia of that vision and humanizing its ethical response to the poems themselves. When he finally loosens the reins on his wit in his response to her in a postscript to his 1726 translation of *The Odyssey*, he acknowledges as much:

> After answering my harmless similes, she proceeds to a matter which does not regard so much the honour of Homer, as that of the times he lived in; and here I must confess she does not wholly mistake my meaning, but I think she mistakes the state of the question. She had said, the manners of those times were so much the better, the less they were like ours. I thought this required a little qualification. I confess that in my opinion the world was mended in some points, such as the custom of putting whole nations to the sword, condemning kings and their families to perpetual slavery, and a few others. Madam Dacier judges otherwise in this; but as to the rest, particularly in preferring the simplicity of the ancient world to the luxury of ours, which is the main point contended for, she owns we agree. (p. 312)[30]

By the time Pope published these lines, Madame Dacier had been dead for six years. Before the end of her life, she and La Motte had met for supper at the house of a mutual friend and officially ended the *Querelle d'Homère* by drinking a toast to Homer.[31] For all the elegance of the gesture, it is not clear that the dead Greek poet was more honored by the peace than he had been by the battle.

DAVID WRAY

NOTES

1. Montesquieu, *Œuvres complètes*, vol. 1, ed. R. Caillois (Paris: 1949). French and English orthography are silently regularized in quotations. All translations unless noted otherwise are my own.

2. Pascale Casanova, *The World Republic of Letters,* trans. M. B. DeBevoise (Cambridge: Harvard University Press, 2007).

3. Jonathan Swift, *A Tale of a Tub* (London: John Nutt, 1704).

4. Marc Fumaroli, *La Querelle des Anciens et des Modernes* (Paris: Gallimard, 2001): 260–61.

5. Joan DeJean, *Ancients against Moderns: Culture Wars and the Making of a Fin de Siècle* (Chicago: University of Chicago Press, 1997): 69.

6. Anne Dacier, *L'Iliade d'Homère* (Paris: Chez Rigaud, 1711), All page numbers are from vol. 1.

7. Julie Candler Hayes, *Translation, Subjectivity, and Culture in France and England, 1600–1800* (Stanford: Stanford University Press, 2009): 121–40.

8. Lawrence Venuti, *The Translator's Invisibility: A History of Translation* (London and New York: Routledge, 1995)..

9. Greek text of the *Iliad* is from Thomas W. Allen's 1902 Oxford Classical Texts edition.

10. Richard Lattimore, *The Iliad of Homer* (Chicago: University of Chicago Press, 1961).

11. John Ozell, *The Iliad of Homer* (London: Bernard Lintott, 1712). The reader who examines this volume will be surprised to find what looks like a prose translation. Ozell, in his introduction, makes it clear he has translated Homer into blank verse, the metrical form of Milton's epic poetry. And with line-breaks properly restored, the translation does in fact fully conform to the conventions of eighteenth-century blank verse. The printer's format thus does not represent the translator's intention, and quotations in this essay taken from the 1712 edition have accordingly been reformatted as verse. See pp. 312–15.

12. James Redfield, "The Proem of the *Iliad*: Homer's Art," *Classical Philology* 74 (1979): 95–110.

13. Sidney Lee, "John Ozell." *Dictionary of National Biography* (London: Oxford University Press, 1895).

14. Lattimore's "vain" is an undertranslation. Remarkably, Lattimore joins Dacier, Ozell, and Pope in altering Homer's order so as to put Zeus's asseverance of present sincerity ahead of his assurance that no agency will ever revoke his assent.

15. Antoine Houdar de la Motte, *L'Iliade* (Paris: Chez Gregoire Dupuis, 1714).

16. Simone Weil, *Simone Weil's* The *Iliad* or the Poem of Force: *A Critical Edition,* ed. James P. Holoka (New York: Peter Lang, 2003) (orig. 1940).

17. On the "dampening" effect of the poetic plural, see Leo Spitzer, "Die klassische

Dämpfung in Racines Stil," *Archivum Romanicum* 12 (1928): 361–472.

18. Samuel Johnson, *The Lives of the Most Eminent English Poets*, vol. 4, ed. Roger Lonsdale (Oxford: Oxford University Press, 2006): 17.

19. Samuel Taylor Coleridge, *Biographia Literaria*, vol. 1, ed. James Engell and W. Jackson Bate (Princeton: Princeton University Press, 1985): 19.

20. Gerard Manley Hopkins, *Selected Letters,* ed. Catherine Phillips (Oxford: Oxford University Press, 1990): 28; Maynard Mack, *Alexander Pope: A Life* (New Haven and London: Yale University Press, 1985)..

21. Mack, 266–68.

22. Pope continued to revise his translation. The lines here quoted reproduce his final version of 1743. In the first edition, the opening two verses ran: "The Wrath of *Peleus'* Son, the direful Spring/Of all the *Grecian* Woes, O Goddess, sing!"

23. Pope's overall estimation of Dacier's *Iliad* is generous and critical in equal measure: "She has made a farther Attempt than her Predecessors to discover the Beauties of the Poet; tho' we have often only her general Praises and Exclamations instead of Reasons. But her Remarks all together are the most judicious Collection extant of the scatter'd Observations of the Ancients and Moderns, as her Preface is excellent, and her Translation equally careful and elegant" (p. 49).

24. Quoted, with references to variant versions, in Joseph M. Levine, *The Autonomy of History: Truth and Method from Erasmus to Gibbon* (Chicago: University of Chicago Press, 1999): 99.

25. Richard E. Bourdette, Jr., "'To *Milton* lending sense': Richard Bentley and *Paradise Lost*," *Milton Quarterly* 14 (1980): 37–49.

26. Matthew Arnold, *On Translating Homer* (London: Longman, Green, Longman, and Roberts, 1861): 11.

27. H. A. Mason, "Arnold and the Classical Tradition," *Arion* 1 (1962): 89–97.

28. Pierre Carlet de Chamblain de Marivaux, *L'Homère travesti ou l'Iliade en vers burlesques* (Paris: 1714): xv.

29. Emmanuel Schwartz, *The Legacy of Homer: Four Centuries of Art from the École Nationale Supérieure des Beaux-Arts, Paris* (New Haven: Yale University Press, 2005): 36.

30. Alexander Pope, *The Odyssey of Homer*, vol. 2 (London: Bernard Lintot, 1726).

31. Arthur A. Tilley, *The Decline of the Age of Louis XIV* (Cambridge: Cambridge University Press, 1929): 349.

INDEX

This is a consolidated name index of printers and publishers to 1800, translators, editors, authors, former owners, and other individuals or presses appearing in item entries and item descriptions only. Forms of names are from the Library of Congress Name Authority File and the Consortium of European Research Libraries Thesaurus. In some instances cross-references are provided from commonly-used forms. The titles of works by or attributed to Homer other than the *Iliad* and the *Odyssey* are also included. References to BHL numbers are in bold for individuals named in the entry.

Set in
Quarto roman & Greek types, with
Garamond italic and Epigrammata Titling.
Photography by Michael Kenny. Copyedited by
Michael W. Phillips Jr. Printed on Mohawk paper
by Capital Offset. Design & typography
by Jerry Kelly.